The Effective Enforcement of Planning Controls

GU00976099

The Effective Enforcement of Planning Controls

Second Edition

Denzil Millichap, LL.M.

Butterworths
London, Dublin, Edinburgh
1995

United Kingdom	Butterworths, a Division of Reed Elsevier (UK) Ltd, Halsbury House, 35 Chancery Lane, LONDON WC2A 1EL and 4 Hill Street, EDINBURGH EH2 3JZ
Australia	Butterworths, SYDNEY, MELBOURNE, BRISBANE, ADELAIDE, PERTH, CANBERRA and HOBART
Canada	Butterworths Canada Ltd, TORONTO and VANCOUVER
Ireland	Butterworth (Ireland) Ltd, DUBLIN
Malaysia	Malayan Law Journal Sdn Bhd, KUALA LUMPUR
New Zealand	Butterworths of New Zealand Ltd, WELLINGTON and AUCKLAND
Puerto Rico	Equity de Puerto Rico, Inc, SAN JUAN
Singapore	Reed Elsevier (Singapore) Pte Ltd, SINGAPORE
South Africa	Butterworths Publishers (Pty) Ltd, DURBAN
USA	Butterworths Legal Publishers, CARLSBAD, California and SALEM, New Hampshire

A CIP Catalogue record for this book is available from the British Library.

First edition 1990

ISBN   0 406 04801 0

Jacket designed by Wendy Millichap

Printed and bound in Great Britain by Clays Ltd, St Ives plc

Dedication

The author and the jacket designer dedicate this to the
memory of their mother.

Foreword

I am very pleased to be able to introduce the much-awaited
second edition of this valuable work. I first became aware of
Denzil Millichap's work in this field late in 1988 when I was
preparing my report on planning enforcement. He combines
an academic approach with practical experience on both
the public and private sides of the profession. As well as some
useful discussions, I gained much assistance from his pioneering
studies (along with Jeffrey Jowell) of enforcement practice,
published in the Journal of Planning Law in 1983 and 1986.

Some two years elapsed before Parliament decided to
implement most of my recommendations in the Planning and
Compensation Act 1991. The first edition of this work emerged
when the Bill was under consideration, and as a result only
limited treatment was possible. Contemporary reviews were
highly favourable, but rightly anticipated the need for a new
edition at an early stage to take on board the changes. The
present edition is therefore most opportune. It contains a
comprehensive discussion of the law and practice following the
1991 Act and subsequent case law.

As I emphasised in my report, a major obstacle to effective
enforcement is not so much the lack of weapons, but lack of
understanding of how to use them. Investigation and effective
enforcement of the law, with proper respect for individual
rights, is never going to be easy. In planning, the problems are
compounded by the complexity of the substantive law, and the
potential rewards for wrongdoing. This book will make a vital
contribution to understanding of the subject, particularly for
those concerned in day-to-day enforcement. It displays a profound
appreciation of both the strategy and the detail of the law, and
tackles the practical problems head-on.

I welcome it whole-heartedly. I only regret that such a book
was not available in 1988 when I started my report. It would
have made my task much easier.

Robert Carnwath
Royal Courts of Justice
June 1995

Preface

In producing the second edition I have sought to follow a key aim of the first – providing a thorough, practical and innovative analysis of the legal and organisational framework of enforcement. I do not, therefore, merely seek to set out what the law is – I also try to show how new ways of using it can help achieve the remediation of a breach in an effective way. I focus on the key problems and issues that prevent effective action. A central element in all this is the perception of, and attitude towards, enforcement among a wide range of actors. That is why Chapter 1 retains its expansive treatment of the subject: that is why I have expanded further on issues such as the effective presentation of prosecutions before the magistrates' court: that is why I stress the importance of the 'planning trinity' – a concept that puts enforcement alongside forward planning and development control.

Case law has helped define the real impact of the 1991 reforms. The more positive approach to granting injunctive relief is evident from the Court of Appeal in its examination of the new statutory provisions for planning injunctions. Conclusions based on an unreported Crown Court decision and close analysis of the breach of condition notice provisions, however, indicates that some LPAs may be putting too much faith in this more limited reform: the inbuilt limitations (legal and practical) affecting the breach of condition notice power are discussed in some detail. An example of the possibility of innovative use of the new provisions is to be found in the discussion of planing contravention notices. Authorities may find it useful to employ pro forma section 106 obligations during any discussion with a contravener as a result of a 'time and place' offer; this will at least help to gauge the bona fides of any 'undertaking' he may offer to address the problem. More detailed analysis of the 'nullity' dilemma (largely the product of some wayward High Court decisions) is provided. This suggests that litigation may provide an answer: however, legislation (as suggested in the Carnwath Report) is likely to be the only effective way of eliminating the 'pettifogging' that is still to be found in the case law at first instance.

I have not set out pro forma enforcement notices in this edition. This may appear perverse. However, my justification for this is that it may at least force officers to think more critically about the wording of any notices that they see being offered as pro formas. In various parts of the text I discuss the risks of relying on pro forma notices and following them blindly. (Those provided by the DOE have their faults as the text indicates.) What I have provided in the appendicised materials, however, are excerpts from the Police and Criminal Evidence Act 1984 Codes of Practice. Code C (addressing the questioning of suspects) will often have a bearing on the investigation of contraventions that directly involve criminal law liability. Such materials are unlikely to be at hand in the planning department and so are provided here.

I would like to thank Ray Jackson and the other partners in the Property Department of Linklaters & Paines for allowing me time to work on this edition.

Denzil Millichap
30 June 1995

Contents

Table of statutes

Table of rules and regulations

List of cases

PARA

PARA

PARA

1 Changing perceptions and the organisational response to enforcement

1.1 PERCEPTIONS OF ENFORCEMENT

The effective enforcement of planning control is not merely a matter of dealing with legal detail. Although a great deal of this book is devoted to explaining the legal rules relating to enforcement another important aspect that is covered focuses on perceptions of enforcement and how they need to be changed. Current perceptions detrimentally affect the handling of enforcement cases from the strategic to the day-to-day levels. There have recently been reforms to the legal framework (reflecting many of the recommendations suggested by Robert Carnwath in his report[1]). Yet effective enforcement requires more than a change to the legal framework: effective enforcement also requires a more fundamental realignment of attitudes and perceptions – among planners, lawyers, elected members, the magistracy and even the complaining neighbour. Changing perceptions is thus an underlying theme of this book and in this introductory chapter I indicate the issues which such a changed perception of enforcement must comprehend and how that ties in with organisational reform. The legal regime does not implement itself – that is the task of organisations and individuals within those organisations. So until enforcement casts off its 'cinderella' status it will never be 'effective'. The consequences of this are significant for planning and other local authority functions. This is why the notion of the planning trinity is important in encapsulating the change of attitude required.

1 *Enforcing Planning Control*, HMSO, 1989.

1.2   THE PLANNING TRINITY

Forward planning has always been perceived as the most prestigious aspect of planning. Development control has somewhat improved its status over the years. Yet enforcement, the third element in the planning system, is definitely viewed as a poor relation. In terms of career prospects, with the professional bias of planners towards the grand vision of the development plan and the nuts and bolts of negotiations with developers, it is obvious why the hard grind of the enforcement officer is accorded little importance. Invariably the caseload is concerned with 'minor' problems, it involves technical questions of law and the enforcement officer is on site, dealing with contraveners and complaining neighbours for much of the day. Such work does not, most planners consider, offer the challenges of a 'real' planning job.

That perception is, of course, misguided. Any regulatory regime requires an enforcement arm to deal with those situations where the rules have not been obeyed. Forward planning and development control would be pointless activities if landowners were able to contravene the controls with impunity. Even the Department of the Environment (DOE) policy (PPG18, para 4) recognises that the 'integrity' of the planning system relies on effective enforcement. (Related issues of deterrence, punishment etc are examined in a discussion, in chapter five, of 'systemic' material considerations.) So a better view of these three planning functions is to treat them as interrelated and inseparable: forward planning cannot be a realistic activity unless development control decisions on the ground reflect the aspirations of the forward planning section; development control is potentially an exercise in futility unless it can count on an effective enforcement unit to deal with contraventions; enforcement cannot work properly unless development control (especially conditions and planning agreements) is carried out conscientiously and applies plan policies that will withstand an appeal to the Secretary of State. Problems with forward planning policy and development control decisions will cause problems for enforcement: enforcement cannot be expected to put right errors created by the other elements in the planning trinity. Mutual support, feedback and constructive criticism are thus elements necessary for the planning function to perform effectively; such elements are central to an appreciation of enforcement that sees it as one of the three indivisible elements in the planning trinity.

Enforcement policies in the development plan are one aspect of applying the concept of the planning trinity. Thus particularly important planning policies can be supported by effective enforcement action (with section 54A adding weight to the local planning authority's (LPA) case on appeal.) Policies may also cover the need for (in particular circumstances) effective enforcement mechanisms and/or monitoring provisions: development control practice is thus administered with a view to ensuring that enforcement action will be more effective. Feedback is important. Problems may indicate a strategic flaw in the resourcing and/or co-ordination of the trinity of planning functions. Enforcement failure may be caused by out of date policies or inefficient development control practice. On the positive side the organisational responses adopted by forward planning and development control may also furnish models of how the organisation of enforcement can be reformed. Standardised documentation, well-designed administrative procedures, manuals, delegated decision-making etc are thus clearly appropriate bureaucratic responses to the enforcement caseload.

The planning trinity, as elements in the following discussion demonstrate, is the concept that can help us appreciate the nature of the problem and the outlines of a solution. It counters the simplistic view that the needs of the enforcement system cannot solely be met by just adding another ex-policeman to the payroll. The planning trinity requires a strategic approach to enforcement – because the planning trinity explicitly recognises that enforcement is a strategic activity beset by strategic limitations. It is time that this third element in the planning trinity was also accorded an organisational status commensurate with its importance and the complex nature of the task. It is an issue that was discussed by Carnwath[1]. DOE policy also now acknowledges that this is a key factor:

> 'Unless they have done so recently, all LPAs are recommended to carry out a thorough review of the effectiveness of their procedural arrangements for planning enforcement; and, where necessary, to introduce revised arrangements'[2].

Yet before change at the organisational level can be made it will be necessary to change perceptions. So before examining the factors relevant to proposals for an organisational response, the enforcement personnel (and any allies!) will have to plan their 'hearts and minds' campaign. So who are the targets and how are they to be approached?

4   **1.2** *Changing perceptions*

1 *Enforcing Planning Control*, HMSO, 1989, pp 26–27.
2 PPG18, para 22. Recommendation 14 by Carnwath suggested that 'consideration should be given to the preparation of a practice manual for authorities on all aspects of enforcement work.' The DOE appears to have rejected the idea of producing such a manual – though a few authorities have done so as part of their response to the enforcement workload.

1.3 WHOSE PERCEPTIONS?

In planning a campaign to achieve organisational reform and to ensure an appropriate status and resourcing for enforcement it will be necessary to focus on those individuals and groups whose perceptions need to be changed. Of immediate relevance will be perceptions of enforcement held by members of the planning department. Those who can influence the other key targets are clearly the principal concern here.

1.3.1 Perceptions in the planning department

In one sense all levels of planning staff need to be converted. In practice it will be the senior and middle-level officers whose support will be necessary in order to achieve support for organisational reform. In the longer term (at the stage of implementing the reforms) however, the rank-and-file members of the department will need to be persuaded of the value of enforcement in helping them do their tasks. As noted earlier both forward planning and development control sections will benefit from an effective enforcement section and so evidence of past problems and how future changes will benefit these sections will be relevant in winning over these groups.

1.3.2 Perceptions in other departments

Organisational change may well affect other departments in the authority and significant changes will probably need the support of other Chief Officers. Winning the hearts and minds of these will be easier once the key personnel in the planning department are behind reform. Where enforcement activity can overlap with other departments (as discussed here) the benefits for those other departments can be demonstrated and solutions to problems that may have seemed intractable may be possible. Again the idea is to describe the problem and provide realistic solutions.

1.3.3 Perceptions among elected members

Elected members are ultimately responsible for policy and resources and so their enthusiastic support is vital. Initially the focus should be on those influential members whose experience of planning enforcement and planning control can be the basis for a well-prepared presentation. The picture needs to be painted in terms appropriate to the interests of those members – 'electoral' considerations may well be an important factor. Once this groundwork is laid the relevant members who control the purse strings should be targeted. As noted elsewhere the aim should be to produce a realistic picture of the problem with practical solutions and proposals. Long-term issues such as monitoring, feedback and updates should be covered – to ensure continued support for the changes that are implemented.

1.3.4 Perceptions held by lawyers

Research on enforcement often reveals that the legal department is perceived as being a 'problem'[1]. Sometimes the traditional reticence of local authority lawyers in their advice on the use of public law powers is responsible for this perception. In some cases it may be a way of protecting lawyers from a barrage of (unfamiliar) extra work. However, some local authority lawyers do take a more positive approach to enforcement problems and so also adopt a 'strategic' viewpoint. Obtaining the support of the legal department will be easier if planning law specialists are already employed: however, where this is not the case it may be possible to show how the details of a new approach (such as the use of manuals, pro forma documentation etc) will avoid the more common errors that can lead to embarrassing mistakes which the lawyers are then asked to sort out. Organisational reform should thus be portrayed as a way of reducing enforcement problems and so reducing the number of problem cases that require legal input. Organisational reform may involve a re-evaluation of the importance of appropriately skilled legal personnel. The lawyer involved in enforcement work should ideally be aware of the full range of enforcement powers available, the strengths and weaknesses of such powers and in particular the ability to use creative legal thinking. He must also be conversant with the range of powers of an enforcement nature in other parallel regimes in the 'environmental law' field. Such attitudes mirror the value of adopting an 'environmental law' approach. This wider perspective parallels the 'environmental problem' approach (see para 1.5.1) which the LPA should adopt. A further element (an important aspect of implementation) is the appropriate handling of prosecutions. Here the aim is to change perceptions of the prosecutor who handles enforcement contraventions in the criminal courts. Such perceptions constitute an important target since effective enforcement relies on the efficacy of the ultimate sanction – a prosecution in the criminal courts. However, the perceptions of planning contraventions held by magistrates may help to explain problems encountered in achieving appropriate penalties at this late stage in an enforcement case. Changing those perceptions relies on prosecutors first changing their own perceptions about the type of case they are handling. Magistrates have great difficulty in dealing with breaches of regulatory law of this type. There is no obvious 'victim' of the crime and what seems to be happening is the persecution of enterprising individuals battling against an officious local bureaucracy. The presentation of cases involving breaches of planning control thus requires considerable thought. The 'communication skill' involved in presenting cases to the magistrates' court is one key area where the LPA (particularly the Legal Department) can make significant improvements. The issues that need to be addressed clearly and cogently in such prosecutions are discussed in chapter nine. Enforcement manuals (for the legal department) should perhaps concentrate on the special factors (discussed in chapter nine) that have to be noted and brought to the attention of the magistrates. This will need some tact no doubt as advice on prosecution technique may not be well-received by some prosecuting lawyers. However, this particular restraint is clearly one that must be tackled effectively.

1 For a discussion of enforcement based on empirical data the following reports are of interest: J Jowell and D Millichap, 'Enforcement of Planning Control in London' [1983] JPL 644; J Rowan-Robinson, E Young and I McLarty, *The Enforcement of Planning Control in Scotland* Scottish Office, Edinburgh, 1984; J Jowell and D Millichap, 'Enforcement of Planning Law: A Report

and Some Proposals' [1986] JPL 482; J Rowan-Robinson and E
Young,'Enforcement – The Weakest Link in the Scottish Planning
Control System' (1987) 8 Urban Law and Policy 255; J Jowell and
D Millichap, 'Enforcement: The Weakest Link in the Planning
Chain' (in M L Harrison and R Mordey, *Planning Control:
Philosophies, Prospects and Practice* Croom Helm, London, 1987).
The topic has now become a relatively popular theme for
undergraduate and postgraduate dissertations. Perhaps perceptions
of enforcement and its importance are also changing in academia.

1.3.5 Perceptions held by the courts

The 1991 reforms have, largely, increased the maximum fines
to £20,000. In most cases the provisions now make specific
reference, where relevant, to the importance of any 'financial
benefit' linked to the crime in the computation of any penalty.
Yet many magistrates' courts still appear to impose fines that
are woefully inadequate. However, in addressing this problem
it must be remembered that the DOE (as a part of the executive
arm of government) faces constitutional hurdles that preventing
it from telling the magistracy (part of the judicial arm of
government) how to fulfil its role. So the independence of the
judiciary from the other two arms of government can produce
problems when it comes to designing and implementing
mechanisms that help 'educate' the Bench. Such education, in
order to meet the demands of a criminal law code that extends
to regulatory action which seems to have little to do with the
'traditional' criminal law, seems an indispensable element. A
more realistic approach that does not offend against the principle
of the separation of powers depends on those who have direct
access to the Bench being able to make the case for meaningful
penalties as strongly as possible. (This is why the previous
paragraph emphasised the importance of prosecutors *themselves*
being 'educated' about the special characteristics of planning
contraventions.) In some cases the LPA may have elected
members on the Bench and these can act as conduits for
information – perhaps even arranging for briefings on the
importance of planning (and other environmental) controls.
However, the most likely source is the prosecuting lawyer.
Changing perceptions of planning contraventions appears to be
a task that is primarily up to the prosecutor handling
prosecutions under the planning legislation. These issues,
discussed in the chapter on securing compliance with the

enforcement notice, are vitally important as a failure to communicate the range of relevant issues to the magistrates is largely the reason for low criminal penalties. There is also the allied problem of perceptions held by some of the judiciary dealing with civil law actions involving enforcement issues. This applies largely to one special area of concern. The problem here is the approach taken as regards the 'nullity' principle and the powers on appeal to correct errors in enforcement notices. Flawed enforcement notices may be corrected on appeal by the inspector if this would not cause injustice: unfortunately contraveners can often persuade first instance judges to employ a rather outmoded interpretation of the legal principles and then declare the notice (even though shorn of its defects) a nullity. This was an issue to which Robert Carnwath devoted his attention: he recommended changes to the legal framework that would help ensure that a more pragmatic and enlightened approach was taken by the High Court. (The Court of Appeal, the House of Lords and some High Court decisions do employ a more appropriate interpretation.) Unfortunately the legislative changes recommended by Carnwath to address this problem were not taken up in the 1991 reforms. So at present, given the lack of clarifying/amending legislation, one of the important aspects of effective enforcement is the approach taken by the LPA and the DOE to the 'nullity' issue when it is raised on appeal before an inspector and before the High Court. Some members of the Bench cling to perceptions that encourage the 'pettifogging' approach to legal analysis that can often dissuade the LPA from taking action in the first place. In order to stop the pettifogging it would seem that LPAs (perhaps jointly with the DOE and the Inspectorate) will have to look at this issue again and plan a campaign of action. This is one issue that perhaps requires action at the institutional level – though individual court cases that touch upon 'nullity' do offer individual LPAs the opportunity to influence the case law principles and put an end to the pettifogging. The legal issues related to this problem are discussed in detail in the chapter on appeals.

1.4 DEFINING PROBLEMS, SUGGESTING SOLUTIONS

Strategic action is not only required in order to use enforcement powers effectively. Achieving organisational reform will also require considerable planning in order to win over those who hold the purse strings. The first element in the strategy will be to define the problems arising from the current (ineffective) organisational response to enforcement. The Ombudsman may well provide pertinent examples. One case (288/B/86) concerned the handling of a vehicle-related breach of control by an LPA. In 1975 the council had issued an enforcement notice dealing with the use of a field for the repair and rebuilding of cars. The council had taken legal proceedings for non-compliance of the notice on seven separate occasions – fines of £1,107 had been imposed. One of the persons responsible had gone to prison twice and the other once. The council had obtained an injunction to restrain the brothers' continuing defiance of the notice which had led to their imprisonment for 28 days for contempt of court. The saga had had no effect upon the use and the field continued to be used for storage of between 100–300 vehicles. In June 1986 the council had decided to grant planning permission for a limited period. The owner of the neighbouring site complained to the local government Ombudsman. He found that the council had not considered two other possibilities namely purchase of the land and relocation of the scrap yard elsewhere. Also the council could have used powers under section 178 of the 1990 Act to carry out the steps required by the enforcement notice at the expense of the two operators.

The Ombudsman found that the decision to abandon enforcement proceedings and to grant planning permission (which only achieved a limited environmental improvement) amounted to maladministration. This was because the council had not pursued every avenue available to prevent the continuance of the brothers' business. Illustrations such as this one of the failure to organise enforcement will help to show the benefits of taking on the concept of the planning trinity and a strategic approach. No doubt there will also be well-known examples of enforcement cases that have been the cause of bad publicity for the LPA – cases that have caused problems for both officers and elected members. The examples need to be chosen carefully and explained in a way that is not going to lead to defensive action by particular officers – the focus must be on the organisation's shortcomings – not those of individuals. (The above example shows a strategic failure to take account of all planning and non-planning powers.) Such cases should illustrate the themes of the 'strategic' approach as the next step is to suggest practical solutions.

Proposals for reform should be realistic. Staff costs must be presented in a way which shows how the benefits (to senior officers, other planning staff and elected members) of the new response will constitute value for money. This may well mean that the whole strategy of changing perceptions may well have to take account of particular sensitivities of key members. Election time is often a season of increased enforcement activity: this factor may be relevant in the timing of the campaign and the content of any reasoned discussion of the problem and possible solutions. It will almost invariably mean winning over senior staff (both within and outside the planning department) to the cause: with environmentalism continuing to have its impact on the organisation of local authority departments the benefits of effective planning enforcement will be increasingly relevant to a number of local authority departments.

Monitoring progress will be essential. Problems in implementing the strategy, failures and successes need to be covered. Indeed, any solution and implementation process must take a realistic view. Elected members must be given clear information about the fundamental restraints: the normally weak nature of the criminal sanction, the intractable problems posed by the determined contravener etc. Such factors will often evade the solutions offered by any organisational reform. Elected members and others must be made aware of the limitations – though naturally these should not obscure the benefits. Regular (quarterly or more frequent) updates on enforcement – both individual cases and the broader picture will be relevant features of keeping enforcement visible.

1.5 TACTICAL ENFORCEMENT AND ORGANISATIONAL REFORM

A strategic awareness of the problems facing enforcement and any reforms required to make it effective must also be complemented by an awareness of the ways in which enforcement personnel should approach their work at the tactical level. They must be aware of the various sanctions and strategies available to them (in a reformed organisation) in order to make best use of the changes achieved. The deployment of these sanctions etc in an effective manner is thus a complementary aspect of the strategic approach. In effect we are now concerned with tactics. Tactical deployment of the various sanctions available must become second nature to enforcement personnel. The greater use of stop notices, the use of the works-in-default power, the role of enforcement agreements, the timetabled processing of enforcement cases, the use of extra-legal sanctions etc should figure in this. Some of these issues can be discussed in the context of general principles: the following principles may be of use to the LPA.

1.5.1 An 'environmental problem'

A breach of planning control may often be viewed as an 'environmental problem'. By this I mean that effective enforcement is not just about issuing an enforcement notice whenever a recalcitrant contravener refuses to comply. Effective enforcement encompasses the ability to deploy a range of sanctions. Those sanctions will not be solely planning-based. An important principle of the strategic approach is thus the ability to view a breach of planning control as an 'environmental problem'. Seeing a breach of planning control as a 'environmental problem' helps the LPA to appreciate the fact that parallel (sometimes overlapping powers) exist which can also be used to deal with a breach of control. Indeed, if the broader viewpoint afforded by the 'environmental law' perspective is adopted, it becomes all too obvious that the planning regime (despite its wide scope) should not be taken as the sole means of dealing with a breach which has planning (and other) implications.

1.5.2 Other regulatory agencies

A further development of the 'environmental problem' perspective is to acknowledge that the enforcement team in the planning department may benefit from liaising with other 'regulators'. A breach of planning control (especially where it is the result of a planned contravention by a determined contravener) may well involve not only other environmental law contraventions: it may also involve contravention of other statutory regimes – business rates may be unpaid, tax and excise duty may be unpaid, there may even be more serious criminal activity involved. In such cases contraventions of other controls may be important in responding tactically to the problem: the powers of the other authorities may be more effective in putting a stop to an unauthorised use (eg an illegal drinking and gambling club) than planning powers. Other regulatory authorities may therefore be more than willing to take the necessary steps and solve the (planning) problem confronting the LPA.

1.5.3 Proportionate enforcement

One of the important features affecting enforcement success is the 'professional' contravener whose activities are a source of income and for whom planning control (as with other forms of regulation) is merely a troublesome detail of doing business. Often such contraveners will be familiar to other 'regulators' and may be known to ex-policeman enforcement officers from earlier days. The problems that these contraveners pose are significant: unfortunately they can often be the cause of considerable pressure to 'do something' and often lead, unfairly, to a conclusion that the enforcement team is not up to scratch. At the other end of the spectrum is the 'negligent' contravener who is willing to remedy the breach and for whom 'informal' enforcement action will suffice. Between these two there is a varied range of situations – with different levels of difficulty for the enforcement team. As contraventions give rise to a widely differing set of circumstances it is important that the response is matched to those circumstances. In an area where the bulk of contraventions are resolved by informal enforcement or the early stages of formal enforcement the LPA's approach will generally favour the 'persuasive approach'. Yet even these authorities will need to have in place the strategies and organisational ability to deal with the recalcitrant contravener. Where circumstances warrant and the law permits, the authority will then be able to respond appropriately when there are indications that they may be faced by a more determined contravener.

   One aspect of this is appreciating the signs of problems to come and taking appropriate action early to persuade the contravener that it is in his interests not to play around. This robust enforcement stance (which relies on officers being fully aware of the full range of the legal and other sanctions available to them) may not necessarily be palatable to all authorities and personnel. A more conciliatory approach is likely to be taken in rural authorities. Perhaps their motto is that of Orlando in *As You Like It* (Act two, scene seven, line 118): 'let gentleness my strong enforcement be'.

Such an approach however, despite being generally effective in many cases, can be inappropriate when the LPA comes up against a determined contravener protecting a profitable breach of control. So, even in rural authorities where aggressive action is not the norm, the ability to deploy a full range of 'environmental law' sanctions will still be important.

1.5.4 Extra-legal pressure

The LPA should also bear in mind that an 'environmental problem' may be resolved by measures other than those provided for by 'the law'. The legal sanction is not the only penalty which can be effective in influencing behaviour. One good example of this is where the contravener's breach of planning control involves activity which could adversely affect someone in a superior legal position (ie someone who can force the contravener to mend his ways). Such a person may not welcome the fact that there is a 'breach of the law'. In certain circumstances it is the sanction of adverse publicity that can be a basis for resolving a problem: though even here it must be admitted that the background threat of legal sanctions is perhaps still important in convincing the contravener (or the superior legal interests) that the economic benefits of the contravention are outweighed by the disbenefits arising from a bad public image. Viewed from the strategic point of view then enforcement should encompass tactics (not solely legal in character) that can deal with problems. Some problems can be tackled by various legal mechanisms which derive from different regulatory functions of the local authority: thus not only is planning control relevant but also building control, environmental health legislation etc. But 'the law' is not always the answer. The strategic view also reminds us that a 'problem' is also amenable to action by means other than 'the law'.

1.5.5 The enforcement skills, acquisition and deployment

The organisational response needs to take account of the availability and co-ordination of the various skills that may be required to handle an enforcement case. If those skills are not held by those likely to be involved in enforcement or are badly co-ordinated or applied, then the organisational response will be defective. These enforcement skills are:

(a) Investigation/fact-finding skills (ascertaining the fact, nature and scope of the breach). The LPA must be able to rely on the raw data about an alleged contravention as part of its assessment of a problem.

(b) Planning skills (applying knowledge of the planning regime to the circumstances to deal with cases where the fact of breach is unclear and whether a breach merits remedial action or merely needs to be regularised by a permission).

(c) Legal skills (applying a comprehensive knowledge of planning law to the facts of a particular case, advising on difficult issues of planning law, providing creative legal solutions, preparing and presenting cases before the magistrates).

(d) Communication skills (these range from the ability to obtain information from potential contraveners to explaining to other officers, inspectors on appeal and the magistrates' court the gravity of the problem: these skills are needed by a range of enforcement personnel and are not normally well-developed in a desk-bound planner or lawyer).

Recruitment and training must therefore take account of any deficiencies arising from poorly developed skills or a failure to integrate those skills in an effective enforcement strategy. Perhaps the most important skill (especially at the stage of creating support for a planned organisational response to enforcement) is the last one – communication. It is important in winning support for change and is crucial to proper implementation. There must be a feedback loop that helps to identify deficiencies in the mechanisms that reflect the planning trinity: then the LPA can develop strategies for addressing those problems. The broader point is, however, based upon an understanding of how the enforcement skills need to be reflected in the organisation of enforcement for the particular LPA. The authority that lacks personnel with the necessary enforcement skills or fails to integrate those skills in an effective manner will not be effective. It will suffer from problems of communication and tardy decision-making/implementation.

1.5.6 Routinising administration

Giving enforcement the back up of an ordered and routinised

system that supports decision-making and the use of the sanctions available is clearly an important aspect of design. Where activity can be standardised then time-savings will result and the more difficult issues to be faced can be allotted appropriate attention. The other aspects of the planning trinity may well furnish examples of how to improve the administration of enforcement. This should encourage the production of clear and comprehensive procedures for dealing with the various stages of an enforcement case – both within the planning department and within the legal department.

1.5.6.1 *The enforcement manual*

The discussion of enforcement skills indicates the potential for error in liaison between and within organisations. The organisational links both within and between departments should thus be clearly established (taking into account the needs for effective liaison and co-ordination) and set down in a document. For ease of convenience I shall refer to such a document as the enforcement manual. The enforcement manual can be expanded and improved through 'feedback' from individual officers whose activity is covered by the manual. It survives the loss of individual members of the bureaucracy: it thus ensures the learnt wisdom of officers is not lost when they depart. The enforcement manual thus is an important resource which not only guides experienced personnel through the more difficult cases but also acts as a comprehensive training manual for new staff. It may be tempting to throw trainee planners into the deep end with enforcement; however, it is an acceptable strategy only if they have adequate back up in the form of an enforcement manual to help them with the general (and, sometimes, the more specific) issues. The enforcement manual (especially if it is comprehensive and contains summaries regarding the legal basis for action and the limits of the law) is also a very useful 'bible' to quote to complaining neighbours, elected members and officers from other departments who are not fully aware of the problems involved in enforcement.

The manual should also be the appropriate place for pro forma letters. Standard procedures should also be set out. Of course, it is impossible to predict every sort of eventuality that may arise. A routine procedure has its limits when confronted with a case that gives rise to novel issues. However, the routine is, at least, a starting point. It enables the officer to pinpoint the unusual. Situations that fall outside the rules can often help improve those rules. Routine procedures should thus be updated and adapted to suit a wide variety of situations. Adequate procedures for monitoring and assessment are highly desirable elements in any system: these may also find a place in the enforcement manual.

1.5.6.2 *Computerising enforcement*

In the last few years information technology (IT) has become increasingly important for effective enforcement. The hardware (personal computers particularly) is now more widely available at reasonable cost: an increasing range of software packages is available. Both personal computers (offering the stand-alone or small network solution) and mainframes can now support packages that can perform a differing range of administrative tasks from logging calls, diarising visits, recording compliance checks, suggesting enforcement options and even offering tailor-made advice on legal and planning matters. Letter writing, the production of various types of legal documentation and other written materials can be processed very efficiently – avoiding the delays of the departmental typing pool. Officers can easily and very quickly produce crisp and impressive warning letters etc and ensure that these are followed up by visits: the software is invariably easy to use and can be accessed by non-enforcement staff in order to follow up enquiries when the enforcement personnel are not in the office. Such packages (ranging from detailed and flexible stand-alone packages such as cCOPE to the latest ICL add-on module) can dramatically improve the effectiveness of the administrative response to the enforcement workload. Any LPA reviewing its organisational response to enforcement must examine the range of options in IT that are available to it and give IT a key role in any proposed changes. The ability of such packages to produce updating reports on enforcement activity, statistics etc is also an important element in being able to keep the enforcement profile high.

1.5.6.3 *Administrative back up*

The enforcement personnel also need an efficient administrative team. At the early stages of a case it is the general efficiency of the administrative staff in the planning office that is important. Reliable records, reliable systems to 'call-up' time-limited permissions, reliable systems to monitor conditions and agreements are all aspects of normal administrative practice. As an enforcement case progresses, however, the work generated as a result of taking enforcement action (both informal and formal) will itself require efficient administrative back up. Sending out pro forma letters may well be the task of the enforcement officer: however, when the stage of issuing notices and sending copies to various officers in the authority is reached, it will be necessary for such administrative tasks (solely concerned with the enforcement function of the LPA) to be carried out efficiently. In a large enforcement team there might be room for an administrator who is primarily responsible for such tasks. It is he or she who should then ensure that the paperwork is up to date, that any relevant documentation is properly recorded, 'reminders' (eg to make site visits) are followed and warning letters are despatched. In most cases, however, such administrative tasks will be undertaken by the enforcement officer, planning officer, or legal officer, as appropriate. With IT support this can be done relatively efficiently.

1.6 THE GOAL OF EFFECTIVE ENFORCEMENT

The notion of the planning trinity is perhaps the starting point for tackling the challenge of organisational reform. It is a message that requires communication throughout the LPA – particularly the planning and legal departments. It is a concept which requires a strategic view of enforcement to be taken and a concept which puts enforcement on a par with the other two aspects of the planning trinity (forward planning and development control). Implementation will mean a greater co-ordination of the necessary enforcement skills and mechanisms to ensure that the administration of enforcement is streamlined – leaving officers with more time to address the more difficult tasks posed by the determined contravener and more complex breaches of control. Strategic enforcement will enable the LPA to improve its activity both in forward planning, development control and, of course, enforcement. Enforcement will then be less of a 'fire-fighting' exercise that is determined by the insistent complainant: it should develop into a more coherent response of the planning department as a whole where the wider interests of the community in protecting the planning interests of the area are given greater weight. In this way enforcement can start to be more pro-active and address priorities in a more effective and consistent way. It will be able to deploy the most appropriate responses to particular situations and be able to provide options appropriate to the demands of the case. Those options will cover the whole spectrum of formal and informal, legal and extra-legal weapons that are available to the LPA and other agencies whose interests coincide. In this way the enormous variety of contraventions and contraveners can be matched by a similarly wide range of effective enforcement responses. Appropriate action can thus be selected and implemented with a minimum of delay, and with full knowledge of the costs, risks and benefits of such action. The likelihood of resolving the problem at the most opportune moment will increase significantly: this will produce cost savings, a better image for enforcement and improvements in the planning function across the board as all concerned make the planning trinity a tangible reality. This will further improve the perception of enforcement among planning personnel. Enforcement will then start to become more of a central element of the LPA's planning strategy and not merely be seen as a clearing house for complaints handled by 'environmental policemen'.

2 Contraventions – discovery and investigation

2.1 REACTIVE AND PRO-ACTIVE ENFORCEMENT

LPAs normally find that neighbour or public complaint produces more than enough cases without having to search for contraventions by pro-active action. However, some pro-active action should be undertaken. The planning trinity will be undermined if important planning conditions (that are likely to be contravened) are not monitored in an effective fashion by the LPA. In some cases (as with conditions relating to trees) there is almost an enforcement duty placed on LPAs by virtue of statutory language stressing the 'amenity' value of certain important planning interests. Additionally the Ombudsman tends to regard a failure to have monitoring procedures to ensure compliance with conditions as a failing constituting maladministration[1]. Seen from this viewpoint a reactive approach to enforcement is not the way to meet obligations as regards protecting the public interest that is represented by planning. Monitoring can thus be all but a legal obligation for the LPA and pro-active enforcement should thus not be seen merely as an optional activity.

1 See reports 667/H/80 and 181/H/81.

2.1.1 Pro-active enforcement – planning agreements

The monitoring of planning agreements is less well established than for conditions. This may be an acceptable state of affairs where the agreement merely provides for a one-off transaction (the transfer of land etc); however, where the agreement has long-term conditional commitments or restrictions there should

19

be more formal methods for overseeing the situation[1]. (Detailed aspects of the enforcement of agreements will not be discussed here – see chapter fourteen for a discussion of the issues.) Of course, elements such as phasing conditions would tie in with on-site controls and monitoring. The legal nature of the agreement (since it should have been properly drafted so as to ensure that the obligations are enforceable against subsequent purchasers of the land) also helps to ensure that the contracting party who wants to then sell it on will want to be sure that he or she has met his side of the bargain. Prospective purchasers would usually point out any 'problems'. Yet this consideration does not play a part if the contracting party is the freeholder who wishes to maintain a long-term interest in the premises. If such a contracting party is under restrictive obligations (eg not to use certain premises in a certain way) or even conditional positive obligations (eg to restore the premises to a certain standard on the happening of a specified event) he may be able to ignore those obligations if the local authority fails to monitor the situation. Thus an important element of using planning agreements is ensuring that the legal provisions are matched by administrative/bureaucratic mechanisms that provide adequate monitoring of the planning situation. The planning trinity provides a useful viewpoint on the monitoring of planning agreements. An important, long-term obligation can be matched up with a monitoring clause by which the landowner is required to supply an authoritative statement of continuing compliance: this may be an obligation met, in practice, by an appropriate professional advisor so that such statements can be accepted at face value. LPAs cannot just rely on the planner/lawyer involved to keep it under review; those officers may well leave the authority before the need for monitoring becomes unimportant.

1   The use of a planning obligation as a 'monitor and mitigate' mechanism that can help reduce the risks of unforeseen adverse impacts prejudicing the interests of the community is perhaps an aspect of planning obligations that will become important. For further discussion of this topic see my Lawyer's Aside column in *Planning*, 8 July 1994.

2.1.2   Pro-active enforcement – other elements

Information sources external to the planning department can be used in the monitoring process. Parish councils, amenity groups, conservation area advisory committees etc can all be involved in a constructive effort (as part of their general involvement in the planning process) to help with the monitoring of conditions and agreements. They also provide, along with neighbours, a warning system for unauthorised developments. Other organisations within the local authority can be brought into a system that provides some monitoring of developments. Devoting resources to such sources of information also would be desirable to counterbalance the problem of 'differential enforcement' which effectively means that the more salubrious areas are better protected by the vociferous middle-classes able and willing to report breaches of control[1]. In terms of serving the planning interests of all the inhabitants of the area such a concern for more a 'democratic' enforcement stance is warranted. The underlying idea of 'enabling' those outside the planning department to detect breaches of planning control is clearly an appropriate technique given the importance of that term in local government today.

1 See the 1987 discussion by Jowell and Millichap of 'differential enforcement' (para 1.3.4, note 1).

2.2 NEIGHBOUR COMPLAINTS

The aggrieved neighbour however, remains the primary source of information regarding breaches of control. Many authorities will find that such a source provides more than enough work for the enforcement team. The reactive approach to enforcement (taking enforcement action in response to information from sources outside the local authority) does however have disadvantages. Neighbour disputes may well be the cause of a complaint made to the authority. Sometimes the authority is asked to take enforcement action against a problem that has both private law and public law aspects to it. One example is found in the PAD reports (3 PAD 386): here the LPA was persuaded to take action against a plywood board measuring 66 inches by 52 inches which was supported on two wooden posts – directly opposite and very close to a window. The aggrieved neighbour had failed to have the board removed by legal action (up to the Court of Appeal) and so then managed to persuade the LPA to take action. The enforcement notice was upheld – after some delay by the appellant.

The individual aggrieved neighbour is also supplemented by the amenity group. If a vocal amenity group (prior to elections!) is especially persuasive it may well force a 'political' decision that has little basis in planning law. Amenity groups in conservation areas may, therefore, be dangerous animals forcing decisions on vulnerable councillors and taking up valuable time from handling breaches of control in other areas (the differential enforcement problem). The LPA should therefore try to deal with the negative aspects of neighbour complaints by ensuring that hasty decisions are not taken by members but that officers are able to provide appropriate analysis where the recommendation to approve development retrospectively has not been followed.

2.2.1 Educating the whistleblower

To some extent the 'preventive education' of groups (and to some extent possible contraveners) may be a useful tactic. Thus letting amenity groups know the limitations of enforcement (possibly by an edited version of the enforcement manual) and the extent to which legal issues about development produce problems may enable councillors to withstand pressure from such groups. This education of amenity groups (and the aggrieved neighbour) may also have positive benefits if their energies are enlisted in handling enforcement cases that are taken on by the council. Neighbours should be schooled in the need for concrete evidence regarding the breach. Such evidence is necessary (and this should be communicated to neighbours) in order to deal at appeal with the inspector's misgivings about whether or not action is justified. Magistrates also need to see the 'victim' of any contravention: since the environment cannot always be easily portrayed in this light the unfortunate neighbour is often the next best 'victim' (see further, chapter nine on presenting prosecutions before the magistrates' court). LPAs that stress, to the aggrieved neighbour, that they may have to stand up before the inspector or the court may also find that the complaint is not so serious after all. So educating the whistleblower sometimes reduces the number of enforcement cases that have to be taken up.

2.2.2   The administrative response to complaints

Efficient logging of complaints and the efficient follow-through with such action as is necessary is naturally an important aspect of handling an enforcement case. The benefits of routinised enforcement and IT have already been mentioned and these are naturally relevant here. Heightened awareness among the public (citizens charters may have had some impact) mean that LPAs need to have an effective administrative response to complaints. Enforcement manuals may be relevant as (in terms of communicating with complainants and other external sources) it may be appropriate to produce edited versions of such manuals so that such external sources of enforcement work are aware of the enforcement process. Such documentation may also be the basis of leaflets to potential contraveners (where a particular section of the community generates particular types of activity): this may help educate the negligent contravener and prevent breaches of planning control.

2.2.3 Planning policy and the multi-cultural community

In some cases the legitimate interests of an identifiable ethnic community will justify the adoption of planning policies addressing those interests. Some authorities, for example, have more generous policies regarding extension of dwelling houses in areas where the population is predominantly from a community where large families are an integral feature of that community's life. If standard policies (designed to accommodate the nuclear family of modern western society) are applied then this may not only lead to more contraventions but may also lead to the dissolution of that community. Forward planning policy should therefore address such special concerns – not only from the viewpoint of that community's planning interests but also from the viewpoint of 'enforcement avoidance'.

2.3 CONDITIONS

A prerequisite for the enforcement of a condition is its precise formulation. This is even more important if the LPA wants to have the option of using the breach of condition notice provisions. There are two perspectives here. First is the formulation of conditions that are legally valid. Second is the formulation of conditions that accord with DOE advice: such advice is more stringent than the legal criteria so LPAs, given the fact that enforcement action (other than breach of condition notices) is appealable to the DOE, will need to give that advice considerable attention. However, the DOE's policy stance is not foolproof as regards the interpretation of the law: circulars have made mistakes as to the law – so the LPA may find that expert legal advice suggests that the legal analysis of the DOE could be challenged if it were to be used by the DOE in quashing a condition. The legal validity of conditions is thus an important issue to examine – but this should be done on the basis of a critical legal eye being applied to the relevant central government advice.

2.3.1 LPA standard conditions

The LPA's standard list of conditions should be refined to address problems discovered over the years. (Feedback from enforcement, an aspect of the planning trinity perspective, should be a standard feature that also helps improve the standard list.) However, the standard list will rarely deal with every situation. Unusual situations arising at the development control stage should thus be given special attention. An experienced planner familiar with the wording of conditions should therefore be available to ensure that site-specific conditions are properly constructed: this may require some 'screening' procedure to be set up. Junior planners should also be effectively supervised when site-specific conditions are being drawn up. Where the matters being conditioned are either complex or unlikely to find the support of the Secretary of State then authorities should consider concluding a planning agreement with the owner/developer.

2.4 INVESTIGATING AN ALLEGED CONTRAVENTION

Once the whistle has been blown on a possible contravention of control the LPA's enforcement team should swing into action with the standardised response. This should be set out comprehensively in the enforcement manual, or for those employing IT, prompted by the software package. An on-site assessment (after the necessary preparation using the planning register etc) will normally be needed. Written requests for information may also be utilised: a discussion of the three principal powers allowing the LPA to require written responses to questions about the legal and planning status of the land follows the discussion of entry powers. The steps to be taken to ascertain information should be set out in procedure notes (whether computer-generated or otherwise): this information will naturally include data about the planning status of the site recorded in the LPA's own records. (Liaison with other departments may also be appropriate where the breach appears to involve other 'environmental' regimes: again, this is an item for the LPA's procedure notes etc.) A purpose-designed checklist should routinely be employed by the investigating officer going on site: this means that those issues that are always relevant are always covered and the basic information clearly set out for the file, computer record or whatever. If entry onto the site (or a neighbouring site) is appropriate the officer should go prepared with a suitably comprehensive written authorisation so that the various statutory powers governing entry can be cited.

2.5 ENTRY POWERS

The 1991 reforms provided for special entry powers for enforcement purposes. These cover mainstream enforcement. For the more specialised sub-regimes the reader should refer the particular chapter in question where the specific statutory provisions are noted. Para 2.5.5 discusses those cases where the general-purpose power under section 324 is still relevant.

2.5.1 Entry without warrant

Special powers to enter land without a warrant for the purposes of enforcement action are given by section 196A (with supplementary provisions in section 196C). (The general-purpose powers formerly available under section 324 are now not available for the purposes of mainstream enforcement.) Section 196A(1) provides that the officer exercising this right must:

   (a) be duly authorised in writing by the authority;
   (b) exercise the right to enter at a reasonable hour;

(c) have reasonable grounds for using the powers;

(d) not enter any building used as a dwellinghouse as of right unless 24 hours' notice of the intended entry has been given to the occupier.

The purposes for which entry under this provision can be sought comprise:

(a) ascertaining whether there is or has been a breach of planning control on the land *or any other land*;

(b) determine whether any enforcement powers under Part VII of the TCPA 1990 would be exercised in relation to that *land or any other land*;

(c) determining how such powers should be exercised in relation to that land *or any other land*;

(d) ascertaining whether there has been compliance with any requirement imposed as a result of any such enforcement power having been exercised in relation to the land *or any other land*[1].

This power therefore deals with mainstream enforcement activity – action against breaches of planning control in the limited technical sense of that term. In section 196C there are supplementary provisions – for example the officer must, if so asked, produce evidence of his authority and state the purpose of his entry before so entering (section 196C(1)(a)). Compensation is payable under the provisions of the TCPA 1990 for damage done to chattels (section 196C(3)). Obstruction of an officer acting under these entry powers is a summary offence punishable by a fine up to level 3 (section 196C(2))[2].

1 TCPA 1990, s 196A(1)(a), (b), (c) and (d) respectively.
2 See para 9.6.11 for the standard scale of fines.

2.5.2 Police escort

An important element in the supplementary provisions is section 196C(1)(b): this allows the officer exercising the rights of entry under section 196A or 196B to 'take with him such other persons as may be necessary'. This can cover a wide range of purposes but in the light of the risks of personal violence the most relevant use of this provision would be to ensure that uniformed police can escort the authorised officer in cases where there is a significant risk of violence. The appropriateness of requesting such an escort should be an element addressed specifically in any enforcement manual etc dealing with compliance checks and site visits in general.

2.5.3 Warrant search

Under section 196B the authority may apply to the local magistrates' court for a warrant to enter land for any of the purposes allowed under the ordinary entry powers. Such an application to the magistrates must show that either:

(a) admission to the land has been refused or a refusal is reasonably apprehended; or
(b) the case is one of urgency.

Demonstrating that a 'refusal is reasonably apprehended' may require some background information about the person in occupation and his past record as regards contravention of planning or other controls. A profitable contravention is clearly likely to be the sort of situation where a determined contravener will be likely to refuse admission. Such factors are similar in many respects to those factors that will show a 'pattern' of non-compliance for the purposes of a statutory injunction restraining an 'apprehended' breach: see chapter nine's discussion of the statutory planning injunction. The holder of the warrant must be duly authorised in writing by the LPA: it would be prudent to supply the magistrates with information as to due authorisation. The warrant can be used once – within one month from date of issue. Entry must be at a reasonable hour unless the case is one of urgency. The urgency criterion would tie in to breaches that cannot easily be remedied or significantly affect the character of the land: for example the felling of a tree, the destruction of an important unlisted building or the installation of hardstanding on rural land. The LPA must be able to illustrate an urgency case by reference to the impact on the 'victim' otherwise the magistrates will not be able to understand what all the fuss is about: educating the Bench is discussed in detail in chapter nine. The legal arguments must therefore be fully illustrated by concrete planning arguments which portray the position clearly and graphically. The existence of forward planning policies will be useful, as will past appeal decisions or even criminal prosecutions affecting the land or the contravener. Procedure notes should address such issues to ensure that applications are fully supported. The supplementary provisions in section 196C also apply to warrant searches.

2.5.4   Section 324 entry powers still relevant

Investigation of any land with a view to:

(a) taking action under section 106(6) for breach of a planning obligation;
(b) issuing a wasteland notice (section 215); or
(c) action under the advertisement control regime;

still fall under the powers of section 324. This is the effect of section 324(1)(c) of the TCPA 1990 which provides that the LPA may 'at any reasonable time enter any land for the purpose of surveying it in connection with – . . . any proposal by the local planning authority . . . to . . . issue any . . . notice under . . . Part III (other than sections 94 and 96), or Chapter 2 or 3 of Part VIII' of the TCPA 1990. Section 324(3) of the TCPA 1990 also grants additional entry powers related to action against flyposting under section 225: these are additional to those in section 324(1) and can be exercisable if the land is occupied and the power to deal with flyposting could not be exercised without entry.

The 'any proposal . . . to . . . issue any notice' is a key term in the section 324 power as it defines the precondition that must be satisfied in order to use these powers. It has been subject to judicial analysis in a case where it was argued that a 'proposal to acquire' land required the authority to make a formal resolution or have an unequivocal intention to do so[1]. The court rejected this interpretation. Such an interpretation would, in the enforcement context, conflict with the obvious need for the authority to have first-hand information on which to base its decision about enforcement. So 'proposal' would *not* seem to require some explicit authorisation on the part of the local authority – merely an intention to do something which depends on an investigation providing relevant information (eg evidence of a breach of control). If proof of the inspector's authority is required he must produce it before entering[2]. The 'inspector' may only demand admission to the land (though this only covers 'occupied land') if 24 hours' notice of the intended entry has been given to the occupier[3]. Other supplementary provisions cover damage to land etc. There is no provision for warrant search in sections 324 and 325.

1 *R v Secretary of State for the Environment, ex p North Herefordshire District Council* (1989) 88 LGR 109. The phrase 'proposal to acquire' occurs in section 8 of the Caravan Sites Act 1968.
2 TCPA 1990, s 325(1)(a)
3 TCPA 1990, s 325(1)(b).

2.5.5 Requisitions for information

Written requests for information about the planning or legal status of the land etc may come at this stage or later (eg when enforcement notices are being prepared for issue and service or criminal proceedings are being considered). The service requirements for enforcement notices mean that a reasonable effort on the part of the authority to identify persons with an 'interest which in the opinion of the authority is materially affected by the notice' must be made. This does not require the authority to find every ownership interest in the land. Indeed the test is primarily one of ascertaining those interests 'materially affected' by the notice. The further gloss on this test is that it is only an interest 'which in the opinion of the authority' is materially affected by the notice. This does not mean that the authority can, capriciously, form an 'opinion' that only X will be 'materially affected' when other persons are known or suspected to be involved in the breach of control or otherwise connected by means of legal ties to the land. Again it may be the understandably cautious attitude of legal officers in the authority that gives rise to such careful attention to detail. In contrast I have heard of one authority at least which does not even bother with requisitions for information and, apparently, has had no problems with its enforcement notices! Such a robust attitude however may not always be possible.

The overly cautious attitude that may be too prevalent does need to be tempered somewhat. The fact that painstaking investigation is not necessarily required may not be widely appreciated: the misconception seems to have arisen in at least one Ombudsman investigation. Thus in a report criticising Birmingham City Council[1] the Ombudsman stressed that under planning law the authority only had to make 'reasonable inquiry' – there was no need to go through the lengthy procedures adopted by the officers (legal and non-legal) in trying to trace every owner. One planner concerned thought that the LPA could not take action until the names and addresses of *all* owners and occupiers were known. This may be a common misunderstanding – unwittingly fostered perhaps by cautious staff in the legal department.

1 87/B/230 – reported at [1989] JPL 287.

2.5.6 Principal requisition powers

There are three main powers (discussed in detail below) by which authorities may require information from those connected with the contravening activity or with legal interests in the land:

(a) TCPA 1990, section 330;
(b) Local Government (Miscellaneous Provisions) Act 1976, section 16;
(c) TCPA 1990, section 171C.

The requisition power is not only useful in terms of achieving its main purpose of gathering information about 'material interests'. It also has a subsidiary aspect. The issue of such a notice (by reason of its 'legal' nature) may help to convince contraveners that the authority is taking the issue seriously. Sometimes then the issue of a requisition for information may have a 'catalytic' effect on the enforcement process and help produce a speedier resolution of the problem.

2.5.7 Section 330 notice

A local authority may use a section 330 notice 'for the purpose of enabling . . . [it] to make an order or issue or serve any notice or other document'[1] under the TCPA 1990[2]. This section may thus be used at any time since 'enabling' would seem to cover the process prior to authorisation of enforcement action. The authority may therefore use the procedure at a very early stage while still assessing the situation. Use at an early stage may be desirable where the officers handling the case consider that either:

(a) a section 330 notice might have a 'catalytic' effect; or
(b) there might be difficulty getting the necessary information from those served with the notice.

In the former case the possible boost of serving a 'legal' notice is useful per se. Those who have inadvertently breached control may well try to resolve the problem with the LPA once they get the letter from the legal department. In the second case an early start will enable the authority to keep to an enforcement schedule and show (the inspector or magistrates if necessary) that it has acted reasonably despite problems with non-replies.

1 TCPA 1990, s 330(1).
2 P(LB&CA)A 1990, s 89(1) applies TCPA 1990, s 330 for the purposes of the P(LB&CA)A 1990 as it applies for the purposes of the TCPA 1990.

2.5.7.1 *Information that may be requested*

Six items of information may be requested under a section 330 notice. These are:

(a) the nature of the interest in the premises of the person on whom the notice is served;

(b) the name and address of any other person known to him as having an interest in the premises;

(c) the purpose for which the premises are being used;

(d) the time when that use began;

(e) the name and address of any person known to the person on whom the notice is served as having used the premises for that purpose;

(f) the time when any activities being carried out on the premises began.

The LPA may therefore ask the person served to state whether his interest is freehold, leasehold or by licence: the period of such interest can also be requested. If the authority uses the legislation's wording as regards 'activities' the response to this particular question will often be disappointing. A person receiving such a question as to his 'activities' is often at a loss as to what it means: the authority should therefore expand on this particular phraseology and, where possible, describe the actual contravening use or building operations as is appropriate. If the authority merely parrots the statutory phrase the recipient will often not know what is being asked of him. At least the recipient who fails to respond cannot use the excuse that the notice was unclear. Pro forma, commercially-available versions of requisition notices can often encourage officers to use rather technical language and so they should be used with care.

2.5.7.2 *Persons on whom notice may be served*

A section 330 notice may be served on any:

(a) occupier of any premises;
(b) person, who either directly or indirectly, receives rent in respect of any premises.

The section's use of the term 'premises' (rather than the more normal phrase 'land') may cause problems of interpretation. There is no definition of 'premises' in the TCPA 1990. Other legal definitions vacillate between it being land (where land does not include buildings), land and buildings, or just buildings. If 'premises' means only buildings then the scope of section 330 is cut down where the authority wishes to seek information from the 'occupier' of land on which there are no buildings. Contravening uses of green belt land with no buildings may thus be one type of serious breach which could give rise to this problem. The sidenote to the section uses the word 'land' so it could be construed widely so as to cover buildings[1]. The problem is made more difficult as there is criminal liability for failing to comply with the section – here the courts would apply a restrictive interpretation because the interpretation of the term has a direct bearing on criminal liability.

1 'Power to require information as to interests in land'.

2.5.7.3 *Penalties*

Those served with a notice are liable for:

(a) failure to respond within 21 days of service (or such longer time as may be specified in the notice, or allowed by the local authority);
(b) knowingly making any misstatement in respect of the information requested[1].

Liability under the first offence is summary only (it is not a case that can be heard by the Crown Court). A fine up to level 3 on the standard scale (see para 9.6.11 for the current scale). The second is triable either way and is punishable in the magistrates' court by a fine not exceeding £1,000; in the Crown Court the penalties are a fine and/or imprisonment for a term not exceeding two years. Whether or not a mandatory injunction under section 222 of the Local Government Act 1972 would be granted to compel a response in situations demanding urgent action is something which may need to be examined – see chapter nine's discussion of injunctions.

1   TCPA 1990, s 330(2).

2.5.7.4   *Planning (Listed Buildings and Conservation Areas) Act 1990 functions*

By virtue of the P(LB&CA)A 1990, section 89(1) a number of provisions from the principal Act (ie the TCPA 1990) apply for the purposes of the P(LB&CA)A 1990 as they apply for the purposes of the TCPA 1990. Six different sections are covered by this provision. Section 330 is one of those provisions and thus the LPA should be aware that enforcement action under the P(LB&CA)A 1990 also gives rise to the section 330 power.

2.5.8   Local Government (Miscellaneous Provisions) Act 1976, section 16

This power has advantages over the power that is contained in the planning legislation. First, the penalties are more severe for failing to respond and so there is more encouragement for a prompt response. Second, the time period for replying is shorter. Third, there is no difficulty over interpreting 'premises'. It is, however, focused on the legal issues at stake – basically the ownership interests.

2.5.8.1   *Overview*

The power is expressed to arise where the authority (with a view to performing a function conferred by any enactment) considers that it ought to have information connected with any land. Those who may be served comprise:

(a) the occupier of the land;
(b) any freeholder, mortgagee or lessee;
(c) any person who directly or indirectly receives rent for the land;
(d) any person who, under an arrangement with a person interested in the land, either
  (i) manages, or
  (ii) arranges for the letting of the land[1].

The range of persons who can be served is thus much wider than that covered by a section 330 notice (occupier, person receiving rent). A person with a superior interest in the land may well be interested in the breach of control (the existence of which would be signalled by the issue of a section 16 notice since it must state which function of the authority is relevant). Giving such 'information' to those able to exert pressure on the contravener or his immediate landlord may itself have useful side-effects.

1 Local Government (Miscellaneous Provisions) Act 1976, s 16(1).

2.5.8.2 *Contents of notice*

A section 16 requisition must specify:

(a) the land;
(b) the function which the authority wishes to perform;
(c) the enactment which confers that function;
(d) the period for replying (which shall not be less than 14 days).

A section 16 notice may require the recipient to supply, within the period stated, the following information:

(a) the nature of his interest in the land; and
(b) the name and address of each person whom the recipient believes
  (i) is the occupier of the land; or
  (ii) falls within the descriptions set out above in sub-paras (b) to (d) of the previous paragraph.

2.5.8.3 *The sanction*

The penalty for non-compliance with a section 16 notice is a fine not exceeding level 5 on the standard scale[1]. In terms of section 16 non-compliance there are two offences – failure to respond within the stated period is the first. The second consists of furnishing information which the accused either knows to be false, or is made recklessly and contains a false statement.

1 Local Government (Miscellaneous Provisions) Act 1976 s 16(2). See para 9.6.11 for the current scale of fines.

2.5.9 Planning contravention notices

One of the problems of the enforcement regime has been getting information from and talking seriously to contraveners – without getting involved in formal enforcement. Carnwath suggested a 'contravention notice' which would act in this way and section 171C introduced the 'planning contravention notice' (PCN). This is more focused on the planning situation than the previous mechanisms discussed above. The Carnwath proposals indicate that this is a mechanism appropriate in certain circumstances and offers the possibility of earlier negotiations with the alleged contravener to resolve any problem. The PCN thus has two distinct roles. It can be used to:

(a) obtain information; and/or
(b) arrange a meeting at which the recipient can discuss the problem and possibly negotiate a remedy.

2.5.9.1 *Who can be served?*

Section 171C(1) indicates that a PCN can be served on:

(a) owners;
(b) occupiers;
(c) those with any other interest;
(d) those carrying out operations on the land;
(e) those using the land for any purpose.

This provision is not tied just to those who have 'normal' legal interests in the land. Builders and squatters/trespassers (for example) can also be served with such notices (if they are carrying out building, engineering, mining or other operations on the land or are using it). The power to serve arises '[w]here it appears to the local planning authority that there may have been a breach of planning control in respect of any land. . .'. The impact of this statutory provision is illustrated by *R v Teignbridge District Council, ex p Teignmouth Quay Company Ltd* where a PCN was quashed by the High Court because there was in fact no apparent breach of control: the LPA had merely wanted to verify information regarding the statutory undertaking[1].

1   (1994) Times, 12 December.

2.5.9.2   *Contents of a PCN*

The PCN can require that the person served:

(a) make a statement as to whether or not the land is being used for any purpose specified in the notice;

(b) make a statement as to whether or not any operations or activities specified in the notices are being or have been carried out on the land;

(c) make a statement as to when any use, operations or activities began;

(d) give the name and address of any person know to him to use or have used the land for any purpose or to be carrying out, or have carried out, any operations or activities on the land;

(e) give any information he holds as to any planning permission for any use or operations or any reason for planning permission not being required for any use or operations;

(f) state the nature of his interest (if any) in the land and the name and address of any other person known to him to have an interest in the land.

These items of information are *specific examples* of what may generally be required of the person served: there are two general categories of information (section 171C(2)) which can be the subject of a PCN. These can be split into four specific types of information – to illustrate the general scope of the PCN requirements. Thus the person served may be required to give information about:

(a) any operations being carried out on the land;

(b) any use of the land;

(c) any other activities being carried out on the land; and
(d) any matter relating to the conditions or limitations subject
to which any planning permission in respect of the land
has been granted.

The PCN is thus, essentially, a way of obtaining a planning
'snapshot' from which an accurate planning description of
the site and any activity on it can be produced. If the breach is
a change of use then the questions should be able to elicit
the appropriate information about that change of use – whether
it is unauthorised development of a breach of condition/
limitation. The LPA should be crystal clear in setting out what
information is required: as already stressed above the questions
should avoid the technical language used by the legislation and
deal in specifics that will be comprehensible to the recipient. So
the DOE's pro forma PCN (see circular 21/91, appendix to annex
1) should be used with care just like any other pro forma
requisition notice. Pro forma notices can, therefore, be self-
defeating in this particular situation as they invariably utilise
the rather technical legal language of the statute rather than
inviting the LPA to translate the legal rules into more intelligible
questions.

2.5.9.3 *Sanctions for non-compliance*

It is an offence not to comply with any requirement for
information in such a notice. (Failure to turn up at a meeting
suggested in a PCN invites no sanction under sections 171C or
171D: see below on the time and place aspects of the PCN.) A
complete failure to provide information within 21 days, without
reasonable excuse, is subject to a maximum fine of £1,000; the
penalty for making a false or misleading statement in reply is
also a summary offence: a fine of up to £5,000[1]. There is a further
sanction in that failure to comply may also reduce the amount
of compensation payable for subsequent wrongful service by the
LPA of a stop notice. In reality the LPA may well have an
informal policy of not prosecuting for non-compliance as little
may be gained from the costly pursuit of a conviction: naturally,
this realistic approach should not be made public.

1 TCPA 1990, ss 171D(4) & 171D(6) respectively.

2.5.9.4   *The time and place offer*

The second role for which a PCN may be used (if the LPA so wishes) is to give notice of a time and place (section 171C(4)) at which:

(a) any offer which the person served may wish to make to apply for planning permission, to refrain from carrying out any operations or activities or to undertake remedial works; and

(b) any representations which he may wish to make *about the notice*;

will be considered by the authority. The statute talks of the authority considering the representations: it would seem necessary (unless the LPA envisages the contravener making representations to committee) to make standing orders giving planning officers the power to hear such representations on behalf of the LPA. Should criminal proceedings be taken on the basis of information produced at such an interview the contravener will employ every technical device available. The comments below on PACE are also relevant.

2.5.9.5   *Pro forma undertakings under section 106*

The time and place option may not be as widely used by LPAs as the information option. However, it does offer the LPA an opportunity to gauge the intentions of the recipient and even secure compliance with planning control via a cost-effective mechanism. The time and place offer may also have a catalytic effect in speeding up the handling of the case – an underlying aim of the legislation. The reference in the legislation to an 'undertaking' should ring a few bells with the enforcement team: a meeting may be the occasion for asking the contravener to commit himself to a planning obligation under section 106 – the provision under which a 'unilateral undertaking' may be given. (The possibility of this was hinted at by Carnwath (page 67).) The specifics will vary according to the circumstances but the basic aim is to see if a contravener's protestations about his bona fides are in fact real. Officers should, in this case, present him with a unilateral undertaking under section 106 which has been prepared by the LPA in advance. It should encapsulate the offer made to refrain from carrying out activities or to undertake remedial works. If the contravener has the legal capacity to give such an undertaking then his failure to sign a deed of undertaking to that effect would indicate to the authority that he was stalling: he need not be required to do so there and then but if he does not do so within a period judged reasonable then the LPA can move on to more formal action. (A reasonably worded undertaking should not be objectionable if the contravener is serious about complying with planning control.) This strategy can therefore act as a catalyst in the process or help the LPA take proportionate enforcement action. The LPA solicitor will be able to advise on the content of the draft undertaking: in practice it would often be complete except for the 'compliance' date and description of action required. The solicitor will also advise on the professional conduct rules that apply if the LPA solicitor is present during such a meeting.

2.5.9.6 *PACE caution*

As noted in para 9.3.1 the LPA officer investigating a contravention (eg while visiting the premises in question) may well have reasonable grounds to suspect that an offence (eg contravention of listed building control) has taken place. Case law indicates that the codes under the Police and Criminal Evidence Act can apply to the activities of LPA officers such as the enforcement officer. Since a time and place meeting may actually provide 'reasonable grounds' for believing that an offence has taken place the LPA will be advised to caution the contravener. Naturally this is not necessary if the contravention is only a mainstream breach for which criminal sanctions only arise where the enforcement notice is not obeyed. However, the cautioning of the contravener may itself be a useful catalyst in obtaining a more compliant response from the contravener and may in fact be used 'liberally' by some LPA officers in order to gain a psychological advantage. This may be relevant in situations where a standardised unilateral undertaking is being used. Other PACE requirements should also be noted and the best place for incorporating the details of such duties is the enforcement manual. The Appendix contains extracts from the PACE codes that may be relevant to the work of the enforcement team.

2.6   WHICH NOTICE?

The notices are subtly different. Section 16 notices are primarily concerned with legal title etc: they are perhaps more relevant when checking on ownership of the land concerned – perhaps with a view to the technical aspects of the notice or a prosecution. Section 330 shades over into planning issues. The planning status of the land is the real focus of PCNs. The different penalties and periods allowed for replies are a factor in choosing the relevant notice: Carnwath suggested 14 days for answering a PCN but the legislation in fact provides a 21 day period. The choice of notice may also depend on the catalytic impact of the notice and its capacity to provide a speedy idea of the alleged contravener's bona fides. A section 16 notice may be more appropriate if these concerns are more relevant in the particular case. There are authorities who take a more liberal view of the various provisions and in fact ask questions which fall outside the ambit of the relevant provision. (This may be said to be creative use of the legal powers but many LPA solicitors would feel uncomfortable about such action.) From the viewpoint of effective enforcement such tactics may be of interest to other LPAs though naturally such an approach could lead to problems later if the contravener used such examples of LPA practice as an argument (before an inspector or the courts) against the merits and legality of enforcement action.

It appears that (after an initial enthusiasm) the use of PCNs is declining. Perhaps this was due to an over-optimistic assessment of their likely success: the low fines for non-compliance with the information requirements and the problems posed by the determined contravener or the over-legalistic/ technical framing of questions may be reasons for the decline. (Perhaps the word 'contravention' suggested that it was a mechanism whose primary use was to stop breaches of planning control – much like an enforcement notice.) Experience with the PCN does illustrate the need for a more sophisticated approach to the appropriate choice of mechanism. (The later discussion of breach of condition notices has some bearing on this aspect of the reforms.) Every enforcement power has its strengths and weaknesses. The effective LPA will ensure that its staff are given guidance on how to use the various powers to the best effect.

2.7   LAND REGISTRY SEARCH

The LPA may also apply to the Chief Land Registrar of the appropriate district land registry under the Land Registration Acts 1925, section 129 for particulars of persons with legal interests in the land affected by a breach of planning control. When used in appropriate cases it is an efficient means of gaining information as to those with mortgagee, freehold or long leasehold interests in the land. It should be considered when the contravener and other parties involved in a breach have been tardy or inconsistent in replies to requests for information. It is also very useful when it comes to establishing (for the purposes of a prosecution against relevant owners) the ownership interests in the land. Such information can overcome the problem of having to prove ownership in a way which avoids having to rely on the presumption of continuing ownership: the case of *R v Ruttle, ex p Marshall* illustrates problems with this element in the prosecution case[1].

---

1   (1989) 57 P & CR 299. See chapter nine's discussion of prosecution proceedings for non-compliance with enforcement notices.

2.7.1   Fax and telephone searches

There are five telephone centres which can handle enquiries regarding any registered title in England and Wales. These are:

Croydon: 0171 312 2332
Durham: 0191 301 0019
Gloucester: 01452 511117
Lytham: 01253 840011
Stevenage: 01438 788887

A general description of procedures and telephone numbers for further advice are given on HMLR notes PRL004 and PRL005 (telephone) and note PRL006 (fax). Rules for using these procedures should be set out in the legal department's enforcement manual so that the importance of having evidence as to ownership is given proper attention at the appropriate stage.

2.7.2   On-line searches

Searches (via a PC connected by an ISDN line and terminal adapter) can be made of HMLR's computer-held records. Such 'direct access services' as the HMLR terms them will involve an IBM compatible PC (286 or better) with hard disk and at least 640K RAM, running MS-DOS 3.3, 5 or 6. Such hardware requirements may have implications for the choice of hardware/ software by the enforcement team for computerising the administration of its enforcement work: clearly the use of such direct access services by the local authority needs to be seen in terms of the needs and priorities of other departments and specialities. The enforcement team may therefore wish to add its comments to any proposal for establishing such a link with HMLR as the benefits may be of relevance to the enforcement workload of the LPA. For further details the LPA should contact the Director of IT, 32 Lincoln's Inn Fields, London, WC2A 3PH (tel 0171 917 8888).

2.8   DEFINITIONAL PROBLEMS

The site visit and/or responses to written requests for information should provide a clear basis on which the LPA can then properly consider the use of its enforcement powers. Where a breach of a planning condition is involved the LPA now has the option of using the breach of condition notice (BCN). The powers relating to the BCN procedure are discussed in chapter three. The present discussion focuses on the preliminary legal issues affecting the basis of the enforcement discretion under mainstream enforcement. In turning to the exercise of the enforcement discretion the basic elements of that power must be examined. The LPA may issue an enforcement notice under section 172(1) when 'it appears to them (a) that there has been a breach of planning control; and (b) that it is expedient to issue the notice, having regard to the provisions of the development plan and to any other material considerations'. The following discusses the first precondition – the 'apparent breach' issue. The legal issues related to the exercise of the discretion in terms of the 'expediency' factor (the enforcement merits) are left to chapter five.

2.8.1 'Where it appears to the local planning authority'

The 'appears' standard does not require that the LPA be convinced beyond all reasonable doubt that a breach of control has occurred or that they must conclusively find it expedient to take action. Some evidence of a breach of planning control will suffice – bearing in mind the powers given to them to investigate the situation and gather such evidence. Administrative law principles suggest that some investigation and appraisal of the situation (both legal and planning) is thus implicitly required of the LPA if the 'apparent' breach test is to be met. Invariably however authorities will take more than sufficient pains to inform themselves of the relevant issues and so get past the first 'legal' hurdle. Mistakes may happen. Even thorough investigations might not reveal the true facts: sometimes the legal position (chapters three and four examine aspects of this) is not crystal clear. With changes of use that could rely on the 28 or 14 day periods in the GPDO the LPA should try to ascertain the intention of the person responsible[1]. From such information they can then judge if the change is going to keep within the 28 or 14 day limit or exceed it and so constitute a change of use requiring permission[2]. The LPA need not wait until the relevant period has been exceeded. However, if a reasonable amount of investigation and appraisal has been carried out then the 'apparent' breach of control (even if the authority is mistaken) will still give rise to the valid exercise of discretion. If an 'apparent' breach is thus mistakenly attacked (there is in fact no breach) in an enforcement notice the authority should withdraw the notice as soon as the error is confirmed: a claim for costs (see chapter seven) will otherwise be risked.

1 See [1993] JPL 296 for a ministerial decision on an enforcement notice where the LPA was found to be entitled to rely upon the initial appearance of a market use to find that the intention was to establish a permanent market: DOE ref T/APP/C/91/P1805/612625.
2 *Tidswell v Secretary of State for the Environment* (1977) 34 P & CR 152 illustrates the appropriateness of the LPA forming (as part of the 'apparent breach' test) an opinion as to the intention of the person responsible to stay within the temporary use provisions of the GPDO.

2.8.1.1   *'Apparent breaches' and estoppel*

An extreme example of the LPA not even having a basis for using its enforcement powers because there was no 'apparent breach' is found in caselaw involving the PCN power (see para 2.5.9.1). The language of that provision is very similar to that found in section 172. In the context of enforcement notices any argument about the lack of any 'apparent breach' will normally surface at the appeal stage before an inspector. However, they can also be raised by way of a legal challenge (via judicial review for example) against the notice. In both cases the term 'estoppel' will often be used. This may be a slightly misleading use of terminology originally used in the context of private law, not public law. The idea of estoppel is to prevent someone using a legal remedy or sanction because to do so would be 'unfair'. However, if there has not been a breach of control (as an inspector might conclude) then that is a simple legal issue based on an interpretation of the facts at hand. Only if those facts have already been the basis of a pre-existing decision (eg by another inspector on appeal) is it more accurate to say that the LPA is estopped from alleging an apparent breach of control. (Only then is it 'unfair' to come to a different conclusion when the same facts have already been authoritatively examined and been the basis of an earlier decision.) So it is therefore important that the LPA ensure that any previous appeal decision that seems to cover the same planning issues can be distinguished. The discussion in *Thrasyvoulou*[1] on the 'issue estoppel' principle is relevant here. If the circumstances of the earlier appeal are different (eg the appellant had lied in the earlier appeal about the date on which the development commenced in breach of control) then issue estoppel will not operate. It is up to the appellant to demonstrate that the new enforcement notice is founded on facts that have already been 'disproved' by an earlier appeal. The LPA should therefore examine a possible issue estoppel argument to see if it really applies; a 'change in circumstances' or a 'mistake' (by the Secretary of State) may enable the LPA to counter-attack a contravener's assertion of 'issue estoppel'. For an example of an estoppel argument succeeding on an appeal to the DOE (second enforcement notice alleging intensification from B1 to B2 of use on land covered by an earlier notice) see 9 PAD 466, T/APP/C/93/E2015/630717. The inspector found that there was no significant change in the planning position since the last enforcement notice had been quashed by the previous inspector and so the appeal succeeded.

1 *Thrasyvoulou v Secretary of State for the Environment* [1990] 2 AC 273, 88 LGR 217, HL.

2.8.2 'That there has been'

Since even very minor building operations can constitute development it would appear that a very small preliminary act of operational development will be enough to satisfy this precondition. Once the building works start there is a breach – the structure or building need not be completed before it can be said that 'there has been a breach'. (The language in section 171B(1) (where the phrase 'substantially completed' is used) should not be thought to qualify this rule. The 'substantially completed' rule only applies to time limits for taking enforcement action in respect of operational development: it has no bearing on whether there has been a breach of control in the first place.) The 'preliminary works' approach is evident in appeal decisions. In one appeal (3 PAD 182) the appellant had (inter alia) put down footings: the enforcement notice relating to the footings was upheld – the inspector treated the footings as the obvious precursor to the erection of a building. Since the siting of a building was inappropriate the inspector rejected the appellant's arguments and upheld the notice. He said 'the only purpose to which the footings could be put would be as foundations for some building. In this position a building would, in my opinion, be obtrusive and difficult to screen. Nor was the siting of any proposed building discussed with the council's planning officers. In these circumstances the retention of the footings would appear to serve no useful purpose, and for that reason permission should not be granted'. Thus the authority need not wait until the whole breach has been completed if the breach (of the operational development kind) is clear at an early stage. Intention would also (as with change of use breaches) appear to be a relevant factor.

A practical example of the problem of a fully constituted change of use breach is found in the *Hobday* case[1]. Here a market use was commenced. Under the GDO a temporary market use for 14 days in any calendar year falls within permitted development provisions. The council (before the use had continued past the 14 day limit) resolved to issue an enforcement notice. The court held that this was an invalid exercise of the power since, at the time of the resolution, there was no apparent breach of control.

1   *R v Rochester upon Medway City Council, ex p Hobday* [1989] 2 PLR 38.

2.8.2   'Breach of planning control'

This is a term of legal art and is defined in section 171A. It covers:

> '(a) carrying out development without the required planning permission; or
> (b) failing to comply with any condition or limitation subject to which planning permission has been granted. . .'.[1]

The definition therefore is restricted to mainstream enforcement and does not cover other forms of contravention of planning control. Unauthorised development or breach of condition are the two forms of contravention which enforcement notices and related mainstream powers can address.

1   TCPA 1990, s 171A(1).

2.9   TIME LIMITS

Mainstream enforcement action must be commenced within certain statutory time limits. The 1991 reforms altered the rules – banishing the 'pre-1963' rule to a welcome oblivion and replacing it with a rolling ten-year time bar. There are now two periods to be aware of and these are encapsulated in the four-year rule and the ten-year rule.

2.9.1   Time-barred breaches – four-year rule

Section 171B sets out a number of time limits on taking enforcement action. Two types of breach are covered by a four-year rule. The first (section 171B(1)) is unauthorised operational development. In such a case 'no enforcement action may be taken after the end of the period of four years beginning with the date on which the operations were substantially completed'. LPAs, in the case of unauthorised operational development therefore have to be careful about the four-year rule when the breach is being investigated some time after substantial completion of the relevant works. The second situation subject to the four-year rule covers breaches 'consisting in the change of use of any building to use as a single dwellinghouse'[1]. Time runs from the date on which the change of use occurred. There is also a special rule relating to mineral planning which is retained by virtue of the TCPA 1990, section 315 (which grants powers to the Secretary of State to modify statutory provisions relating to minerals) so that pre-existing rules found in regulations from 1971 still apply despite the 1990 consolidation[2]. So in the case of non-compliance with a condition or limitation affecting a permission for mining operations time runs from the date when that non-compliance has come to the knowledge of the mineral planning authority[3].

1 TCPA 1990, s 171B(2).
2 Town and Country Planning (Minerals) Regulations 1971.
3 Ibid reg 4.

2.9.2 Time-barred breaches – ten-year rule

The third category of breach is covered by a ten-year time bar. This is a residual category and so covers all other types of breach: effectively all unauthorised changes of use (except to a single dwellinghouse) become lawful uses once they have been established for ten years. Breaches of conditions are also now subject to the ten-year time bar.

2.9.3 Time-barred breaches – lawful development or use

The TCPA 1990, section 191(2) and (3) provides that where enforcement against a breach of control that is time-barred then the development or non-compliance with a condition will be lawful. The LPA that starts to take action in such cases will thus often be met with arguments regarding the factual basis for establishing a claim for a certificate of lawful use or development. By virtue of the TCPA 1990, section 191(6) the lawfulness of any matter covered by such a certificate shall be 'conclusively presumed': this will prevent the LPA from taking enforcement action in respect of such matters. The other advantages (compared to established use certificates) to the landowner of the new certificates are explained in circular 17/92, para 5. As regards enforcement action however, an established use certificate has a similar effect to that of the new certificate of lawful use or development. Established use certificates are still relevant as regards their conclusivity on any matters covered by such certificates: see the Planning and Compensation Act 1991 (Commencement No 11 and Transitional Provisions) Order 1992, SI 1992/1630, art 3(2) which provides for the former section 192(4) to continue in force. Established use certificates can also be converted into certificates under section 191: the procedures are set out in Annex 1 to circular 17/92, para 40. For reasons of space a discussion of certificates under sections 191 and 192 and established use certificates is omitted.

3 Unauthorised development

3.1 INTRODUCTION

The first general category of planning breach comprises 'unauthorised development'. However, in order to appreciate that a situation involves 'development' that is 'unauthorised' the officer will also have to be aware of those situations where (for instance) planning permission is not required for development or where such permission has been granted by (inter alia) the legislation. Since the focus of this book is enforcement a full discussion of the legal rules regarding 'development' is left to general texts on planning control and planning law. The following focuses on the more relevant and common problems that are likely to confront the LPA in the enforcement setting.

3.1.1 No 'development' involved

There are a number of situations where no 'development' occurs even though physical works are carried out or there is a change in the use of the land/buildings in question. The TCPA 1990, section 55(2) sets out instances – both in relation to operational development and change of use development. Fuller discussion of these 'exemptions' is delayed until the issues of operational and change of use development are reached. Discussion of those situations where the carrying out of 'works' does not constitute development appears in paras 3.2.1 et seq. The parallel discussion in relation to changes of use appears in paras 3.3.3 et seq: this is a longer discussion since it focuses on the way in which the Use Classes Order (UCO) operates. LPA officers should thus note that whereas the 'exemption' from planning control in respect of operational development (on the basis that no 'development' is involved) is quite brief – see the TCPA 1990,

section 55(2)(a), (b) and (c) – the important exemption in respect
of uses (no 'material' change of use involved where the change
relates to uses within same use class) is rather more involved.
Although the General Permitted Development Order (GPDO)
has a similar practical effect to that of the UCO the underlying
conceptual basis is different. In the former permission is granted
for certain types of operational development: in the latter there
appear those situations where there is no 'development'. There
is no grant of planning permission effected by the UCO since its
purpose is to set out those occasions where there is no
development. Confusion on this point is not uncommon – trainee
planners especially should be made aware of the subtle, though
important, difference.

3.2   OPERATIONAL DEVELOPMENT

LPA personnel should be conversant with the definition of
'development' in section 55(1) of the TCPA 1990. That definition
states that 'development' means:

> 'carrying out of building, engineering, mining or other operations in,
> on, over or under land, or the making of any material change in the
> use of any buildings or other land'.

The legislation thus focuses on two different types of activity:
the first is 'operational' development and the second is
'change of use' development. As space does not permit an
analysis of 'operational development' in its various forms
the discussion now turns to those instances where statute
determines that there is no 'development' arising out of specific
'operations'.

3.2.1 Operations not constituting development

The TCPA 1990, section 55(2) sets out certain categories of use
and operation which do not involve development. The discussion
here is on those 'operations' excluded from the ambit of the term
'development'. The LPA must, if confronted by activity that
could fall into these categories, examine the situation carefully.
The most important exemption is the first – internal works to
buildings.

3.2.2 Internal works and minor exterior works

By virtue of section 55(2)(a) the carrying out of the following do not constitute development, these are works for:

'(a) the maintenance, improvement or other alteration of any building,
(b) where such works
  (i) affect only the interior of the building or
  (ii) do not materially affect the external appearance of the building . . .'.

This provision does cause problems because the statutory language applies a distinction (between the 'interior' of a building and its 'exterior') that is not always easy to apply in practice. Problems arise with a large structure whose design incorporates an atrium or large open space that is roofed over (partly or wholly). The problem with such structures (shopping malls and office blocks are a common example) is that it is difficult at first sight to decide if the walls fronting onto the open space are on the 'outside' or are on the 'inside' of the building. A ministerial decision relating to the MetroCentre addressed the problem of interpreting this provision and provides us with a workable solution to the problem. It appears that the 'enclosed space test' is the best way of applying the rule in section 55(2)(a). This suggests that the walls etc of such a structure are 'external' only if they separate the external environment (with its wind and rain) from an internal environment that is largely unaffected by normal weather changes because of its enclosed nature. Insignificant openings to the external environment can be discounted. Such a test thus focuses on the largest coherent structure rather than the smaller component units (eg shops) in order to help us determine what is the 'building' for the purposes of this provision in the TCPA 1990. See further my discussion of this concept (which must be kept distinct and separate from the 'planning unit' concept) in *Planning*, 9 December 1994. (If the building is a listed building of course then the works might be subject to listed building control – but that is another matter.)

3.2.3 'Other operational development'

There has been little litigation on what type of development falls within this category. It is a residual category that would appear to be a 'sweeping-up' clause to cover forms of developments of an operational kind not covered by the three main named categories. LPAs should not forget this category when faced with activity that does not neatly fall into the established main categories. Indeed, it is possible that the removal of a substantial tree could fall into this residual category since 'arboricultural operations' could be a specialised type of development (affecting the character of the land) falling within this residual category.

3.3   MATERIAL CHANGE OF USE

The second limb of the definition of development focuses on the 'material change of use' of land. That concept gives rise to considerable problems because of the terms 'material', 'use' and (even) 'land'. In assessing whether or not development is involved in a 'use' situation the authority will therefore have to take account of these complexities. However, before turning to these issues we shall first examine those instances where the legislation simplifies things by specifying those instances where there is a material change of use. The legislation gives two clear examples of such development. Thus section 55(3)(b) of the TCPA 1990 states:

> 'the deposit of refuse or waste materials on land involves a material change in its use, notwithstanding that the land is comprised in a site already used for that purpose, if –
> (i) the superficial area of the deposit is extended, or
> (ii) the height of the deposit is thereby extended and exceeds the level of the land adjoining the site.'

The more common term that would be applied here is 'tipping'. Thus by virtue of this provision tipping may constitute a material change of use rather than operational development. The second statutory example of a material change of use precedes this subsection. Section 55(3)(a) of the principal Act thus states:

> 'For the avoidance of doubt it is hereby declared that for the purposes of this section – . . . the use as two or more separate dwellinghouses of any building previously used as a single dwellinghouse involves a material change in the use of the building and of each part of it which is so used;'.

3.3.1 Dwellinghouse conversions

The subdivision/conversion of one dwellinghouse to form two or more is a common problem for the LPA. The provision set out above thus helps to clarify the legal position somewhat so that the planning consequences (increased density of occupation etc) can be taken into account and enforcement action taken if 'expedient'. The problem that arises for the LPA is often one of finding the breach: after this there may be difficulty with establishing whether or not there is an established use as two or more separate dwellinghouses. The effect of enforcing against the use (causing homelessness) is also an important issue which illustrates the general principle that enforcement involves strategic issues – in this case the need to consider the enforcement problem in the light of other local authority functions.

3.3.2 Display of advertisements

Another provision that 'clarifies' the basic definition of 'material change of use' is to be found in section 55(5) of the principal Act. Unfortunately this 'clarification' brings into the discussion rather complex issues. Such issues are not usually uppermost in the minds of planning and legal officers of the LPA and they arise from the manner in which the mainstream planning regime and the interlocking subsidiary regime of advertisement control interact. That provision states:

> 'Without prejudice to any regulations made under the provisions of this Act relating to the control of advertisements, the use for the display of advertisements of any external part of a building which is not normally used for that purpose shall be treated for the purposes of this section as involving a material change in the use of that part of the building.'

This clearly indicates that the display of an advertisement may well constitute a 'change of use' development. Such development could relate to the external part of a building used for the display of an advertisement. Additionally, it should be noted that a change of use may arise from the display of an advertisement on open land – a field normally in agricultural use for example: the mixed-use (agricultural and advertising) so created would fall within a very common category of breach affecting agricultural land. The statutory provision should not be interpreted as restricting the generally-applicable rules as to what constitutes a material change or, for that matter, operational development. The provision does not explicitly deal with operational development in respect of the display of an advertisement and might therefore be interpreted in a way to indicate that such activity cannot fall under the 'operational' limb of mainstream planning control. However, since this provision clearly recognises the principle that one limb of the development definition may apply then there seems to be no reason why works carried out in the course of displaying an advertisement could not also constitute 'operational development'. These aspects are considered in more detail in chapter twelve which is devoted to the enforcement of advertisement control.

3.3.3   Uses that do not constitute development

The other way in which the legislation attempts to simplify matters is by setting out three instances where the use of land does not involve development. These provisions thus enable the LPA to determine that no 'unauthorised development' has occurred (because there is no 'development' involved) and thus no basis for enforcement action exists. (The possibility that the change may, however, contravene a planning condition or a planning agreement/obligations should not be overlooked.) These three provisions cover:

(a) incidental dwellinghouse uses;
(b) agriculture/forestry uses;
(c) the operation of the Use Classes Order.

Where the use under examination falls within these particular categories then enforcement action cannot be taken as there is no development. The impact of these exemptions is thus very important to note.

3.3.3.1 *Incidental dwellinghouse uses*

Section 55(2)(d) states that the following use does not involve development:

'the use of any buildings or other land within the curtilage of a dwellinghouse for any purpose incidental to the enjoyment of the dwellinghouse as such.'

The problems that arise from this provision are related to the 'hobby' use that turns into something more than just a pastime. Examples of such problems are discussed later when attention turns to a number of common problems with uses in breach of planning control.

3.3.3.2 *Agriculture/forestry use*

The use of land for agriculture or forestry is most relevant to enforcement activity when land that is not built upon is used for a purpose which is quasi-agricultural. The problem is intensified by the operation of the GPDO which permits some operational development if it is for agricultural purposes. Authorities on the urban fringe may thus have many instances of bogus 'agricultural exemptions' based on both this statutory provision and the provisions of the GPDO. The definition of agriculture is broad and covers:

> 'horticulture, fruit growing, seed growing, dairy farming, the breeding and keeping of livestock (including any creature kept for the production of food, wool, skins or fur, or for the purpose of its use in the farming of land), the use of land as grazing land, meadow land, osier land, market gardens and nursery grounds, and the use of land for woodlands where that use is ancillary to the farming of land for other agricultural purposes, and "agricultural" shall be construed accordingly.'

LPAs faced with dubious examples of the agricultural exemption will have to examine carefully the 'primary use' of the land in question to see whether the broad definition given to agriculture applies. The problem of 'hobby' farms often arises. The authority may therefore face the direct opposite of the problem that arises with the 'incidental dwellinghouse use' problem noted in the previous section. Whereas a breach of control arises on residential premises when a hobby becomes a commercial activity it is the change from 'commercial farming' to 'hobby farming' that is a problem with this exemption. In the domestic situation the contravener will try to show he is engaged in a hobby – not a business: whereas as in this situation the contravener will try to show he is engaged in commercial farming activity and not a hobby! Authorities will also need to be alert to problems of interpretation where the related term of 'agricultural unit' has to be applied to specific circumstances. This term is different from the similar term 'planning unit' and some care is required in situations where either term is applied to agricultural land.

3.3.3.3 *Use Classes Order*

The most far-reaching 'exemption' in relation to change of use development is that found, primarily, in the Use Classes Order[1]. This order is supplemented by further provisions in the GPDO 1995[2] which tie in with the use classes to give further 'exemptions' from planning control. The GPDO's provisions grant exemption from control by giving planning permission for certain changes of use between specified use classes. The UCO relies on the following provision in the TCPA 1990 for its effect – section 55(2)(f) thus states that there is no development in respect of the use of land:

> 'in the case of buildings or other land which are used for a purpose of any class specified in an order made by the Secretary of State under this section, the use of the buildings or other land or, subject to the provisions of the order, of any part of the buildings or the other land, for any other purpose of the same class'.

The 'order' mentioned in that provision is the UCO. The UCO thus enables the LPA to determine that no development has occurred where the new use and the old are in the same class. Officers should also note that the use classes are not, however, determinative when the following are involved:

(a) changes involving uses not specified in the use classes – here the sui generis use problem still requires an assessment of 'materiality';

(b) changes from a use in one class to a use in a different class will still have to be tested against the 'material change of use' principle: such changes are not automatically 'material'[3].

The use classes are construed in a relatively restrictive fashion by the courts and so a use that is not obviously contained within a class may well be outside the rules regarding use classes[4].

1 Town and Country Planning (Use Classes) Order 1987, SI 1987/ 764.
2 Town and Country Planning (General Permitted Development) Order 1995, SI 1995/418.
3 *Rann v Secretary of State for the Environment* [1980] JPL 109.
4 *Tessier v Secretary of State for the Environment* [1975] JPL 39.

3.4 USES – SOME IMPORTANT CONCEPTS

The operation of the legal principles relating to uses can only be understood if the officer applies certain judge-made principles. These principles derive from the need to supplement the bare bones of the legislation with more substantial and workable tools that enable the legal principles to operate effectively. Such tools help with the interpretation of the terms 'land' and 'use' – problems noted in the introduction to this discussion. These tools comprise the following concepts:

  (a) the planning unit;
  (b) primary/ancillary uses (the related concepts of composite/ mixed uses can also be subsumed within this topic).

3.4.1 Planning unit

The planning unit is a necessary tool since it helps to define the 'spatial' extent of the analysis when the LPA wishes to determine if a 'material change of use' has occurred in relation to 'land'. (It is not a concept, however, that should not be applied to situations outside the scope of the statutory provision to which it applies. It should not, for example, be employed when addressing issues related to operational development (such as the 'interior/exterior' dichotomy found in the TCPA 1990, section 55(2)(a) which is discussed above in para 3.2.2.)) The legislation does not give any guidance as to how large an area should be taken into account when looking at the 'land' to see if there is a material change of use. The legislation does not offer any help as to this 'spatial' dimension and so the courts have developed the concept of the 'planning unit' to help interpret this provision (the 'use' limb of the definition of development in section 55(1)). In the case of *G Percy Trentham v Gloucestershire County Council*[1] Lord Justice Diplock said at 513:

> 'What is the unit which the local authority are entitled to look at and deal with in an enforcement notice for the purpose of determining whether or not there has been "a material change in the use of any buildings or other land"? . . . I think for that purpose what the local authority are entitled to look at is the whole of the area which was used for a particular purpose, including any part of that area whose use was incidental to or ancillary to the achievement of that purpose'.

The link between the occupation of an area of land (the 'planning unit' problem) for a specific 'purpose' and the primary/ancillary use problem is illustrated in another case. Thus in *Wealden District Council v Secretary of State for the Environment and Colin Day*[2] Ralph Gibson LJ said that he would accept:

'. . . that the question whether a particular additional use was ancillary to or included within the primary use of the planning unit was to be determined objectively in the sense that the purposes for which land was used had to be determined according to all the evidence, in addition to evidence of what the occupier said was his purpose, including evidence of what was being done on the land and the assessment of the relationship of that activity to the primary use.'

Although a full examination of these two concepts (planning unit and primary/ancillary uses) is inappropriate it is important to stress that their interrelation is clear. In assessing the legal issues surrounding a material change of use breach the LPA may well find it necessary to examine carefully both these issues. Although not a theme given much prominence in the case law it would seem that the concept of 'purpose' is, fundamentally, concerned with the activity on the land that has an 'economic' aspect to it – whether production of goods or services or their consumption. It is not necessary to state the planning unit in the notice – *Hawkey v Secretary of State for the Environment*[3].

1   [1966] 1 All ER 701, [1966] 1 WLR 506.
2   [1988] JPL 268 at 274.
3   (1971) 22 P & CR 610.

3.4.2   Determining the planning unit

With a use breach it is therefore necessary to be clear as to the spatial extent of the 'land' under examination: if the boundaries of the 'land' are drawn narrowly (catching only an ancillary use which is located on one specific part of a large site) the erroneous conclusion might be drawn that the ancillary use is the primary use for that small site. This would suggest that there is a material change of use when in fact there was not. Identifying the proper unit is thus very important and often tied up with the problem of identifying primary and ancillary uses. The case of

Burdle v Secretary of State for the Environment is usually taken as the most useful summary of the principles[1]. This case stresses that a key aspect of the planning unit concept is the 'unit of occupation': for many purposes the 'spatial' dimension of the enquiry will thus be determined by reference to the manner in which the land is occupied by the person carrying on that use. The occupier may be engaged in a number of activities on the land. In most cases those activities will be subordinate (the planning term is 'ancillary' or 'incidental') to a main use. The situation can then be further complicated if the range of uses to which the occupier puts the land covers uses that are not ancillary to one primary use. Thus there may be two or more primary uses on the land occupied by the user. In this case there may be two or more planning units (each smaller than the unit of occupation). Where such complications arise the concept of primary uses may be difficult to employ here since the *Burdle* case suggests that two or more 'primary' uses may co-exist and be so dependent on each other that in effect there is a composite use. Thus a 'composite' use might well be found to exist if there is, in fact, no clear and rigid physical separation between those uses and they are linked together in terms of economic viability. This is one indication that the 'spatial' problem and the 'category' of use problem cannot really be separated from each other.

The difficulties facing planning authorities are evident from appeal decisions and case law. Thus in one case a site had been developed as a winter base for travelling showmen[2]. Four enforcement notices were issued. Each notice related to the whole site – even though the site was occupied by different people. The deputy judge held that it was quite valid to issue the notice in relation to the whole site. By way of contrast however, it should be noted that the case of *Johnston v Secretary of State for the Environment* took a different line when it came to a large number of garages split up into separate ownerships[3]. It may well be that the *Rawlins* case involved a clear 'joint' effort in the breach of control (missing in the *Johnston* case) such that the total area was an appropriate focus for the authority. This illustrates perhaps the need to look at the nature of the 'economic' and 'organisational' aspects of the breach of control when assessing the correct planning unit. In the *Rawlins* case the breach involved concerted activity by the owners such that their individual units of occupation became subsumed under the larger planning unit: the 'economic' and 'organisational' interdependence of the contraveners in the *Rawlins* case was something that was missing in the *Johnston* situation.

1 [1972] 3 All ER 240, [1972] 1 WLR 1207.
2 *Rawlins v Secretary of State for the Environment* [1989] JPL 439.
3 (1974) 28 P&CR 424.

3.4.2.1   *The 'enforcement unit'*

Perhaps the caselaw will need to develop a concept of the 'enforcement unit' which more clearly addresses the relevant factors for LPAs when determining the appropriate area of 'land' that should be covered by an enforcement notice[1]. Since there are often (as with the *Rawlins* case) two different 'tiers' of owners whose economic interests in the land vary (eg from the landlord interested in the rents received to the occupiers actually using the land for their benefit) this may also be important for understanding that the 'enforcement unit' may well vary according to the identity of the recipient of the notice: this is because his landholding (and so his liability as regards the contravention) will often be different from the landholding and contravention of another recipient. The tenants will clearly be responsible for their respective breaches. The landlord, however, will also be responsible for the whole site and so the enforcement notice served on him should reflect such factors. So if the landlord as well as the tenants are both responsible for the contraventions then their different role and different landholdings will need to be taken into account in the drawing up of the relevant enforcement notices. The enforcement notice served on the landlord would cover the whole site and require him (inter alia) to eject the occupiers from the land and remove all structures etc. The enforcement notices directed to the individual contravening occupiers would be tailor-made for each occupier and require them to cease using the land for the contravening use and remove all structures etc. Effective enforcement in cases such as *Rawlins* (where there are different levels of ownership interests involved in the contravention) will thus require a much more sophisticated approach involving notices directed to the individual units as well as the unit which forms the aggregated whole.

In *Richmond-upon-Thames London Borough Council v Secretary of State for the Environment* the point was stressed that an enforcement notice could relate to part of a planning unit[2]. However, there are practical and sound planning reasons why the LPA should rarely restrict the notice to part of the land occupied by the contravener on whom a notice is served. If the notice only covered part of the property, the contravening use could be moved to another part not covered by the notice and the contravener would not commit an offence of non-compliance. It is therefore better to cover all the land under the control of the contravener who is responsible for the breach. Where possible mistakes as to the 'enforcement unit' have been made then the authority should ensure that speedy action is taken to rectify the error: in this respect the discussion in chapter seven on the correction power and the comments in chapter six on the 'nullity' issue should be scrutinised. It is particularly important to note that the legal rules have not yet been fully explored and explained by the courts so mistakes can easily happen: yet errors should not be automatically seen as fatal – the correction power is a very important aspect of 'damage limitation' and authorities should endeavour to use it to the full.

1   This concept may have to be developed in order to deal with a failure by the legislation to define what is meant by the 'land' in the enforcement provisions. The 'planning unit' is employed to deal with a similar problem in the provisions dealing with the definition of development. However, it is unlikely that the two concepts are identical since their statutory context is quite different. See further on this problem (where sites are split up into multiple leased units by the landlord) the discussion in my Lawyer's Aside column in *Planning*, 24 March 1995. Suggestions there regarding the breadth of the 'steps' that can be required in an enforcement notice (eg requiring the landlord to use his private law powers to eject tenants in breach of planning control, to provide the LPA with copies of all leases or licenses etc) should also be noted.
2   [1988] JPL 396.

3.4.3   Primary/ancillary uses

The above discussion necessarily made use of the terms 'primary' and 'ancillary' uses. The following looks more closely at these, and related, 'categories' of use. The primary/ancillary use dichotomy is important both when the LPA is applying the UCO to a situation and when it is concerned with those uses that are not 'classified' under that order – the sui generis uses. The focus in both cases must be on the primary (economic) purpose to which the land comprised in the planning unit is put: it is that economic purpose which largely defines the use and indicates its planning/environmental impacts. Such ancillary uses as may also be evident will not affect those impacts – if they do then, almost by definition, they are not ancillary or incidental and should be treated as primary uses. Thus when applying the

UCO to a case the appropriate class for the 'old' (primary) use is examined together with that of the 'new' (primary) use: if both primary uses are within the same class then that change of use is not 'material' – it will not constitute development (TCPA 1990, section 55(2)(f)).

The LPA officer may find a situation confusing where an ancillary use occupies a discrete part of a building: an office canteen might be assumed to be a 'restaurant' (A3) use – it sells food to be eaten on the premises. However, since its clientele, its economic viability and other such factors are identified with that of the office to which it is appended such a canteen has only an ancillary restaurant use: its primary use is B1 office use. Again the 'economic' links that seem to be relevant to some aspects of the planning unit concept (see the above discussion) seem to be relevant here. If the canteen started to open its doors to customers who were not employees and stayed open beyond office hours then that canteen use would have assumed a separate identity in 'economic' terms: it thus would probably have attained 'primary' use status. A new planning unit would have been created with a separate and distinct use – A3. There would now have been a material change of use of that portion of the land used by the canteen and enforcement action could be taken because this would be 'unauthorised development' of that canteen area. (Similar factors may help explain decisions about farm shops that take in produce from outside rather than just selling produce produced by the farm.) However if the office canteen was to be turned into a creche for children of employees that would not be a change to class D1(b) since it would still be tied to the primary office user and thus still be primary office itself.

3.4.4   Inclusive and ordinarily incidental uses

The UCO incorporates a rule to the effect that a use which is both:

(a) included in; and
(b) is ordinarily incidental to any use in a class specified in the Order is not excluded from the use to which it is incidental merely because it is specified in the UCO as a separate use[1].

This rule seems to be a narrower statutory version of the 'ancillary use' concept devised by the courts. So even if a use does not fall within the terms of this special statutory rule regarding 'incidental use' status it may well benefit from 'ancillary use' status under the case law. The use of the term 'ordinarily' is the important restriction. It makes this particular statutory rule more 'objective' in its ambit.

1   Town and Country Planning (Use Classes) Order 1987, SI 1987/ 764, art 3(3).

3.4.5   Intensification

The discussion of the planning unit illustrates some of the difficulties confronting the LPA. Another problem arising from the nature of the concept of 'use' is that although increased activity on land may have quite dramatic effects on the environment there is no 'change' of use if the use remains the same or is within the same use class. Planning primarily focuses on the 'quality' of the use and not its 'quantity'. Of course if the use is carried on in reliance on a planning permission the LPA should have taken steps (at the development control stage) to deal with the risk of intensification. Environmental damage can thus be handled by conditions that restrict impact: if this is inappropriate then permission should be refused because the 'use' exhibits fundamental 'characteristics' that conflict with adjoining users. A problem for enforcement, however, is where a use develops gradually. At first it may be quite innocuous and the operator explains that the 'nuisance' element will not be much of a problem. To a busy officer such reassurances may be acceptable. However, the LPA must ensure that the fundamental character of the 'nascent' use is understood and that adequate action is taken at an early stage to control the expansion of the use and attendant problems.

If intensification does lead to a new use being carried out then enforcement action can be taken. However the authority should try to handle such problems early on by effective development control decisions, co-ordination of activity with other departments (eg Environmental Health) and monitoring of compliance with either informal or formal enforcement action. In an Ombudsman case a good example of 'intensification' problems can be seen. This case (*Southampton City Council* 87/ B/1230) arose out of an application in respect of a use which expanded. The use also involved noisy machinery to cut stone.

Planning permission was granted subject to conditions including the requirement that doors to the building housing the machinery be closed when the machinery was in use. Complaints were made of excessive noise and other operational development on the site. The complainant was visited by the environmental health officer and was told that noise abatement notices could be used to deal with the problem. The complainant was asked to make a diary of contraventions. The planning department also failed to make arrangements for continued observation – these would seem to have been desirable given that the condition regarding the closure of the doors constituted a continuing obligation (always a category of obligation that needs monitoring). A noise abatement notice was issued. The Ombudsman suggested that compliance with this should have been monitored and that the council should consider taking enforcement action against any outstanding breach of control. This case illustrates that certain types of use may expand in response to business needs and that the potential for expansion should be more carefully considered when planning permission is granted. Again we see that the development control function must be adequately organised. The monitoring of compliance with controls is also something that this case emphasises.

3.4.6   Subdivision, sui generis uses

Where premises are used for a purpose that falls within one of the use classes then the use of any part of the premises for that same use is not 'development'[1]: this provision expressly excludes the subdivision of a dwellinghouse – this will still constitute 'development'. However, it should be noted that this provision does not operate to catch those instances where the 'use' concerned is not one which is a 'class specified in an order made by the Secretary of State'. The terms of section 55(2)(f) do not, therefore, cover uses that fall outside the classes in the UCO: sui generis uses cannot take advantage of the provision. Sui generis uses therefore are still subject to the rule in the *Winton* case[2]. Subdivision of premises used for such a use into smaller units used for the same use may thus be amenable to enforcement action. If the subdivision, as a matter of fact and degree, is found to have had the effect of amounting to a material change of use then enforcement action could be taken against the landlord and the tenants of the subdivided units. (As noted above the 'enforcement unit' for the notices would vary according to whether the recipient was the landlord or the occupying tenants. See para 3.4.2 on such 'two-tier' contraventions.)

1 TCPA 1990, s 55(2)(f).
2 *Winton v Secretary of State for the Environment* (1982) 46 P & CR 205, [1984] JPL 188.

3.5 PARTICULAR USE BREACHES

There are some particular examples of breaches of control relating to unauthorised changes of use which deserve highlighting. These examples are of particular interest since they illustrate some of the strategic and tactical issues which the LPA will need to address.

3.5.1 Vehicle repair

This discussion of particular use breaches will start with a favourite topic of enforcement personnel – vehicle repairs. Such activities often go hand in hand with related 'scrap materials recycling' uses and so involve a number of different but related activities on one site. In looking specifically at vehicle repair breaches it will become apparent that this subject gives rise to a number of issues of general concern. The first is the relevance of neighbour complaint to enforcement work: liaising with the aggrieved neighbour (and, perhaps, the ward councillor) is an important aspect of handling the breach. Monitoring of the site can be a task partly undertaken by neighbours. The proper 'handling' of the aggrieved neighbour is thus an important element highlighted by vehicle repair cases. Liaison with other agencies (eg the police) may be relevant if the activity affects the highway. The local knowledge (and contacts) of the ex-policeman enforcement officer may be very useful in dealing with vehicle repair breaches; he may be aware of some of the characters involved from his earlier work of enforcing *criminal* law. His communication and investigative skills will also be of use when dealing with the more recalcitrant type of offender. Moving away from the small-scale operation problems may be found with noisier repair/maintenance activity. Spraying and steam-cleaning operations can produce problems with 'emissions'. Dealing with such problems may have unwanted side-effects: here the parallels with breaches arising from restaurant uses and their 'emissions' are relevant. Extractor fans and ducts may deal with the problem for the operator and some neighbours but the installation of such equipment may be inappropriate on a listed building or in a conservation area. Thus dealing with one problem (eg emissions under the Environmental Protection Act (EPA) 1990) may still involve problems with other planning interests. Again, car-spraying is an activity which may well involve another agency – the Health and Safety Executive. This form of breach thus emphasises the importance (noted in chapter one) of being able to approach contraventions involving planning control as 'environmental problems' whose solution may involve the use of powers available under other regimes. Strong evidence of a neighbour complaint is an important element in getting favourable results before the various appeal fora – magistrates, inspector, the High Court, the Ombudsman. Clear and concrete evidence of the 'damage' caused by a breach will thus not only help the authority gain a higher fine against a convicted contravener but is important to substantiate the validity of using enforcement powers against such activity if the contravener takes up the matter before fora other than the magistrates' court. Vehicle repair breaches thus illustrate many of the issues (organisational etc) that confront the LPA in its enforcement activity. The discussion of other problem breaches involving uses that follows looks at more specific issues and cites both inspectors' decisions and court cases as a way of illustrating some of the issues that may be faced by the planning authority when dealing with an enforcement problem.

3.5.2   Scrap-yards

Scrap-yards need particular attention by all planners since the term 'scrap-yard' is generally too broad a category to describe the different uses that may be carried on. Often the activity will be a B4 use. An inspector's decision reported at [1989] JPL 130 examined a site being used for the recovery of non-ferrous material from scrap[1]. Enforcement action was taken against the use of a site: it was described as a 'scrap-yard'. About 95% of material coming on to the site was non-ferrous. The metallic constituents and ferrous and non-ferrous metals were separated and the non-ferrous metal was sorted by type, grade and quality and then cut, bailed or organised as necessary into manageable lots. Eventually all the material would be removed. Although the contravener accepted that he was registered as a scrap-metal dealer it was argued that this did not prove that the appeal site was a scrap-yard. The planning authority argued that the activity on the land fell within the definition of 'scrap-yard'. The inspector noted that the use of definitions 'used in other legislation may help in understanding, but does not determine the issues in these grounds of appeal'. The inspector concluded that the use of a site was not as a scrap-yard (which he accepted would be a sui generis use) but was primarily 'for the recovery of non-ferrous metal from scrap': the activities on the site, the inspector found, fell within the definition of 'industrial process' given in article 2(b) of the UCO. He also found that the particular process carried on fell within the description in Class B4(c) – 'recovery of metal from scrap or dross or ashes'[2].

This appeal is interesting in that it is an example of the DOE's general position that stresses (rightly) the point that definitions in other legislation are not determinative when construing specific terms in planning legislation. Such definitions may help but they must be treated with care. The decision also emphasises that planning authorities have to be careful with certain types of uses that have a 'processing' aspect to them. In this case the 'scrap-yard' was in fact a site for an 'industrial process' in Class B4. LPAs should also note the controls exercised over scrap-yards under the EPA 1990 as regards waste management. Contraventions of planning control may well also involve contraventions of EPA 1990 provisions regarding waste handling and treatment and action under the EPA 1990 may well be more effective in resolving contraventions. Waste management licensing under the EPA 1990 has not been introduced as rigorously as it might: operators can claim exemptions from licensing if they comply with various conditions and limitations. (The exemptions operate like 'permitted development' rights in the planning system and so the operator claiming the exemption must be sure that he complies with the various conditions that prescribe such exemptions.) There is therefore scope for dealing with problem sites via the EPA 1990 controls if the LPA staff can liaise with colleagues in the environmental health department.

1 T/APP/C/87/5720/0013.
2 The Town and Country Planning (Use Classes) (Amendment) Order 1995, SI 1995/297 has deleted Class B4 (along with classes B5 to B7) from the UCO 1987. In some cases then the activities found in a scrap-yard may well fall under B2 – general industrial.

3.5.3 Mobile cafes

One example of caravans being used in a manner leading to a breach of control is the mobile cafe (often found on lay-bys but sometimes on the forecourts of business premises in tourist areas). Here the special enforcement procedure relating to Crown Land may apply – see chapter fourteen. The notice would allege a material change of use – 'use of the land for the stationing of a caravan for the purpose of selling refreshments and associated vehicle parking for customers'. If the vehicle can be moved around then the authority should allege a mixed use as highway and stationing etc. The site plan must cover the whole lay-by. Handling this type of breach may well require an agreed 'policy' between the highway authority and the planning authority. Different authorities will have different objectives – thus the need to co-ordinate and liaise. A useful discussion of the issues can be found in 'Stopping for a Snack? Mobile Snack-bars and the Law' by DW Williams [1983] JPL 23. (A related issue that may arise with mobile cafes is that of the 'roving' breach – ie the temporary use of small parts of one piece of land for a contravening use. Tackling this sort of breach and its variants is something which is touched on in para 3.5.9 below.)

3.5.4 Residential uses

Changes to and from residential use are of particular concern to authorities since the impact on local amenity may be quite pronounced. Breaches involving residential accommodation are, by virtue of the impact on residential amenity, likely to be brought to the attention of the authority by aggrieved neighbours. Yet some breaches may be more difficult to detect: working from home gives rise to detection problems and 'proof' problems. The aggrieved neighbour may therefore be an important source of information. In addition DOE policy has long recognised that the doctor working from home should not be unnecessarily subjected to the rigours of planning control. However, this does not prevent the LPA from taking action where the planning issues so warrant. The LPA has to draw the line somewhere and, as a matter of fact and degree, determine that the level of office use in a house goes beyond that which is 'ancillary' to the domestic use. The LPA has to look therefore at home-based uses and bear in mind the ancillary/primary use concept, the issues relevant to the planning unit, the possibility of sui generis uses and the 'materiality' of the change of use. Percentage floor area is not necessarily the definitive guide – the planning authority must take into account a large number of issues.

3.5.5 Hobby uses and leisure plots

Hobbies and leisure plots are similar problems. In the first case a 'hobby' may sometimes develop into a non-residential activity – even though it is carried out on residential premises. In the second case the use of agricultural land for leisure purposes (connected with horse-riding, holiday homes/chalets etc) means that land is changed from agricultural use to a variety of other uses that have a leisure-based purpose. The term 'hobby farm' is perhaps the bridge between these two types of contravening uses and on that basis they can be treated as problems of a similar nature.

As regards the establishment of hobbies on residential premises the legislation allows for uses incidental to the dwellinghouse to be carried on (as long as that is within the curtilage) since no development is involved – TCPA 1990, section 55(2)(d). However, interests and pastime can sometime develop into money-making activities – even if the original intention of the limited commercial activity was to defray expenses. Once the commercial element comes in the 'incidental' nature of the hobby is lost. Yet even an intense hobby use can involve development even if there is no significant commercial element. The particular circumstances of the 'hobbyist' may thus mean that the incidental use of the house for the 'hobby' changes into a use that is more properly considered a commercial use in its own right. Car-repairing breaches are good examples of such hobby/commercial uses. The neighbours may well complain vociferously but the noise and detriment to visual amenity may not be of a level to persuade an inspector that the threshold has been crossed and that there is now a mixed commercial/residential use of the premises. The contravener need merely state that the cars belong to friends or family and this will, apparently, be enough for many inspectors. If no elaborate equipment is in evidence on the inspector's site visit then this too will help the appellant win. An example of such a problem is found in an appeal decision quashing an enforcement notice issued by Northavon District Council (DOE ref T/APP/G0120/C/86/562/P6[1]). The de minimis test will thus be applied by inspectors to help them reach such decisions – even if 10–12 cars a month are involved. To counter such arguments the authority would have to find evidence of (for example) advertising in the planning paper, statements from customers who were not 'friends', reliable counts as to the volume of cars, names and addresses of customers (perhaps the skills of ex-policemen may be relevant here). If customers paid for more than the expenses of the 'hobbyist' then this might indicate a commercial element. The zealous enforcement officer might even be tempted to take along his own car for attention (when off duty) to see what the response is. Multiple garages (for instance attached to blocks of flats) offer a good opportunity for the enterprising car mechanic. At this level of use, however, it is difficult for him to sustain the argument that he is using all the garages for domestic purposes. The extension of a domestic garage to accommodate a car-repairing activity might also be a good indication of a commercial element. Of course the deemed application for permission will raise issues of amenity, traffic hazard etc. Personal circumstances (eg unemployment) may persuade an inspector to grant permission – however the authority should put forward stringent conditions to prevent intensification and ensure that once the personal circumstances no longer pertain that the more appropriate standards are applied to the site.

The second category normally involves the conversion of farmland into a 'leisure plot'. This term is commonly used by planners but care should be taken in using it in enforcement notices and in justifying action against such uses. Since it is a very wide term the more precise character of the use should be set out: it is a term that, like 'scrap-yard' (see above) should be given more precise expression because of its over-broad nature. *Shephard and Love v Secretary of State for the Environment and Ashford Borough Council* is one case discussing the problems with this term: *Pittman v Secretary of State and Canterbury City Council* is also relevant[2]. Using the term 'leisure plot' in an enforcement would not appear to render the notice hopelessly ambiguous – as in the *Shephard* case. Leisure plots should be distinguished from uses where a commercial concern takes over farmland for the pursuit of leisure activities by those who have no proprietary interest in the land. In such cases the mixed use should be described by reference to the particular (commercial) leisure activity in question. An appeal decision involving hang-gliding on farmland illustrates the difference - 9 PAD 498.

1 Reported in [1987] JPL 146.
2 [1992] JPL 827 and [1988] JPL 391.

3.5.6 Pet animals

Another form of 'hobby' that can easily develop into a commercial use is the breeding of cats, dogs etc. Again the problem here is determining the threshold – when does an activity incidental to use of the dwellinghouse become a primary use? In the *Wallington* case the inspector had determined that the appellant be allowed to keep six dogs at his house: enforcement action had been taken against the keeping of 44 dogs[1]. The court held that the inspector was entitled to have regard to what people normally do in dwellinghouses to help ascertain whether this use was of a non-residential nature. The inspector had held that even keeping six dogs would exceed the number normally kept in domestic circumstances. The court did mention the problem of using a fixed 'headcount' – the size of a litter of puppies might be a good reason for setting the limit at six dogs. Examples of dog-breeding problems examined on appeal can be found in 9 PAD 410, 495 & 549.

1 *Wallington v Secretary of State for Wales* [1990] JPL 112.

3.5.7 Tipping

The deposit of material onto land may be a matter which authorities often try to control by action under the planning regime. The problem here is that the scope of the planning regime over such activity is a little imprecise. If the material is 'waste material' or 'refuse' then its deposit will fall within the ambit of the system – though it may well benefit from permitted development status. Some of the intricacies of the system are covered in a separate chapter (which also deals with the related activity – mining – see chapter fourteen): for the purposes of this discussion, however, it is pertinent to note that the deposit of material on land also falls within the ambit of a licensing system under the EPA 1990 (which modifies the regime originally set up under the Control of Pollution Act 1974) if that material is 'controlled waste'. The EPA controls are, in many ways, wider ranging than those of the planning regime. One example of this is found in the definition of terms. Thus under the EPA 1990 a tipping activity is regulated if the material being deposited is 'controlled waste'. This illustrates how an 'environmental problem' may fall under regimes other than planning: see chapter fourteen on 'tipping' breaches under the TCPA and the EPA.

3.5.8   Haulage depots, builder's yards etc

A range of uses involving 'open land' can often cause problems. Vehicle parks, haulage depots, builder's yards, agricultural machinery yards are examples of such uses which require precision in the drafting of notices and care also from any related action by development control staff etc. The grant of certificates of lawful use will need to be carefully managed so that the specific nature of the use in question (and any buildings associated with it) are very carefully described. Usually this will involve the LPA imposing limitations on such a certificate: the boundaries of the land to which the certificate relates should be clearly set out and the detail and level of use defined very carefully. Unless these precautions are taken in granting such certificates the occupant will be able to make significant changes in the nature of the use without going outside the terms of the certificate. This will make enforcement almost impossible - unless other environmental law controls can be used to deal with the problem. Advice on the granting of certificates of lawful use and development in circular 17/92 (paras 22–28) is relevant here and should be studied where sui generis uses of land of this type are encountered. Appeal decisions reported in the JPL or PAD reports (or elsewhere) should also be examined as these will often show up problems that may not be foreseen by the LPA. Where one large site has been split up into a number of smaller units on which contravening uses of this type have been established then the LPA is probably faced with a 'two-tier' contravention against which action is required both at the landlord tier and the tenant tier: the discussion of the planning unit earlier in this chapter is relevant.

3.5.9 'Roving' use breaches

One problem that may well crop up is the 'roving' breach. By this I mean a breach of control on land which is tackled by an enforcement notice whose terms are very precise as to the 'area' affected by the breach. Such a notice may define the breach of control as the change of use of a small piece of the land concerned (often this concerns a field or other open site): however, after the notice has been upheld on appeal the contravener merely migrates to another 'small piece' of the land. This 'new' activity may not be covered by the prohibition in the effective enforcement notice. One way of dealing with this is to allege a change of use to mixed use of the whole 'planning unit': this means that wherever the roving breach appears on the planning unit there will be a breach of control. (This would seem to be limited, however, to contiguous sites which can be treated cumulatively as one piece of 'land' for the purposes of planning control and enforcement. Any sites separated from land on which a breach has occurred could not legitimately be said to be the 'land' in respect of which a breach of planning control has occurred. The fact of separation would appear to be a key factor here – though there is not a reported case of an enforcement notice aggregating different areas of separate plots of land in this way.) Another possibility is to specify the breach of control by reference to the small area of the land which is currently affected by the breach but require that the contravener remove all 'equipment' etc used for the breach from the larger unit of land covered by the notice. The removal requirement thus covers the whole area owned by the person responsible for the breach but the breach is defined by reference to a smaller portion of the land – that area directly affected by the breach at the time of issuing the notice. This means that although the contravener may later move to another small piece of land he will be in breach of the mandatory requirement to remove his 'equipment' from the larger area of land to which the notice relates.

Authorities may come across a variant of this problem if a contravener owns adjacent properties (eg two terraced houses) but commences a use in breach of control in only one. There is a good chance that the contravener will switch the contravening use (in response to enforcement action) to the next-door property. In such circumstances the LPA may consider alleging that the 'land' for enforcement purpose is both (contiguous) properties: the unauthorised change is to a mixed use (single-family residential and house in multiple occupation for example). In effect both properties are treated as one piece of land for the purposes of taking enforcement action. This prevents the operator just moving the contravening use next door (as he could easily do if the notice merely covered the one house). For these purposes the control of both properties by the one owner is an important argument in substantiating this approach since normally separate houses would be treated as separate entities for planning purposes. A more conventional approach (though still slightly novel for many authorities I suspect) is to attack a roving breach with both enforcement and stop notices (with the latter taking effect immediately) as soon as possible after each 'migration'. Instead of allowing the contravener to play the system the planning authority should thus consider using more coercive mechanisms. This takes us to the 'ultimate' weapon for dealing with roving contraventions – the injunction.

3.5.10 Injunctions

Another possible line of attack is to seek a statutory injunction. (This remedy is discussed in detail later in chapter nine. However, the 'roving' breach problem is a convenient place in which to mention some aspects of the use of injunctions.) One variant of the 'roving' breach is where the use migrates to different properties which are owned by different people. The planning authority may thus find itself chasing a contravening use along the highways and byways in a rather futile attempt to control the contravening activity which is so profitable for the contravener. This sort of activity may be a prime candidate for making use of special enforcement policies in the development plan – a topic raised also in the fuller discussion of injunctions in chapter nine. Such policies might well address such problems and lay the basis for injunctive proceedings. The provisions of section 187B are particularly relevant in this discussion of 'roving' breaches because they provide for 'apprehended' breaches of control to be restrained by injunction. However, it is important to note an example of an injunction (under the Local Government

Act 1972, section 222) being used to deal with a 'roving' breach. This is the case of *A-G (ex rel East Sussex County Council) v Morris* and is particularly relevant as regards the area covered by the injunction – a matter of some importance with those prone to move around contravening planning control[1]. Here the contravener failed to comply with an enforcement notice and after several prosecutions he moved to an adjacent part of the same plot of land. New notices were served and further prosecutions and fines followed. The court held that an injunction could be granted relating to *all land within the county of East Sussex* since the contravener had flouted the authority and used delaying tactics to impede enforcement of the law. It was accepted by the court that this was an unusual form of relief but the circumstances warranted a perpetual injunction covering the whole of the county planning authority's area. Since the law relating to injunctive relief has moved on a little since then the planning authority wishing to deal with a 'roving' breach in such a manner should find it less difficult to gain such relief – especially where the authority can show a good case for suspecting an 'apprehended' breach of control. This will often involve showing a pattern of breaches and previous conduct of the contravener will be important in persuading the court to grant relief.

Examples of contraveners whose activities might be tackled via injunctions include fly-tippers and fly-posting outfits. These can often be a source of complaint and significant environmental impact. Such professional 'roving' contraveners may well be highlighted in the enforcement manual or IT-based procedures that the LPA uses to routinise enforcement activity. Indeed, the nature of the breach and the character and conduct of the contravener may indicate that injunctive action of this nature is the only effective form of enforcement and should figure at an early stage in any enforcement episode. The *Morris* case also provides a useful starting point for dealing with such problems since an injunction covering the whole area subject to the LPA's jurisdiction might be needed: this is especially relevant given the more generous statutory provisions that cover the injunctive remedy provided under the planning legislation[2].

---

1 [1973] JPL 429.
2 See the discussion in chapter nine of *Runnymede Borough Council v Harwood* and *Croydon London Borough Council v Gladden* noting judicial recognition that the provisions for statutory injunctions were intended to give LPAs greater scope in dealing with contraventions.

4 Breach of control – non-compliance with condition or limitation

4.1 INTRODUCTION

The second type of breach comprises the failure to comply with any condition or limitation imposed on a grant of planning permission. An initial point to bear in mind is that the act or omission that corresponds to the non-compliance may in fact not be an activity that constitutes 'development'. Thus a breach of this type can be quite different to an 'unauthorised development' breach which was discussed in the preceding chapter. A good example of a breach under this category that does not actually constitute development is non-compliance with a condition requiring that a scheme of landscaping be approved by the authority before any development takes place. Although commencement of works on site is itself activity involving 'development', the breach of control is the failure to obtain prior approval of details. When requiring compliance with such a condition the LPA will thus often require the contravener to take 'steps' which are not acts of 'development': compliance with such a condition means that a landscaping scheme has to be submitted. Clearly, the submission of a scheme for approval is not an activity that constitutes 'development'. Breaches of condition thus serve to remind the LPA that the kinds of action that may be required by an enforcement notice are as wide-ranging as those that can be required by conditions. This is a point of relevance later when the discussion turns to the statutory requirement of 'specifying' the steps to be taken in an enforcement notice.

4.2 CONDITIONS PRECEDENT

A problem that may often face the LPA arises from the use of 'conditions precedent' in planning permissions. A Grampian condition is an example of such a condition – one that requires prior action, usually by the developer (action which does not constitute beginning development in reliance on the permission) before works covered by the permission can begin. Normally they are phrased negatively – 'no development shall be carried out until...'. If the development is commenced without complying with such a condition then this is treated as a breach of condition[1]. On a related note the Court of Appeal decision in *Whitley & Sons v Secretary of State for Wales* demonstrates the pragmatic approach taken (as regards the question of whether or not such works are a valid start on development in order to keep the permission alive) with works which commence implementation in breach of control[2]. The Court of Appeal, without wanting to provide a 'charter for developers to ignore conditions which are intended to be complied with before a planning permission is implemented', indicated that works constituting commencement of development (if carried out before the general time limit of, normally, five years) could be in breach but still count as valid commencement. The court indicated that the planning merits could then, if necessary, be sorted out by the Secretary of State on an appeal against enforcement action taken against the breach of condition. This rather generous approach contrasts with earlier authority that had doubted whether non-complying works could validly be counted as commencement. However, this decision's factual circumstances may perhaps (in a later case) be distinguished. In this case the developer had submitted schemes (covering working, restoration and landscaping) for approval, followed by limited works to implement the permission, *both* before the expiry date. Prior approval conditions (a very common form of condition precedent) are discussed below.

1   *Clwyd County Council v Secretary of State for Wales and Welsh Aggregates* [1982] JPL 696.
2   (1992) 64 P & CR 296.

4.3   BREACH OF LIMITATION

The LPA does not have to decide if the breach concerns a condition or limitation: as long as a 'proviso' (to use a neutral term covering both conditions and limitations) is contravened the LPA can take action. As regards enforcement notices the

TCPA 1990, section 173(1)(b) merely requires that an enforcement notice states 'the paragraph of section 171A(1) within which, in the opinion of the authority, the breach falls'. Therefore there is no need to state that the relevant proviso is a 'condition' or a 'limitation'. As the DOE's model notices indicate the LPA need only state, for example, that the breach is under 'section 171A(1)(b)' in order to meet the requirements of section 173(1)(b). The LPA is therefore not obliged to address the rather conflicting case law on what constitutes a 'limitation' for the purposes of the planning legislation. As noted in para 4.7.1 below a breach of condition notice (BCN) can tackle non-compliance with a limitation by virtue of a statutory rule of construction.

4.4   PLANNING APPEALS AND JUSTIFIABLE CONDITIONS

Since the LPA will find itself (on an enforcement notice appeal) having to 'justify' the condition that is the subject of enforcement notice action then clearly the DOE policy on conditions will have relevance. That is why the term 'justifiable' condition is used to discuss these policy issues. The DOE's policy framework means that the LPA will have to 'justify' the condition on appeal if it wishes to enforce compliance. It should be remembered that there is quite a difference between a condition that is legal and one that is acceptable (ie 'justifiable') to the Secretary of State. If a condition fails the criteria set out by central government then an appeal against any enforcement action based on a breach of that unacceptable condition is likely to be successful. Authorities risk an award of costs for 'unreasonable behaviour' if they take enforcement action in such circumstances.

4.4.1 PPG1 and justifiable conditions

A restatement of central government policy as regards 'justifiable' conditions is found in PPG1, paragraphs 46 and 47. These state:

> 'The ability of local planning authorities and the Secretary of State to impose conditions on a planning permission can enable many development proposals to proceed where it would otherwise be necessary to refuse planning permission. The sensitive use of conditions can improve the quality of development control and

enhance public confidence in the planning system. To achieve these ends conditions should be used in a way which is clearly seen to be fair, reasonable and practicable. Conditions should only be imposed where they are

necessary	(12–15)
relevant to planning	(16–19)
relevant to the development to be permitted	(20–21)
enforceable	(22–24)
precise	(25–28)
reasonable in all other respects.	(29–35)

In considering whether a particular condition is necessary, one key test is whether planning permission would have to be refused if the condition were not to be imposed. If not, then such a condition needs special and precise justification. The same criteria and test should be applied in deciding whether to dispense with an extant condition.'

(The numbers in parentheses have been added by the author and refer to the relevant paragraphs in circular 1/85 where the tests are more fully analysed.)

4.4.2 Enforceability – government advice

Of particular relevance here is the issue of enforceability. The advice of central government found in paragraphs 22–24 of circular 1/85 should thus be carefully studied by all planning staff. The courts, however, have emphasised that a condition that is difficult to enforce is not ultra vires: a condition would have to be impossible to enforce and thus flawed by *Wednesbury* unreasonableness in order to be struck down on legal grounds[1]. Such caselaw serves to remind LPAs etc that policy arguments regarding conditions must be treated separately from the legal rules.

1 *Chichester District Council v Secretary of State for the Environment* [1992] 3 PLR 49.

4.4.3 Unjustifiable conditions – government advice

Appendix B to circular 1/85 lists 14 specific examples of conditions which are unacceptable. Clearly, if the condition which the authority seeks to enforce falls under these categories then the LPA will find it very difficult to win on appeal if the appeal option is used by the recipient of an enforcement notice.

4.5   LAWFUL CONDITION

The 'justifiability' of the condition in terms of DOE policy is not
the only factor affecting enforcement decisions. The lawfulness
of the condition is the other key factor to take into account. If the
condition contravenes the legal rules regarding the power to
impose conditions then it will be void as ultra vires. The leading
case on this is *Newbury District Council v Secretary of State for
the Environment*[1]. The case illustrates the point that although
the statutory words granting a discretion to a LPA may appear
to be very wide there are general principles of administrative
law that enable the courts to interpret such provisions in a way
which is more restrictive than the words alone may seem to
warrant. Thus, although the discretion to impose conditions is
framed widely ('such conditions as they think fit') the courts
have over the years developed general principles which limit
this discretion. There are three main principles which will
apply when considering the legality of a condition. A condition
will be ultra vires unless it:

   (a) serves a planning purpose;
   (b) fairly and reasonably relates to the permitted development;
        and
   (c) is not unreasonable – in the *Wednesbury* sense of the
        term.

If the condition is ultra vires then the LPA must take into
account the two possible consequences. First the planning
permission may remain in force – with the ultra vires condition
severed. In this case then there is no breach of condition because
the condition does not exist. Whether or not a condition can be
severed from the permission depends upon whether the condition
is a fundamental aspect of that permission or whether it deals
with some extraneous or minor matter. Thus in one of the
leading cases on this issue, *Hall & Co Ltd v Shoreham-on-Sea
UDC* it was felt that a condition requiring the applicants to
construct a road on their own land and then allow the public a
right of way over it was ultra vires and void for unreasonableness[2].
The second possibility is that the permission is also invalid
because the ultra vires condition is so central to the permission
that it cannot be separated from it without causing the whole
permission to fall. In this situation the court would find that the
development in question has taken place without permission.
However, this would not necessarily mean that the contravener

would be at the mercy of the LPA. There may be questions as to 'lawful development' (with the certification procedure under section 191 coming into play).

If the implementation of the vitiated permission was recent (so making lawfulness difficult to show) the court may entertain arguments based on some notions of equity – operating to prevent the LPA from depriving the contravener of the benefit of the contravening development. This possibility is hinted at in a case involving an ultra vires permission relating to mineral extraction[3]. One member of the Court of Appeal suggested that if the LPA argued in favour of its own permission being declared a nullity then such a stance would not be treated sympathetically by the court. However, this obiter comment overlooks a fundamental aspect of the planning system. This is connected with the tripartite set of interests involved: the landowner, the public interest and the LPA (as guardian of the public interest). The suggestions that there are only two issues at play (the landowner's property interests and the LPA's role) ignores the principal concern of the planning regime – the public interest which the whole system is there to protect. So the public interest should not be conflated with the actions of the LPA since there are often occasions where the LPA can misjudge the public interest and harm both the interests of the community and the private landowner. The discretion of the court to grant relief (to any party) cannot easily be explained (especially in the context of public law) by reference to equity arguments derived from private law where there are only two interests at stake. There are additional problems with using analyses that rely on an 'absolutist' interpretation of terms such as 'nullity', 'voidness' etc: such problems, in the context of the 'nullity' issue, are discussed in more detail below when the powers of correction granted to the appellate are dealt with. The proper approach of the courts must therefore be to consider a wider range of factors than were cursorily noted in the Court of Appeal: there is particularly the need to consider the importance of 'good administration'. A form of equity that would over-emphasise private rights would be just as inappropriate as an analysis that allowed the LPA to employ draconian enforcement sanctions that prevented the Secretary of State from using his powers to consider the merits on appeal. After all the Secretary of State is better suited to balance the range of interests involved and so the court should perhaps come to a decision that enables the Secretary of State to address the issues and sort out the conflicting demands of 'fairness'. Such issues lead naturally on to a discussion of 'estoppel' in the context of conditions.

1   [1981] AC 578, [1980] 1 All ER 731.
2   [1964] 1 All ER 1.
3   *Mouchell Superannuation Fund Trustees v Oxfordshire County Council* [1992] 1 PLR 97. For a more detailed discussion of the unbalanced nature of the analysis see the comments in my Lawyer's Aside column, *Planning*, 10 July 1992. If 'estoppel' and related notions are to be imported from the private law then the fundamental differences between the private law and public law contexts need to be recognised and reflected fully in the 'translation'.

4.6   CONDITIONS PROTECTED BY ESTOPPEL

Estoppel arguments have surfaced in the enforcement field in relation to the power of the LPA to take enforcement action – the *Thrasyvoulou* case as discussed in para 2.8.1.1. Another instance of estoppel arguments being available (this time benefiting the LPA) may be found in the enforcement of conditions. One aspect of this issue (the landowner being 'estopped' from challenging a condition by virtue of his prior acceptance of it) was examined by the Secretary of State in an appeal decision in 1982[1]. This appeal was dealing with an application to discharge a condition which restricted a display of advertisements. The appellant had agreed to such a condition being imposed before the application: this, the council argued, meant that the appellant was estopped from applying to the Secretary of State to have that condition discharged. The Secretary of State stated that there could be a basis for an estoppel on the grounds of such an 'agreement' if 'the LPA dealing with the application can be shown to have acted upon it and thereby to have altered their position to their detriment.' A similar line of thinking has also surfaced in the Divisional Court. It has accepted that a landowner who has, at an inquiry, undertaken to do something will be estopped from arguing that that undertaking (whose content is encompassed by the subsequent grant) is unenforceable against him[2]. However, the arguments employed relied heavily on principles of equity (from private law) and are somewhat suspect when blithely applied to a public law field where there are significant differences. (Such concerns are evident in other caselaw on estoppel in the planning field and indicate why those decisions are less willing to apply an estoppel argument benefiting the landowner[3].) In the case of estoppel working against the landowner because of his promises made at the application/appeal stage there is also the problem of dealing with a future purchaser of the land. Presumably the courts would be loath to find that he was also bound by the undertaking; this likely reticence would parallel the rules from the private law as regards equity. The LPA is taking on the risk, when enforcing such an undertaking, that the court might now be less willing to apply by analogy such a deceptively simple argument based on equitable principles to the public law setting. (Enforcement would be by injunction presumably as a failure to mirror the undertaking in a condition would mean that it is not a breach of condition/limitation.) The message is clear: the LPA must ensure that any such 'undertakings' offered at inquiry are turned into section 106 obligations if such obligations are to be enforceable.

1 [1982] JPL 733 (Oxford City Council, DOE ref APP/5353/A/81/10093).
2 *Hildenborough Village Preservation Association v Secretary of State for the Environment* [1978] JPL 708.
3 See chapter five on estoppel being used to prevent the LPA issuing an enforcement notice.

4.7 BREACH OF CONDITION NOTICES

The introduction of the BCN power was aimed at giving the LPA the opportunity of a fast-track enforcement option which would avoid the delay of an enforcement notice appeal. However, this new sanction (because of its specific ambit and streamlined procedures) has a number of limitations which may well be relevant in an enforcement situation; where these limitations apply perhaps the more established route (enforcement notice) should be used. The practical limitations on the BCN power are set out below after the discussion of the BCN provisions.

4.7.1 Relevant permission and condition(s)/limitation(s)

If there are a number of permissions in similar terms the LPA will need to be reasonably clear as to which has been implemented in order to be sure that the relevant condition has been breached. A PCN might be an appropriate means of dealing with any confusion regarding multiple permissions – TCPA 1990, section 171C(2) appears to cover enquiries seeking to determine which is the 'implemented' permission and the condition that appears to have been breached. One BCN can cover multiple conditions and limitations and the BCN provisions do cover breaches of limitations. This is clear from the TCPA 1990, section 187A(13)(a) which provides that for the purposes of section 187A the term 'conditions' includes limitations. Consequently, breach of a proviso in, for example, the GPDO regarding distances and other qualifying factors, can also be tackled by a BCN.

4.7.2 Two types of BCN: two categories of contravener

The LPA may serve a BCN on any person:

(a) carrying out or has carried out the development; *or*
(b) having control of the land.

The TCPA 1990, section 187A(3) then refers to the person on whom a BCN has been duly served as the 'person responsible'. However, since the legislation has two different categories of recipient the LPA must be careful to ensure that, before serving the BCN, it is clear which is the relevant category of contravener in the context of the particular breach. The need for a careful choice as to the recipients is emphasised by the fact that a BCN served on a person 'having control' of the land can only require that person to comply with 'conditions regulating the use of the land': see the TCPA 1990, section 187A(4). So in addition to two categories of contravener there are also two types (differently worded) of BCN. Complications can increase where both types of BCN are needed. The LPA may therefore, in order to prevent confusion arising from this tiny detail, wish to focus on the two types of BCN (and their appropriate recipients) in the enforcement manual: different pro forma BCNs would also be a good idea – clearly marked to ensure that they are not served on the wrong category of contravener. (Given the importance of the criminal sanction the LPA must be careful about such niceties otherwise the sanction of criminal proceedings may be worthless.)

As to the meaning of 'person having control of the land': this would normally indicate some direct physical and legal power over the use of the land. This would be the occupier of the land in many cases but also, potentially, the occupier's landlord if he has a great deal of control via the lease or licence. The reference to a person carrying out the development might cover any person ordering builders etc to do such work: it would also seem to cover the builder himself. This interpretation is strengthened by the specific reference in subsection (13)(b) to the phrase 'carrying out development'. Someone falls within the definition of carrying out development by 'causing or permitting another to do so': see para 9.6.5 for a discussion of the meaning of 'cause or permit'.

4.7.3 BCN requirements

The BCN requires the person served to secure compliance with such of the conditions as are specified in the notice – section 187A(2). The notice shall also 'specify the steps which the authority considers ought to be taken, or the activities which the authority considers ought to cease . . . ' – subsection (5). Planning conditions requiring works (which were supposed to have been carried out prior to occupation, for example) need to be reflected in appropriately worded BCNs. This is clear from an unreported case where a conviction was quashed by Truro Crown Court when the defendant had not complied with a BCN requiring that a 'sewage treatment plant is installed in accordance with approved plans'[1]. The plant had not been installed because the site in question was the subject of an ownership dispute. The planning condition (for construction of a dwelling) was in this form: 'before the dwelling hereby permitted is occupied, a Bio-Disc Treatment Unit shall be sited in accordance with the approved plan'. The Crown Court held that the prosecution could not rely on a failure to cease occupation when that was not a step specified in the BCN. The BCN should therefore have also included the additional step 'to cease occupation of the premises until the Bio-Disc Unit is sited'. This sort of situation (and possibly many other cases where conditions are tied to occupation) is one where the LPA may well want to under-enforce by not requiring occupation to cease. This is possibly why the BCN in this case only partially covered the situation and so failed to substantiate the prosecution case. If under-enforcement is important then the LPA will probably have to use an enforcement notice: see below on the limitations of the BCN power.

1 *Quinton v North Cornwall District Council* 11 May 1994, Truro Crown Court.

4.7.4 Compliance period

Not less than 28 days must be allowed for compliance; time runs from the date of service of the notice: TCPA 1990, section 187A(7)(a). This compliance period may be extended (during the currency of the period) by the LPA serving notice to that effect on the 'person responsible'.

4.7.5 No appeal – criminal sanction

An offence is committed by the 'person responsible' if:

(a) 'any of the conditions specified in the notice is not complied with'; and

(b) 'the steps specified in the notice have not been taken or, as the case may be, the activities specified in the notice have not ceased[1].'

However, there will be a defence to a prosecution if it can be shown that either the activities specified in the notice are not being carried on or that the 'person responsible' had taken 'all reasonable measures to secure compliance with the conditions specified in the notice'[2]. The interpretation of this defence may involve a range of factors. Impecuniosity can be pleaded but the magistrates should not be unduly influenced by this factor[3]. If the 'person in control' is a landlord with rights under the lease to take action against the tenant who contravenes planning control then a failure to use those sanctions may be difficult to explain away. Given the underlying purpose of the enforcement powers in ensuring compliance with planning control it is arguable that 'all reasonable measures' is to be construed in the light of the importance of protecting the public interest against planning contraventions. 'Reasonable measures' in this situation should thus perhaps encompass taking action under the private law which may leave the landlord out of pocket. To construe the term narrowly would, otherwise, allow the landlord to profit out of the contravention by the tenant. This would clearly be contrary to the underlying aims of the legislative scheme. It may also invite analysis of provisions under general principles of criminal law regarding aiding and abetting (see para 9.6.10 on such liability). The courts will no doubt have to face such issues in considering defences raised by landlords under this provision. In the case of a person responsible who is alleged to have been in control of the land it is a defence for such person if he proves that he no longer has control of the land[4]. This would mean that there would be little point in serving a BCN on a builder who had completed all work on the site by the time the notice was served. The offence is only summary – punishable by a fine up to level 3[5].

1 TCPA 1990, s 187A(8).
2 TCPA 1990, s 187A(11)(a).
3 *Kent County Council v Brockman* [1994] JPL B27 (dealing with the similar section 179(3) defence in respect of non-compliance with an enforcement notice of doing 'everything he could be expected to do to secure compliance with the notice').
4 TCPA 1990, s 187A(11)(b).
5 TCPA 1990, s 187A(12). See para 9.6.11 for the scale of fines.

4.7.6 Presentation of BCN prosecutions

Comments regarding the range of issues that need to be addressed fully and clearly when handling prosecutions under the planning legislation are set out more fully in chapter nine. Such issues must be addressed by the prosecutor if a fine of an appropriate level is to be won.

4.7.7 Limitations of the BCN provisions

The first issue to note is that the discretion to use a BCN is couched in much more demanding terms than that which frames the enforcement notice discretion (discussed in chapter five). Section 187A(2), in dealing with planning permissions subject to conditions, indicates that the LPA may serve a BCN '. . . if any of the conditions is not complied with . . .' There is no 'apparent breach' test in this language. The LPA must be clear that a breach has occurred or else it will face arguments from the recipient on this point before the Bench. This feature sets the tone for the BCN provisions as a whole: the LPA must be much more aware of the special nature of this new weapon and take account of practical restrictions on its use of these powers. The framing of the discretion indicates, for example, that conditions must now be clear and unambiguous – otherwise enforcement by way of the BCN route may well prove hazardous. This takes us back to the planning trinity issue and the need for

forward planning and development control activity to work in
harmony with enforcement.

4.7.7.1 *Interpretation by the criminal courts*

Another practical issue relates to the criminal courts and their
approach to the interpretation of planning permissions etc. Can
the LPA be reasonably sure that (particularly as regards the use
of the BCN powers) it will secure, if necessary, a conviction in
the criminal courts on the back of the relevant planning condition?
Naturally the LPA may wish to chance its arm and hope that the
recipient complies and/or does not notice that the condition in
question would possibly be viewed critically by the Bench. If a
condition and/or the related BCN would permit a number of
interpretations then prosecution is a risky enterprise. The
criminal courts tend to favour the accused in interpreting any
official order which is said to be the basis of the contravention.
Imprecise conditions could therefore lead to a failure in the
magistrates' court. Some conditions may therefore not be
sufficiently precise to justify a BCN prosecution.

4.7.7.2 *Interaction of administrative and criminal procedures*

Another factor is the interaction between the criminal courts
and administrative procedures. The LPA will have to take
account of the likely response of magistrates to a claim that the
condition in question is being appealed to the Secretary of State.
This may lead to the magistrates adjourning proceedings pending
the appeal. The Court of Appeal in *R v Newland* indicated
(exceptional) circumstances for granting an adjournment[1]. In
*R v Beaconsfield Magistrates, ex p South Buckinghamshire
District Council* the court held that magistrates should normally
not grant an adjournment as the penalty could reflect the fact
that an appeal was pending[2]. (In fact the court then held that
the adjournment granted in this case was appropriate because
the defendants were old and in ill health and the LPA had
delayed in taking enforcement action. The latter factor indicates
the importance of keeping up momentum and being prompt in
the processing of enforcement cases.)

1   (1987) 54 P & CR 222.
2   (1993) 157 JP 1073.

4.7.7.3 *Under enforcement*

Another problem with the BCN procedure in particular is that in some cases the breach of condition is not wholly objectionable. Planning circumstances since the original grant of permission may have changed somewhat – making the planning case for the condition in question less strong. At the time of the breach there may be a good planning case for modifying the terms of the condition. However, the BCN procedure does not allow the condition to be modified by way of under-enforcement: the BCN is an 'all or nothing' procedure that lacks the flexibility of the enforcement notice. The BCN must be worded so as to 'secure compliance' with the condition in question (section 187A(5) of the TCPA 1990). As the *Quinton* case illustrates this can be quite onerous if a *Grampian* condition has been breached: full compliance is required if that condition is to be remedied yet this can be *Wednesbury* unreasonable or, at least, provide the contravener with a 'reasonable measures' defence under section 187A(11) if a prosecution is undertaken. In some cases therefore the LPA will be faced with conflicting legal requirements. If the LPA wishes to under-enforce it will have to use an enforcement notice.

4.7.7.4 *No self-enforcement on sale*

One advantage of an enforcement notice is that the underlying contravention is highly visible when it comes selling the land: any hopes that the contravener may have of selling the land will be confronted by solicitor's enquiries as to the contravention. Enforcement notices are, in this way, self-enforcing. BCNs are not registrable as land charges and so do not produce such an incentive. If the purchaser's solicitors fail to ask the relevant questions of the vendor then 'market forces' will not work in the LPA's favour. BCNs (like enforcement notices and stop notices) are entered on the register for such documents under section 188 of the TCPA 1990 but this is not routinely examined by purchasers. BCNs are only removed from the register if they are quashed by a (civil) court: see art 26(3)(b) of the Town and Country Planning (General Development Procedure) Order 1995.

4.7.7.5 *Punishment, not remediation*

The BCN relies on the threat of a criminal sanction in order to persuade the contravener to comply. On its own therefore the BCN (if ignored by the recalcitrant contravener) will not necessarily lead to remediation. A successful prosecution (given the low ceiling on the penalty that can be imposed) may not in fact persuade the contravener to remedy the breach. In this light the BCN's power is a rather weak form of punishment. Additionally, since the works in default powers under section 178 (allowing direct action when an enforcement notice is disobeyed) do not apply, it is not really a mechanism whose fundamental structure is designed to ensure remediation when used as the sole enforcement weapon. (Such a criticism may also be levelled at the proposition that criminalising planning contraventions will, of itself, reduce the problems of enforcement faced by LPAs.) The LPA could seek a mandatory injunction under section 187B. Yet even though the courts have indicated that, in general, they will be more willing to grant relief under section 187B than under the Local Government Act 1972, section 222 the position as regards mandatory injunctions may still be more restrictive. The courts may follow the established case law on mandatory injunctions – so making them more difficult to obtain than prohibitive injunctions. (See chapter nine on securing compliance with the enforcement notice for a more detailed discussion.) So if the LPA wants to ensure that the contravention is remedied it may find itself having to supplement the BCN by other more mainstream action such as an enforcement notice and the works in default power. This possibility may therefore merit attention in any procedure notes or manual: perhaps an assessment of the chances of securing remediation by the BCN procedure alone will have to be made so that situations involving the more recalcitrant contravener can be tackled by the more remediation-centred remedy of the enforcement notice.

4.7.7.6   *No stop notice*

A stop notice cannot be issued if a contravention is tackled only by way of a BCN. A severe breach affecting the local amenity may therefore continue until the BCN takes effect (at least 28 days) and for some time thereafter if the contravener ignores the notice. In cases that merit swift action to stop the impact an enforcement notice and stop notice may have to be used – as alternative or additional sanctions.

4.7.7.7   *BCNs – not a panacea*

The above limitations indicate that LPAs should use BCNs to deal with those breaches of condition whose impacts etc are likely to be fully addressed by this type of action. BCNs are not a replacement for mainstream enforcement action: they are designed to be a specialised form of enforcement action for specific situations and, in the light of the penalty available, for the less persistent contravener. Their limitations are clear and unless the LPA is willing to take a risk and accept some setbacks when using this power it should not automatically use the BCN procedure for all breach of condition cases. They are particularly unsuited to dealing with breaches of *Grampian* conditions. The enforcement manual and enforcement personnel should be clear as to the limitations of the BCN procedure: effective enforcement requires that the available weapons in the enforcement armoury be used wisely and that the risks involved in using certain weapons for purposes for which they are not ideally suited are appreciated.

4.8 PROBLEM CONDITIONS

Conditions that satisfy the tests of 'legality' and 'justifiability' are likely to be amenable to enforcement action – whether by breach of condition notice (as just examined) or by enforcement notice. Yet this does not mean that conditions failing these tests cannot be subject to some enforcement action. The informal enforcement techniques (where persuasion and bluff are employed rather than resorting to formal legal notices etc) may result in the condition being enforced and activity detrimental to planning interests being tackled even though the condition may in fact be susceptible to a challenge on legal grounds or planning merits. The more adventurous LPA may well take a robust view of action in such cases and even take formal enforcement action – well aware of the risks of failure but counting on a significant level of success in terms of its overall enforcement objectives. Such an authority will, naturally, ensure that such an approach is taken with open eyes: officers who take a more adventurous stance on the use of the available powers will risk censure if elected members are given a false view of the chances of success. Risk-taking is not fundamentally wrong for the enforcement team: the positive and negative aspects of such a strategy must, however, be made clear to senior officers and members. There are conditions that meet the tests of legality and justifiability and yet prove difficult for the enforcement team. In terms of effective enforcement the LPA should perhaps bear these conditions in mind and address the issue in procedure notes etc.

4.8.1 Prior-approval conditions

A condition may be difficult to enforce by reason of the difficulty
in setting out the 'steps' required by the notice in order to
remedy the breach. The difficulty is not only one of 'legality' but
also 'justifiability' – the tests relevant to the validity of conditions
may also be applied to the 'steps' required by an enforcement
notice. Breaches of a condition precedent (such as prior approval
of a landscaping scheme) have been treated differently by the
courts. If one step requires that work cease and only recommence
after a scheme for landscaping has been 'agreed with the local
planning authority' then this may be found to be ultra vires the
enforcement discretion – *Kaur v Secretary of State for the
Environment*[1]. Conditions precedent which rely on either:

   (a) approval of details, or
   (b) prior agreement with the LPA

may thus be difficult to enforce. The most obvious 'steps' that
could be required in an enforcement notice would be those that
closely mirror the terms of the condition that has been breached.
However the restrictive interpretation placed on the legislation
by the courts (evident in *Kaur*) is something which the LPA
should bear in mind.

   The case of *Murfitt v Secretary of State for the Environment*[2]
indicates the problems with enforcement action which addresses
breach of a prior-approval condition. If the enforcement notice
merely requires agreement with the LPA of a remedial scheme
then *Kaur* indicates that this could well be struck down by the
inspector. The LPA might argue for the use of the correction
power: however, the uncertainty regarding the 'nullity' principle
suggests that the LPA should ensure that the enforcement
notice is drafted so as to include provision for the matter to be
decided by the Secretary of State if the LPA and the contravener
cannot reach agreement.

   This problem perhaps raises the question as to whether the
LPA should start to draw up a standard list of 'enforcement
notice steps': such a list would often be closely allied to the
standard list of conditions. The *Murfitt* case reminds us that
those conditions that involve extra procedural elements should
also be the occasion for enforcement notice steps that are
similarly structured. Such a list would also be of use in
formulating breach of condition notices where complex conditions
(eg those that require works to be carried out before occupation)

would also be mirrored by requirements set out in breach of condition notices that are similarly phrased.

1 [1990] JPL 814.
2 [1980] JPL 598.

4.8.2 Landscaping conditions

Landscaping conditions also fall into a second category of problem breaches – conditions commonly contravened. Often a residential or commercial development is completed without the landscaping. The circular on conditions (1/85) discusses landscaping conditions in paragraphs 40–41. It suggests that a landscaping condition on a residential development might require that no start on the last few houses be made until the landscaping has been substantially completed. However, even this advice needs to be applied carefully: what, for example, does 'substantially' completed mean? The circular also suggests that occupancy be tied to completion of landscaping. This advice is followed up with model conditions. Landscaping conditions that rely on the 'occupancy' tactic work well if the solicitors acting for prospective purchasers realise the impact of the condition. Purchasers, if properly advised, should not be willing to buy houses etc whose premature occupation would give rise to a breach of control.

4.8.3 Limited period permissions

A planning permission relating to a use that may be harmful to a sensitive locality will often be granted subject to a condition requiring its cessation after a specified time[1]. If the use continues after that specified time then there will be a breach of planning control. The safest course of action for the authority when drafting the notice is to phrase the breach in terms of a breach of condition and not a material change of use[2]. A defect of this nature, however, would probably not cause the notice to fall since the discretion to correct the notice would probably be exercised so as to deal with this problem. The LPA that has made this mistake, however, would seem to have a good chance of convincing an inspector to use the inspector's correction power and rectify the error – see chapter seven's discussion of this power.

1 TCPA 1990, s 72(1)(b).
2 The DOE's preferred description – see for example an appeal decision reported in [1978] JPL 724.

4.8.4   Conditions restricting permitted development

Permitted development rights can be cut down by either:

(a) an article 4 direction; or
(b) a condition attached to an implemented planning permission.

In such cases the carrying out of the activity is no longer permitted under the GPDO and so it will involve unauthorised development. If permitted development rights have been taken away by a condition attached to a planning permission, the LPA find it difficult to resist (on appeal) the deemed application for planning permission if the condition is contrary to central government policy. Authorities should therefore be hesitant about enforcement where the condition is likely to be 'deleted' by the inspector on appeal. The courts have also indicated that a condition must be clear and unequivocal in order to have such an impact[1]. In a similar vein the restriction of permitted development rights by an article 4 direction is less likely to be upheld in an enforcement case if the article 4 direction is widely drawn. A more carefully drafted direction which deals with defined problems in a discriminating fashion is preferable. Paragraphs 66–69 of circular 1/85 discuss the attitude of the DOE to conditions that restrict the operation of the GPDO and the Use Classes Order.

1 *Dunoon Developments Ltd v Secretary of State for the Environment* (1992) 65 P & CR 101.

4.8.5   Non-compliance with approved plans

If a development is carried out which does not conform to the terms of a planning permission there can be a problem in defining the type of contravention that has occurred. This is naturally relevant because it then has an impact on the relevant time limits that might apply. The Court of Appeal in *Handoll v Warner Goodman Street* has indicated that a permission cannot be said to have been implemented where the building in question (a bungalow) was 90 feet west of the location approved by the LPA[1]. There was therefore no breach of an agricultural occupancy condition because the permission containing this condition had not been implemented. (The court criticised the approach in *Kerrier* and held that it was wrongly decided[2].) However, since such problems seem to commonly arise with rural dwellings there is a clear risk that LPAs can miss the boat and then fall foul of the four-year time bar relating to unauthorised development.

If the *Kerrier* approach (representing a more favourable line of thinking) is no longer available perhaps the answer lies in using the power to grant retrospective planning permission. Such powers relate to development either carried out without permission or without complying with some condition subject to which planning permission was granted (TCPA 1990, section 73A(2)). A planning condition can be imposed on such a permission (section 70 powers to impose conditions also apply to sections 73 and 73A applications): this is then the condition which can be the basis of an allegation of a breach of condition (eg agricultural occupancy). Additionally, subsection (3) states that such a permission 'may be granted so as to have effect' from the date on which the development was carried out. The permissive 'may' (rather than a 'shall') indicates that the permission need not be back-dated to the date when the development was 'carried out'. The LPA may therefore, if there are potential time-limit problems with any condition on a retrospective application, avoid these by not back-dating the permission too far.

All such applications would have to be made by a 'friendly party' of course. Some authorities have persuaded their Chief Planning Officers to fill out the forms. There is no requirement that the applicant under section 73A have a legal interest in the land: however, proprietorship certificates etc will be required of course. Naturally, the contravention of such a condition imposed on a retrospective permission is going to be assessed on the (inevitable) appeal by the Secretary of State in the light of the planning arguments; these will also include possible 'hardship' arguments by the present occupiers. However, at least this offers a way of addressing the merits by way of enforcement action that does not stretch the law as it now stands. It is clearly most relevant where the contravener would otherwise profit from his own contravening activity.

1 (1994) Times, 26 December.
2 *Kerrier District Council v Secretary of State for the Environment* (1980) 41 P & CR 284. The Divisional Court held that the Secretary of State was wrong to quash an enforcement notice dealing with a breach of an agricultural occupancy condition when the bungalow as built contained a basement not approved by the LPA. The Secretary of State found that the 'material differences between the bungalow as built and the plans as approved in 1973 meant that the bungalow had been built without any planning permission at all' (at 286). The court's approach was based on the principle that the occupiers of a building that was not fully complying with the relevant permission should not be able to benefit from their failure to comply by arguing that any occupancy conditions did not bite.

4.9 LOCAL PLANNING AUTHORITY STANDARD CONDITIONS

Where issues are finely balanced (especially if aesthetic issues raised by listed buildings, conservation areas, green belt etc are relevant) it is the well-informed judgement of elected members that will be an important factor. Inspectors will generally be loath to label well-informed and tenable decisions of elected members as 'unreasonable' from the costs point of view. The enforcement of conditions affecting such 'interests of acknowledged importance' will thus involve a greater degree of latitude and less risk of a costs award against the LPA. The subjectivity element that is inherent in such issues is thus something that is relevant in the formulation and use of the standard list of conditions. Of course enforcement action taken to support conditions protecting amenity interests may not survive the deemed application for planning permission when the notice is appealed – the inspector may reduce the protection afforded by the condition in question by substituting another. If that is something which happens frequently (both in enforcement and ordinary planning appeals) then it may be necessary to reappraise the standard list.

4.9.1 Ombudsman-proof conditions

The Ombudsman's caseload often involves problems arising from the imposition (and monitoring) of conditions. In one case[1] a condition had been imposed on the grant of planning permission requiring that 'all construction traffic shall make use of the proposed new road and no use shall be made of' the private highway adjoining the site. This condition was being breached by heavy vehicles and plant. The Ombudsman did not find maladministration in the council's failure to take enforcement action. However he felt that the council might have done more to detect the alleged breaches of the condition either by arranging periods of observation by their own officers or enlisting the support of residents who were prepared to observe and give evidence. He also went on to find that the imposition of the condition itself amounted to maladministration. The Ombudsman suggested that conditions should not be imposed if they cannot be expected to be enforced. The non-monitoring of compliance with conditions has been criticised before – see for example reports from the early 1980s (references 667/H/80 and 181/H/81). The imposition of a defective condition will also be grounds for a finding of maladministration (656/C/82). These Ombudsman cases thus illustrate the need for a more strategic approach to enforcement such that conditions imposed at the development control stage are then monitored appropriately.

1   15/C/84, Kingston-Upon-Hull City Council, [1986] JPL 138.

5 Enforcement notices – discretion, law, policy and practice

5.1 INTRODUCTION

Once the LPA is satisfied that there is an 'apparent' breach of control then it will consider whether or not to exercise the enforcement discretion[1]. That discretion is exercised within a framework of planning policy derived both from the local plan and central government advice – with the former attaining a greater importance now that the TCPA 1990, section 54A has created a statutory emphasis on decision-making that accords with relevant local plan policy. The discretion given to the LPA is, as with other discretions under the planning legislation, wide. However, it is not an unfettered one which enables the LPA to turn a blind eye to factors that must be taken into account. The legal parameters relating to the discretion are therefore important aspects of effective enforcement and require some examination.

1 TCPA 1990, s 172(1)(a) sets out the precondition for the exercise of the power to issue an enforcement notice: the LPA '. . . may issue a notice (in this Act referred to as an "enforcement notice") where it appears to them . . . that there has been a breach of planning control'.

5.2 THE DISCRETION TO ISSUE

The LPA's enforcement power is framed in wide terms – they may issue an enforcement notice 'where they consider it expedient to issue the notice, having regard to the provisions of the development plan and to any other material consideration'. The 'expediency' element emphasises the very free hand given the LPA in deciding whether or not to take action and, implicitly, the precise nature of the action – ie the requirements set out in the notice. It is therefore similar to the development control power under the TCPA 1990, section 70. However, the wide discretion cannot be interpreted in isolation – the 'literal' breadth of the discretion must be tempered by judicial comments as to the manner in which discretionary powers are to be exercised, the rest of the language in section 172(1)(b) noted in the excerpt above and other relevant statutory provisions and fundamental aims of the legislation. Thus generally applicable principles of administrative law will be applied. The need to consider all relevant considerations and ignore irrelevant considerations; the need to avoid manifestly unreasonable (in the *Wednesbury* sense) action; the requirement that the decision must not frustrate the object and purpose of the statute conferring the power[1]: all these principles (discussed more fully in chapter eight's treatment of the discretion underlying the stop notice provisions) apply to the exercise of the statutory discretion under which authorities are empowered to issue enforcement notices.

1 *Padfield v Minister of Agriculture, Fisheries and Food* [1968] AC 997.

5.2.1 The elements in the discretion

The elements in the enforcement notice power can be conveniently split up into the following phrases:

(a) may issue a notice if they consider it expedient to do so;
(b) having regard to the provisions of the development plan;
(c) and to any other material considerations.

5.3 'MAY ISSUE A NOTICE IF THEY CONSIDER IT EXPEDIENT TO DO SO'

Judicial review of *inaction* is difficult to sustain unless (for example) the breach relates to a condition whose imposition was particularly important and was a major reason for issuing a permission. In such circumstances the decision not to take action would need to be justified – otherwise it would risk being categorised as arbitrary and capricious. Thus in one case (*Perry v Stanborough (Developments) Ltd*) the court stressed that

Parliament had expressly left the enforcement of planning control by means of an enforcement notice to the discretion of the LPA[1]. That principle does, however, need to be applied in the light of general principles of administrative law that a discretion is given to an authority for a purpose and if they fail to consider (taking into account only the relevant matters) the issue of whether or not to exercise such a discretion then they may well be in breach of the preliminary duty to consider exercising that discretion.

The LPA will rarely find itself in a position where failure to exercise the discretion to issue an enforcement notice could be challenged in the courts. They may well face an Ombudsman investigation which could examine in greater detail whether the elected members of the council were given all relevant facts when deciding not to take such action. Failure to issue a notice in time (eg because of the four-year rule) might be attacked by an Ombudsman referral – maladministration by 'delay' or 'incompetence'[2].

1 [1978] JPL 36.
2 Delays in taking formal enforcement action can easily lead to an adverse finding by the Ombudsman.

5.4 'HAVING REGARD TO THE PROVISIONS OF THE DEVELOPMENT PLAN'

Looking solely at the 'have regard to' standard we would immediately think of the section of the TCPA 1990 dealing with development control decisions[1]. Old case law reminds us that this means that the LPA should not 'slavishly adhere' to the provisions in a development plan or other material considerations, for example, central government advice[2]. With the TCPA 1990, section 54A the picture has significantly changed. Section 54A states that:

> 'Where, in making any determination under the planning Acts, regard is to be had to the development plan, the determination shall be made in accordance with the plan unless material considerations indicate otherwise.'

The decision to take enforcement action by way of an enforcement notice is clearly caught by this section because of the express wording in section 172 regarding the materiality of the development plan. Section 54A's emphasis on the plan thus means that both the decision in principle to issue an enforcement notice and the precise contents of that (eg its requirements and compliance period(s)) will therefore normally have to accord with relevant policies in the development plan, if any. For the LPA concerned with effective enforcement this is not to be seen as a restriction; it should be viewed as a support in handling breaches of planning control in a way that accords with local circumstances. So the enforcement task of the LPA will be much easier to carry out if there are 'enforcement policies' in the development plan addressing important 'enforcement considerations'. These should tie in with the key elements of the plan's strategy. They should thus make clear how important a particular policy or set of policies is to the LPA. In justifying its exercise of the enforcement discretion (before the inspector or before the courts) the LPA will then be able to use the section 54A 'presumption' in favour of action in accordance with the development plan to justify both taking action and also the precise terms of that action.

Section 54A thus means that the LPA (and other decision-makers) should 'normally adhere' to the development plan's policies if relevant to the enforcement situation at hand. The development plan thus now assumes a greater role in enforcement and this is clearly to the benefit of the LPA when justifying its actions (and, more importantly, the contents of its enforcement notices) before an inspector. Yet this boost should not be taken as allowing the LPA's development plan policies on enforcement issues to override other relevant considerations. Section 54A has a 'let-out clause' (the last five words of the excerpted quote above) which does allow, if there is justification for doing so on planning grounds, the inspector to override planning policy. The law regarding the section 54A proviso (in the context of the development control sub-regime) is not too illuminating. Also there is no explicit guidance on the application of the proviso to enforcement decisions in DOE policy. The nearest we have is the guidance in PPG1 (paragraphs 25 to 31) on the development control function – which must be relevant by analogy. The terms of that guidance, when applied to enforcement appeals, would therefore indicate that inspectors should have a very clear-cut case for overriding the plan (see further on this para 5.6.7 below). Consequently, the LPA, if there is an appeal must press the inspector to be clear and comprehensive about his reasons for not following development plan policy on enforcement if he is minded to apply the section

54A proviso. The section 54A 'presumption' also has a bearing on the range of factors which the civil courts will take into account when considering an application for a statutory injunction (see chapter nine) as the planning arguments favouring the grant of such a remedy will be stronger if the LPA can utilise the development plan and make reference to the section 54A presumption.

This discussion emphasises the importance of seeing enforcement as an indivisible element (along with the other planning functions such as forward planning) in the 'planning trinity'. It also leads on to those material considerations which may both be reflected in plan policy but which also have a 'weighting' that is of even greater importance. Even with section 54A there are, therefore, certain planning interests whose importance to the enforcement discretion may point to a decision apparently in conflict with plan criteria.

1 TCPA 1990, s 70(2).
2 The 'slavishly adhere' phrase is often used to designate the improper emphasis that, prior to TCPA 1990, s 54A, might mistakenly have been placed on the development plan: it comes from case law (*Simpson v Edinburgh Corpn* 1960 SC 313). Although now not directly relevant because of section 54A the phrase does, however, provide, with adaptation, the useful paraphrase ('normally adhere') found in the text of this paragraph.

5.4.1 Conservation area policies

As noted below the exercise of enforcement powers under section 172 will have to take account of the requirements of the conservation area test in section 72(1) of P(LB&CA)A 1990. Additionally the LPA may well have conservation area policies in its development plan whose content will naturally be relevant to the exercise of the enforcement discretion[1]. Further, leading on from earlier comments on the importance of enforcement policy, it is perhaps not surprising that conservation area enforcement policies may also be relevant here. The LPA that aims to be effective with its enforcement activity will therefore need to ensure that the forward planning aspect of the planning trinity supports the conservationist aims of the conservation area regime. Such policies should have been formulated in accordance with the requirements of section 72(1) with its heightened emphasis on conservation area interests. A problem here is that the forward planning element of the planning trinity may not have properly reconciled the different language from all these provisions. Indeed, the 'special attention' language of section 72(1) possibly indicates a statutory weighting favouring conservation area interests above the interest of ensuring that decision-makers 'normally adhere' to the development plan when making planning decisions: section 54A, as suggested above, creates that 'normally adheres' duty as regards the decision-maker. Such complications have surfaced in case law on listed building decision-making in the development control field (see next paragraph). Other case law illustrates that it is permissible, on good planning grounds, to allow a development that harms a conservation area[2]. The conservation area test does not therefore impose an overriding duty to conserve: the LPA that treated section 72(1) in this way would be committing an error of law. PPG15 policy also stresses that the emphasis on conservation can be overridden[3]. However, when (on appeal) the contravener or inspector address such issues the LPA will clearly be able to rely on the statutory wording of section 72(1) to substantiate a need for clear and comprehensive arguments justifying a decision that harms a conservation area.

1   See chapter eleven for a detailed discussion of conservation area enforcement notices and the complex provisions of the conservation area test in section 72(1).
2   *Wansdyke District Council v Secretary of State for the Environment* [1992] JPL 1168.
3   PPG15, para 4.19 notes the strong presumption against the grant of planning permission that would harm a conservation area but states that 'in exceptional circumstances the presumption may be overridden in favour of development which is desirable on the ground of some other public interest'.

5.4.2   Listed building policies

There is no listed building test that, by virtue of an express statutory rule, applies to the enforcement discretion exercisable by the LPA. Clearly the LPA must take account of a contravention's impact on a nearby listed building if that impact is significant in listed building terms: such an impact would be material to the enforcement discretion as a matter of principle. However, at the appeal stage there is a statutory test (similar in many respects to that for conservation areas) which will kick in and affect consideration of the deemed application for planning permission. The P(LB&CA)A 1990, section 66(1) addresses the special protections given to a listed building even when the building itself has not been the subject of the contravening development. This provision can therefore affect a deemed application for development – even when that application is not made in respect of a listed building. This provision requires that the inspector or Secretary of State pay 'special regard to the desirability of preserving the building or its setting or any features of special architectural or historic interest which it possesses'. Arguments before the inspector should therefore address this statutory test and the LPA should, at the forward planning stage, ensure that its development plan does not encourage conflicting approaches. Where a breach of planning control has an impact on such interests then the existence of such provisions in the development plan would clearly be of relevance to the exercise of the enforcement discretion. The clear implication is that such interests should also be protected by *enforcement policies* relating to such features.

The potential for conflict between development planning policy and the statutory emphasis on preservation of listed buildings is a factor that forward planning should address. Within the development control context such a conflict has been recognised[1]. Arguments on appeal will therefore need to address the possible conflict between the statutory emphasis on preserving listed buildings and the development plan emphasis (section 54A is naturally relevant) on factors affecting an enforcement appeal involving a listed building.

1 *Heatherington UK Ltd v Secretary of State for the Environment* [1994] EGCS 118.

5.5 'AND TO ANY OTHER MATERIAL CONSIDERATIONS'

This catch-all phrase covers a number of other relevant matters. For the purposes of this discussion it may be pertinent to distinguish three different categories of 'other material consideration'. These are:

(a) central government policy;

(b) considerations that are material by virtue of other explicit statutory provisions ('statutory considerations');
(c) other material (enforcement) considerations.

Such factors can serve to justify action which appears to conflict with the development plan policies on enforcement. This is the effect of the section 54A proviso regarding 'material considerations' that 'indicate otherwise'. This is most relevant on appeal. The LPA should be prepared to argue against the invocation of the section 54A proviso where the appellant argues that material considerations indicate that a more lenient attitude to the contravention should be taken. In light of decisions in the courts on section 54A and ordinary planning appeals it is clear that, at present, the degree of justification required by inspectors to override plan policy is not that great[1].

---

1 *St Albans District Council v Secretary of State for the Environment* [1993] 1 PLR 88 thus produced the judicial comment that the PPG1 advice on section 54A introduced a gloss on the statutory wording that was not a legal requirement.

5.6 CENTRAL GOVERNMENT POLICY

Central government policy on enforcement is primarily concerned with ensuring that formal enforcement is only taken as a last resort after a long process of negotiation, advice and help. The main sources of advice on mainstream enforcement are PPG18 and circulars 21/91 and 17/92. Key elements of that advice are the focus (found in PPG18) on detrimental impacts on the local amenity and the importance of not unnecessarily harming the economic functioning of small businesses. If the contravention involves a small business then central government advice stresses the importance of being helpful and sympathetic to the contravener. An example of such advice is found in PPG18, paragraph 16:

'... the LPA should aim to agree on a timetable for relocation which will minimise disruption to the business and, if possible, avoid any permanent loss of employment as a result of the relocation'.

However, the LPA should always remember that DOE policy is addressing planning issues at a generalised level and the very local focus of enforcement, in the light of all relevant considerations, may justify action in conflict with such policy.

Such action would not be per se unlawful: if the difference in approach can be justified on appeal then the LPA's stance will be vindicated. It is therefore important to be aware of the legal parameters affecting government policy in the context of appeal as an assessment of such factors will be relevant to the LPA's use of its enforcement powers.

5.6.1 DOE policy and enforcement appeals

The relevance of central government policy and its application and interpretation in particular circumstances are matters which the courts have examined in recent years. The advice on enforcement is particularly laissez faire. Circulars, as the courts remind us, are nationally applicable statements of general policy that must be interpreted as a whole. They must be adapted and applied in the light of local circumstances – *Surrey Heath Borough Council*[1]. Advice from central government can often be partial in its orientation and fail to tackle a number of particular issues[2]. The advice on enforcement is particularly interesting since its terms are very wide-ranging and do not address certain types of enforcement situations that commonly confront the LPA.

1 *Surrey Heath Borough Council v Secretary of State for the Environment* [1987] JPL 199.
2 One example is the lack of explicit guidance in PPG2 or elsewhere on the relevance of the cost-benefit analysis advocated in circular 21/91, Annex 3 to the use of the stop notice discretion. This is highlighted in the litigation involving Wendy Fair Markets: *R v Elmbridge Borough Council, ex p Wendy Fair Markets* [1994] EGCS 159 (see chapter eight on stop notice).

5.6.2 DOE policy and the courts

The policy contained in circulars, policy guidance notes etc is recognised by the courts as being a 'material consideration' for the purposes of development control decisions. Such policy is equally capable of being 'material' when it comes to the enforcement function as the phrase 'material consideration' is to be found in section 172. When a notice is appealed then central government policy may well attain a greater prominence

— both in terms of the deemed application for permission and in terms of the enforcement issues themselves. As has been stated above, the advice of central government as regards enforcement action is broadly drawn. If an inspector were to 'slavishly adhere to'[1] central government policy on enforcement he may find himself committing an error of law: recent case law has increasingly criticised the manner in which some policy pronouncements in circulars have been formulated, interpreted or applied. The following looks at some of the major issues arising from the interpretation and application of DOE policy.

1 See para 5.4 above.

5.6.3 Local plan policy

The inherent potential for conflict between the terms of central government policy and local government policy (found in the development plan) is a fundamental aspect of enforcement notice appeals. With section 54A the LPA is now in a stronger position if its development plan has credible policies directly supporting their action. Of course, the 'weighting' ascribed to such plan policies may be a matter which the inspector views differently if DOE advice is considered to be more appropriate. If development plan policies include 'enforcement policies' then the LPA can insist, at the appeal, on the inspector applying them unless there are good planning reasons for not so doing. The advice in PPG1 regarding section 54A may well provide the LPA with the basis of an argument that the appellant provide 'compelling arguments' showing that his contravention should be treated in a way contrary to the plan: such an argument, the LPA might assert, should have to show that the development makes a 'particular contribution' to 'some local or national need or objectives [and] is so significant that it outweighs what the plan has to say about it'. Such language (from PPG1, paragraph 30) points to a 'public interest' justification whose benefits are so marked that the plan policy on enforcement is seriously flawed. The following looks at some relevant principles of the case law — that pre-dates the introduction of section 54A: the *Wycombe* case is the common strand that links most of these points together[1].

1 *Wycombe District Council v Secretary of State for the Environment and Queensgate Developments Ltd* [1988] JPL 111 (QBD).

5.6.4   Lawful policy

Where central government policy is being used and interpreted it must be policy relating to planning matters. This principle is number one of eight in the *Wycombe* case. Government policy cannot, therefore, make something that, in terms of the enforcement power and other provisions governing decision-making, is not a 'material consideration' into a matter which the decision-maker should consider. If the inspector incorporates an error of law from a circular into a decision then the LPA will have very good grounds for challenging that decision.

5.6.5   Lawful policy must be considered

If the policy relates to a relevant consideration then it must figure in the decision-making process. This is the second principle in the *Wycombe* case. In terms of the Secretary of State's policy on enforcement that policy advice is rather generalised and largely relates to the 'hands off' approach. This policy must be considered: however, its application to a particular case would have to be tempered by the specific circumstances of that case. Such policy can be considered – but the weighting attributed to it may be minimal. Lord Hoffman (in the *Tesco* case) was of the view that a planning authority is entitled to give a material consideration no weight if that is a decision based on rational planning grounds[1]. In practical terms the distinction between minimal weight and no weight will often be non-existent.

1   *Tesco Stores Ltd v Secretary of State for the Environment* (1995) Times, 13 May.

5.6.6   Correct interpretation

Both the inspector and the LPA must correctly interpret and understand the nature and content of the policy. This is the third principle in the *Wycombe* case. This may be difficult for a decision-maker where the policy is vague, contradictory or only partial in its scope: such problems do arise with the DOE's enforcement policy. The requirement set out in the *Wycombe* case to 'understand the nature and content of the policy' would seem to allow for challenges where the inspector or the Secretary of State has, by virtue of questionable assertions appearing in the decision-letter, indicated that a rather shaky grasp of DOE policy has affected the decision-making process. The courts have indicated that it is they who have the final say on what the policy advice *really* means. Thus in the cases of *Surrey Heath Borough Council v Secretary of State for the Environment* and *ELS Wholesales (Wolverhampton) Ltd* and *Crownbrae Ltd v Secretary of State for the Environment and Cheltenham Borough Council* the point is stressed that, in effect, the courts can supply 'objective' interpretations of policy[1]. This is tempered to some extent by the courts' willingness to allow the decision-maker some latitude in applying policy to facts (where 'fact and degree' judgments are necessary).

1 [1987] JPL 199 and [1987] JPL 844 respectively.

5.6.7 Normally adhere to the plan

It is clearly an error if the inspector were to be guilty of 'slavish adherence' to DOE policy – the fourth principle in the *Wycombe* case. However, in the light of section 54A this principle takes on an extra dimension. In effect we can borrow the 'slavish adherence' terminology and conclude that section 54A requires that the inspector (as well as any other decision-maker) should 'normally adhere' to the plan. (See also para 5.4 on this point.) So if the plan has contrary policy to that set out in the circular we might conclude that (normally) the plan will prevail. The rule that a circular should not be applied mechanically to every case without regard to the particular circumstances now has to take account of the primacy of plan policy. The advice on 'timetabling' and helping the contravener locate alternative premises is thus not to be applied in a mechanical fashion when the circumstances of a case (including any plan policies that are relevant) are inappropriate for such treatment.

5.6.8 Relevance and weight of considerations

An important aspect of policy is its function of giving 'weight' to certain considerations. If those considerations are 'relevant considerations' in law then the circular may validly ascribe to them a weighting which is higher than that given to local plan policies. Assessing the relevance and weight to be accorded to the policy as against the relevance and weight to be attached to other relevant considerations is a matter for the determining authority in a particular case and the determining authority alone. This is the fifth principle in the *Wycombe* case. However, this principle may need further elaboration by the courts in the light of those considerations which already possess a 'statutory weighting'. (The *Heatherington* case is an example of such a development in the case law: see para 5.4.2.) Some 'material considerations' are more 'material' than others. This is apparent when we recognise that on many occasions the enforcement powers in the legislation may be exercised within the context of the conservation area test or the listed building test[1].

1   P(LB&CA)A 1990, ss 72(1) and 16(2) and 66(1) respectively.

5.6.9   Departures from policy – reasons

If the determining authority (here the focus is on the Secretary of State) departs from the policy contained in the development plan in a particular case he has to set out his reasons for doing so. This is the sixth principle in the *Wycombe* case. The reasons must be sound, clear-cut and intelligible. Authorities should note, however, that reasons can be briefly stated – the seventh principle in the *Wycombe* case. Also the courts tend to give a certain amount of latitude to the appellate body – thus minor inconsistencies and a moderate amount of muddled analysis may not be a strong enough basis for challenge. If the inspector appears to be uncertain about the manner in which he should approach a subject the LPA should clearly and cogently point the way forward (preferably with written submissions – even at an inquiry). If the inspector then fails to follow the advice he may have laid the basis for a challenge on a point of law – failure to interpret the law properly.

5.6.10   Adequate reasons for departing from policy

If reasons for departing from policy were substantially wrong or irrelevant then a challenge to the decision could be made: this is the first standard in the eighth principle in the *Wycombe* case. Adequate reasons are important because the recipient of the decision ought to know where he stands in relation to a particular decision. The underlying rationale is important. The requirement to give reasons that are adequate is (per Lord Denning) 'to enable the parties and the court to see what matters [the decision-maker] has taken into consideration and what view he has reached on the points of fact and law which arise'[1]. This emphasis on 'transparency' in decision-making (to borrow a term from civil law jurisdictions) is something which is increasingly emphasised in administrative law decisions and the planning case law.

1 *Earl of Iveagh v Minister of Housing and Local Government* [1964] 1 QB 395 at 410.

5.6.11 Adequate reasons for making an exception to policy

If an exception is made to a particular policy then a challenge may be made if the reasons are substantially wrong or irrelevant: this is the second standard appearing in the eighth principle in the *Wycombe* case. Many policies will make express provision for exceptions: the policy on enforcement activity has very few explicit exceptions. The implicit exceptions (which should be pointed out to the inspector) deal with special planning interests – listed buildings, conservation areas etc. Where such exceptions apply then the authority should ensure that adequate reasons (based on the special interests concerned and other relevant factors, for example, enforcement policies in the local plan) are clearly spelt out to the inspector.

5.6.12 Radical departure from an earlier decision

In the case of *London Borough of Bromley v Secretary of State for the Environment and Cope* a further principle was developed[1]. This case cited the *Wycombe* principles and then set out a further ground by which the court might be asked to review a decision. (It should be noted that the court in *Wycombe* stated that the list was not exhaustive. Thus the LPA may well be able to develop and expand upon the principles set out here.) The *Bromley* case states that if the Secretary of State is going to make a radical departure from an earlier decision, he must give sound, clear-cut and intelligible reasons for so doing, or else he will be taken to be acting irrationally. This principle may not be applicable to many enforcement policy cases: it is more relevant to the issue of the deemed application of planning permission. LPAs should note this decision and its possible relevance to enforcement.

1 [1990] JPL 53.

5.7   ENFORCEMENT CONSIDERATIONS

5.7.1   Environmental factors

Planning control is a very wide-ranging form of regulation that overlaps with 'environmental' legislation. If there is a breach of planning control the impacts of that breach on planning interests are relevant enforcement considerations. Even if those factors could be tackled by other non-planning powers this 'overlap' does not mean that taking enforcement action under planning control is unlawful. The parallel point in terms of development control was made in the case of *Gateshead Metropolitan Borough Council v Secretary of State for the Environment*[1]. As long as an impact (which need not be directly land-use related and physical in nature) gives rise to issues relevant to the exercise of planning enforcement powers the LPA can use such powers to deal with the problem. That is the legal rule – as long as a breach of planning control has planning enforcement impacts it can be tackled by enforcement notices etc. However, the presence of effective enforcement powers under a non-planning regime capable of dealing with the planning impacts is a material consideration – just as the existence of powers to regulate emissions to air under the Environmental Protection Act 1990 is a material consideration in dealing with a planning application for a power station. The LPA may consider, on the information available to it, that planning enforcement is still expedient because action under other powers may not be taken as quickly or as effectively. The Secretary of State or his inspector may of course come to a different conclusion on appeal – but that is not a legal issue it is a matter of (political) judgement.

1   [1994] 1 PLR 85, CA.

5.7.2   Planning enforcement and other regimes

The legality of taking action under enforcement provisions of the planning legislation (even when other non-planning powers are available) is demonstrated in the case of *Wallington v Secretary of State for Wales*[1]. Mr Malcolm Spence QC, (Deputy Judge) held that the use of an enforcement notice to control a breach of planning control that involved a noise nuisance was intra vires the LPA. He noted PPG1, paragraph 22 (a version since superseded) and said (at 119) that there:

'. . . might well be a number of situations in which it is perfectly possible to seek to deal with an unsatisfactory situation by means of the planning legislation and/or by means of other legislation. What would be wrong, as suggested in para 22 of Planning Policy Guidance No 1, would be to refuse planning permission or serve an enforcement notice on a basis that does not constitute a planning consideration.

That was what has not happened in this case because the high degree of noise which emanates from these premises, as found by the inspector in paragraph 28 of his decision letter, certainly was, in his judgment, a planning consideration. Accordingly, it was perfectly possible and proper for the planning authority to proceed by means of the planning machinery, namely, service of an enforcement notice, albeit they might if they wished, and if it had been thought that they could substantiate a case, have proceeded in another way'.

Case law, however, still shows how inspectors are prone to take advice from PPG1 and fall into error. This is when they interpret the PPG as laying down a rule that if other non-planning powers exist then planning enforcement powers should not be utilised. The so-called principle of 'non-duplication' (PPG1, paragraph 35) is the unfortunately phrased criterion that may encourage this erroneous view: LPAs should be quick to point out that case law and paragraph 37 of the PPG provide a more accurate summary of the position:

'Provided a consideration is material in planning terms, however, it must be taken into account in dealing with a planning application notwithstanding that other machinery may exist for its regulation.'

Substitute 'breach of planning control' for 'planning application' and the statement applies just as much to enforcement. This argument is also relevant to the use of enforcement notices in tackling breaches of advertisement control (where development has also been involved) – see chapter twelve.

1 [1990] JPL 112.

5.7.3 Deterrence, integrity and other systemic enforcement factors

LPA officers are well aware of the political pressure from elected members to 'do something' when a contravention severely affecting the amenity of an area has occurred. Such cases often lead to calls for swift and draconian action against the 'lawbreaker'. Yet such concerns seem to be absent in DOE policy and often an appeal may founder because the LPA cannot demonstrate in an objective fashion a severe detrimental impact. Perhaps this is due to the standard analyses of 'material consideration' which concentrate on the physical, land-use impacts of development. Such impacts are clearly the most common type of consideration relevant to the planning function and the planning trinity. However, an analysis of that key statutory term 'material consideration' does require acknowledgement that there is another important category of 'material consideration'. This category is concerned with the wider issue of the effective operation of the planning system in protecting the community against inappropriate development. Such 'systemic' considerations are an important supplementary category – as is clear from well-known examples of planning consideration that fall into this category. Precedent and prematurity are examples of the 'systemic material consideration' category. Enforcement provides us with a third – one which is found in DOE policy and ties in with the 'deterrence' and 'punishment' language often encountered at the local level.

An ever-present systemic consideration that is material to all enforcement decision-making is the need to ensure that the planning system is respected by those it regulates. This factor (recognised by the DOE as such in PPG18, paragraph 4) is the need to ensure that the 'integrity' of the planning system is not harmed by a failure to take effective action. It is clear that a number of breaches (especially of the same type and highly visible) in a locality could undermine respect for the effectiveness of planning control in protecting local amenity etc. Elected members may use more emotive language to characterise this problem. Yet, when viewed from the 'systemic' angle it is clear that such factors are relevant as regards their relationship to 'integrity'. It is clear that such issues can, in terms of section 172(1), be used to justify enforcement action. Naturally the weight to be ascribed to such factors varies and often the issues will be seen as less damaging to the 'public interest' if the matter goes to appeal. However, this does not change the legal position – the 'integrity' aspect of effective enforcement action is a factor relevant to section 172(1) and, as with other 'material considerations' must be taken into account. This is especially relevant when justifying action before the inspector.

5.7.4 Hardship

The hardship of the individual faced with enforcement action is a material consideration – though normally it will be outweighed by the need to protect the wider interests of the community. On occasion however severe hardship may justify modified enforcement action. LPAs must, however, be aware of the wider interests at stake. The archetypal example of the aged home-owner putting in double-glazing and falling foul of listed building control is even celebrated in the *Journal of Planning Law*[1]. This case shows the perils of treating hardship as a reason for being over-generous. The inspector relented in his decision and allowed uPVC to be retained. The elderly occupant however left the premises soon after and the house was put up for sale. This means that the breach will not be rectified even though the new occupants will not have a 'hardship' argument. The answer to hardship arguments is thus not to drop enforcement action but to postpone it by way of a planning agreement which 'bites' when the facts justifying the hardship argument are no longer relevant. If the person concerned moves then the new occupiers will have to remedy the breach. In considering hardship arguments LPA officers should therefore bear in mind the need to protect the long-term interests of the community as well as allowing the short-term interests of the deserving case to be reflected in decision-making procedures.

1   [1992] JPL 709.

5.7.5 Statutory enforcement considerations

Certain considerations are 'material' to the exercise of enforcement discretions by virtue of special legislative provisions. The conservation area test in section P(LB&CA)A 1990, section 72(1) is relevant whenever 'any power' under the planning legislation is being exercised in relation to land within a conservation area. Those criteria are thus 'considerations' that are relevant to the exercise of the enforcement power where the land on which the breach has occurred is within a conservation area. The test requires that 'special attention' be paid to the conservation area's interests when exercising planning powers in relation to land within such an area: case law on this provision has largely focused on development control decisions but it is clear that the statutory emphasis on conservation means that conservation interests are given a much greater weighting than the more normal 'material considerations'. That weighting is evident in the 'special attention' phraseology: thus it might be said that the conservation area's interests are '*special* material considerations' whereas most other planning issues are merely 'material considerations'. A more detailed discussion of the conservation area test is set out in chapter eleven.

5.8   DELEGATION OF ENFORCEMENT POWERS

Giving a decision to a single officer is permissible. Giving an elected member some veto over proposed decisions to take enforcement may lead to problems[1]. However, there are ways of ensuring that speedy decisions can be taken without running foul of the legal rules governing delegation. The courts can sometimes take a lenient view on the authorisation requirements. Thus in one case it was held that the authorisation of a stop notice could also be interpreted as the authorisation of the enforcement notice on which it relied. Here the council had invalidly authorised one enforcement notice and then, at a later date, authorised the stop notice. The court, rather kindly, interpreted the stop notice authorisation as covering the second (valid) authorisation of an enforcement notice[2].

1 See para 5.8.2 below.
2 *R v Rochester upon Medway City Council, ex p Wendy Hobday* [1989] JPL 17.

5.8.1   Decision-making 'arrangements'

LPAs may 'arrange for the discharge of any of their functions . . . by a committee, a sub-committee or an officer of the authority'[1]. The importance of making adequate 'arrangements' is underlined in an appeal decision where a compromise agreed in principle between the authority and the appellant had not been finalised because of administrative problems – committee approval of the compromise was delayed[2]. The appellant succeeded in his application for costs. The decision letter stated:

'It may be that the internal procedures of the council inhibited them from arriving at a decision promptly, but a procedural difficulty is not in my view sufficient to make the local planning authority's conduct reasonable in all the circumstances of the case.'

Emergency procedures should thus be used where time is important – this not only covers serious breaches but also conclusion of compromise arrangements that precede the determination of an appeal.

In *Swishbrook Ltd v Secretary of State for the Environment and Islington London Borough Council*[3] the LPA (exercising its powers to make a discontinuance notice under the advertisement regime) had not explicitly authorised any particular officer of the council to issue and serve such notices. The notice had been signed by 'David Lewis' – though it was not stated who he was on the notice. Mr Lionel Read (sitting as Deputy Judge) said (at 140):

'That could, and did not, mean that no one could issue and serve them. It meant that any officer could issue and serve them on the authority of the council provided that the nature of his office was such that, in the ordinary course of events, he might properly exercise that authority. Mr David Lewis was the Acting Borough Solicitor. He was plainly qualified to exercise that authority.'

This may be sufficient to help another LPA deal with 'technical' arguments in a similar situation. However, it is not good administrative practice to allow such challenges (which can delay effective enforcement action) to be made. It should be always borne in mind that delegation to a single member of the council does not come within the broad terms of the power to delegate. This is clear from the *Hillingdon* case: so a decision made in such a manner would be subject to challenge[4]. This is just the sort of point that the zealous solicitor acting for a contravener would attack. A possible solution to the problem of ensuring quick but accountable decision-making is suggested in para 5.8.3.

1 Local Government Act 1972, s 101(1).
2 North Shropshire District Council, DOE ref T/APP/C/88/N3210/3-4/P6, decision letter dated 15 March 1989, 4 PAD 392.
3 [1990] JPL 137.
4 *R v Secretary of State for the Environment, ex p Hillingdon London Borough Council* [1986] 2 All ER 273n, [1987] JPL 717, CA.

5.8.2 'Member-veto'

The problem of ensuring quick but accountable decision-making is sometimes tackled by using a 'member-veto'. This may not be the term employed within the LPA but it reflects, in many cases, the reality of the situation. Thus the power to authorise enforcement (or any other function of the authority) is given to an officer: however, this is tempered by requiring (whether de facto or de iure) that the officer gain the approval of a senior member of the council – usually the chairman or vice-chairman of the appropriate (sub-)committee. In this case the function has been discharged by an officer and a member; the reality is often that the member has the de facto power to veto a decision he does not like. Proving that this is so (where this is not discernible from the standing orders or other documentation) would, of course, be difficult. Thus in one case[1] the court upheld the issue of a notice under a standing order which empowered an officer 'with the written approval of the Mayor or the Chairman of the appropriate Committee . . . [to] give such instructions as may be reasonable'. This decision allows a member to have a veto over an officer's proposed exercise of a planning function. This means that in substance the decision is taken by an officer and a member of the council – not an 'arrangement' that is covered under the Local Government Act. Such doubts seem to have persuaded the court (in a non-planning case) to strike down a decision to grant a tenancy of a council house to a recently divorced councillor[2]. The chief officer had stated that he would not have made such a decision had it not been for the pressure applied by the chairman and vice-chairman of the relevant committee (whom he was obliged to 'consult'). Here the dominant role played by the chairman in particular meant that the terms of section 101 had not been met. The court in this case then seems to have seen through (because of evidence from the officer) the sham and found that, de facto, the councillor had a veto over the exercise of the function. In such a case it cannot be argued that the authority had set up a committee of two (comprising a member and an officer): the Local Government Act[3] disqualifies a local government officer from being a member of a committee or sub-committee of an authority.

One way of dealing with the problem of urgent decision-making and yet retaining adequate democratic control is to set up a number of emergency committees comprising two members of the council. One such committee, established in line with the Local Government Act's relevant provisions, could then handle emergency planning matters. However, this would still have to comply with the obligations placed on committees, sub-committees and councils generally to afford access to the public to meetings. This would seem to make it difficult for emergency decisions (that might only be practical 'over the phone') to be made. In such circumstances the authority might well use the two-stage procedure noted below (working parties and officer-delegation).

1 *Fraser v Secretary of State for the Environment* [1988] JPL 344.
2 *R v Port Talbot Borough Council, ex p Jones* [1988] 2 All ER 207.
3 Local Government Act 1972, s 104(1).

5.8.3 Working parties

An authority is entitled to set up informal bodies such as working parties to serve an ancillary function in helping with the work of an authority[1]. Such 'ancillary' bodies would seem to fall under the provisions of the Local Government Act which empower the local authority to do anything 'which is calculated to facilitate, or is conducive or incidental to, the discharge of any of their functions'[2]. Such working parties would not seem to have primary decision-making powers since such powers would not be 'subsidiary powers of local authorities' – to use the phraseology of the sidenote to the section. Decision-making powers under the planning legislation are primary, not subsidiary, powers and so the authorisation of enforcement action cannot be carried out by such bodies. However, they can act as 'sounding boards' enabling a sole officer (given delegated powers to take action in an emergency) to assess the views of key councillors. Such bodies could thus assess a situation and weigh the arguments for and against a particular course of action and make known their views on a particular issue. This would give the officer with the emergency powers the confidence that his decision would not be totally at variance with the mood of the elected members of the council.

The meetings of such working parties are not caught by the requirements to admit the public – section 100 ff of the Local Government Act 1972. Such meetings could even be held over the telephone: perhaps between two senior planning committee councillors who together constitute the emergency working party. Their deliberations and conclusions would then be taken into account by the sole officer given the power to take action in emergencies. Standing orders would thus describe the first stage as merely a fact finding and general discussion of the issues exercise but indicate clearly that the decision was solely that of the officer. This would enable quick decisions to be taken within a reasonably accountable system of political control without infringing the limits placed upon decision-making by the legislation. It is very important to separate the two-stage nature of the process in standing orders otherwise it might be suggested in court that the working party's views did in fact determine what the officer subsequently decided. This would be likely to run foul of the case law which requires that de facto decision-making power should reside with the institutions/ persons allowed to have such power under the legislation.

1   *R v Eden District Council, ex p Moffat* (1988) Times, 24 November.
2   Local Government Act 1972, s 111.

5.8.4   Delegation to officers

Local authorities (members and officers) may understandably be reluctant to delegate enforcement authorisations to officers. Officers may not wish to have such controversial decisions thrust upon them. The above has suggested one way of achieving accountability but with time-savings. However, there are occasions where enforcement action can solely be handled by officers. One form of enforcement that can be delegated is enforcement which is ancillary to or supportive of enforcement action already authorised by members. Such ancillary action can thus be specifically (or by general description) stated in the main enforcement authorisation: thus officers may, at their discretion, be given powers to take action under the works in default power and take action before the magistrates in respect of non-compliance with the enforcement notice. This saves going back to committee but yet retains the advantage of some 'political' control. Another form of enforcement decision which can easily be given to officers is the 'negative' decision not to enforce. In fact this power is exercised anyway by many officers: they may turn a blind eye to a breach or decide that it is not worth bothering committee with a problem. However, it is with 'positive' enforcement action that the main problems occur. If an authority does not have many delegated decisions (eg at the development control stage) going to officers then it is unlikely that enforcement authorisations will be delegated. However, if an authority uses delegation in respect of many development control decisions then it may be worthwhile trying to get some enforcement powers delegated. The most obvious candidate for this is the breach of condition (especially those that are covered by 'enforcement policies' in the local plan, eg landscaping). In the Carnwath Report we see an even more robust approach. He thus says (page 26):

> 'Provided appropriate procedures are established for liaison between Departments and with members, I see no reason why the formal action, even in contentious cases, should not be taken by officers.'

5.9 RATIFICATION OF DECISIONS

Decisions that are ultra vires cannot be given validity by ratification. An example in the case law illustrates this point. In *R v Rochester upon Medway City Council, ex p Hobday* the authority had invalidly authorised enforcement action against a use[1]. It was held that a later resolution of the council could not ratify the decision made earlier since that decision was ultra vires.

1 [1989] JPL 17 (the case also dealt with stop notices).

5.10 ESTOPPEL AND THE COURTS

Although the notion of 'estoppel' comes from private law and its principles of 'equity' it has come to be used in the public law realm. In the planning field it is reflected in a concern that a power given to a public authority cannot be prejudiced by reason of some 'unfairness'. It can also operate against the landowner. However, the best known situations are where the courts have construed a written response (that no planning permission is required) to a planning application as a determination that permission is not required[1]. The courts may also accept that the action of the officer was, in the circumstances, to be seen as the action of the LPA[2]. Since the estoppel point will often be argued before the Secretary of State or his inspector – the appellant arguing that (for example) the enforcement action taken is invalid – the courts have also accepted that whether or not there is an estoppel may be a 'fact and degree' matter for the Secretary of State[3]. Another form of estoppel is concerned with the preventing the LPA from asserting that a contravention has occurred when the facts relied on have already been examined in detail (eg on appeal) and led to a finding that there is no breach. Reference is often made to the concept of 'issue estoppel', 'cause of action estoppel' or res judicata in this respect: this type of estoppel is noted in chapter two. The possibility of estoppel being used against the appellant contravener is also discussed in chapter two and may well be relevant to the issues discussed in this chapter.

1   *Western Fish Products v Penwith District Council* [1981] 2 All ER 204, 38 P & CR 7.
2   *Bedfordia Plant Ltd v Secretary of State for the Environment* [1981] JPL 122; *Lever Finance Ltd v Westminster City London Borough Council* [1971] 1 QB 222, [1970] 3 All ER 496.
3   See the *Bedfordia Plant* case, note 2 above.

5.10.1   Estoppel and the Ombudsman

The LPA is not immune from wider arguments based on 'unfairness'. The Ombudsman may well consider that the giving of erroneous advice and the later 'reversal' of that advice by taking enforcement action constitutes maladministration. So the LPA may face sanctions even if they have not been faulted on legal grounds. Since planning is such a complex subject a member of the public will often rely on the expert opinion of a planning officer. This advice may be sought over the telephone or at the planning enquiry desk. Unfortunately the advice may be inaccurate – the complexity of the situation may not have been fully communicated to the officer or he may have made an error in interpreting the situation. The officer may preface his remarks with caveats as to the provisional nature of his conclusions. The enquiry desk may sport a plaque stating that any opinions voiced by an officer are not binding on the authority. Such precautions however, will not be sympathetically taken by the disgruntled member of the public[1]. Hence the risk of an Ombudsman case. Further precautions can be taken: development control manuals that give a sound basis for analysing a situation can prevent many errors when used properly. Trainee staff can thus rely on the 'distilled wisdom' of their more senior colleagues. Circulars can often be good guides to a rather complex system – these should be available. Local plans (if well-indexed) can be very useful sources (naturally) of information about the likely attitude of a committee to a development. Ready access to accurate information is thus one important response to this problem. Estoppel problems should thus arise less frequently and thus create fewer practical problems for enforcement.

1   See *Tidman v Reading Borough Council* (1994) Times, 10 November which illustrates that the court will not entertain a negligence claim based on erroneous advice from a planning officer over the phone regarding the planning situation relating to a site.

6 Formal action after authorisation

6.1 INTRODUCTION

The legal aspects of enforcement action involving breach of condition notices have been described earlier in chapter four's discussion of non-compliance with conditions and limitations. However, enforcement notices will remain the primary weapon in mainstream enforcement should formal action be required. This chapter examines the procedures for producing a valid enforcement notice and then serving it on the appropriate persons. Precision and accuracy are necessary elements in this process. However, the need for precision should not be elevated to a degree which brings the whole procedure to a grinding halt whilst, for example, every conceivable ownership interest in the land is traced and finalised. The authority should concentrate on taking reasonable steps to ascertain ownership interests. It should be remembered that the enforcement regime is reasonably tolerant of mistakes as to service. For example, a stop notice is not invalidated by reason of bad service of a copy of the underlying enforcement notice – if the LPA 'took all such steps as were reasonably practicable to effect proper service'[1]. The 'reasonably practicable' test indicates that the LPA need not expend disproportionate resources in obtaining information about 'material interests'. Furthermore, should a compensation claim be made and validated the claimant will not be able to recoup his losses in full if his failures to reply to requisitions are relevant (see discussion of the stop notice power in chapter eight). The LPA should therefore be reasonably robust about problems encountered in gathering information: yet this is not to say that the legal niceties are irrelevant – merely that the LPA should ensure that legal advice does not overstress the 'negative' elements of enforcement. Such a stance is almost second nature to careful lawyers – yet with most situations it is an attitude which may unnecessarily delay effective enforcement. As noted in chapter one the perceptions of enforcement by the legal department is one of the factors that needs to be tackled when addressing reform and the organizational needs of enforcement. The lawyers must also develop a positive attitude to enforcement – a 'can do' attitude rather than a 'the law does not permit that' attitude. Such an approach ties in with the general theme of this book which stresses that the enforcement function of the LPA deserves a degree of consideration equal to that devoted to forward planning and development control. Planning law is a technical area and enforcement is often fraught with difficult legal issues: effective enforcement thus requires that the legal department also adopt a positive approach to the planning trinity and provide the pro-active advice on planning law issues that is necessary.

1   TCPA 1990, s 184(8).

6.2   THE LEGAL DEPARTMENT

The legal advisors to the LPA have a difficult task. With present staffing problems it may be difficult for the authority to retain (let alone recruit) lawyers with the necessary skills. Those that are asked to deal with enforcement face one of the most complex fields of law. Even with the recent reforms of the enforcement system it is still pertinent to bear in mind that comments from the Bench still appear which point to the over-technical approach to the legal aspects of enforcement. Thus in *West Oxfordshire District Council v Secretary of State for the Environment*[1] Graham Eyre QC (sitting as Deputy Judge) stated:

'It is perhaps remarkable that nearly four decades had passed since the enforcement notice machinery first emerged in the Town and Country Planning Act 1947 during which time the legislature had made substantial amendments to the statutory provisions so as to remove or substantially reduce the powers of the courts to intervene on arid technical grounds, and yet this court has been treated to a rehearsal of somewhat arid technicalities most of which have a ring of nostalgic, in its true sense, and largely unwelcome familiarity.'

Apart from the (over)technicality of enforcement itself (discussed in paras 6.7 et seq) the planning lawyer involved in enforcement issues will have to contend with the ever-developing field of planning law in general. Developments in the planning law field at large will almost always have relevance to enforcement work since the limits of the planning system as a mechanism for controlling human activity set out the very bounds of the enforcement power.

1 [1988] JPL 324 at pp 324–5.

6.3 PRELIMINARY LEGAL ISSUES

The input from the legal department is primarily one of dealing with standard 'legal' issues. However, this does not mean routine involvement on every legal aspect of enforcement in every case. Legal input can be 'routinised' in much the same way as the basic administration of enforcement can be routinised. If effective legal input is provided at the stage of designing enforcement systems in the LPA then members of the enforcement team and other planning officers can handle most of the 'routine' legal issues. Planning officers who are less experienced but able to draw upon adequate and comprehensive guides to such issues should be able to deal with them without involving the legal department. Yet appropriate systems (eg screening cases by experienced officers to ensure that those with more complex legal problems are handled appropriately) should be employed to ensure that the legal department is brought in before the situation gets out of control. Departmental chauvinism must not be allowed to disrupt the necessary flow of information and requests where circumstances warrant. It should not be seen as a weakness if the planning officer concerned is unable to resolve a problem himself. It is always much better to ensure that any potential issues are screened and examined by legal officers to ensure that any risks of falling down on fundamental points later on are minimised.

6.4 THE ENFORCEMENT REPORT

The drafting of an enforcement notice consequent upon an authorisation should be a straightforward issue if the authorisation and the attendant details are adequately set out for the officer (whether from the legal department or not). The LPA must ensure therefore that the officer given the task of drawing up the enforcement notice receives an authorisation which can easily be translated into an enforcement notice. The focus initially then is really upon the enforcement report which will normally precede the authorisation. The word 'normally' is advisably employed since it is not too uncommon for officers at a committee meeting to be 'surprised' with an authorisation made out of the blue by the committee. It may well follow a committee's rejection of a recommendation of the planning officer to grant (retrospective) permission for a development – especially where the anger of neighbours has been aroused and this has been particularly felt by elected members. 'Surprise' authorizations (unless tackled by adequate procedural rules which mitigate the potential disasters that they can produce) may be one reason why the legal department receives authorisations which are difficult to implement effectively and efficiently. The hard-pressed legal department must therefore be able to rely on much of the work having been done already. The enforcement report and authorisation should contain all the necessary and up-to-date information required by the draughtsman of the enforcement notice. Generally, there is no need for the report (unless difficult issues of planning law are raised) to be vetted by the legal department: again the relevance of screening procedures is clear.

The use of standardised procedures by the planning officers with standard steps, standard reasons for issuing the notice, and other such procedures is important. This should mean that the enforcement notice authorisation and the necessary details for its drafting and issue will be proof against any challenge in front of the inspector (except on policy grounds of course) and the courts. Where no such mechanisms exist for ensuring that authorisations and reports are adequately structured then it may be necessary to have a preliminary vetting of such reports by legal officers.

6.4.1 Standardised formats for notices

The standardisation and routinisation of procedures is a useful bureaucratic response not only for the planning department but for the legal department. In this respect the legal department is already furnished with model enforcement notices produced by the DOE. (Circulars 21/91 and 17/92 will be available within the planning department so they are not reproduced here. Note, however, comments at appropriate points in this text on the need to use such models carefully and to amend some of the language used in the models (eg in relation to the use of stippling or hatching when showing the area covered by the enforcement notice). The LPA is less likely to blindly adopt unsuitable models if it has to translate those available into its own procedure notes so that the notices reflect the peculiarities of the particular systems put in place for effective enforcement.) Using model enforcement notices (this also applies, of course, to stop notices and breach of condition notices) means that the officer concerned will then be given a relatively easy task of translating the information set out in the report and the authorisation onto the body of a notice itself.

If the situation does not clearly fall into the established patterns set out in standard procedures and forms then the officer may have to consider such issues afresh. Ideally, of course, where an enforcement issue gives rise to novel problems the strategy of the LPA should have been discussed at the pre-authorisation stage so that both the legal and planning personnel reach agreement as to the appropriate strategy. If the issue is one merely of deciding on a particular form of words for the steps required then it may not even be necessary to involve the legal department if the planning department can deploy reasonably experienced personnel who are aware of problems of drafting. Where such novel situations do occur and mistakes are made then the appropriate steps should be taken to ensure that procedures are tightened up and the stock of 'distilled wisdom' that comprises the enforcement manual is amended accordingly. The enforcement manual not only serves as a useful teaching aid for planners but also for legal staff and helps to ensure that both departments (and this will be the normal situation since integrated enforcement teams are unlikely to be that common) maintain a good working relationship and thus ensure a high degree of confidence in the capacity of the other to deal with enforcement issues.

6.5 ENFORCEMENT NOTICE – MANDATORY ELEMENTS

The legislation requires that an enforcement notice contain certain items of information. These mandatory elements are discussed below. Circular 21/91, Annex 2, paragraphs 5-13 discuss these issues from the viewpoint of the DOE – the advice serves as a useful checklist for the LPA.

6.5.1 'Stated' elements

The TCPA 1990, section 173 requires that the LPA state:

(a) the matters which appear to constitute the breach of planning control; and
(b) whether the breach comprises:
    carrying out of development without the required planning permission; or
    failing to comply with a condition or limitation subject to which planning permission has been granted.

The requirement to 'state' such factors is a change from the previous language which required that the LPA 'specify' the matters constituting the breach. Case law under the old (higher) standard should therefore be seen in this light: this is one example of the statutory changes following the Carnwath Report that were supposed to reduce the unnecessarily technical approach of the courts (especially at High Court level) to enforcement. Indeed, this theme of simplification is carried through in the DOE advice in circular 21/91 with its 'plain English' model notices set out in the three appendices to Annex 2. As regards this part of the enforcement notice therefore the LPA should be more confident about withstanding legal challenges on the wording used.

6.5.2 Subjective test of validity

Section 173(2) seems to introduce (from the case law) the very subjective test of validity as regards the elements discussed in para 6.5.1. A notice complies with the requirement to 'state' the matters which appear to constitute the breach if 'it enables any person on whom a copy of it is served to know what those matters are'. This is a statutory version of a case law principle from *Miller-Mead*[1]. This appears to mean that if there is any single person (served with a notice) who understands what the notice is saying when it states the matters constituting the breach of control then the notice cannot be challenged by any other person for failing to state those matters. However, this would seem, for practical purposes, to be limited to administrative uses of the notice (eg on appeal to the DOE, judicial review proceedings etc): if an ambiguous notice was relied on before the criminal courts then the LPA might have problems. If it was prosecuting someone whose subjective knowledge was not as complete as the person whose state of mind is relevant for section 173(2) the court would be very likely to take this into account. Although the subjective test of validity is useful for certain purposes it does not solve all the problems of the LPA.

1   *Miller-Mead v Minister of Housing and Local Government* [1963] 2 QB 196 (Lord Upjohn).

6.5.3   'Specified' steps and activities

Section 173(3) states that the notice shall specify:

'the steps which the authority require to be taken, or the activities which the authority require to cease . . .'

Such requirements must be either of the following two purposes (section 173(4)):

   (a) remedying the breach; or
   (b) remedying any injury to amenity which has been caused by the breach.

These elements are still subject to the more stringent 'specify' requirement. The legislation standard is therefore still relatively high. However, this should be seen in the light of the correction and variation powers accorded to the Secretary of State or inspector on appeal.

6.5.3.1   *Some statutory examples of enforcement notice requirements*

Section 173(5) gives four examples of requirements that may be specified. This is not an exhaustive list of what a notice may require and should not be taken to limit the statutory language as regards 'steps'. (The wide scope of 'steps' is discussed below in para 6.5.3.3.) Section 173(6) makes specific reference to breaches involving demolition of a building: the notice may require the construction of a building ('replacement building') which is as similar as possible to the demolished building. Section 173(7) gives further guidance as to what the replacement building would comprise. LPAs should note that where such a requirement is specified then planning permission is treated as having been granted by virtue of section 73A in respect of such development if all the requirements of the notice relating to such construction have been complied with. Since this is a deemed grant of permission the LPA may be asked to provide some documentary evidence that such a permission does exist (eg to a potential purchaser). This should be unnecessary if the LPA confirms compliance with the notice in their replies to enquiries: the legal rule in section 173(12) in conjunction with the enforcement notice and the fact of compliance constitute adequate proof of the permission and its terms.

6.5.3.2 *Under-enforcement*

Full flexibility is introduced into the system right from the beginning as regards partial enforcement. Thus the LPA can under-enforce by specifying steps to be taken in order wholly or partly to remedy the breach or remove or alleviate any injury to amenity. Such flexibility is, however, not found in the provisions relating to BCNs (see chapter four).

6.5.3.3 *The wide scope of the 'steps'*

An enforcement notice's requirements can relate to both 'steps' and 'activities'. The above indicate in very general terms the wide range of matters that can be covered by the 'steps' in an enforcement notice. Most of the matters covered, naturally enough, relate either to activity which is required of the contravener or prohibitions on activity. That activity is often of a kind which would fall under the heading of 'development' – be it operational or change of use. However, it should always be borne in mind that the term 'steps' should not be equated with 'works', 'operations' or 'uses'. A step (eg when dealing with a breach of a condition requiring the submission of plans for approval) may require action on the part of the contravener which does not fall within the scope of 'development' as that term is understood in its technical sense. Thus a step may well require that the contravener submit plans or negotiate with the authority to resolve a problem before resuming an activity which does fall within the ambit of the term 'development'. It could even encompass a requirement that the contravener provide a bond (where mineral extraction is at the heart of the problem). A step could also require the landlord of a multiply occupied site involving a 'composite contravention' to terminate all leases and licenses under which the contraventions are carried out. A related step could require him to furnish the LPA with a copy of the lease/licence so that they can then know what steps the landlord can take under the terms of the lease or licence. A step could even require the owner to execute a planning obligation whose terms are included with an enforcement notice. (Given the changes to section 106 and the developing case law on the legal limits on the content of planning obligations, such a step should not now be seen as legally objectionable: the DOE may well, of course, object on policy grounds to using section 106 in this way but that is not something which would necessarily win the day if the LPA has enforcement policy in the development plan to support its approach.) 'Steps' is thus a term of very wide application and the LPA should consider how the 'steps' appropriate to the situation should be framed – though always bearing in mind the limitations placed on the content of such steps by the legislation[1]. As long as the steps fall within the terms of the provision set out in the legislation the LPA is fully justified in law in setting out such steps in an enforcement notice.

When framing such steps the authority should use the list of standard conditions (employed for development control purposes) as a model. If that list is scrutinised the authority will be able to appreciate the sort of actions that may validly appear in its enforcement 'steps'. Indeed the parallel with development control strongly suggests that the authority should produce a standard list of enforcement steps: this makes for consistency and effectiveness in the exercise of its enforcement powers.

1   The steps must therefore be for certain 'purposes' as discussed above and, implicitly, they must serve a planning purpose that is related in some way to the contravention. This 'relationship' standard is similar to that used for 'material considerations' in *Stringer v MHLG* [1971] 1 All ER 65. Indeed, the case law on the legal limits of planning conditions and planning obligations is probably the most relevant source of the legal rules on what a 'step' can legally constitute. Naturally, the rules as to what is 'legally'

permissible will be less constraining on the LPA than the policy rules from the DOE as to what is 'justifiable'. The inspector may therefore not think it 'expedient' to include steps in an enforcement notice which, although lawful, would contravene the policy limits set by the DOE. The discussion of the 'legality' and 'justifiability' of planning conditions (chapter four) is therefore of analogous relevance to this issue.

6.5.4   The 'specified date'

The notice must 'specify' the date on which the enforcement notice shall take effect: sometimes practitioners will refer to this point in time as 'the date of effectiveness' since that more clearly indicates the function of that date[1]. The LPA should, as a matter of administrative policy, normally set the 'specified date' at about 35 days or so after effecting service of the last copy of the notice. This will allow enough time to deal with any hiccups affecting such service without having to redate the notices. The legislation requires that service be 'not later than 28 days before the specified date'[2]. Clearly, and this is reflected in the pro forma notices, the authority will meet this requirement by specifying a specific date in the notice.

1   TCPA 1990, s 173(8).
2   TCPA 1990, s 172(3).

6.5.5   The 'specified' compliance period(s)

The enforcement notice 'shall specify the period within which any such step as is mentioned [above] is to be taken and may specify different periods for the taking of different steps'[1]. What is a 'period'? In an appeal decision an inspector examined a notice which required an unauthorised use to 'cease immediately'. The inspector held that this did not satisfy the requirement for the notice to specify a period for compliance. He decided it was a nullity but still decided that the most appropriate course was formally to quash the notice[2]. Perhaps the authority wishing to achieve 'immediate' cessation should specify a period in terms of 'hours' (or even minutes!) in order to get round this approach. Of course the authority would then have to ensure that the time of service was accurately and unambiguously ascertainable if such a short period is to be effective. On appeal of course the inspector may substitute a longer period. However, if such a breach does warrant a minimal compliance period it would seem very likely that a stop notice is required.

Where there are multiple steps required by the notice the authority may wish to set multiple compliance periods. However, this may well cause problems for enforcement staff who have to monitor compliance with the notice. The LPA may therefore be advised (if administrative backup is a little shaky) to choose just one compliance period: this should be the date appropriate for the most time-consuming step. The courts have upheld a notice that did not state the compliance period: however, here the compliance period could be determined from the other information (the final date for compliance and the date on which the notice came into effect) and so the notice did supply the information[3].

1   TCPA 1990, s 173(5).
2   London Borough of Croydon, DOE ref: T/APP/C/88/L5240/021/P6 dated 7 September 1989.
3   *King and King v Secretary of State for the Environment* [1981] JPL 813.

6.5.6   Matters 'specified' by regulation

Certain matters that need to be specified in an enforcement notice are prescribed by delegated legislation – not the TCPA 1990.

6.5.6.1   *The 'expediency' reasons*

The reasons for issuing the notice fall into this category[1]. The actual phrase used in the regulations is 'reasons why [the LPA] consider it expedient to issue the notice'. The processes leading up to the authorisation of enforcement action should have produced defensible reasons for taking action: the comments regarding the need for procedures to take account of 'surprise' authorisations following a committee decision contrary to officer advice to grant retrospective permission should also ensure that adequate reasons are available in this situation. The range of 'material considerations' that cover the use of the enforcement power provide a suitable number of potential reasons for taking such action. In addition to the standard land-use impact reasons the LPA should also note the 'systemic' category of enforcement considerations. The most important of these is protecting the 'integrity' of the planning system (see para 5.7.3).

The circular suggests that such reasons be included in the text of the enforcement notice[2]. The three model enforcement notices in Annex 2 of the circular also set out the expediency reasons in the body of the notice. These reasons do not limit the argument of the authority at appeal since the appeal will trigger a deemed application for permission and so wider arguments of planning policy will arise if there is an appeal: however, if the authority has been lax in its statement of reasons it may face an application for costs on appeal – so it is best to be right first time around.

1 Town and Country Planning (Enforcement Notices and Appeals) Regulations 1991, SI 1991/2804, reg 3(a) made under the TCPA 1990, s 173(10).
2 Circular 21/91, para 12.

6.5.6.2 *The precise boundaries of the land*

The regulations state that this may be done 'by reference to a plan or otherwise'[1]. Usually an Ordnance Survey plan is the basis for identifying the land by a plan. The circular suggests that a minimum scale of 1/2500 be used[2]. The DOE model notices include wording which suggests that the verbal description of the property relates to land shown 'by a suitably coloured outline'. However, this advice may be impractical in many cases: LPAs will invariably have to produce upwards of a dozen copies (for service, internal use and at appeal) so it might be better to use shading, stippling or other similar methods of identification. This makes reproduction of the plan a much less tedious process. The importance of clearly and correctly showing the extent of the land covered by the notice in the plan attached to the notice is illustrated by an appeal decision[3]. Three metres of land along the western edge of the site, including the perimeter fence were outside the areas defined on the plan. Also part of a Portakabin (the removal of which was required in the notice) was outside the boundary shown on the plan. The inspector accepted the argument of the appellant that enlargement of the notice site area did not fall within the powers of the inspector under section 176(2): the notice was quashed – presumably on the basis that there would be 'injustice' to the appellant (though this is not clear from the report). This was done even though the inspector noted that the courts stressed that the powers to correct notices should be used 'whenever possible'.

The decision seems to be a little harsh for the authority since it would not seem to cause 'injustice' for the notice to be altered: the appellant had not noticed the error – it was only when the inspector did a site visit that the error came to light. As long as the enlargement would not take in land owned by a person not served with a copy of the notice it is difficult to see what 'injustice' would have been caused by the correction of the notice and, perhaps, allowing the appellants time to rework their arguments. (The discussion in para 6.7.1 et seq is relevant here.) Apart from the lesson to be learned by authorities as to the risk of using inaccurate plans it also demonstrates the need to argue more forcefully against the over-technical application of the law and a rather narrow interpretation of the 'injustice' criterion.

1 Town and Country Planning (Enforcement Notices and Appeals) Regulations 1991, SI 1991/2804, reg 3(b) made under the TCPA 1990, s 173(10).
2 Circular 21/91, Annex 2, para 13.
3 Knowsley Borough Council, DOE ref T/APP/C/87/V4305/007-8/P6, dated 2 September 1988.

6.5.6.3 *Multi-let premises contraventions*

In considering what area of land should be covered by a notice the LPA's concern is with 'the land to which the notice relates'. This, as the following example shows, may not be a question whose answer can be explained easily in terms of the 'planning unit'. (Hence the suggestions in para 3.4.2 that the term 'enforcement unit' be used instead to avoid confusion with the term 'planning unit'.) The LPA will no doubt be aware, from practical experience, of some breaches of control which, in effect, are the result of a joint enterprise by both the landlord of the site and (short-term) tenants of the individual units. ('Redundant' light industrial or agricultural buildings on a site near a town are often split up this way.) In such a case the LPA is not faced with one contravener who has full control of, and the dominant economic interest in maintaining, the contravening use. In such a case there are two tiers of contravener. The landlord's prime concern is indirectly benefiting from the contraventions of his occupiers and arranges relations with them for that purpose. His interest is thus in collecting the rent from the contravening occupiers: they are directly concerned with making their contravening uses pay their way. What is appropriate in such cases is to take a similarly 'two-tiered' approach which mirrors the two levels of contravener involved and their different economic interests in the contravening uses. One enforcement notice should be directed against the whole site and be served on the landlord: individual subsidiary notices should then each be directed against the individual occupiers of the smaller sites. Copies of those subsidiary notices should also be served on the landlord (see para 6.6.3.2). In such a case then the 'two-tier contravention' can only be addressed by 'two-tier enforcement notices' addressed to different (but complementary) areas of land and the different 'owners'. There are therefore, in effect, two different situations for applying the 'planning unit' concept. Unfortunately the notion of the planning unit encourages the LPA and others to think of just a single piece of land when tackling an enforcement problem. Yet as this type of contravention example shows it is not accurate to assume that an enforcement problem can only result in action against a single piece of land defined in one enforcement notice. (See also para 3.4.2 for related comments on the need to tailor the requirements of the two types of enforcement notice to the recipients.)

The related problem of the mixed use breach also requires that the largest area under the ownership of the (single in this case) contravener be specified in the notice as the land to which the notice 'relates'. This enables the LPA to prevent the owner (eg of a farm on which a caravan park has been unlawfully established) from just shifting the specific site around the farm (see also para 3.5.9 on this). From both these cases it is clear that the 'planning unit' can in fact be an unnecessary distraction which could well cause problems. (Another example where the planning unit concept has caused confusion is to be found in the Ministerial decision relating to the MetroCentre: see the discussion referenced in para 3.2.2 above.) The 'multi-let premises contravention' problem is particularly unsuited to any 'planning unit'-based analysis and so that concept should be used with great care when change of use breaches of a complex kind involving various occupiers on one large site are involved.

6.6 ENFORCEMENT NOTICE – MANDATORY PROCESSES

In addition to substantive rule regarding the contents of enforcement notice the legal regime also sets down certain procedural steps.

6.6.1 Proper authorisation

Adequate 'arrangements' must be made to ensure that the authorisation of enforcement action is properly carried out. The final paragraphs of chapter five discuss the relevant issues.

6.6.2 Issuing a notice

The production of an enforcement notice (its 'issue') is authenticated once the document is signed by the 'proper officer' of the local planning authority. The term 'proper officer' is found in the Local Government Act 1972, section 270(3). Therefore an officer must be appointed for this particular purpose – to issue enforcement notices. By virtue of the Local Government Act 1972, section 234(1) any notice which a local authority is authorised to issue may be signed on behalf of the authority by the 'proper officer of the authority'. A facsimile signature is sufficient to enable section 234(2) of the Local Government Act to operate so as to deem that the document has been duly issued by the authority[1]. A facsimile produced by any process – usually a rubber stamp of the signature of the Chief Executive or the Borough Planning Officer – is thus appropriate. An enforcement case *Fitzpatrick v Secretary of State for the Environment*[2] gives one example of this. An enforcement notice had been endorsed with the facsimile signature of the District Secretary by one of his staff. The council, by resolution, had instructed the District Secretary to issue the notice. Such a resolution constituted an 'arrangement' by which the authority could validly carry out its functions – section 101(1). The facsimile signature fell squarely within the ambit of section 234(2).

---

1 Local Government Act 1972, s 234(2).

2 [1990] 1 PLR 8, CA. The background to this case illustrates some of the problems facing authorities. Litigation involving the appellant started in 1977.

6.6.3 Service of copies

The service of copies of the enforcement notice involves the following issues:

(a) the service of copies of the notice cannot be less than 28 days before the date of effectiveness – a failure here would be late service[1];
(b) effective service – service 'shall' be effected in respect of certain people[2] – a failure here would be cause problems for the authority although some are not insurmountable;
(c) every copy served must be accompanied by an explanatory note[3] setting out specified items of information.

The *Porritt* case indicates a benevolent interpretation of the 28 day requirement[4]. Copies of a notice were served 27 days before the 'specified date'. The inspector rejected the argument that the notice had not been properly served since there was no prejudice. The Divisional Court upheld that decision.

1 See para 6.5 regarding the 'specified date' in an enforcement notice.
2 TCPA 1990, s 172(2).
3 Town and Country Planning (Enforcement Notices and Appeals) Regulations 1991, SI 1991/2804, reg 4 – made under the TCPA 1990, s 173(7)(b).
4 *Porritt v Secretary of State for the Environment* [1988] JPL 414.

6.6.3.1 *Those to be served*

Those who should be served with a copy of the notice comprise:

(a) the owner of the land to which the notice relates;
(b) the occupier of the land to which the notice relates;
(c) any other person having an interest in the land, who, in the opinion of the authority has an interest materially affected by the notice[1].

The definition of 'owner' is given in the TCPA 1990, section 336(1): this means a person who is entitled to 'receive the rack rent of the land, or where the land is not let at a rack rent, would be so entitled if it were so let'. Thus a freeholder who has let the land at less than full economic rent will not fall within the definition. The term 'occupier' is left undefined. However, the courts have established that it is the degree of control over the land that is a major determinant when assessing 'occupation'. If the degree of control is negligible then the person will not be an occupier for the purposes of this provision[2].

1   TCPA 1990, s 172(2).
2   *Scarborough Borough Council v Adams* [1983] JPL 673.

6.6.3.2   *'Material interests'*

The third category is designed to catch those who may not fall under the 'owner' or 'occupier' categories. So where the authority considers that a person other than an 'owner' or 'occupier' will be 'materially affected' by the notice then they are required to serve a copy of the notice on such a person. It should be noted that the phrase is not 'objectively' framed – that is to say the 'materiality' of an 'interest' is a matter of judgment on the part of the LPA. If the LPA determines (on a proper assessment of the evidence) that a person's legal interest in the land will not be 'materially affected' then they are not obliged to serve a copy of the notice on that person. Often this is not realised by local authorities – even legal staff overlook the effect of this when seeking to establish all the 'material interests'. This is evident from one Ombudsman report where the Ombudsman criticised the over-zealous (and thus long-winded) efforts of a legal department in seeking to get exact details of all ownership interests[1]. The Ombudsman report stated that under planning law the authority only had to make 'reasonable inquiry' – there was no need to go through the lengthy procedure adopted by the legal and 'client' department. The Ombudsman's simplification of the duty to ascertain material interests may be subject to some criticism: however, in terms of its general orientation it is a useful precis of the 'spirit' in which such issues should be tackled by the LPA. This is not to say that authorities can rely on cursory examinations and pay little regard to making reasonable enquiries: it could be a basis for criticism on appeal or even before the courts if a cavalier attitude were taken as regards the duty to serve copies of notices on those with 'material interests'. However, the point should be stressed – the over-cautious legal department may (mistakenly) inhibit speedy action where this is warranted. In cases where there is a 'multi-let premises contravention' (as discussed above) then the landlord should also receive copies of all the subsidiary enforcement notices served primarily on the contravening lessors/licensees of the individual units[2].

1 Birmingham City Council, 87/B/230, reported in [1989] JPL 287.
2 *Rawlins v Secretary of State for the Environment* [1990] 1 PLR 110, CA.

6.6.3.3 *Service on the landlord*

The LPA has to bear in mind the nature of the relationship between the tenant (who is contravening planning control) and his landlord. Freeholders and other landlords may well have quite an important role (under the terms of a lease or licence) to play in the management and control of the property. Their 'superior titles' may not actually involve them (or entitle them) in active management of the land. Sometimes this justifies service and issue of notices on the landlord that address his particular role in the contravention. If his involvement is less direct (merely turning a blind eye to the contravention rather than positively encouraging the 'entrepreneurial spirit' of his tenants) the LPA may find it advantageous to serve copies of notices on the landlord (and even more superior titles). This action may have the effect (if followed up by correspondence and visits etc) of persuading the landlord to take action under the private law (leasehold) arrangements between him and the contravener. The authority may thus be able to put pressure on those able to enforce covenants in leases about the use of the leased premises. Service of copies of notices on the landlord does not invalidate the notice – as long as the LPA has reason to believe that the landlord's interest will be 'materially affected' by the notice they are, in fact, obliged to serve the landlord with a copy of the notice. The landlord could well argue that his economic interests in the land (reflected in the rent paid by the contravening tenant) warrant his knowing of the contravention. Indeed, this can be seen from the LPA's angle as an argument which suggests that the landlord should be served with a specific 'landlord's enforcement notice' requiring him to use all his private law remedies under the lease to stop the contravention. Most modern leases have requirements that the tenant comply with planning law: one of the 'steps' could therefore be to require the landlord to supply the LPA with a copy of the lease or licence under which the contravening tenant occupies the land. This would have a direct bearing on ensuring speedy compliance with the tenant's enforcement notice and so would not appear to be objectionable: see the earlier arguments on the wide scope of enforcement notice 'steps'.

6.6.4   Effective service

Service can be carried out under the TCPA 1990[1] or the general powers granted by the Local Government Act 1972[2]. Service under the TCPA 1990 in respect of ordinary individuals (not corporate entities) may be effected by the following methods:

  (a) delivering the document personally to the recipient;
  (b) leaving it at the usual or last known place of abode of the person;
  (c) leaving it at an address for service which has been given by the person;
  (d) sending the document in a prepaid registered letter (or by recorded delivery) addressed to the person at his usual or last known place of abode;
  (e) sending it by the postal methods above to the address for service which has been given by the person.

Where service is required to be made in respect of a corporate body then the following methods should be used:

  (a) delivery to the secretary or clerk of the company or body at the registered or principal office; or
  (b) sending it in a prepaid registered letter (or by recorded delivery) addressed to the secretary or clerk of the company or body at the registered or principal office.

1   TCPA 1990, s 329.
2   Local Government Act 1972, s 233.

6.6.4.1   *Post or personal?*

Personal ('by hand') delivery should be used wherever possible. The officer delivering the document should try to get a signed receipt and also set out in writing for the 'file' the details of what was delivered, to whom, the time etc. The identity of the person accepting service (name and status – owner, occupier, etc) is also useful information to note down. If postal service is used the LPA must be aware of the problems that can be encountered and the legal rules that apply by virtue of the Interpretation Act 1978 (see the next paragraph). As regards these problems it should be recognised that the difficult contravener will often refuse to sign for recorded delivery items: one look at the local authority's envelope will often give rise to the answer 'gone away'! If ordinary post is used then the intended recipient may boldly state that he never received the letter – and this may often work when such an assertion is made to the magistrates (see the next paragraph on postal delivery for details of the 'rules'). If resources permit then the LPA may have to arrange for personal service, or service by 'affixing'.

6.6.4.2 *Postal service*

The service of documents by post is covered by generally applicable legislation – the Interpretation Act 1978, section 7. Thus service is deemed to be effective by properly addressing, pre-paying and posting a letter containing the document and, unless the contrary is proved, service is deemed to have been effected at the time at which the letter would be delivered in the ordinary course of the post. Thus section 7 creates a presumption in favour of service. This presumption may be rebutted by contrary evidence. Thus if it is proved (and usually this will be relevant in proceedings before the magistrates' court) that a letter has been returned marked 'undelivered' then the presumption is rebutted *Hewitt v Leicester City Council*[1]. The addressee of the letter (the accused) thus faces the burden of proof in this instance. If the local authority proves that the letter has been properly addressed and posted then the court would, without proof of non-service, have to find that there has been delivery *Cooper v Scott-Farnell*[2]. This provision applies to local authorities and includes the Common Council of the City of London and planning boards[3].

1 [1969] 2 All ER 802.
2 [1969] 1 All ER 178.
3 Local Government (Miscellaneous Provisions) Act 1982, s 33(8) and (9).

6.6.4.3   *Service on persons 'interested' in land*

Service on a person having an interest in the land and whose name cannot be ascertained after reasonable enquiry will be taken as properly carried out if the following steps are taken[1]. First the document must be addressed to such person either by name or by description ('the owner', 'the occupier'). Second the relevant premises must be described. Third the document must be sent or delivered in the manner specified in the paragraphs (a) to (e) of para 6.6.4. Alternatively, the document may be served in the following manner. First, it and the envelope must be inscribed clearly and legibly with the words 'Important – This Communication Affects Your Property'[2]. Second, it must then either:

    (a) be sent to the premises in a prepaid registered letter or by recorded delivery and is not returned to the authority sending it; or
    (b) be delivered to some person on those premises; or
    (c) be affixed conspicuously to some object on those premises.

If the documents are 'affixed conspicuously' on the premises it is best to take two photographs (one close up to identify the notice and one at middle distance to show the notice on the premises) to help prove service.

1   TCPA 1990, s 329(2).
2   TCPA 1990, s 329(2)(b) and the Town and Country Planning General Regulations 1992, SI 1992/1492, reg 13.

6.6.4.4   *Service on owners and occupiers*

Service on any 'owner' or 'occupier' of premises will be taken as properly effected if either of the following two methods are used[1]. In the first method the document must be addressed to such person either by name or by description ('the owner', 'the occupier'). Then the relevant premises must be described on the copy of the notice. Third the notice must be sent or delivered in the manner specified in (a) to (e) of para 6.6.4. The DOE's model forms for enforcement notices do not actually include specific places for the names and addresses of the owner or occupier. Such items of information will appear on the DOE's model covering letter. This would seem to be sufficient under the terms of this provision since it would be overly pedantic to argue that the inclusion of the appropriate details on the covering letter did not mean that the copy of the notice was not properly addressed etc. The other method of service comprises the following steps. First the copy of the notice and the envelope must be inscribed clearly and legibly with the words 'Important – This Communication Affects Your Property'[2]. Second it must then either:

(a) be sent to the premises in a prepaid registered letter or by recorded delivery and must not be returned to the authority sending it; or
(b) be delivered to some person on those premises; or
(c) be affixed conspicuously to some object on those premises.

If the documents are 'affixed conspicuously' on the premises it is best to take two photographs (one close up to identify the copy of the notice and one at middle distance to show the notice on the premises) to help prove service under this provision.

1 TCPA 1990, s 329(2).
2 TCPA 1990, s 329(2)(b) and the Town and Country Planning General Regulations 1992, SI 1992/1492, reg 13.

6.6.4.5 *Unoccupied premises – interested persons and occupiers*

In the following circumstances another form of service is possible. This applies where:

(a) the document is required to be served on all persons having interests in, or being occupiers of premises; and
(b) it appears to the authority that any part of that land is unoccupied.

In such circumstances service will be taken to be duly carried out in respect of occupiers and those having interests *in the unoccupied part of the land* if the following is done. First the document must be addressed to 'the owners and any occupiers' – with a description of the land that is unoccupied. Then the copy of the notice must be affixed conspicuously to some object on the land[1].

1 TCPA 1990, s 329(3).

6.6.4.6 *Service of documents – Local Government Act 1972, section 233*

There is a general provision dealing with the service of documents found in the Local Government Act 1972. This is available as an additional means of serving documents under the enforcement regime in the Planning Acts[1]. In respect of those who have been identified by name there are three main methods of effecting service of a document. These are:

(a) delivering it to the person;
(b) leaving it at the 'proper address';
(c) sending it by post to the person at the 'proper address'[2].

In the case of a company or other body corporate then the document may be given to or served on the secretary or clerk of that body. In the case of a partnership then it should be given to or served on a partner or other person having the 'control or management' of the partnership business[3]. The term 'proper address' is normally the last known address of the person. However, if the person is a body corporate then service should at the address of the registered or principal office of the body[4]. In the case of a partnership then the 'proper address' is the address of the principal office of the partnership. Where the company is registered outside the UK then the 'proper address' is the principal office of the company within the UK. Similarly, where the partnership carries on business outside the UK then its principal office within the UK serves as its 'proper address'. If the person to be served with the document has previously specified the address within the UK (other than his 'proper address' as an address at which either he or someone on his behalf will accept 'documents' of the same description as the 'documents' to be served then that address is to be treated as the 'proper address'[5].

1 Local Government Act 1972, s 233(10).
2 Ibid, s 233(2).
3 Ibid, s 233(3)(a),(b).
4 Ibid, s 233(4)(a).
5 Ibid, s 233(5).

6.6.4.7 *Name or address unobtainable*

Where the name or address of any owner, lessee or occupier of land cannot after 'reasonable inquiry' be ascertained then service may be carried out (under the Local Government Act power) in the following way. The document should either be left 'in the hands of a person who is or appears to be resident or employed on the land' or it should be left 'conspicuously affixed to some building or object on the land'[1]. This would seem to rule out postal service as an option as the section seems to distinguish between service 'by delivering' a document and service 'by leaving' it. Section 233(2) uses both phrases and this seems to indicate that they are mutually exclusive and do not overlap. The phrase 'after reasonable inquiry' would seem to depend on the circumstances. However, it might be possible that the service of a requisition for information in a proper manner which does not lead to any response might constitute 'reasonable inquiry'. In such a case service of a copy of an enforcement notice would then be possible under section 233(7) of the Local Government Act 1972 by leaving it in the manner described above. Where workmen are carrying out works to an empty building (eg converting a single dwelling house to flats) then they would seem to be 'employed on the land' and could thus be served with either a requisition for information or a copy of an enforcement notice under this provision.

1 Local Government Act 1972, s 233(7).

6.6.5 Service of accompanying documents

Every copy of an enforcement notice served by an LPA must be accompanied by an explanatory note that comprehensively explains the rights of appeal to the recipient – the scope of the documentation is set out in the regulations[1]. The LPA will be able to comply with these requirements by enclosing the DOE's booklet on enforcement appeals with the copies of the notice, and using the DOE's model enforcement notices which include an annex outlining the rights of appeal and referring to the DOE's booklet[2].

1 Town and Country Planning (Enforcement Notices and Appeals) Regulations 1991, SI 1991/2804, reg 4.
2 Circular 21/91, Annex 2, para 18. See the three appendices to Annex 2 of the circular for the three model enforcement notices.

6.6.6 Appeal forms

The authority should also (though this is only set out in the circular and so is not a requirement of the law) enclose an appeal form and a duplicate copy of the notice.

6.7 DEFICIENCIES OF SUBSTANCE AND PROCEDURE

The thorny problem confronting the LPA when concerned with errors as to substance and procedure is the subject of the following discussion. In dealing with flaws in the *contents* of the enforcement notice officers will invariably come across the interminable discussions relating to nullity and invalidity. Officers may be pleased to hear that this treatment will not attempt to reconcile conflicting cases on this subject but instead attempt to cut through the Gordian knot by a brief examination of fundamentals. (A more critical approach might well start with the proposition that the more interventionist decisions (largely High Court) are a misguided attempt to simplify the rules regarding flawed decision-making by employing rather simplistic and dogmatic principles.) The following thus focuses on important principles of administrative law and judicial comments (especially by the Court of Appeal and the House of Lords) over the years which indicate that the courts should consign this particular area of 'pettifogging' to history. Unfortunately there are still High Court decisions that retain an affection for rather dogmatic legal analysis and so result in enforcement notices being quashed even when they are put right by the use of correction powers at the appeal stage[1].

1 An example of the interventionist orthodoxy is found in *McKay v Secretary of State for the Environment* [1994] JPL 806. For an overview of the arguments against this and similar case law see my item in *Planning*, 27 January 1995.

6.7.1 Errors of substance

The traditional analysis of the impact of flawed decision-making in the enforcement field relies heavily on an 'absolutist' view of the power to take enforcement action. The argument runs like this. If the LPA fails to follow the requirements in the legislation (eg those regarding the items of information that must be 'specified' in the notice) then the document so produced may be so unintelligible that it does not, as a matter of law, constitute an enforcement notice. The purported notice is thus a 'nullity' and no action by an inspector to 'correct' it on appeal can make it into a proper notice. If the error is not substantial the notice is merely 'invalid' and can be cured on appeal by the inspector. This line of thinking is generally attributed (as far as enforcement case law is concerned) to the comments of the Court of Appeal in the case of *Miller-Mead v Minister of Housing and Local Government*[1]. Whether this is in fact a fair summary of various statements made by different members of the Court of Appeal is debatable. Lord Denning, for instance, was rather careful to point out the problems caused by an over-technical approach. It is also relevant to point out that now the approach of administrative law in general to problems of flawed decisions and notices has changed somewhat from this received wisdom. Such analyses often use the term 'vitiated' to cover defective decisions or actions: this more closely accords with the present legislative framework regarding enforcement notices where the vitiating factors ('defect, error or misdescription') may now be overcome by the exercise of the correction power if there is no injustice to the appellant or to the LPA[2]. The House of Lords (in another enforcement case) in fact supports an approach to flawed decision-making that is much more pragmatic about the role of the courts and critical about the rather simplistic approach that language such as 'nullity', 'void' etc engenders. The House of Lords thus has, since *Miller-Mead* taken a quite different line. Lord Hailsham (using an analysis generally supported by academic commentators of administrative law) thus had this to say about the traditional, absolutist approach:

'In this appeal we are in the field of the rapidly developing jurisprudence of administrative law, and we are considering the effect of non-compliance by a statutory authority with the statutory requirements affecting the discharge of one of its functions. In the reported decisions there is much language presupposing the existence of stark categories such as "mandatory" and "directory", "void" and "voidable", a "nullity", and "purely regulatory". Such language is useful; indeed, in the course of this opinion I have used some of it myself. But I wish to say that I am not at all clear that the language itself may not be misleading insofar as it may be supposed to present a court with the necessity of fitting a particular case into one or other of mutually exclusive and starkly contrasted compartments, compartments which in some cases (eg "void" and "voidable") are borrowed from the language of contract or status, and are not easily fitted to the requirements of administrative law.

When Parliament lays down a statutory requirement for the exercise of legal authority it expects its authority to be obeyed down to the minutest detail. But what the courts have to decide in a particular case is the legal consequence of non-compliance on the rights of the subject viewed in the light of a concrete state of facts and a continuing chain of events. It may be that what the courts are faced with is not so much a stark choice of alternatives but a spectrum of possibilities in which one compartment or description fades gradually into another. At one end of this spectrum there may be cases in which a fundamental obligation may have been so outrageously and flagrantly ignored or defied that the subject may safely ignore what has been done and treat it as having no legal consequences on himself. . . . But in a very great number of cases, it may be in a majority of them, it may be necessary for a subject, in order to safeguard himself, to go to the court for declaration of his rights, the grant of which may well be discretionary, and by the like token it may be wise for an authority (as it certainly would have been here) to do everything in its power to remedy the fault in its procedure so as not to deprive the subject of his due or themselves or their power to act. In such cases, though language like "mandatory", "directory", "void", "voidable", "nullity" and so forth may be helpful in argument, it may be misleading in effect if relied on to show that the courts, in deciding the consequences of a defect in the exercise of power, are necessarily bound to fit the facts of a particular case and a developing chain of events into rigid legal categories or to stretch or cramp them on a bed of Procrustes invented by lawyers for the purposes of convenient exposition.[2]'

I have quoted at length from an important judgement because unfortunately the 'rigid legal categories . . . invented by lawyers for the purposes of convenient exposition' are inherently attractive to all who want to simplify the rules relating to flawed notices. However, as Lord Hailsham suggests, such categories (with their 'absolutist' approach) should be the exception rather than the rule and instead the courts (and others) should employ a more 'relativist' interpretation of terms such as 'nullity'. The High Court and Court of Appeal do often reflect this approach in their decisions. Unfortunately the High Court, on occasion, may also produce decisions that conflict with this approach: this leads to the courts intervening too readily in appeal decisions and striking down notices that have, by use of the correct powers, been cured of their original flaws. One important case in the enforcement field that points to the possibility of a clean break with the interventionist orthodoxy is that of *R v Tower Hamlets London Borough Council, ex p P F Ahern (London) Ltd*[4].

1 [1963] 2 QB 196, [1963] 1 All ER 459.
2 TCPA 1990, s 176(2)(a).
3 *London and Clydeside Estates Ltd v Aberdeen District Council* [1979] 3 All ER 876 at 883 d–j.
4 [1989] 2 PLR 96.

6.7.1.1 *The Ahern case*

Mr Justice Roch stated:

> '. . . the law has progressed . . . to the point where the pettifogging has stopped, where artificial and nice distinctions understood only by lawyers no longer prevail, and the Act can be read so that it means what it says, namely that the Secretary of State may correct *any* (which is my emphasis) defect or error in an enforcement notice if he is satisfied that the correction could be made without injustice to either party to the planning appeal.'[1]

The *Ahern* case clearly reflects the concern of the courts to do away with the old technicalities. It also indicates that the discussion as to whether a flaw in a notice is so fundamental as to lead to its being a nullity is something which has to be examined by reference to the facts of the case and by reference to the wide power granted to the Secretary of State or his inspector on appeal. The stress in the excerpt quoted above as to the width of the correction power is very important to note. Clearly, the legislation does provide a mechanism whereby a flawed notice can be corrected on appeal. In view of the *duty* placed upon the appellate decision maker 'to get the enforcement notice in order' it is becoming clearer that the number of occasions on which a vitiating flaw in an enforcement notice renders such a notice so flawed as to be a worthless scrap of paper will be considerably fewer than the traditional analysis would have accepted[2].

1 [1989] 2 PLR 96 at 109.
2 *Hammersmith London Borough Council v Secretary of State for the Environment* (1975) 30 P & CR 19, at 21.

6.7.1.2 *The correction power*

Where an appeal is made against a vitiated notice the correction
and variation powers are available. It would seem consistent
with the statutory framework to view such powers in wide terms
such that only the most fundamentally flawed notice could fall
outside the correction power. Indeed, the LPA (as suggested
later on in the discussion of appeals) will be well advised to
ensure that any flaws in the notice are handled by way of the
correction power at the earliest point in the appeal proceedings.
The *early* use of the correction power during an appeal enables
the appellant to make the necessary adjustments to his appeal
grounds and supporting facts so as to avoid any injustice. This
is clearly in the interests of good administration and prevents
the abuse of the appeal system by the contravener[1]. The criteria
relevant to the issue of whether an enforcement notice is
fundamentally vitiated might primarily rely upon whether the
owner, occupier etc affected by the enforcement notice is able to
make use of the statutory right of appeal. It might therefore be
an important factor to consider whether the persons who *would*
have been entitled to appeal had the notice been *properly* drawn
up and served are in fact parties to the appeal against the
relevant enforcement notice. If they are not then a correction
would be unfair since it would affect their property rights
without their being able to appeal against the notice to the
Secretary of State. However, it should be noted that under the
regulations the LPA must give notice (if there is to be an
inquiry) of the appeal to '... occupiers of properties in the locality
of the site to which the enforcement notice relates and to any
other persons who in the opinion of the authority are affected by
the breach of planning control. . .'[2]. If the extension of the area
of land (as proposed by the inspector by way of his correction
power) would affect those who have in fact been made aware of
the appeal then it would be possible to argue that such a
correction could be made.

   If those affected were given the opportunity to make their case
to the inspector (an adjournment of a few weeks may be
necessary however) then the courts may even take a pragmatic
view of the rules in such a case. If such owners were not aware
of the appeal however and were thus not able to make their case
then any correction would probably cause injustice. Fundamental
errors as to the appropriate area covered by the enforcement

notice may thus still give rise to a fundamental vitiating error – but this would not necessarily be the case in all circumstances.

1   Note the language in the Supreme Court Act 1981, s 31(6) regarding the interests of 'good administration' and judicial review proceedings.
2   Town and Country Planning (Enforcement Notices and Appeals) Regulations 1991, SI 1991/2804, reg 8 deals with public notification of the appeal.

6.7.1.3   *Absence of correction power*

If the notice is not appealed then the courts may be justified in imposing a more exacting standard when assessing the effects of a vitiating error. The LPA has a discretion to withdraw a notice before it becomes effective and arguably this power must be exercised where the LPA is aware or should reasonably be aware of an error in the notice. Failure to exercise the withdrawal power may thus be a basis (if the authority could reasonably have been expected to exercise that power) for an assertion by the appellant (by means of judicial review, for example) that the enforcement notice is fundamentally vitiated. The discretionary nature of relief would naturally involve consideration of good administration if there is delay – the criterion in the Supreme Court Act 1981. It might therefore be the case that the duty on the appellate decision-maker to get the notice in order is paralleled by a similar duty on the LPA to withdraw a flawed notice where it might reasonably be expected to do so. If the notice has taken effect then the substantive validity of the notice is something that can be raised before the criminal or civil courts before whom the notice may later appear. This particular aspect of vitiated notices is discussed below.

6.7.1.4   *The 'nugatory' notice – interpretation in the criminal courts*

The concept of 'nullity' can produce problems in the legal analysis of an enforcement notice's status if an 'absolutist' interpretation of that term is adopted. As suggested above the term 'nullity' is really a relative term: just because there are fundamental flaws (which can be corrected on appeal) we should not automatically conclude that the notice is just a worthless scrap of paper. The concept of a 'nugatory' enforcement notice is one which is not found in case law or DOE policy. It is a concept that I use to describe an enforcement notice (this also applies to a breach of condition notice or stop notice) whose value in a criminal prosecution is restricted. The concept thus reflects the different standard of interpretation placed on an enforcement notice when it is a principle element in a prosecution case. Since the criminal courts will favour the defendant in construing the evidence presented the LPA should always be aware of the risks of prosecuting for non-compliance with an enforcement notice where that notice would not be construed in a favourable manner by the Bench. A notice may be clear to the LPA and the inspector: both parties may rely on their specialised knowledge in construing a notice. However, this 'insider knowledge' will not necessarily be employed or accepted by magistrates when faced with an enforcement notice whose technical terms may be unfamiliar. If such terms can be construed in favour of the defendant then the risk that the magistrates will so construe it is very real. That is why a 'nugatory' enforcement notice needs to be carefully assessed by the LPA: it may be immune from judicial review by the courts, it may have survived an appeal before an inspector but if it goes to the magistrates it may well fail.

It is therefore important to remember that there are two standards of interpretation: these two standards should be kept in mind by the LPA officers. A notice might, even if vitiated by some flaw, still be a notice but the interpretation of it before the criminal courts could effectively make the notice worthless – hence the term *nugatory*. Thus the LPA may well have an effective enforcement notice in the strict legal sense but in terms of practical results its interpretation may be so adverse for the purposes of ensuring compliance that in practical terms the enforcement notice is just a scrap of paper. Before the civil courts (eg when suing to recover sums expended under the works in default power) a more liberal interpretation will generally be allowed. Therefore a flawed notice before such a forum as this will not be quite so ineffective. (The notion of 'relative' validity is thus also evident here in explaining the distinction between 'nugatory' and 'vitiated' enforcement notices.) It is therefore important to examine the enforcement notice which still suffers from vitiating flaws (which might not have been corrected on appeal, or were actually caused by badly considered corrections and variations on appeal) from the correct standpoint.

6.7.1.5 *Strategic litigation and institutional co-operation*

The LPA must be prepared to be clear and forceful (in submissions to the inspector) as regards the breadth of the correction powers and the problems of flawed enforcement notices. Only by insisting on the proper interpretation of the legal principles (ie requiring him to adopt a 'relativist' interpretation of nullity rather than an absolutist interpretation) can the LPA be reasonably sure that the public interest will not be harmed by unnecessary 'pettifogging'. In this way it can cut the Gordian knot which hampers enforcement. The LPA should follow up the lead given by the *Ahern* case and so sidestep the 'pettifogging' that is inherent in the interventionist orthodoxy encouraged by some courts' interpretation of the nullity principle. If necessary this will have to be followed through in submissions to the court: LPAs must be prepared to 'shadow' the Secretary of State (who will be the principal party in any challenge by the contravener against an inspector's decision) and ensure that the Secretary of State argues the case effectively. (From a strategic viewpoint of course it may be desirable for the various LPA associations, the Inspectorate and the DOE to ensure that all relevant decisions reflect this approach and that litigation is conducted on a coherent basis. Strategic enforcement can therefore, on occasion, involve the LPA in 'strategic litigation' where the problem is primarily one of wayward judicial authority.) If the more appropriate analysis prevails in the courts and on appeal to the Secretary of State then the opportunity for the contravener to make an unmerited challenge to the validity of a notice will be considerably lessened. Such a strategic approach at the institutional level should be something which the Inspectorate and the DOE would welcome since clearly it is not cost-effective to have to start all over again with a new enforcement notice when the flawed enforcement notice could easily have been corrected without injustice to the appellant.

6.7.1.6   *Legislative change*

The problems caused by the over-technical and interventionist orthodoxy were discussed in detail in the Carnwath Report. Unfortunately the suggestions made by Carnwath regarding legislative action to clear up the confusion were not followed. Perhaps legislation is the only long-term answer (leaving 'strategic litigation' etc to perform a stop-gap role). It may seem excessive to explore this option here as it is hardly relevant to the daily activity of LPAs on the enforcement front. However, effective enforcement must encompass legislative action to deal with real problems. This interventionist approach of some High Court decisions is a real problem. Such decisions make the headlines and lead to LPA lawyers and planners attempting to reconcile the case law. Since this is impossible (the two approaches being totally incompatible) the result is often a delay in taking action and further ammunition for those who see enforcement as an over-technical exercise which is too expensive to undertake in many cases. Attacking the roots of such erroneous perceptions may well involve legislative action: effective enforcement should not be afraid of venturing into this realm.

6.7.2   **Errors of procedure**

Procedural errors will arise in respect of authorisation, issue and service. In respect of the first two it is vital that adequate internal procedures are employed. The internal rules applicable to the issue of the notice must be clear and appropriate to the task. Authorities should not allow the hint of any error to be the basis of litigation, however spurious.

6.7.2.1   *Errors in service*

An appellant may appeal against the notice on the ground that copies of the enforcement notice were not served as required by the TCPA 1990, section 172. He may do so where he hopes to show that there has been substantial prejudice caused to either himself or another person who was not so served. Where such issues are raised on appeal the LPA should ensure that the issue of substantial prejudice is proved by the appellant. It would seem from the case law that whether or not there is substantial prejudice is a matter of fact and degree for the decision-maker[1]. Clearly, the LPA should forcefully require proof of substantial prejudice.

1 *Mayes v Secretary of State for Wales* [1989] JPL 848.

6.7.2.2 *Accompanying documents*

Where the LPA fails to include information as to the rights of appeal (as required by the legislation) then this failure may be serious. If an appeal against a notice is made by an appellant and the interests of a person not made aware of the rights to appeal are not prejudiced then the LPA may be able to argue that the interests of good administration indicate that the error was not fundamentally vitiating. In *London and Clydeside Estate Ltd v Aberdeen District Council* the authority failed to include a statement in writing of the rights of appeal relating to a compulsory purchase matter[1]. The House of Lords held that the certificate which should have been accompanied by such a statement was invalid. However, this case is of wider importance since it does include a valuable discussion of the problems of the absolutist interpretation of concepts such as 'nullity' etc. As noted above this case (especially in the light of the legislative changes to the enforcement regime since *Miller-Mead*) is invaluable in supporting a more pragmatic approach to the legal principles regarding flawed decision-making.

1 [1979] 3 All ER 876.

6.7.2.3 *Latent nullity and prosecutions*

Procedural errors (lack of proper authorisation etc) may have occurred but by their nature they will not be errors which will appear on the face of the notice. If such errors are not investigated by way of an appeal to the Secretary of State the contravener may receive a notice that on the face of it is not vitiated but, on further investigation, might be found to be a nullity. However, a declaration that the notice is a nullity would require examination of the background situation by a civil court. The defendant contravener is thus not permitted to go into issues as a latent nullity during a criminal trial[1]. The LPA is not therefore required to prove regularity and procedure as these are matters which should have been addressed in other proceedings.

1   *R v Wicks* (1995) Times, 19 April, CA. This case reviews conflicting dicta and authority and is thus a useful overview of the different arguments. See also the discussion of stop notices and issues of vires in chapter eight.

7 Enforcement action – appeals and review

7.1 INTRODUCTION

The LPA may feel that the right to appeal is often abused by contraveners and serves only to delay the coming into force of the enforcement notice. The statutory provision[1] whereby the enforcement notice is suspended pending a final determination or withdrawal of the appeal means that the enforcement notice cannot 'bite' until such final determination etc. Since a contravener is likely to request that the appeal be handled by means of a public inquiry the delay may be considerable. However, there are options available, if the circumstances permit, to reduce the impacts of that delay. First the LPA has the option of using the stop notice procedure (see chapter eight) which enables the LPA to require the cessation of 'activities' involved in a breach of control. The stop notice's requirements are not suspended by an appeal. Second the LPA may be able to use the breach of condition notice as a way of dealing with the breach: hopefully it will be a swifter form of redress in most cases; unfortunately, of course, the recalcitrant contravener may well play the system in this situation as well. Third the LPA could seek a planning injunction under section 187B. The LPA may also combine these weapons (eg an enforcement and stop notice combined with a breach of condition notice). The LPA does therefore have it in its power to deal swiftly with 'activities' involved in a breach of planning control (where, of course, the various legal technicalities are not a problem) and also restrict the ability of the contravener to use appeals to the courts as a further delaying tactic – since leave is now required to appeal by virtue of the TCPA 1990, section 289(6).

---

1 TCPA 1990, s 175(4). In the case of appeals to the High Court and further the notice may, by order of the court, have effect (in full or in part) pending the final determination of the appeal. The 1991

reforms thus allow the LPA to argue the case for continued protection of planning interests against activities etc even though an enforcement notice may be challenged.

7.2   THE APPELLANT AND THE NOTICE OF APPEAL

The legislation[1] defines the range of potential appellants in these terms:

'A person having an interest in the land to which an enforcement notice relates or a relevant occupier may appeal to the Secretary of State against the notice, whether or not a copy of it has been served on him.'

The term 'relevant occupier' is defined in subsection (6) to mean a person who:

'(a) on the date on which the enforcement notice is issued occupies the land to which the notice relates by virtue of a licence; and
(b) continues so to occupy the land when the appeal is brought.'

Thus those with a freehold or leasehold interest and those occupying by a licence may appeal. With the latter it may be important to note that the date of *issue* (not service of copies) of the notice is a key date. The statutory formula also means that those who have been served with a copy notice do not necessarily have the right to appeal against it – the LPA may have served those whom it (mistakenly) believed would be materially affected by the notice but do not in fact fall within the scope of the provision under discussion here. This formula also means that an appellant need not have been served with a copy of the notice. Such a person may raise this as an appeal ground: however, neither he (nor any other person) is entitled to raise again (in any proceedings instituted after the making of the appeal) the fact of non-service on the person who appealed[2]. The statutory formula means that trespassers cannot appeal against an enforcement notice.

1   TCPA 1990, s 174(1).
2   TCPA 1990, s 175(5).

7.2.1   Time limits for the appeal

The appeal must be made by written notice to the Secretary of

State. This need not be on the appeal form supplied. The appeal is validly made if given to the Secretary of State before the date of effectiveness or if sent in a properly addressed and prepaid letter posted to him such that, in the ordinary course of post, it would be delivered to him before that date[1]. The Secretary of State will not accept appeals received after this date as the time limit is construed strictly[2]. Official practice is to provide photocopies of envelopes so that the date of posting is evident – the LPA will normally be able to rely on the DOE to screen out late appeals. The case law indicates that an appeal arriving at the DOE *on* the date of effectiveness is out of time[3]. Some authorities timetable their notices so that the 'specified date' is a Monday or Tuesday: the reason for this seems to be that the badly advised appellant may therefore (if he uses the postal service) leave things too late and fail to ensure that the notice of appeal arrives *before* the date of effectiveness. The LPA however should not assume that the tactic of choosing a Monday or a Tuesday (or, for that matter a public holiday) as the date of effectiveness will necessarily catch out the unwary appellant. If the appellant delivers the notice by hand through the post-box of the DOE then as long as that is done before the 'specified date' then the appeal will be validly made[3]. The former rules regarding making an appeal had been held to mean that an appeal lost in the post is not 'made': *R v Secretary of State for the Environment, ex p Jackson*[4]. However, the statutory language now may have modified that rule. The appeal is made 'by sending . . . to' the Secretary of State the notice of appeal such that it would normally arrive before the appeal period expires. If the post is delayed but the notice is received then this would seem to mean that the appeal is properly made. However, does the language (by virtue of the phrase 'send to') imply that the notice must actually be received in order to qualify as being made? If the letter is lost in the post has it been 'sent to' the Secretary of State? The *Lenlyn* case (addressing the unamended provision) did take a hard line on the wording of the wording then in force. It might be possible that a lost appeal is also construed as not being 'made' since no notice is received. (Practice at the DOE is to check on whether the appellant can prove that he posted the appeal notice properly; if that is the case they will treat that appeal as made even though it has not been received at all.) Fax transmission of an appeal is quite possible – the fax number is 0117 987 8782: since details can be sent along later (the DOE will request these) a short-form notice of appeal can be made on one sheet allowing the tardy recipient of a notice to make a last minute appeal: he must appeal before midnight of the day before the notice is to take effect to make a valid appeal. LPAs checking on whether an appeal has been made at the last moment should therefore contact the general enforcement enquiry number – 0117 987 8075.

1 TCPA 1990, s 174(3).
2 *Lenlyn Ltd v Secretary of State for the Environment* [1985] JPL 482.
3 *Howard v Secretary of State for the Environment* [1975] QB 235.
4 [1987] JPL 790.

7.2.2   Grounds of appeal – screening

Normally the appellant will state the grounds of appeal and the facts in support of such grounds on the standard form notice. However, section 174(3) of the TCPA 1990 states that an appeal need be only made 'by notice in writing' to the Secretary of State – thus the LPA may not receive a statement of facts until the appellant has responded to the Secretary of State's formal request for such a statement. Whether the standard form of appeal is used or whether the appellant provides information in another manner, it is important that the grounds on which the appeal is made and the supporting facts are carefully scrutinised. Again this might be an appropriate stage for screening the enforcement case at this stage: if the LPA considers that the appellant is acting unreasonably or has not complied with the statutory requirements as to the information required by the Secretary of State then they should clearly indicate the errors and refer to the possibility of an application for costs in respect of any expense which might be incurred on the part of the LPA in dealing with such issues. Screening by an experienced officer at this stage allows the validity of the grounds of appeal to be scrutinised not only with a view to their substantive merits but also with a view to ensuring that the council's case for an award of costs can be substantiated if it, at a later stage, makes a costs application. Such an application (as is noted below) is only likely to succeed if the LPA has given a clear warning of the 'unreasonable conduct' by the appellant.

The delegated legislation dealing with the appellant's production of a statement of the grounds of appeal and the facts on which he proposes to rely is found in regulation 5 of the 1991

Regulations[1]. When the Secretary of State notifies the appellant of the duty to supply the statement of the grounds for appeal and the supporting facts the appellant then has 14 days in which to comply with such a notice. In the primary legislation there is a provision which empowers the Secretary of State to determine an appeal without reference to a ground where the ground is not supported by a statement of fact; this is found in section 174(5) of the TCPA 1990. Circular 21/91, Annex 2, paragraphs 27–30 set out the DOE's approach to the appellant's statement of facts etc in support of his appeal. The Secretary of State may give notice to the appellant requiring him to deliver his statement of grounds of appeal and brief statement of supporting facts within 14 days of the Secretary of State sending such a notice. The LPA may wish to make a case for the early use of these powers where the conduct of the appellant indicates that the DOE should also be more insistent in its dealings with him.

The DOE (in the circular) notes that both LPAs and appellants can be tardy in producing the written statements to be used at inquiries (paragraphs 30 and 31–32 respectively). If the LPA considers that the appellant's statement is 'insufficiently informative or detailed for the purposes of the public inquiry' (the phraseology is taken from paragraph 30) then it should formally request that the powers in the 1992 Rules be exercised to require a 'statement of relevant matters' and a statement of case[2]. The following paragraphs examine the grounds of appeal that may be relied on in an appeal.

1 Town and Country Planning (Enforcement Notices and Appeals) Regulations 1991, SI 1991/2804.
2 Town and Country Planning (Enforcement) (Inquiries Procedure) Rules 1992, SI 1992/1903, rr 7 and 8.

7.2.2.1 *Ground (a)*

'that, in respect of any breach of planning control which may be constituted by the matters stated in the notice, planning permission ought to be granted or, as the case may be, the condition or limitation concerned ought to be discharged'.

When faced with an appeal on this ground the LPA will be concerned primarily with the planning merits of the application for planning permission or modification of the condition. Since very many enforcement notices arise from neighbour complaints it is important that the LPA can produce cogent and substantiated evidence from neighbours who have complained about the breach. Such evidence can throw light upon the concrete adverse impacts arising from the breach of control. Naturally, if the breach of control affects particularly important planning interests (listed buildings, conservation areas etc) then the impact of the development on such interests will be relevant. Again, it is important to stress that the special 'tests' that may be appropriate when such interests are involved should be used by the LPA to counter the arguments by the appellant that planning permission ought to be granted[1]. Similarly, the suggestion that a condition which has been breached should be discharged will also need to be countered by concrete and cogent evidence to the contrary. The mobilisation of the aggrieved neighbours, amenity groups etc to help the LPA substantiate a case for rejecting the appellant's contentions cannot be underemphasised.

1 See the discussion in chapter ten and chapter five of issues relevant to listed buildings.

7.2.2.2   *Ground (b)*

'that those matters [stated in the notice] have not occurred'.

Where such a ground is relied on by the appellant the LPA will have to be in a position to produce contrary arguments – this will involve a mixture of legal and planning analysis. It is important to note that where this ground is used then the appellant must demonstrate that that ground is made out – *Nelsovil Ltd v Minister of Housing and Local Government*[1]. The appellant need only prove his case on the balance of probabilities – *Thrasyvoulou v Secretary of State for the Environment*[2]. Where such a ground is relevant the local authority may therefore have to look at issues which have been discussed earlier in this book – established uses, intensification, and other similar issues in dispute which deal with the problem of whether development has occurred and whether that development requires express planning permission. As discussed in chapter two the LPA may be able to raise an estoppel argument against the appellant (see next paragraph) arguing this ground.

1   [1962] 1 All ER 423, [1962] 1 WLR 404.
2   [1984] JPL 732.

7.2.2.3   *Ground (c)*

'that those matters (if they occurred) do not constitute a breach of planning control'.

If this issue has already been fully examined and (in a previous enforcement appeal for example) the conclusion does not favour the appellant then the LPA should be able to argue that the appellant is estopped from using this ground of appeal. If this is the only ground pleaded then the LPA has the option (in addition to using an estoppel argument before the inspector) to apply to the court for a declaration that the appeal is invalid. The LPA may also be able to persuade the DOE that this is the case.

7.2.2.4   *Ground (d)*

'that, at the date when the notice was issued, no enforcement action could be taken in respect of any breach of planning control which may be constituted by those matters'.

This involves the operation of the ten and four-year rules. A mixture of fact and law will therefore be involved in dealing with this ground.

7.2.2.5   *Ground (e)*

'that copies of the enforcement notice were not served as required by section 172'.

Where problems of service are raised the LPA should ensure that adequate details as to the alleged errors are given by the appellant. If the allegation is that copies of the notice were served late then the authority should ask for clear evidence as to late service. If the allegation is based upon non-service on either the owner/occupier or another person with a 'material interest' then proof that the person in question was not served should be required by the LPA. Where the LPA has ensured that its service procedures are up to the task then they should be able to deal with most allegations of non-service. If the appellant does demonstrate that the person on whom a copy should have been served was not so served then the LPA should ensure that the Secretary of State is made aware of section 176(5) of the TCPA 1990 which empowers the Secretary of State to 'disregard that fact if neither the appellant nor that person has been substantially prejudiced by the failure to serve him'. The arguments will therefore largely focus around the phrase 'substantially prejudice' when it comes to the exercise of that power by the Secretary of State.

7.2.2.6   *Ground (f)*

'that the steps required by the notice to be taken, or the activities required by the notice to cease, exceed what is necessary to remedy any breach of planning control which may be constituted by those matters or, as the case may be, to remedy any injury to amenity which has been caused by any such breach'.

The key phrase here is 'what is necessary'. The legislation does not use a 'reasonableness' standard (rather unusually) but this 'necessary' standard. In arguing an appeal on this ground the LPA should therefore be keen to ensure that the appellant's arguments are relevant to 'necessity' rather than reasonableness.

7.2.2.7   *Ground (g)*

'that any period specified in the notice in accordance with section 173(9) falls short of what should reasonably be allowed'.

Where the appellant relies upon this ground in his appeal the LPA should focus on the term 'reasonably' and the particular element of the 'public interest' factor involved in a consideration of reasonableness. Clearly, the disruption of business activity arising from compliance with an enforcement notice is a factor to take into account if it is of a scale and kind to be relevant to the 'public interest': however, the weight to be given to that factor will vary according to the circumstances. If the LPA considers that the damage (eg pollution, amenity impacts etc) to planning interests is severe then the relevance of such 'public interest' factors will be perhaps more relevant to assessing what is 'reasonable' in terms of the compliance period. If the appellant has clearly been 'playing the system' by his appeal and none of his other grounds of appeal have any merit then the LPA may be able to argue that the contravener might reasonably have been expected to start searching for alternative premises very soon after being informed by the LPA that enforcement action was envisaged. In certain circumstances then the compliance period specified in an enforcement notice can be 'reasonably' short since the time taken to deal with an appeal against such a notice will necessarily add many months to the compliance timetable. Therefore it may be arguable that, in the context of the time taken for an appeal to be decided, the period allowed in the notice for the carrying out of steps can be quite short.

7.3 APPEAL BY WRITTEN REPRESENTATIONS

The written representations methods will have its attractions for the LPA. This method is faster and cheaper than determination by way of a public inquiry. However, the LPA should be aware of the inherent problems that arise from adopting the written representation procedure. Possibly because the written representation procedure is more low-key and less 'visible' there is a temptation on the part of officers to deal with issues in a less thorough manner. With public inquiries the LPA's case will have been vetted by, in many cases, legal staff (possibly counsel) who take on the advocacy role during the inquiry. This means that the arguments and evidence provided by the planning officers will have been viewed from a fresh angle and inconsistencies and omissions will (hopefully) have been noted and set right. Such 'internal review' is not necessarily very common with written representation proceedings. This means that the presentation of a case by (inexperienced) officers may lead to errors and omissions appearing in the arguments and evidence produced by the LPA. Such problems may have been in the mind of the court in the case of *Ricketts and Fletcher v Secretary of State for the Environment and Salisbury District Council*[1]. Here the court was examining an appeal relating to development control issues which had been handled by the written representations procedure. The Deputy Judge stated that he:

'. . . would be the last person to point to the shortcomings of that procedure. The procedure was appropriate in very many cases. It has very considerable administrative advantages in terms of time and cost. As a procedural mechanism it was wholly to be supported.

On the other hand there was no doubt than an inquiry did give to the parties an opportunity to test the material rather more directly, effectively and efficiently. That seemed to be an inherent characteristic of an appeal by way of inquiry as against an appeal by way of written representation.

The general problem was that there were many cases coming by way of appeal to this court which on analysis demonstrated that material was not sufficiently tried or tested, or indeed that the material was not tried or tested at all. Thus there had been an increase in the number of cases where recourse was had to this court in order to make submissions on documents, their interpretation, their shortcomings and matters of that kind'[2].

These comments also illustrate that the case made out by the appellant may not be thoroughly tested when written representations are employed to deal with the appeal. The procedure also generally gives rise to less input from the 'aggrieved neighbour' and other amenity groups who may be very interested in the appeal. Often the input of such parties at the public inquiry form of proceeding provides another useful angle on the issues to be examined. The LPA should therefore consider whether there are gaps in its handling of appeals by way of written representation and take appropriate steps to deal with such problems. This may involve clearer guidelines from experienced officers as to the content of the LPA's case. Other options include a closer examination of statements produced by aggrieved neighbours etc to see if their arguments raise any novel points. The LPA may also consider whether an internal review procedure (vetting of reports by a special officer – planning or perhaps legal) is warranted.

From the viewpoint of effective enforcement action the LPA needs to be aware of the risks of employing the written representations procedure. Not only must it ensure that its own case and that of the appellant are thoroughly examined but it will also be necessary to subject the decision letter to close scrutiny. The 'low-key' nature of this procedure is likely also to affect the manner in which the inspector deals with the issue. The temptation on the part of the inspector to deal with the issues in rather a 'brusque' fashion should therefore be tackled by the LPA ensuring that its representations are fully and forcefully made. When the decision letter is produced particular care should be taken in its scrutiny to ensure that no substantial errors have been made.

1   [1988] JPL 768.
2   Ibid, page 772.

7.4 HEARINGS

The determination of appeals by way of a hearing is not that common. It is designed to be a half-way house between the full-blown public inquiry and the written representations method. It is suitable for appeals that do not raise matters that are likely to be contentious. Since enforcement notice appeals often deal with contentious issues (eg matters of established use, etc) this may explain why such a procedure is not commonly employed for enforcement notice appeals. DOE advice as to the use of such hearings (circular 21/91, Annex 2, paragraph 25) in the enforcement context is in the following terms:

> 'Where the dispute is solely about the planning merits of the notice and the appeal, or the requirements of the notice or the period for compliance, and there has been a request to be heard, it may be appropriate to proceed by way of an informal hearing rather than a public inquiry. The less formal procedure of an informal hearing makes it inappropriate in any case where there is a dispute on evidential facts, or on most legal grounds in section 174(2).'

The LPA will also prefer to subject the appellant and his witnesses to cross-examination – even perhaps asking the inspector to use his various powers (eg subpoena) to require a thorough investigation and testing of evidence to be undertaken (see below on the witness summons procedure).

7.5 PUBLIC INQUIRIES

The appellant is very likely to opt for the public inquiry format. Indeed, if the appeal will involve arguments about facts then the DOE may decide that the appeal should be heard by way of public inquiry even where the appellant does not so request. In such cases the DOE generally considers that the resolution of such disputes requires oral evidence tested by cross-examination. According to the Annual Report and Accounts for the Year Ended 31 March 1994 produced by the Planning Inspectorate 36% of enforcement notice appeals were handled by way of public inquiry (para A2.6 of the report). Written representations accounted for 59.5% and hearings accounted for 4.5%. (Figures relate to decisions made by inspectors – which account for 99% of all appeals.)

7.5.1 Streamlined procedures

Ordinary planning inquiries have benefited from changes in practice which have been reflected in provisions of the relevant rules. Enforcement inquiries have also been subject to similar change so the improved rules regarding early production of proofs of evidence etc are important elements in speeding up the appeal stage of an enforcement case. Circular 17/92, Annex 3 (comprising 12 paragraphs) outlines the main changes introduced by the 1992 Rules.

7.5.2 Evidential issues

Disputes between the LPA and the appellant as regards issues of fact are very common in enforcement notice appeals. Where such disputes arise within the context of a public inquiry then the provisions of section 250 (subsections (2) to (5)) of the Local Government Act 1972 apply. Evidence can be given on oath. The inspector may admit hearsay evidence[1]. In dealing with issues of fact raised by the appellant in his evidence the LPA should always be mindful that the appellant is under a burden to establish the existence of any ground of appeal which he relies on in his case. Thus the need to satisfy the tribunal (the inspector or the Secretary of State) as to the ground advanced is something which the LPA may wish to stress in its own submissions. Case law[2] has this to say on the burden of proof in relation to grounds of appeal advanced by an appellant:

> 'whether or not the burden had been discharged and a ground of appeal made out would almost inevitably involve the tribunal in matters of fact and degree. This was a world into which the court would not venture unless in relation to the material before it the tribunal had acted perversely in the sense that on that material no tribunal acting reasonably could have reached the conclusion that the tribunal had in fact reached. Of course, if there was no material whatsoever on which to found a conclusion there was perversity par excellence. Allegations of perversity should only be advanced in this court with a due sense of responsibility. It was not a "long-stop" plea when all else failed. The circumstances in which that plea would succeed are likely to be exceptional[3].'

The degree of latitude that the courts will therefore accord to the inspector or the Secretary of State in assessing, as a matter of fact and degree, the evidence brought by the appellant means that the LPA will have to ensure that its best case is presented at the inquiry itself. Action at a later stage (a High Court challenge against the decision letter of the inspector, for example) is likely to be very difficult especially where *Wednesbury* grounds of 'perversity' are alleged.

1 *T A Miller Ltd v Minister of Housing and Local Government* [1968] 2 All ER 633, [1968] 1 WLR 992.
2 *Ferris v Secretary of State for the Environment and Doncaster Metropolitan Borough Council* [1988] JPL 777.
3 Ibid at 780.

7.5.3 Witness summons, subpoena

The inspector has the power to test evidence at an inquiry by using a witness summons requiring a person to give evidence or to produce any documents in his custody. The term 'subpoena' may be used to describe this power though that is not in fact the term found in the legislative provisions[1]. A writ of subpoena may have to be used to compel compliance with a witness summons[2] but hopefully the recipient of the summons will comply without such further powers having to be used. A recipient of a summons who:

> 'refuses or deliberately fails to attend in obedience to a summons issued under this section, or to give evidence, or who deliberately alters, suppresses, conceals, destroys, or refuses to produce any book or other document which he is required to is liable to be required to produce for the purposes of this section, shall be liable on summary conviction to a fine not exceeding level 3 on the standard scale or to imprisonment for a term not exceeding six months, or to both'.

The 'necessary expenses' involved in the recipient's attendance must be paid or tendered to him: such costs can be subject of a costs award by the inspector[3].

1 Local Government Act 1972, s 250(2).
2 RSC Ord 38, r 19 deals with a writ of subpoena in aid of 'an inferior court or tribunal'.
3 Local Government Act 1972, s 250(2)(a) and (4) respectively.

7.6 NEGOTIATIONS PENDING APPEAL

There may be many situations where the contravener seeks to agree a compromise with the local planning authority during the currency of an appeal. He may take this course of action because of advice as to the (insubstantial) merits of his case. The contravener may also find that his dispute with the LPA is preventing him from selling the land. Further, if the LPA has issued a stop notice to prevent unauthorised 'activities' continuing the contravener may wish to 'bargain away' the stop notice by agreeing to a modification of his activities on the land. A fuller discussion of 'negotiated compliance' appears in chapter nine. However, a few words in the context of appeals are relevant.

Negotiations in the setting of an enforcement episode are in some ways analogous to those that can take place during a development control 'dispute'. Both sides can gain from a negotiated compromise which obviates the need for a long and (sometimes) expensive inquiry. In the context of an enforcement problem however, the LPA will need to take account of various issues particular to such a situation. These issues are further discussed in chapter nine but the key point to note here is the manner in which the compromise is effected. It may be all too tempting to handle the compromise by the issue of a planning permission. However, there are good arguments for avoiding this route and instead handling the compromise (primarily) by a planning agreement. This will enable the authority to ensure that terms and conditions of the compromise are contained in a form which enables effective action to be taken at a later stage should things go wrong. Negotiations pending an enforcement notice appeal should therefore be carried out within the framework of a compromise to be consolidated into a planning agreement. The reader is referred to chapter nine for further discussion as to achieving a negotiated solution to an enforcement problem.

7.7 POWERS OF THE INSPECTOR

For the purposes of this discussion it is assumed that the determination of the appeal will be a matter for the inspector. It is important to know the framework within which he acts. In particular, the possibility that the terms of the enforcement notice may need amending is something which is very relevant when it comes to the specific powers granted to the inspector. Comments made earlier regarding the ambit of the correction power are applicable here; to some extent the following discussion will repeat issues raised there. Such repetition is necessary since the points raised by a discussion of the correction power are very important and cannot be overemphasised. The exercise of various powers by the inspector is something to which the authority must pay close attention at the appeal stage. Indeed, the 'material considerations' that are relevant to the exercise of some of these powers (eg the grant of planning permission, the discharge of any condition subject to which planning permission was granted) may well involve consideration of special planning factors, such as the listed building test and the conservation area test, that have statutory 'weighting' (see the discussion in chapter five of such statutory enforcement considerations and the chapters dealing with listed buildings and conservation areas).

7.7.1 During appeal – correction or variation

By virtue of the TCPA 1990, section 176(1) a power is granted to the Secretary of State (therefore exercisable by the inspector by virtue of Schedule 6) to:

'(a) correct any defect, error or misdescription in the enforcement notice; or
(b) give directions for varying its terms'.

Such power is granted 'on an appeal . . . if he is satisfied that the correction or variation will not cause injustice to the appellant or the local planning authority'. It is important to note that the correction or variation powers under section 176(1) do not apply merely to the final decision. The correction or variation powers can be exercised at any stage from the time when the appeal is validly made until its determination. This means that the LPA is in a position to request at any time during the currency of the appeal that such powers be used in order to correct any flaw in the enforcement notice or to vary the terms of the enforcement notice. The latter could be used, for example, to shorten or lengthen the compliance periods or to amend the 'steps' required by the notice. As there is a duty on the inspector 'to get the notice in order'[1] then the LPA is on very strong ground when requesting that the powers to correct a defective notice be exercised.

Naturally, the sooner that such powers can be exercised the better. A variation or correction of the notice at an early stage in the proceedings is less likely to cause injustice to the appellant and thus fall foul of the proviso as to 'injustice'. The LPA should ensure that it is in a position to argue that the appellant (since he will be given enough time to reassess the situation after any such correction or variation) will not be caused 'injustice' by the exercise of the correction or variation powers. (See also the arguments on the 'nullity' issue in chapter six). Indeed, the LPA should be persistent in its analysis of this particular set of powers and point out to the inspector that any allegation of 'injustice' needs to be substantiated and considered in the light of the time that is available to the appellant to digest any amendments to the enforcement notice. Even if the use of the correction or variation powers occurs at quite a late stage in the appeal it is clearly possible for the inspector to rearrange the timetabling of the appeal in such a manner as to deal with any possible injustice that could clearly be caused.

1 *Hammersmith London Borough Council v Secretary of State for the Environment* (1975) 30 P & CR 19 at 21.

7.7.1.1 *Costs implications of the correction or variation powers*

There may of course be costs implications where the exercise of the correction or variation power at the behest of the LPA has caused the appellant to incur reasonable expense unnecessarily. The ambit of the costs power is discussed later on in this chapter. However, in respect of this particular issue it is important to stress that in a complex enforcement case the making of mistakes as to the legal position will not necessarily constitute 'unreasonable conduct' when the LPA wishes to put the situation right by requesting that the inspector use his correction powers. Also, a costs application would have to deal with the 'quantum' issue and the appellant would therefore have to show what expenses were incurred unnecessarily by the 'unreasonable conduct' of the LPA.

The risk of a successful costs application being made against the council in respect of variations and corrections made at the council's behest does, however, become more serious as the appeal progresses. So where the LPA fails to request the exercise of the correction or variation powers until very late in the day, then the risk of a costs application succeeding will be much greater. Thus if the LPA fails to notice legal deficiencies in their approach (perhaps after being warned of them by the appellant) then it would be unreasonable of them to delay unduly in requesting the exercise of the correction power. If the exercise of such a power then results in the enforcement notice being considerably amended (thus rendering some appeal grounds inappropriate and giving rise to other grounds of appeal) then there is likely to be a strong case for saying that the work expended on grounds which are now inappropriate and the extra work needed to deal with the new grounds would be relevant to the issue of 'quantum'. However, as has been stressed already if the LPA is careful to keep enforcement notice appeals under careful scrutiny the risks of a successful costs application by virtue of a late correction or variation should be kept to a minimum.

7.7.1.2 *The DOE's standpoint*

The use of correction or variation powers by the inspector is something which the DOE and the Inspectorate Agency should support. Clearly, the quashing of an enforcement notice in circumstances where its early correction by the inspector is warranted will lead to further expense on the part of the DOE, the Inspectorate and the LPA. The minor administrative cost of carrying out a correction or variation at an early stage in an appeal will be small compared to the administrative expense of the LPA having to issue and serve a second enforcement notice and the DOE having then to process the appeal against such a notice. The advantage in terms of cost savings to the DOE and the LPA should thus be forcefully pointed out when the LPA requests that the inspector exercise his correction or variation powers under the TCPA 1990, section 176(1).

7.7.2 **The power to quash**

The TCPA 1990, section 176(2) empowers the Secretary of State to quash the notice when determining to allow the appeal. The quashing power may also be used where the LPA falls down on processing the appeal and keeping to the timetabling provisions.

In these circumstances therefore the quashing power erases the enforcement notice in toto. The quashing of a notice by reason of the LPA's failure to comply with procedural aspects of an appeal will invariably be preceded by clear warnings of the use of such a power. It will therefore be a case of gross incompetence by the LPA if such warnings are not heeded and the notice is quashed on the basis of non-compliance with statutory procedure.

7.7.3   Grant planning permission

By virtue of the TCPA 1990, section 177(1)(a) the Secretary of State may 'grant planning permission in respect of the matters stated in the enforcement notice as constituting a breach of planning control, whether in relation to the whole or any part of those mattes or in relation to the whole or any part of the land to which the notice relates'. A breach of planning control may, in part, be acceptable to the LPA. However, there may be occasions when a local planning authority which tries to be reasonable in its approach to an enforcement issue ends up creating problems for itself when it comes to defining the various elements required in an enforcement notice. Sometimes then the simplicity of a more blunt approach in an enforcement notice is preferable from the point of view of avoiding mistakes that are difficult to rectify later on. Therefore, it may be necessary to be all-embracing in an enforcement notice as regards the steps required to be taken but then accept that planning permission can be granted for part of the development at the appeal. Where the LPA supports the grant of partial planning permission the precise nature of the proposed grant will be something which they should address during the appeal. As always, the LPA should be careful to ensure that any proposed conditions on a grant of planning permission are themselves up to the standards required for their later enforcement – if that should become necessary.

7.7.3.1   *Relevant considerations*

The TCPA 1990, section 177(2) states that the consideration of a grant of planning permission under section 177(1) carries with it the duty to 'have regard to the provisions of the development plan, so far as material to the subject matter of the enforcement notice, and to any other material considerations'. The wording of this provision is a further reminder to the LPA about 'enforcement policies' in the development plan; if the 'subject matter' of the notice falls within the ambit of such policies then those policies will clearly be (doubly) relevant considerations because of section 54A. It has already been stressed elsewhere that the effective enforcement of planning control requires the co-ordination of all three aspects of the planning trinity (forward planning, development control and enforcement) and in respect of the powers under section 177 this is particularly pertinent. Where the breach of control has taken place on land in a conservation area the conservation area test will apply: if consideration of the deemed application affects a listed building then the listed building test from section 66(1) of P(LB&CA)A 1990 will be relevant. Hopefully the LPA will have in place conservation area enforcement policies and listed building enforcement policies in the local plan to help justify their action. As mentioned earlier, the impact of the conservation area test in those cases where it does have relevance is very important. The LPA should therefore ensure that the impact of the conservation area designation is clearly understood when the powers of the inspector are exercised under the 1990 Act. The systemic considerations relevant to enforcement (maintaining the integrity of the planning system in particular) will also be relevant as 'material considerations' under this provision.

7.7.3.2 *Dwellinghouses and retrospective grants*

One issue to take care with is the need to suggest conditions on the grant of a permission allowing retention of a dwellinghouse to be occupied by (for example) an agricultural worker. If the works are nearly four years old any condition which the inspector imposes controlling occupancy should not be 'backdated' to correspond with the date on which the works were substantially finished. To do so might risk a contravening occupation of the building soon becoming immune from action because of the four-year rule. The LPA should argue for the occupancy condition to take effect from the date of the decision letter: this then ensures that the four-year period starts anew from the grant of permission.

7.7.3.3   *Consideration of multiple deemed applications*

If multiple notices have been issued and a number of different
occupiers and uses are involved the LPA should ensure that the
issues are treated both in aggregate and individually. The
inspector in *Bruschweiller v Secretary of State* failed to consider
each of the deemed applications on their own[1]. The High Court
quashed his decisions (refusal of all deemed applications) since
he was obliged to consider them separately as well as in
aggregate. Indeed, the planning impacts of a number of
contravening uses may well be different (and acceptable) when
compared with the impacts of others or all together. The LPA
will therefore have to prepare its enforcement case (including
its assessment of the situation from the report to committee
seeking authorisation) with this in mind when multiple
contraventions are involved.

1   [1994] EGCS 206. See also *Reed v Secretary of State for the
    Environment* (1993) 65 P & CR 50.

**7.7.4   Discharge any condition or limitation of a
permission**

The power to discharge any condition or limitation subject to
which planning permission is granted is given to the Secretary
of State by the TCPA 1990, section 177(1)(b). The inspector
must take account of the planning issues as they stand at the
time of his decision: he should discharge a condition simply
because it was inappropriate at the time of the original
permission[1]. Again this power arises 'on the determination of an
appeal'. The possible exercise of this particular power is
something which the LPA would need to address carefully. The
justification in planning terms for any condition or limitation
which the inspector may discharge would therefore need to be
set out. This is one situation where the views of the aggrieved
neighbour might usefully be employed to back up the case for
retention of any condition etc, where amenity and other similar
issues are relevant. The power can, however, result in tighter
control over the permitted activity. The TCPA 1990, section
177(4) provides that the Secretary of State may substitute
another condition or limitation for the one discharged and that

this may be 'more or less onerous'. This can, effectively, mean that the contravener who appeals finds himself in a worse position by having a more restrictive permission apply to his activities. This can be done, of course, by a revocation order: however, compensation is payable in such cases. Parliament seems therefore to have thought it appropriate to tighten up on the regulation of activities (without compensation provision) in cases where there is a contravention of control and there is an enforcement appeal. However, LPAs should be aware that the Inspectorate has a policy of letting the appellant know (in a 'minded to' letter) of the proposed substitution of a more onerous condition: the letter asks for the comments of the appellant. This can often result in the appeal being withdrawn. The 'unfairness' of imposing a more onerous condition seems to be one factor underlying such action. Another may be the potential for confusion if the inspector grants a second (more restrictive) permission and leaves the laxer permission intact. If this is a problem the LPA should argue that the inspector can take away the pre-existing and laxer permission by way of a planning condition imposed on the more restrictive permission he proposes to grant[2]. The inspector could also require the contravener to execute a planning obligation preventing him from relying on that earlier permission[3]. The current approach may perhaps be a little surprising since it seems to encourage action which is contrary to the clear intention of Parliament to allow the appellate decision-maker (in an enforcement appeal) to tighten up on control without having to make compensatory payments. A policy that undermines that aim would be in conflict with the legislative provision granting the discretion and so ultra vires.

1 *Bannister v Secretary of State for the Environment* [1994] 2 PLR 90.
2 *Gill v Secretary of State for the Environment* [1985] JPL 710 indicates that such a condition can be imposed on a permission so restricting the rights of the owner to use the various permissions granted under the GPDO.
3 Ministerial policy may traditionally have been against planning conditions requiring the applicant for planning permission to enter into a planning agreement. However, the legality of such a condition has not been fully analysed by the courts. In view of the changes to section 106 and the developing case law such a condition should not now be seen as ultra vires.

7.7.5　Issue certificate of lawful use or development

The inspector or Secretary of State may also issue a certificate of lawful use or development under section 191: TCPA 1990, section 177(1)(c). Where such a power is at issue during the appeal the LPA should particularly address the need for specificity in the terms of any such certificate. The discussion in para 3.5.8 regarding the problems raised by open sites used as 'haulage depots', 'vehicle parks' etc should be noted and the inspector should be referred to the discussion of such problems in circular 17/92. Failure to specify the lawful use carefully will put the local environment at risk from intensification and other changes in the use which will not be amenable to control.

7.7.6　Make an award of costs

Parties to an enforcement appeal should, if they want to seek costs, make an application for costs at the appropriate stage of the proceedings[1]. Normally such an application and the supporting arguments will come at the end of closing submissions by the main parties. (In the case of written representations the circular requires that an application for costs be made to the DOE before the inspector's site-inspection as it should then be clear from the parties' statements as to whether a claim can be substantiated[2].) Annex 5 of the circular also discusses late applications, full and partial awards etc. The costs application must be supported in the normal fashion by reference primarily to the circular. There are particular issues that need highlighting in enforcement cases.

1　Circular 8/93, Annex 1, para 6, indent (1). Annex 5 (addressing the topic of the costs application) devotes seven paragraphs to the relevant issues.
2　Ibid Annex 5, para 3.

7.7.6.1　*Basic principles*

The basic grounds for a costs application are:

    (a)　unreasonable conduct by the other party;
    (b)　which causes the party applying for costs to incur expense unnecessarily.

These fundamental criteria are set out in Annex 1, paragraph 6 of the circular (indents (2) and (3)).

7.7.6.2 *Wasted costs*

The TCPA 1990, section 322A empowers the inspector to award costs which have been wasted by appeal parties through withdrawal of an appeal. This covers situations where the LPA withdraws one or more grounds in its case. Paragraphs 13 and 14 of Annex 1 discuss such orders.

7.7.6.3 *Quantum*

The amount of costs recoverable will be the costs 'necessarily and reasonably incurred in relation to the proceedings'[1]. These provisos are particularly relevant for the LPA which may find that large claims are put forward by professional advisers of appellants. The LPA facing an award of costs should therefore consider (when defending their positions against a costs application) the 'necessarily and reasonably incurred' criteria that are applied to the 'quantum' of costs recoverable. It does not seem 'reasonable' of an appellant to claim the costs of expensive professional advisers on a minor matter which could easily have been handled by written representations. Even if the appellant has been unreasonably led into taking unnecessary action to cover issues that are not relevant it does not seem reasonable of the appellant to then go overboard and employ the most expensive advisers.

1 Circular 8/93, Annex 5, para 4.

7.7.7 Awards against authorities

Authorities who have not complied with government advice on procedure and substance may well find themselves facing a costs application. However, this should not be seen as an excuse for not taking action: in cases where the more subjective impacts of a contravention are relevant the LPA will have greater scope for resisting a costs application. If clear and justifiable development plan policy on enforcement can be called in aid, it is clear that the LPA will also have a stronger argument both on the planning merits of the case and any costs application. The most relevant criterion of those included is the guidance on the unreasonable issue of an enforcement notice (paragraphs 21 to 25 of Annex 3 to circular 8/93. (Other guidance in the circular is not discussed in detail below.)

7.7.7.1   *Unreasonable issue of notice*

The impact of government advice on the 'expediency' of enforcement action will be important in assessing the unreasonableness of taking action. Paragraph 22 of Annex 3 stresses the need for 'care' on the part of the LPA to take account of the legal rules, PPG18's advice on enforcement and 'well-publicised appeal decisions'. Paragraph 22 later accepts that interpreting the law can be difficult and so reliance on a legal interpretation that is later seen to be erroneous will not necessarily lead to a costs award. Paragraph 23 addresses the role of the planning contravention notice in all this. The advice states that it '. . . is not intended that an authority's enforcement decision, when reasonably taken in the circumstances, should put them at risk of an award of appeals costs because they decided not to serve a planning contravention notice'.

Paragraph 24 indicates that issuing an enforcement notice to enable a breach to be regularised would be viewed as unreasonable if there was no 'significant planning objection' to the contravention. The advice in PPG18, paragraphs 5–22 is stated as being relevant to the decision as to the reasonable taking of enforcement action. LPAs should ensure that where they are pushed into action by neighbours then those neighbours should be prepared to write in to the DOE with their 'planning objections'. Again, neighbour complaint can be a very important element at appeal – not only as regards the substantive issues but also in respect of costs. One fundamental issue in all this should not be forgotten by the LPA. The advice is not necessarily comprehensive. Indeed, the costs circular fails to cover the 'systemic' consideration that is found in all enforcement cases (to a lesser or greater degree). This is the 'integrity' factor noted in PPG18, paragraph 4. That paragraph expressly refers to the 'integrity' of the planning system; contraventions, if not effectively controlled, could lead to a perception that planning is a paper tiger. Yet this factor (as important as prematurity, precedent and other similar 'systemic' considerations in the development control context) is ignored in the costs circular. The LPA should therefore consider justifying its reliance (in appropriate cases) on this factor even if it does not fall within the referenced parts of PPG18. It may also be (from the more strategic side of enforcement as part of the planning trinity) relevant to consider how forward planning policy in the development plan can be used as the basis for justifying action in cases where the planning system's 'integrity' is at risk.

Another weakness in the advice is its focus on local amenity impacts. Paragraph 24 requires that LPAs show that '. . . they had reasonable grounds for concluding that the breach of control would unacceptably affect public amenity, or the existing use of land and buildings meriting protection in the public interest . . .'. However, the focus of planning (and this reflects the broader 'environmental law' component that is relevant to effective enforcement) now goes beyond this narrow 'micro-spatial' focus. Planning (under the influence of sustainable development) is now addressing impacts that are beyond those of the immediate neighbourhood, town, city or region. The spectrum of planning impacts ranges from these micro-spatial elements of the continuum through to the macro-spatial elements which reflect global 'amenity' concerns. The relevance of sustainable development to enforcement may not be the principal concern of LPAs at the moment as they struggle to address the demands of sustainability in terms of development plan policy. However, it is clearly possible that the longer term and cumulative impacts of certain types of contraventions will have significance for the macro-spatial dimension even if, at the local level, the breach appears to be of minor significance. For example, a condition requiring the use of sustainably managed timber products would cause 'no harm to amenity in the locality of the site' (as paragraph 5, indent (5) of PPG18 phrases the test for reasonable enforcement action). However, that breach cumulatively and indeed of its own account may well make a significant impact on the wider environmental amenity which is the concern of sustainable development. Again the policy basis for enforcement action (as strengthened by section 54A) may be relevant here in supplementing the narrower focus of the enforcement advice in circulars and PPGs. If LPAs are to resist the constricting effects of that advice they must be able to rely on sound planning and legal analysis that shows how their concerns fall within the legal ambit of their powers and have significance beyond that accorded by DOE statements.

7.7.7.2   *Use of stop notice or BCN*

Although the authority may have disregarded DOE advice and issued a stop notice this would not seem to be a valid ground on which to award costs. There is no appeal against a stop notice (other than judicial review) and so the existence of the stop notice will not be a matter for the inspector on appeal. There will therefore be no expense incurred by the appellant in the handling of his appeal and so no sum compensating him can be awarded. Similar considerations apply to the BCN power: this is perhaps one advantage of the BCN power in that there is no appeal to the Secretary of State and so no costs sanction from that quarter.

7.7.7.3   *Flawed enforcement notices*

An appeal decided on 11 June 1987 raises problems. In this ministerial decision on costs the Secretary of State examined an appeal lodged against an enforcement notice which was technically incorrect. The notice should have been directed to non-compliance with the conditions attached to a planning permission – apparently it alleged an unauthorised material change of use. The Secretary of State stated that the council 'acted unreasonably in considering it expedient to serve the notice, which was palpably wrong, and that they should reimburse your clients the unnecessary expense they incurred in pursuing the matter to inquiry'[1]. Such a conclusion might be seen as increasingly harsh if more emphasis is placed on the power to correct notices (after the *Ahern* case) so that such errors are no longer likely to survive the correction power and so lead to a quashing of notices. However, this case illustrates the need for the LPA to ensure that forceful arguments are advanced at appeal to ensure that the correction power is used (perhaps allowing for the appellant to alter his grounds of appeal) to rectify all but the most flawed of notices.

There are examples however where legal flaws in the notice did not constitute 'unreasonable behaviour' by the LPA[2]. In this appeal the appellant had argued that the LPA had failed to take into account the advice in Annex B of circular 22/80. The council however pointed to the sensitive nature of the site and the use (green belt and non-conforming vehicle-orientated use) and the unco-operative stance taken by the contravener. The inspector found that he could not correct the notice – even though it was his duty 'to get the notice in order' because this would cause injustice: the appellant would be deprived of the opportunity of arguing that there was an established use. However, as 'it may well be that it is only as a result of this inquiry that [the LPA] have become fully informed as to what that primary use is' the inspector concluded that the LPA had not acted unreasonably.

In another costs case it was accepted as relevant by the Secretary of State that the onus of proof in relation to appeals on the ground that the LPA is time-barred rests with the appellant – this would imply that the amount of investigation that may be reasonably required of the authority is less than that required of the appellant[3]. In this case written evidence from the previous owner was made available at a late stage – the council promptly acted on this evidence and withdrew the enforcement notice. This meant that 'the council were able to show a material change in planning circumstances between the issue of the enforcement notice on 10 January 1985 and its withdrawal on 29 November 1985 and it is not accepted therefore that your clients were put to unnecessary unreasonable expense of an appeal by the council's actions'. The council had, until then, relied on a previous decision of the Secretary of State which had indicated that there was a breach of planning control. Their issue of the notice and its late withdrawal did not therefore constitute unreasonable behaviour. The Secretary of State accepted in another decision[4] that:

> 'the facts concerning the use of land and premises and the duration of that use are peculiarly within the knowledge of the owner and occupier and that a local planning authority in deciding to take enforcement action can only act on such information as they themselves have. Therefore, in enforcement appeals the onus of proof rests on the person appealing and it is not for the council to prove the case against an appellant company but for the appellant company to establish the facts and grounds on which they rely.'

1 Huntingdonshire District Council, DOE ref APP/H0520/C/86/1207, reported in [1988] JPL 58.
2 South Buckinghamshire District Council, DOE ref T/APP/N0410/ C/86/2138/P6, decision letter dated 8 November 1987, reported in [1988] JPL 291.

3   Vale Royal District Council, DOE ref APP/L0635/C/85/981, decision
    letter dated 27 May 1987, reported in [1988] JPL 63.
4   DOE ref APP/C/87/Z3635/8, decision letter dated 26 October 1988,
    reported in [1989] JPL 124, at 125.

7.7.7.4   *Judicial review*

Since the decision as to costs is not a decision as to the
enforcement notice appeal but a decision under the Local
Government Act the LPA will have to challenge such a decision
by way of judicial review. Where it considers that the terms of
the discretionary power have been exceeded or not properly
applied then a challenge on ultra vires principles is subject to
the rules and procedures relating to judicial review and not
those relating to the procedures under the TCPA 1990 for
challenging decisions. An example of such a challenge is to be
found in *R v Secretary of State for the Environment, ex p North
Norfolk District Council* where the inspector's reasoning in
making an award was unclear[1].

1   [1994] EGCS 131.

7.7.8   **Awards against appellants**

If the LPA is intending to ask for a costs award then generally
it should have laid the groundwork for such an application early
on: paragraph 6 of Annex 3 to the costs circular emphasises that
the LPA should draw the attention of the appellant to the
relevant facts and to the possible consequences of persisting
with the unreasonable behaviour. This is evident in decisions on
costs[1].

1   For example, Cotswold District Council, DOE ref APP/F1610/C/85/
    3365, decision letter dated 22 April 1987, reported in [1988] JPL 67.

7.7.8.1   *Playing the system*

Paragraph 1 of Annex 3 states that the 'right of appeal is a
statutory right, but it should be exercised in a reasonable
manner'. This statement of principle would seem to support an

application for costs made by the LPA when it considers (with justification) that the appeal should have been handled (more quickly and more cheaply) by written representations rather than public inquiry.

7.8 THE APPEAL DECISION

Another stage (similar to the finalisation of the enforcement authorisation report) where a screening procedure might be instigated is when the appeal decision is received. The most obvious type of decision to screen for legal errors is the decision quashing the notice and granting permission – particularly if the absolutist version of the nullity principle appears to have held sway. The LPA may also wish to screen decisions where notices are upheld but the requirements of a notice are varied. The arguments at the appeal stage may often give some warning of possible legal difficulties which may merit checking when the decision comes in. An appropriate and targeted screening procedure should thus be set up to deal with appeal decisions that are likely to generate legal errors.

7.8.1 Challenges by the contravener

If the contravener challenges a decision to uphold an enforcement notice the LPA may, understandably, wish to take a low-key role. However, such proceedings should be kept under review and the LPA's position should be protected by taking an active (though subsidiary) role. In taking such a position the LPA can then keep under review the position of the DOE and step in where necessary if it considers that the DOE is not adequately dealing with points of law to the satisfaction of the LPA. Conflicts between the LPA and the DOE over a number of issues that affect enforcement (eg the 'statutory' considerations arising from the conservation area test and the listed building test as discussed in chapter five) are clearly areas where disagreement could arise.

7.8.2 Corrections and variations

Where the decision has effected corrections or variations to the enforcement notice then the LPA must ensure that the copies of the enforcement notice kept in the LPA's records are amended. Clearly, apart from complying with the requirements to update the register such amendments are also desirable to ensure that compliance checks by enforcement officers are carried out at the appropriate times. Such checks will also have to be looking for the correct 'steps'. Administrative procedures to make the appropriate amendments consequent upon a varied or corrected enforcement notice are thus very important.

7.8.3 Legal challenges to the appeal decision

Section 289 covers appeals on points of law to the High Court against decisions made in relation to enforcement notice appeals. In *Clarke v Secretary of State for the Environment*, the Court of Appeal emphasised this point when ruling that the Divisional Court judge had been wrong to consider affidavit evidence under section 289 and found that the inspector's findings of fact were perverse[1]. Thus the court should not hear evidence under this section unless it is in support of an argument that the inspector had not properly summarised the issues or had not taken relevant evidence into account. A significant change made to this provision as a result of the Carnwath Report was the introduction of a requirement for leave. This and related changes to the legal principles covering challenges to decisions of the inspector or Secretary of State need to be well-understood by the LPA if the determined contravener is to be prevented from playing the system and delaying enforcement. The principles will also be relevant where the LPA wishes to challenge decisions made on appeal: both decisions relating to the enforcement notice and the grant of planning permission are challengeable under this provision. However, in cases where the appeal decision has been to (mistakenly) find that the notice is a nullity and of no effect at all the LPA will need to use the judicial review route under RSC Order 53 etc. In this case, naturally, promptness is crucial and the judicial review case law on this issue will need to be borne in mind.

1 [1992] 3 PLR 146.

7.8.3.1 *Application for leave*

The application for leave must be made within 28 days from date of receipt of the decision[1]. The applicant must have an 'arguable case' in order to successfully apply for leave[2]. If no miscarriage of justice has occurred then leave will be refused[3]. In addition to the statutory provisions of section 289 there are also RSC provisions and a Practice Direction issued by the Lord Chief Justice on 25 October 1994 (see *The Independent*, 2 November 1994). These address the more detailed aspect of challenging enforcement notice appeal decisions and so will need to be borne in mind by the LPA when challenging or resisting a challenge to an enforcement notice appeal.

If the High Court refuses leave to appeal to it under the TCPA 1990, section 289(6) this refusal cannot then be appealed to the Court of Appeal[4]. The Court of Appeal has no inherent jurisdiction therefore to hear a challenge: the court came to this view on the basis of authority from non-planning regimes and also on a purposive interpretation of the legislation which, as per the 1991 reforms, was aimed at preventing unmeritorious appeals. Although the TCPA 1990, section 289(1) envisages an alternative procedure whereby the Secretary of State for the Environment can be required by a party to state and sign a case for the opinion of the High Court the necessary rules have not been made: this procedure would undoubtedly be useful (given the number of legal issues that are unresolved in the field of enforcement) but is not available in practice[5].

1 *Ynys Mon Borough Council v Secretary of State for the Environment* [1992] 3 PLR 1 following the unreported Court of Appeal case of *Smith v Secretary of State for the Environment* (1987) Times, 6 July.
2 *R v Secretary of State for the Environment and Gojkovic, ex p Kensington & Chelsea Royal London Borough Council* [1993] JPL 139.
3 *PG Vallance Ltd v Secretary of State for the Environment* [1994] JPL 50.
4 *Huggett v Secretary of State for the Environment* (1995) Times, 1 March.
5 *Hoser v Minister of Housing and Local Government* [1963] Ch 428.

7.8.3.2 *Enforcement notice – effective during appeal*

The LPA, at the leave stage, should routinely consider liaising with the DOE in making a case for the court exercising its discretion under the TCPA 1990, section 289(4A) to order that the notice shall have effect (in whole or in part) pending the final determination of the proceedings. Naturally, such submissions will be more likely to succeed if the harm occasioned by the breach can be shown to be significant and the grounds of appeal are based on 'technical' issues: again development plan policy relating to the enforcement action will be relevant and useful – the planning trinity perspective on enforcement will enable the LPA to make a strong case for the court exercising its discretion.

7.8.3.3 *Remission to Secretary of State*

If the appeal succeeds then the court can only remit the matter to the Secretary of State with the opinion of the court for his rehearing and redetermination[1]. He is then able to hear the issues de novo: the Secretary of State will deal with the matter himself and recover the appeal if necessary.

1 RSC Ord 94, r 13(7).

7.9 DEEMED GRANTS OF PERMISSION

The works required by an enforcement notice will often constitute 'development'. There is therefore the small detail of the system ensuring that planning permission is granted for operational development carried out in compliance with an enforcement notice. The TCPA 1990, section 173(12) deals with a common situation involving such development: the 'replacement building' which is required to be built after unlawful demolition. (The TCPA 1990, section 173(6) and (7) address action required by the notice in this respect.) Subsection (12) operates to grant permission (by virtue of section 73A) for the construction of a 'replacement building' where the requirements of the notice have been met. Another use of section 73A is found in subsection (11): in this case permission is treated as having been granted for those elements involved in the contravention that could have been, but were not, tackled by the notice. This provision thus regularises elements of the contravening development (be it operational or change of use) where the enforcement notice has been complied with and (presumably by design) that notice does not require action to deal with such elements of the contravening development.

7.9.1 Mixed uses, deemed permission and intensification

The provisions of the TCPA 1990, section 173(11) can have unfortunate effects if the LPA is not careful in its approach to contraventions involving a range of uses – some of which are acceptable on planning grounds. If the LPA only issues a notice tackling the problem uses it may find that the TCPA 1990, section 173(1) operates so as to give those 'acceptable' uses planning permission. This means that the uses cannot be controlled as regards future intensification because of the impact of this provision. However, intensification is often an underlying problem with a range of uses and so the LPA must be awake to the fact that an acceptable use may become unacceptable later by virtue of intensification. The LPA should therefore be very careful when leaving some uses out of the enforcement notice where those uses could later develop into problems. The TCPA 1990, section 173(11) can all too easily produce problems akin to those of a widely drawn certificate of lawful use: see also the discussion in chapter three. A grant of planning permission (perhaps on appeal) that is tightly constrained may be one answer: the LPA may also argue that the inspector require a planning obligation to be entered into that restricts the ability of the occupier to intensify the 'acceptable' use. The planning obligation would thus constrain the use of the permission granted under this provision.

7.10 THE CONTINUING EFFECT OF AN ENFORCEMENT NOTICE

An effective enforcement notice, like a planning permission, runs with the land to which it relates. The impact of a subsequent permission (that covers development to the notice applies) on the notice is a matter of detail which the TCPA 1990 addresses. The risk also that the owner may try to 'resurrect' the contravention is a similar issue of the long-term impact of the notice.

7.10.1   Notice superseded by later permission

When permission is granted for development which has already been subject of an enforcement or breach of condition notice then the enforcement notice (or breach of condition notice) still remains in existence. The later permission merely means that the relevant notice shall 'cease to have effect so far as inconsistent with that permission'[1]. Thus an authority which decides (after 'service of a copy of an enforcement notice') to grant permission for the contravention should also (where there is an appeal) ensure that the notice is withdrawn. If this is not done then the appellant may still continue with his enforcement appeal and claim costs[2] – see earlier on the costs issue. The fact that an enforcement notice or breach of condition notice has wholly or partly ceased to have effect under this provision does not affect the liability of any person for an offence relating to a previous failure to comply with that notice[3]. The realities of prosecution however may make prosecution in such circumstances a rather academic issue.

1   TCPA 1990, s 180(1)(a); para (b) applies the rule to breach of condition notices.
2   As happened in *R v Secretary of State for the Environment, ex p Three Rivers District Council* [1983] JPL 730.
3   TCPA 1990, s 180(3).

7.10.2   Effect against subsequent development

Even where the requirements in an enforcement notice have been carried out such compliance 'shall not discharge the notice'[1]. The principle that the enforcement notice continues to have effect in relation to the land covered by the notice is given further elaboration in subsection (2). This subsection states that where a notice requires that the use of land be discontinued then that shall be interpreted as meaning that the use shall be discontinued 'permanently'. Such a prohibition operates against a use 'to the extent that it is in contravention of Part III': this provision in the legislation emphasises the importance of the principle (the *Mansi* doctrine) that an enforcement notice should not prohibit any use that is incidental or ancillary to a primary use that can be carried out without being in contravention of Part III[2]. This provision in the statute mirrors that doctrine. The subsection goes on to say that the resumption of a use which has been required to be discontinued will therefore be in contravention of an enforcement notice even though that use was discontinued in compliance with the enforcement notice at an earlier stage.

Subsection (3) deals with the parallel situation where compliance with the notice relates to operational development. Where there has been compliance with an enforcement notice requiring removal or alteration of works but at a later date such works are reinstated or restored then a special offence is committed under the TCPA 1990, section 181(5). Thus a person who carries out any development on the land by way of reinstating or restoring buildings or works which have been removed or altered in compliance with an enforcement notice shall be guilty of an offence. The offence is summary and is subject to a fine not exceeding level 5 on the standard scale (see para 9.6.11 for the current scale of fines). It is important to note that the criminal offences under section 179 do not apply as respect any failure to take any steps required by an enforcement notice by way of removal or alteration of what has been so reinstated or restored. The LPA may of course use its works in default power against such reinstatement or restoration of authorised works. However, the TCPA 1990, section 181(4)(b) requires that if the LPA do propose to take any steps required by an enforcement notice for the demolition or alteration of the building or works then it must 'serve on the owner and occupier of the land a notice of their intention to do so' at least 28 days before taking any such steps.

1   TCPA 1990, s 181(1).
2   *Mansi v Elstree RDC* (1964) 16 P & CR 153. The case of *Swinbank v Secretary of State for the Environment* (1987) 55 P & CR 371 suggests that *Mansi* establishes a rule of construction for those interpreting an enforcement notice addressing a breach involving a change of use. The *Mansi* doctrine therefore tells the court (both criminal and civil) and the inspector how to construe any requirements regarding the cessation of activities: those activities that are ancillary to lawful uses should not therefore be construed as falling within any prohibition.

8   Stop notices

8.1   INTRODUCTION

The following statement from a report of the Commissioner for Local Administration[1] notes a phenomenon that is probably quite widespread amongst local planning authorities. Thus the investigator found that:

> 'Officer E said that it is a matter of "policy" not to serve stop notices. The council has since told me that a stop notice is regarded as a last resort in extreme cases, following a period of negotiations.'

Such a 'policy' not to serve stop notices may often stem from a rather pessimistic picture of compensation liability painted by the legal department. Such a picture is often readily accepted by senior officers unwilling to risk resources. However, as is apparent from the following discussion, compensation liability (especially where the LPA is reasonably well organised as regards the drawing up and issue of enforcement notices and stop notices) is not going to be a major problem.

1   560/H/80.

8.2   THE DISCRETION TO ISSUE – REVIEW BY THE COURTS

Although the power to issue a stop notice is drafted in very wide terms it is not appropriate to think of this discretion as an 'unfettered discretion'. Case law from the rating regime illustrates the care needed when describing discretionary powers (such as the power to serve stop notices – and enforcement notices) that seem to be widely drawn. Thus the Court of Appeal in the case of *R v Rochdale Metropolitan Borough Council, ex p*

194

Cromer Ring Mill Ltd[1] criticised the Divisional Court's use of
the 'unfettered discretion' phrase in connection with a power
under section 9 of the General Rate Act 1967. The Court of
Appeal said that the epithet 'unfettered' was misleading. The
effect of case law (primarily *Wednesbury* principles) meant that
the discretion was by no means an unfettered one. It quoted
with approval the observations of Cumming-Bruce LJ in *R v
Liverpool City Council, ex p Windsor Securities Ltd*[2] where it
was said (in relation to another discretion under the Rating
Act):

> 'In the exercise of that discretion the authority has to behave fairly.
> It must direct itself properly in law. It must direct its attention to
> the matters which it is bound to consider. It must exclude from its
> considerations matters which are irrelevant.'

If the LPA does not obey those rules it may be said to be acting
unreasonably – see *Associated Provincial Picture Houses Ltd v
Wednesbury Corpn*[3]. Likewise the LPA must not so act as to
frustrate the object and purpose of the statute conferring the
power[4]. So a statutory discretion cannot necessarily be accurately
described as an 'unfettered discretion' even if it does, on a prima
facie literal interpretation of the provision concerned, appear to
be very widely drawn.

1   [1982] 3 All ER 761.
2   [1979] RA 159.
3   [1948] 1 KB 223, [1947] 2 All ER 680.
4   *Padfield v Minster of Agriculture, Fisheries and Food* [1968] AC
    997, [1968] 1 All ER 694.

8.2.1   The discretion to issue – practical matters

The stop notice power (although it relies primarily on the rather
unpredictable sanction of a criminal prosecution) can be a very
powerful tool in the authority's armoury. It can only be used
where an enforcement notice has already set out a breach of
planning control (be it operational or change of use in nature)
and requires such breach to be remedied by the cessation of
some activity. The term 'activity' is found in the legislation and
means that a stop notice can prohibit both use breaches and
operational breaches *in flagrante delicto*. A notable feature of
the stop notice is that it cannot be appealed: the only challenge
would be by way of judicial review – the above comments will

therefore be relevant when the LPA is considering the use of this power. Further 'legal' issues arise from the fact that the stop notice is intended to be a short-term expedient to deal with the problem of an activity which needs controlling before the enforcement notice takes effect. Therefore, the LPA must be sure of its legal position as regards the 'underlying' enforcement notice.

8.2.1.1 *Stopping 'relevant activities'*

The LPA may issue a stop notice prohibiting the carrying out of any 'relevant activity' covered by an enforcement where they 'consider it expedient that any relevant activity should cease before the expiry of the period for compliance with [that] enforcement notice[1]'. The term 'relevant activity' means 'activity specified in the enforcement notice as an activity which the local planning authority require to cease and any activity carried out as part of that activity or associated with that activity'. This definition allows the LPA to focus, if it wants to limit its action, on 'ancillary' activities which are, in fact, the main problem in terms of amenity impacts: in effect the stop notice can be designed to 'under-enforce' and so only attack the real problems if the LPA so considers it appropriate. This definition suggests that if the LPA is concerned only with a particular aspect of the contravention in its consideration of a stop notice then any authorisation report should address 'under-enforcement' and consider the practicality of serving a stop notice that concentrates on such aspects of the contravention. Failure to take account of the flexibility provided by the statute could provide ammunition for the recipient to challenge the notice via judicial review proceedings. Naturally the LPA will be able to argue that the practicalities of enforcing (eg by way of a prosecution in the magistrates' court) may justify a simpler blanket notice as proving non-compliance in criminal proceedings may be difficult and so defeat the underlying purpose of the legislation. This issue is another type of 'systemic' consideration which has relevance in the enforcement regime.

1   TCPA 1990, s 183(1).

8.2.1.2 *Activities that cannot be prohibited*

A stop notice cannot prohibit:

    (a) the use of any building as a dwellinghouse[1]; and
    (b) an activity that has been carried out for more than four
        years ending with the service of the notice[2].

In the case of the second limitation any period during which that
activity continued by virtue of a planning permission is not to be
included in computing the four-year period: this avoids problems
caused by time-limited permissions which are then contravened
after the time-limit condition bites. If the notice purports to
prohibit the use of any building as a dwellinghouse yet also
covers lawful prohibitions then it will not be void entirely. The
invalid prohibitions can be ignored – they do not invalidate the
stop notice in toto and so valid prohibitions are still effective.
This is clear from the case of *Runnymede Borough Council v
Smith*[3].

1 TCPA 1990, s 183(4).
2 TCPA 1990, s 183(5). By virtue of subsection (5A) this provision
    does not prevent a stop notice prohibiting any activity consisting of,
    or incidental to, building, engineering, mining or other operations
    or the deposit of refuse or waste materials.
3 [1986] JPL 592.

8.2.1.3 *The expediency criterion – circular 21/91*

Circular 21/91, Annex 3 sets out the DOE's advice on the
'expediency' of stop notice action. Paragraphs 20–24 set out the
cost-benefit analysis which, in the view of the DOE, is the
appropriate way to exercise the broad discretion under section
183. The language in those paragraphs reflects the emphasis on
protecting the local 'neighbourhood' and its amenity. This focus
is clearly aimed at giving weight to very localised impacts –
impacts on local people and their amenity. However, the LPA
may well (from the viewpoint of the wider aspects of planning
and sustainable development) wish to use the stop notice power
to deal with harmful impacts that affect a much wider
'community' than the local neighbourhood. Such a concern is not
'unlawful' given the broad scope of planning control, but clearly
the recipient of a stop notice that is based on such considerations

is very likely to challenge the use of the stop notice power in this way. The more restrictive advice in circular 21/91 will inevitably be used in any such challenge and so the LPA should be sure that it does not prejudice its case by apparently 'ignoring' the circular. The LPA should rather discuss the circular but point out that other factors of a planning nature, not noted in the circular, are even more important than the circular's advice on the local amenity impacts. Litigation involving a market use on green belt illustrates the problems that may be encountered when the LPA prefers to use the discretion in a way which seemingly overrides DOE policy[1]. The circular does contain very useful summaries of the legal position affecting compensation etc which local authorities and others should study. However, it should be remembered that as the service of a stop notice cannot be challenged by an appeal to the Secretary of State then any views he might have about 'expediency' are a matter of his opinion only. As long as the authority is not manifestly unreasonable in its use of a stop notice (so that judicial review of the decision to issue would be possible) then the authority will be safe.

1   *R v Elmbridge Borough Council, ex p Wendy Fair Markets Ltd* [1994] EGCS 159. The High Court upheld the approach of the LPA holding that the circular's advice was advisory and not binding where the LPA had planning arguments justifying its approach. The green belt factors meant that the LPA was entitled to come to a view that the cost-benefit analysis was inappropriate.

8.2.2   Stop notices and special planning interests

There are no listed building stop notices and so a breach of listed building control (that is not accompanied by a breach of 'normal' planning control) cannot be tackled by a stop notice. The authority should consider an injunction if the damage to the listed building will be significant. If a listed building is affected by a normal breach of planning control then a stop notice can be used on the back of an ordinary enforcement notice. If the breach of control involves an 'activity' that has unwelcome effects on a conservation area then the 'character' element in the conservation area test (P(LB&CA)A 1990, section 72) will be relevant in the exercise of the discretion. Since the term 'character' seems to cover both the visual and the use elements of a conservation area then an 'activity' which does not preserve or enhance such elements (cf the wording of the conservation area test) would seem to warrant particular attention from the LPA as regards the stop notice power.

There may be occasions where a stop notice can be used against a use comprising an illegally displayed advertisement. If the advertisement is displayed on an external part of a building (or open land) not normally used for that purpose then there is a material change of use: if it is illegally displayed (ie is not in accordance with the advertisement regulations) then the TCPA 1990, section 222 deemed grant of planning permission will not operate and so there will be an unauthorised change of use of that part of the building. A stop notice (on the back of an enforcement notice) can thus be issued to deal with the problem. If the display affects a listed building or is within a conservation area then clearly the LPA may well wish to take such action. A fuller discussion of advertisement control issues is found in chapter twelve.

8.2.3 Contents etc

A stop notice must:

   (a) refer to the enforcement notice to which it relates[1];
   (b) have a copy of that notice annexed to it[2];
   (c) specify the date on which it will take effect[3];
   (d) state the activity prohibited by the notice[4].

It is important therefore that the authority ensures that the enforcement notice is properly referenced in the stop notice and that a copy of that enforcement notice is attached to it.

1 TCPA 1990, s 184(1).
2 TCPA 1990, s 184(1).
3 TCPA 1990, s 184(2).
4 TCPA 1990, s 183(1).

8.2.4 Construction of a stop notice

A stop notice may incorporate the terms of an enforcement notice and thus be read in conjunction with the enforcement notice if there are problems in interpretation – *Bristol Stadium*

Ltd v Brown[1]. However, a stop notice that relies on an enforcement notice whose description of the breach does not cover the prohibited activity in the stop notice will be invalid.

1   [1980] JPL 107.

8.2.5 'Activity' and 'breach'

The legislation states that the carrying out of any activity 'which is, or is included in, a matter alleged' by the relevant enforcement notice 'to constitute the breach' of planning control can be the subject of a stop notice. This language clearly indicates the necessary nexus between the enforcement notice and the stop notice – an example of which is found above in the note on the *Bristol Stadium* case. The particular key term for analysis here is 'breach'. Any activity that 'is, or is included in, a matter alleged' to constitute the 'breach' can figure in a stop notice. In the TCPA 1990, section 171A(1) we are told that a breach of planning control may consist of the failure to comply with a condition. Thus failure to comply with a condition (if it involves an activity) can be subjected to stop notice action. The clearest example is failure to comply with a condition that restricts the use of land. If a condition dealing with hours of working is breached then failure to comply with that condition would clearly involve an 'activity' which 'is, or is included in, a matter alleged' to constitute the breach of control. The 'activity' would seem to be the use of the premises beyond the stated time.

Where a breach of control involves a condition that requires positive action then it will be more difficult to tackle such a breach by a stop notice. Unless the condition is a condition precedent it will be difficult to justify the assertion that the non-compliance with the condition involves an 'activity'. An 'activity' is something involving positive action and 'inaction' would thus not be covered. However, if the breach involved non-compliance with a precondition (eg the submission of detailed plans etc) then it would seem that commencement of development (the carrying out of building works) would be an 'activity' which 'is, or is included in, a matter alleged' to constitute the breach of control.

8.3 DATE OF EFFECTIVENESS

The notice must contain a date on which it becomes effective[1]. This cannot be later than 28 days from the day on which it is first served[2]. As regards the 'start date' for the prohibitions contained in the stop notice the legislation sets out alternatives. First the stop notice can take effect not less than 3 days from service[3]. This three-day hiatus, however, could well allow the contravener to carry out works whose impact could not easily be remedied. Therefore the second scenario allowed by the legislation envisages that if there are 'special reasons' for so requiring the stop notice may 'specify an earlier date'[4]. In such a case the LPA must ensure that 'a statement of those special reasons is served with the stop notice'[5]. In the case of 'immediate effect' stop notices therefore the LPA *must* ensure that the date of service and the date of effectiveness are the same and both are clearly set out in the notice; a 'special reasons' schedule might routinely be attached to the standard-form stop notice used by the LPA so that there is less risk of a separately produced statement being mislaid or forgotten in such cases. (In ordinary 'three-day' stop notices this schedule can be easily struck out.) However, if the activity is very damaging to planning interests (eg demolition works threatening a listed building) then the authority should consider applying to the High Court for an injunction[6].

1 TCPA 1990, s 184(2).
2 TCPA 1990, s 184(3)(b).
3 TCPA 1990, s 184(3)(a).
4 Ibid.
5 Ibid.
6 See the discussion of injunctive relief in chapter nine.

8.3.1 Entry in the register

The register required by the TCPA 1990, section 188(1) covers both enforcement and stop notices. The development order prescribing the appropriate information is the Town and Country Planning (General Development Procedure) Order 1995, SI 1995/419.

8.4 SERVICE

The authority should serve a stop notice 'on any person who appears to them to have an interest in the land or to be engaged in any activity prohibited by the notice[1]'. The various modes of service of documents on owners, occupiers etc are discussed in chapter six. The legislation clearly envisages the service of such notices on builders etc, 'engaged in' works of construction etc, on the land. Given the breadth of liability for contravention of a stop notice (it also covers those 'causing or permitting' contraventions) it is also important to ensure that professionals not directly engaged in the prohibited activity can be targetted – this can be done by posting a site notice (they would not appear to fall within the provisions of section 183(6) as regards service). Since the ultimate sanction is a prosecution the LPA should naturally try to serve all those who may have to be prosecuted. The comments in chapter nine regarding prosecutions and the position of 'aiders and abetters' (para 9.6.10) also underline the importance of aiming not only at owners and occupiers but also any contractors and professionals directly involved in the contravening activity.

1 TCPA 1990, s 183(6).

8.4.1 Site notice

It is important to note that the authority is empowered to display a site notice where a stop has been served in respect of any land[1]. The site notice should state:

(a) that a stop notice has been served;
(b) that any person contravening it may be prosecuted for an offence under section 187 of the TCPA 1990;
(c) the date when the stop notice takes effect;
(d) the requirements of the stop notice[2].

Site notices should routinely be used since their presence is a good way of helping to ensure compliance with the notice – see the later discussion of prosecutions. Another reason for always using a site notice is that the statutory defence in section 183(3) is more difficult to prove if a site notice has been displayed because then the defendant will find it difficult to prove that he 'could not reasonably have known' of the existence of the stop notice: the statutory defence is discussed below.

1 TCPA 1990, s 184(6).
2 Ibid.

8.4.2   Time of service

The 1991 reforms allow service of the stop notice to be carried out simultaneously with the enforcement notice or afterwards[1]. This has removed the problems created by case law on the unamended provision which raised doubts as to the legality of such service. The stop notice must be served before the enforcement notice takes effect[2]. Where the contravener is unco-operative or his activities on the site increase and make a significant impact on the locality the LPA may well wish to serve a stop notice even when an appeal is in progress: a costs award cannot be made on the basis that the LPA has issued a stop notice. This sanction (available to the LPA because the enforcement notice appeal 'freezes' the enforcement notice and prevents it from taking effect) may thus still be of use in appropriate cases until the enforcement notice is quashed or (as upheld) then takes effect.

1 TCPA 1990, s 183(3).
2 Ibid.

8.4.3   Bad service of enforcement notice

Sometimes a copy of the underlying enforcement notice may not have been served properly. However, if the LPA demonstrates that it 'took all such steps as were reasonably practicable to effect proper service' then bad service will not make the stop notice invalid[1]. This may be important in judicial review or criminal proceedings.

1 TCPA 1990, s 184(8).

8.5 WITHDRAWAL

A stop notice may be withdrawn at any time by serving notice to that effect on persons served with the notice[1]. If a site notice has been put up then a notice of the withdrawal 'in place of the site notice' should be displayed[2]. Since withdrawal may give rise to a compensation claim under section 186(1)(d) the authority should be careful about withdrawing a notice if its issue has caused loss[3]. If the withdrawal is part of a negotiated resolution of a problem the authority should ensure (in the enforcement agreement) that its position as regards compensation liability is protected.

1 TCPA 1990, s 183(7).
2 TCPA 1990, s 184(7).
3 See further on compensation below.

8.6 STOP NOTICE NULLIFIED

A stop notice ceases to have effect in four circumstances and ceases to exist in one – when quashed by the courts as a result of a successful application for judicial review. The first four circumstances are found in the TCPA and apply where:

(a) the underlying enforcement notice is withdrawn or quashed;
(b) the period allowed for compliance with the enforcement notice expires;
(c) notice of withdrawal of the stop notice is served;
(d) the underlying enforcement notice is varied[1].

If the variation covers some of the matters prohibited by the stop notice then the stop notice ceases to have effect in so far as such variation cuts down the ambit of the enforcement notice so as to affect the scope of the stop notice. One point to note is that although the stop notice ceases to have effect when the compliance period for the enforcement notice expires there is no requirement placed on the authority to delete the stop notice from the statutory register of enforcement and stop notices. Only when the enforcement notice is withdrawn or quashed is there an obligation on the authority to remove the entry relating to both notices and everything relating to such notices[2]. When a stop notice ceases to have effect because of withdrawal then it ceases to have effect from the date of first service of the withdrawal notice.

1 TCPA 1990, ss 184(4) and (5).
2 Town and Country Planning (General Development Procedure) Order 1995, SI 1995/419, art 26(3).

8.7 COMPENSATION

Certain persons[1] may be able to claim compensation for any 'loss or damage directly attributable to the prohibition in the notice'[2]. If the underlying enforcement notice is varied then the focus will be on the extent to which the prohibition no longer applies. A claim is possible where any of the following apply[3]:

(a) the enforcement notice is quashed on grounds other than that planning permission ought to be granted for development or that a condition or limitation alleged in the enforcement not to have been complied with ought to be discharged;

(b) the enforcement notice is varied (otherwise than on the basis that permission ought to be granted for development etc) with the result that any prohibited activity ceases to be a 'relevant activity' in the enforcement notice;

(c) the enforcement notice is withdrawn otherwise than in consequence of the grant by them of permission for the development to which the enforcement notice relates;

(d) the enforcement notice is withdrawn otherwise than in consequence of a grant of permission for retention of the development or continuation of the use both without compliance with a condition subject to which a previous permission was granted;

(e) the stop notice is withdrawn.

The LPA whose enforcement notice has been quashed on 'planning policy' grounds alone will not face a compensation claim. If the enforcement notice is a nullity then the first three situations cannot be relevant since there is no 'enforcement notice'. If the stop notice is a nullity then that too would seem to mean that there has not been service of a 'stop notice under section 183'. Logic would also demand that a stop notice that is a nullity means that there is no stop notice: therefore, it cannot be withdrawn and so the fourth basis of liability cannot (where the stop is a nullity) apply. However, in one case[4] the court (illustrating perhaps the more 'relativist' approach to the concept of 'nullity' which is appropriate in cases of flawed decision-making) indicated that the way to deal with this problem was to make an order requiring the LPA to withdraw the stop notice: this would clear the way for the claimant to claim compensation.

1 The category of claimants covers a person who –
   (a) occupies; or
   (b) has an interest in the land to which a stop notice relates at the time when the stop notice was first served (TCPA 1990, s 186(2)).
2 Ibid.
3 TCPA 1990, s 186(1).
4 *Clwyd County Council v Secretary of State for Wales* [1982] JPL 696. The court's approach thus ties in with the more modern analysis advocated by Lord Hailsham (see para 6.7.1) in dealing with flawed notices and decisions.

8.7.1 Scope of claim

The principal basis of a claim will be for 'loss or damage directly attributable to the prohibition contained in the notice'[1]. The amount claimed may include a sum payable in respect of a breach of contract caused by taking such action as is necessary to comply with a prohibition in the stop notice[2]. The costs of the appellant in fighting the enforcement appeal are not 'directly attributable' to the prohibition contained in the stop notice[3] and so cannot be claimed under section 186. Items of expenditure that may lead to compensation payments would include the provision of temporary accommodation while work is held up on office/residential etc development or work to deal with the deterioration of a building left exposed to the elements because of the stop notice's prohibition[4]. If there is a break in the chain of causation linking the prohibition and the loss/damage then the 'directly attributable' requirement will not be met[5]. Interest (calculated from the date of service of the stop notice) is payable on compensation awarded under this section where the stop notice is served after 25 September 1991[6].

1 TCPA 1990, s 186(2).
2 TCPA 1990, s 186(5).

3 *Sample (Warkworth) Ltd v Alnwick District Council* [1984] JPL 670.
4 Ibid.
5 Ibid.
6 Planning and Compensation Act 1991, s 80 and Sch 18.

8.7.2 Claimant's fault relevant

Where the claimant has failed to comply with a notice under the TCPA 1990, sections 171C or 330, or section 16 of the Local Government (Miscellaneous Provisions) Act 1976 and this has a bearing on the compensation payable then that failure or any misstatement made by him in response to such a notice is taken into account when determining the amount of compensation payable[1].

1 TCPA 1990, s 186(5).

8.7.3 Procedure for claiming

This is set out in regulations[1]. The claim must be made in writing (served on the LPA) within 12 months of the decision to vary or quash the enforcement notice or withdraw the enforcement or stop notice. As shown by *R v Secretary of State for the Environment, ex p Hillingdon LBC* the period starts to run the date on which the Secretary of State quashes the notice (even if the LPA challenges that decision in the High Court)[2]. The Secretary of State may 'at any time in any particular case' extend the claim period: this is a change of wording from the previous regulations and probably allows the claim period to be extended even when the extension is exercised after the expiry of the 12 month period set by the regulations[3]. The claim must be made unequivocally but need not actually state the sum claimed[4].

1 Town and Country Planning General Regulations 1992, SI 1992/1492, see especially reg 12.
2 [1992] 2 PLR 91.
3 Town and Country Planning General Regulations 1992, SI 1992/1492, reg 12(2).
4 *Texas Homecare Ltd v Lewes District Council* [1986] JPL 50.

8.8   PROSECUTION

8.8.1   Presentation of cases – changing the perceptions of the magistrate

As with all other criminal proceedings relating to planning contraventions the LPA must ensure that the prosecution case is not only 'legally' up to scratch, the LPA must also ensure that the magistrates are given the full background to the contravention and the importance of the planning system. Failure to attend to this wider picture is largely the reason for unsatisfactory penalties etc. The comments regarding prosecutions relating to non-compliance with enforcement notices in chapter nine should therefore be taken on board. Unless the LPA presents cases in this way the magistrates, for whom planning contraventions are a rarity, will fail to grasp the 'criminality' of the offence. In addition, as there is no obvious 'victim' who has been harmed, they will not grasp the importance of the case. They will, by default, look very sympathetically on the defendant and not take kindly to the LPA prosecutor (who may well be seen as part of an interfering bureaucracy persecuting enterprising local businessmen).

8.8.2   Stop notice – criminal liability

If any person contravenes a stop notice after a site notice has been displayed or the stop notice has been served on him then that person commits an offence[1]. A person also 'contravenes' a stop notice if he 'causes or permits' a contravention: those involved in the chain of command can thus be targeted by the LPA – including any professionals who give direct orders to a workman etc to carry out activities prohibited by the notice[2]. The general law regarding aiding and abetting should also be borne in mind when considering a prosecution: the rules regarding the liability of such parties are not specific to the TCPA but are based on generally applicable statutory and case law principles. (This is also an item discussed in chapter nine.) The penalties before the magistrates' court for a first offence are a fine up to £20,000 and an unlimited fine before the Crown

Court[3]. If the offence is continued after a first conviction then the offender may be convicted of a second or subsequent offence under section 187 by reference to any period of time following the preceding conviction for such an offence[4].

1 TCPA 1990, s 187(1).
2 TCPA 1990, s 187(1B). See the relevant part of chapter nine on the meaning of 'causes or permits': this terminology is frequently found in planning and other environmental law offences.
3 TCPA 1990, s 187(2).
4 TCPA 1990, s 187(1A).

8.8.3 Financial benefit of contravention

The court is specifically required to take account of 'any financial benefit which has accrued or appears likely to accrue to [the accused] in consequence of the offence[1]'. As that provision points out this is an important factor and so the LPA prosecutor should repeat the statutory language (eg 'the court shall in particular have regard to') and then produce solid expert evidence on such financial matters. Such evidence should then be supplemented by other indications of the 'harm' to the 'victim' so that the magistrates can form a view as to the degree of harm caused by the accused and the appropriate penalty that should be imposed.

1 TCPA 1990, s 187(2A).

8.8.4 Specific defence

If the accused proves both of the following:

(a) that the stop notice was not served on him; and
(b) that he did not know, and could not reasonably have been expected to know of its existence

then a defence will have been made out[1]. Clearly, proof of service and conspicuous and continuous display of the site notice are important here. The LPA must ensure that adequate documentary evidence is placed on file by the process server containing the relevant details. Unless he proves that he was not served and that the site notice was not conspicuous when he went on site then he will have difficulty in making out this defence. Aggrieved neighbours may well provide a useful reporting service to ensure that the LPA is able to deal with situations when the site notice is 'vandalised'. Such action, would, of course, be criminal damage and a prosecution against the 'vandal' could also be added to any related contraventions of planning control.

1   TCPA 1990, s 187(3).

8.8.5   Vires arguments

The defendant may assert that the stop notice is invalid (eg by reason of failure to comply with the four-year limitation in section 183(5)). In one case the Court of Appeal held that a defendant could call evidence to show that the activity had started before the limitation period (then 12 months)[1]. If the notice is so flawed that a civil court would quash it as a nullity then the defendant could argue that the whole proceedings are flawed because there is no 'stop notice' on which a prosecution can be based[2]. The Court of Appeal (Criminal Division) in *R v Pettigrove*[3] noted that the legislation provided an:

> '. . . elaborate system for the service of enforcement notices and for appeals. There was no right of appeal against stop notices which were contingent on enforcement notices. Once the stop notice was validly in existence and validly served, then it was the obligation of those to whom it was directed to comply with it. Arguments as to whether the use constituted an ancillary use or any other planning law argument would not be a defence to not complying with the stop notice. Such arguments arose on the appeal against the enforcement notice and that was the proper place for dealing with the matter.'

These comments of the Court of Appeal in respect of criminal proceedings relating to a stop notice clearly indicate that arguments as to *vires* which could have been raised during the enforcement notice appeal should not be raised in the context of a prosecution in respect of a related stop notice. However, this does not necessarily mean that the vires arguments could not be raised in judicial review proceedings brought by a defendant to attack the LPA's decision to initiate a criminal prosecution. It would also seem that vires arguments relating solely to the stop notice can be raised before the magistrates as in *R v Jenner*.

1   *R v Jenner* [1983] JPL 547.
2   *Bristol Stadium Ltd v Brown* [1980] JPL 107.
3   (1990) 62 P & CR 355.

9 Securing compliance with the notice – monitoring, negotiation, prosecution and injunction

9.1 INTRODUCTION

Achieving compliance with the enforcement notice may need a certain 'persistence' on the part of LPA officers. Before examining aspects of the powers to enter land a few words will be devoted to 'softening up' the contravener with appropriate warning letters. In most cases the responsible contravener will comply with the terms of an enforcement notice if he is made aware that the LPA is 'on the ball'. Keeping momentum when handling enforcement cases is thus important at this particular stage.

9.2 WARNING LETTERS

Pro forma warning letters constitute an important bureaucratic tool for the LPA. They serve to give the impression of efficiency and fairness: comments made elsewhere regarding the use of IT in enforcement are relevant here. With IT this bureaucratic tool can be very efficient in terms of officer time as such letters can be produced quickly and on time. In certain cases the delivery of a warning letter in person by the enforcement officer helps to drive home the point that the LPA is taking the issue seriously. The contents of the letter should clearly recite the import of the relevant enforcement notice and the relevant steps and compliance dates. The letter might also finish off with a 'reminder' as to how the criminal provisions might be applied by the magistrates' court should the maximum penalties be imposed for non-compliance. Illustrations of the sanctions available to the LPA would also include the possibility of injunction and the works in default power. An overview of the effect of these sanctions might also serve to illustrate the serious nature of non-compliance. Both the content and the form of the warning letter (crisply produced and 'legal' in appearance) thus serve to help the LPA maintain the aura of efficiency – which, of course, will be mirrored in practice.

9.3   ENTRY POWERS

An important way of gathering reliable information is the site visit. The ex-policeman enforcement officer will normally have the necessary fact-finding and investigative skills for such a task. 'Handling the public' is also something that will be important. If the ex-policeman has worked in the area while in the police force he may even know the contravener from his police work. The legal detail must be observed as regards the scope of the powers: chapter two addresses these – for example, the officer must be 'duly authorised in writing' by his council in order to make use of the powers. The officer should therefore be given a card containing such written authority (quoting the Act) so that occupiers/owners can be sure of his credentials. For non-mainstream enforcement purposes there are different entry powers – please refer to the separate discussions of such regimes.

9.3.1   Police and Criminal Evidence Act 1984

A case relating to trading standards highlighted the importance of statutory criteria relating to the collection of evidence. In *Dudley Metropolitan Borough Council v Debenhams plc*[1] a trading standards officer had not complied with Code B of the Police and Criminal Evidence Act 1984 (PACE) and had argued that this was unnecessary because he was engaged in 'routine enquiries' and so was not carrying out a 'search' as envisaged by Code B. The Divisional Court however concluded that the company had been subjected to a search (at which computer records were taken) and so Code B applied. Since this had not been followed (there had been no written consent to the search nor a statement that anything seized may be produced in evidence) the computer evidence was inadmissible. The impact of this case has been largely nullified, however, by revisions to the PACE codes. Thus paragraph 1.3B of PACE Code B states:

> This code does not apply to the exercise of a statutory power to enter premises or to inspect goods, equipment or procedures if the exercise of that power is not dependent on the existence of grounds for

suspecting that an offence may have been committed and the person exercising the power has no reasonable grounds for such suspicion.

The entry powers under the planning legislation (see chapter two) do not depend on there being any suspicion that an offence has occurred. The requirements of Code B will thus not apply to searches carried out under the planning legislation. Colleagues in the trading standards team will be able to supply a copy of an advice circular on the impact of this paragraph: the document is produced by the Local Authorities Co-Ordinating Body on Food and Trading Standards (commonly referred to as 'LACOTS'). Code C (which deals with a range of subjects including interviewing) may also be relevant when investigating contraventions as it includes the duty to give a caution when there are grounds to suspect that an offence has been committed. Such obligations may appear to be rather 'over the top' but as well as heading off possible technical challenges when a prosecution is at issue the LPA should also be aware that such procedures may have a beneficial effect in some cases. They may make the contravener realise the seriousness of the situation and could have a catalytic effect in bringing matters to a head. Comments on PACE and its possible relevance to the PCN and a meeting (subsequent to a 'time and place' offer) are also to be found in chapter two.

1   (1994) 159 JP 18.

9.4   NEGOTIATED COMPROMISE

At many stages during an enforcement case a planning officer may be confronted with an offer of a compromise. The officer faced with such an offer of compromise must be aware of the options open to him in order to make the best choice in the circumstances. The following deals with the two major options – compliance by permission and compliance by contract. Underlying the choice between them however is the important consideration that the process by which that compromise is made concrete should not prejudice the LPA's main weapon. This comprises the use of enforcement pressure (the co-ordinated and measured use of all available sanctions) against the contravener. A compromise that involves the LPA releasing such pressure at too early a stage is very likely to let the contravener off the hook. Such pressure should only be released once the LPA is assured that the professed sincerity of the contravener will be translated into action to remedy the breach. This is a point examined at the end of the discussion of prosecutions since the measured application of enforcement pressure is something which is relevant to compromises reached at this late stage of the process.

9.4.1 Compliance by permission

The issue here arises out of the conflicting needs of the LPA to be flexible and reasonable and yet to ensure that the calculating contravener does not continue to 'play the system'. Where a particular enforcement episode has indicated that the control of the development and/or the particular contravener will continue to cause problems even after a compromise by means of a planning permission then the LPA should consider a more 'legalistic' form of compromise. In other words, instead of using a planning permission to regularise and/or consolidate a compromise the LPA should ensure that its procedures cover the use of planning obligations under section 106.

9.4.2 Compliance by contract

The advantage of using a planning obligation (entered into by agreement with the contravener) to deal with a breach of planning control is that the LPA will have a greater degree of control over complex compliance action that needs to be undertaken. This is particularly important if the means of remedying the breach involve continuing obligations which give rise to problems of monitoring etc. One-off obligations can easily be kept under review: however, obligations that relate to states of affairs (eg occupation restrictions or maintenance obligations) do require special thought. If the contravener has indicated through his past conduct that he is likely to be a difficult customer then the advantage of using the more robust mechanism of the planning agreement is even clearer. LPAs should thus try to ensure that planning officers unlearn the 'knee-jerk' response to an offer of compromise (especially at the later stages when an enforcement notice is active) by turning to a planning permission: instead they should give some thought to dealing with the situation by means of a planning agreement.

9.4.3 The enforcement agreement

The adoption of this approach in suitable cases will require some 'capital' investment. Both the planning department and the legal department will need to be educated as to the use of such tactics for the effective enforcement of planning control. The general analogy can be drawn between a normal development control function and the use of planning agreements in that sphere and the enforcement function and the use of enforcement agreements. The use of such agreements makes for greater certainty. In particular, LPAs may wish to adapt their use of planning agreements in the wider field to the enforcement area with special regard to the following matters:

    (a) the compliance period;
    (b) the steps required by the notice;
    (c) the contractor;
    (d) monitoring provisions;
    (e) enforcement provisions.

The related use of a pro forma unilateral undertaking under section 106 at the PCN 'time and place' discussion has already been discussed earlier. That illustrates the 'catalytic' value of such meetings and the opportunities of capitalising on enforcement opportunities by using contractual enforcement. In some cases the LPA may find that the contravener's attitude during negotiations is somewhat at variance with his professed sincerity. This should not be viewed as a failure: the LPA at least then is aware that the contravener is stalling and knows that more 'stick' is required since the 'carrot' of offering not to take formal action has failed. So even if negotiation by contract does not result in a section 106 obligation being entered into there will still be benefits for the LPA in terms of knowing what the real intentions of the contravener are. Shortage of space, however, prevents detailed discussion of the contents of such obligations and related issues.

9.4.3.1 *Resource implications for the authority*

If the LPA already uses agreements in the development control sphere then it should not be difficult for them to adapt to such agreements for the purposes of enforcement. Indeed, the enforcement team can copy the example from their development control colleagues and require the contravener to pay the LPA's legal expenses. This will be useful in making the enforcement task take on a higher profile and 'pay its way' in terms of the various indicators of success used in the LPA. This stage of enforcement could even be contracted out to solicitors conversant with planning and the principles of negotiated compliance.

9.4.3.2　*Legal powers and the bargaining situation*

The LPA should ensure that the terms of an enforcement agreement do mirror quite closely the terms of their enforcement notice. Since enforcement agreements will be agreements made 'under pressure' the chances of a disgruntled contravener challenging the validity of such agreements might be more significant than would be the case with planning agreements used for development control purposes. In order to forestall such action the LPA should therefore stick closely to the context set by the enforcement notice in order to show that the agreement is fairly and reasonably related to the enforcement action underlying the use of section 106.

9.5　DIRECT ACTION AND THE WORKS IN DEFAULT POWER

Direct action under the TCPA 1990, section 178 may be the only way of putting things right when the LPA is confronted by the persistent and determined contravener. When the steps required by an effective enforcement notice have not been undertaken within the period(s) allowed in the notice the LPA may use its 'works in default power' to enter the land and take the 'steps' required by the notice itself.[1] The phraseology employed means that the LPA does not have power to take action as regards the 'activities which the authority require to cease' – the second type of requirement in an enforcement notice. However, this does not prevent the LPA from, in effect, making it difficult to carry on such activities by taking steps that involve removal of plant and equipment used in connection with such activities.

Such an approach was possible under the old provisions: the amended legislation does not materially affect the relevant legal principles. Indeed, circular 21/91 advocates such action in Annex 2, paragraph 50:

'. . . where, for example, a storage use is required to be discontinued, and whether or not the notice specifically requires the removal of stored items, it is now open to the LPA to remove those items as a step towards discontinuing the use and continue to remove such items which may appear on the land'.

It would be preferable, however, if the notice was specific about the removal of such plant and equipment: if such items are spelt out in the notice then the magistrates' court is less likely to be sidetracked by contraveners trying to suggest that the LPA has acted ultra vires.

1 TCPA 1990, s 178(1).

9.5.1 Strategic use of default power

A breach of planning control that does involve a use can thus be attacked by means of the default power. The enforcement notice should list the following steps:

'(1) The discontinuance of the contravening use.
 (2) The removal of all plant, equipment, furniture and fittings used in connection with the contravening use.'

(The more specific the LPA can be about the plant, equipment etc the better.) If there is non-compliance with the notice in respect of the second step then the authority can use its default powers to enter the land and, in effect, cause the contravener to cease the use by taking away the 'tools of the trade'. Such action will also be useful in deterring those considering similar types of contravening uses.

9.5.2 Judicial review

The discretion given to the LPA to carry out works in default is subject to judicial review. In the Court of Appeal case of *R v*

Greenwich London Borough Council, ex p Patel[1] the court said
that there was a duty on the authority to investigate the
situation where an owner had not appealed against an
enforcement notice because he had been unaware of it and the
enforcement was upheld as valid. If the authority fails to act
reasonably then the court could consider an application for
judicial review directed against the use of the works in default
power.

1 [1985] JPL 851.

9.5.3 Local authority recovery of sums

The authority may recover from the owner at the time of
carrying out the steps under the default power:

(a) any expenses reasonably incurred by the authority[1];
(b) a sum which reflects their establishment charges[2].

Although this may seem hard on a person who becomes an
owner after the breach has occurred there is provision for such
an owner to recover such sums from those responsible by virtue
of provisions which deem such sums as being 'incurred or paid
for the use and at the request of the person by whom the breach
of planning control was committed[3]'. The LPA can therefore go
against an 'innocent' owner (who should, in any case, be aware
of the notice through his enquiries before purchase) knowing
that he can take up the matter with those who were responsible
as a contract debt.

1 TCPA 1990, s 178(1)(b).
2 Local Government Act 1974, s 36.
3 TCPA 1990, s 178(2)(b).

9.5.3.1 *Expenses as charge on the land – power of sale*

Regulations have provided for the expenses of the LPA to be a
charge that is binding on successive owners of the land to which
the notice relates: the charge takes effect as from the date of the
completion by the LPA of the steps required to be taken by the

notice[1]. The wording of this provision does not appear to extend to the establishment charges element which can be an additional sum to the 'expenses' of direct action. This provision can be the basis for quite effective action in cases where the contravener is particularly recalcitrant. Under the Local Land Charges Act 1975, section 7 any local land charge falling within the terms of section 1(1)(a) of that Act 'shall, when registered, take effect as if it had been created by a deed of charge by way of legal mortgage within the meaning of the Law of Property Act 1925 ...'. This type of financial charge falls within section 1(1)(a) and so the LPA (by virtue of section 7) has the right to the legal remedies of a legal mortgagee: the provisions of the Law of Property Act 1925, section 101 (and related provisions) thus apply such that the LPA has the power to appoint a receiver and a power to sell the land on which the contravention has occurred. Although such powers may be somewhat draconian in the sphere of planning control their existence must be taken into account and consideration given to their use where the contravention continues and the only real solution appears to be compulsory purchase or the use of powers under the Law of Property Act 1925. In many cases where the works of default powers have been used and a local land charge registered the mortgagee powers may in fact be easier to use than compulsory purchase.

1 Town and Country Planning General Regulations 1992, SI 1992/1492, reg 14(2); these regulations are made under the TCPA 1990, s 178(5).

9.5.4 Public Health Act provisions

Section 178(3) empowers the Secretary of State to make regulations applying specified provisions of the Public Health Act 1936 to enforcement action under the TCPA 1990. The Town and Country Planning General Regulations 1992 also serve an enforcement role under this subsection. They apply (with certain modifications) the provisions of three sections of the Public Health Act 1936 to enforcement action: sections 276 (sale of materials), 289 (requiring occupier to permit works to be executed by the owner), and 294 (limit on liability of agents or trustees). Two of these three provisions will be examined below.

9.5.4.1   *Sale of materials*

The LPA is entitled to sell any 'materials' which have been removed by them from any premises when taking steps required by an enforcement notice[1]. It would seem that (given the ambit of the legislation) the term 'materials' means 'building materials'. Once the LPA has removed the (building) materials they must hold them for at least three days. If the owner claims and removes them before 'the expiration of three days' then the authority obviously cannot sell them. If the three-day period passes and the LPA do sell the materials then they must 'pay the proceeds to the person to whom the materials belonged after deducting the amount of any expenses recoverable by them from him'[2].

As will be discussed in chapter twelve dealing with the enforcement of advertisement control the use of the works in default power and the consequent power to sell 'materials' can be a very effective sanction. The use of the sale power means that the LPA can deprive the contravener of the (building) 'materials' which will have been an integral part of the contravention. This is most relevant to situations such as advertising control. However, in the normal range of enforcement actions it may also be relevant to temporary structures or buildings (eg Portakabins) which are an important part of the contravening activity. The LPA thus can be quite 'direct' in its enforcement powers by the use of its power to sell 'materials': its power to sell the land where its expenses become a registered local land charge is another option which should, as noted above, be borne in mind.

1   Public Health Act 1936, s 276(1).
2   Public Health Act 1936, s 276(2).

9.5.4.2   *Agents and trustees*

When the LPA seeks to recover expenses from an owner it should note the special position of agents and trustees. If an owner proves that he:

  (a)   is receiving the rent of those premises merely as agent or trustee for some other person, and

(b) has not, since the date of service on him of a demand for payment had (on behalf of his principal) sufficient money to discharge the whole demand of the authority then,

his liability shall be limited to the amount of such money held by him for that principal. The balance may still be recovered from the principal[1].

1 Public Health Act 1936, s 294.

9.6 PROSECUTIONS

The prosecution of offences under mainstream planning control is not a simple task. For the moment it is important to put to one side the technicalities of the various provisions providing for criminal liability – as well as general principles of criminal law. The main issue confronting the prosecutor is the handling of an enforcement case in a way which overcomes fundamental problems rooted in the perception of such cases by the Bench. For the vast majority of lay (and even stipendiary) magistrates the hearing of a planning case will be a novelty. Such a case will also fall outside the normal framework of criminal proceedings in one important respect. With contraventions of planning control there is no obvious 'victim'. There is no person whose property or person has been violated by another. There is no easy way of measuring the crime and assessing the guilt of the defendant. Planning contraventions are, in this sense, victimless crimes which make the job of the magistrate very difficult when it comes to sentencing. The prosecuting lawyer who overlooks this fundamental point will invariably fail to give the magistrate a clear and convincing picture of the gravity of the offence. So prosecuting lawyers must take special care with prosecutions. The appropriate approach to prosecutions is thus discussed below in considerable detail as it is probably more important than the 'routine' issue of getting the legal niceties right.

9.6.1 Section 179(1) and the 'owner' offence

If the owner is 'in breach of an enforcement notice' then he will be guilty of an offence[1]. The prosecuting authority will have to prove that the defendant was the owner at the time a copy of the notice was served on him in order to prove their case against an owner[2]. A combination of requisitions for information (perhaps Land Registry searches) and the presumption (in criminal law) of continuing ownership will be important here. The owner will be guilty of an offence if any steps required by the notice (other than cessation of a use) have not been taken within the compliance period. The offence is one of strict liability[3]. This is important as it underlines the similarity between contraventions under the planning regime and those under the more specialised regimes of environmental law where the courts have also emphasised the importance of imposing quite high standards on defendants. The accused 'may be charged by reference to any day or longer period of time' (TCPA 1990, section 179(6)). Before the magistrates' court the penalty is a fine not exceeding £20,000: if the case goes to the Crown Court then the fine is unlimited[4]. The choice of venue is firstly a matter for the magistrates. They will hear arguments from both sides. However, even if they decide that it should not go to the Crown Court the defendant may still elect for a Crown Court trial. Since the offence is 'triable either way' – that is, the defendant may elect for a Crown Court trial, the prosecution is not restrained by the six months' limitation period imposed on offences that are only capable of going to the magistrates' court.

There is a special defence available to the owner charged under the TCPA 1990, section 179(2). In order to make out the defence he must show that 'he did everything he could be expected to do to secure compliance with the notice[5]'. This is a high standard: there is no 'reasonableness' standard in the provision which qualifies what he might be 'expected to do to secure compliance'. This could indicate therefore that even if compliance would require legal action against a non-owner (eg trespasser) to remove that person from the site this would be 'expected' of the owner despite the cost. A genuine reason preventing the accused from complying with the notice will be required. In *Kent County Council v Brockman*[6] it was held that the personal and financial circumstances of the defendant were relevant to this defence. A genuinely incapacitated defendant who had done nothing to comply with the notice could still rely on the defence. The court, however, should be rigorous in the proof needed from a defendant claiming impecuniosity.

1 TCPA 1990, s 179(2): subsection (1) sets out what constitutes being

in breach of an enforcement notice as regards the 'owner'. The definition of 'owner' is discussed in para 6.6.3.1.
2 *R v Ruttle, ex p Marshall* (1989) 57 P & CR 299.
3 *R v Collett* [1994] 2 All ER 372: the Court of Appeal was construing the former version of this provision but the conclusions would be the same. The court thus concluded that it was the policy of the legislation to impose absolute liability so as to encourage vigilance on the part of owners, occupiers etc.
4 TCPA 1990, s 179(8).
5 TCPA 1990, s 179(3).
6 [1994] Crim LR 296.

9.6.2 The 'activities' offence

The offence constituted by the TCPA 1990, section 179(4) and (5) has two elements which would normally be kept separate. These provisions are concerned with a failure on the part of those who are not 'owners' to ensure that a prohibited activity ceases. Those who can be found liable comprise any person 'who has control of' the land and any person who 'has an interest in the land to which an enforcement notice relates (other than the owner)'[1]. They must not 'carry on any activity which is required by the notice to cease or cause or permit such an activity to be carried on'[2]. The prosecutor must therefore take care with drafting the information so that the allegation is not bad for duplicity. The meaning of 'cause' and 'permit' is discussed below in para 9.6.5. An example of an authority falling down on the detail is the case of *Holmes v Bradford Metropolitan City Council*[3] where the authority charged an owner under this provision even though the express language of the provision specifically excludes owners. The general defence described below is available to the accused.

1 TCPA 1990, s 179(4).
2 Ibid.
3 (1994) Times, 19 May .

9.6.3 Further offences after section 179(2) and (5) convictions

By virtue of the TCPA 1990, section 179(6) a person may be convicted of a second or subsequent offence by reference to any period of time following the preceding conviction for such an offence. This has somewhat simplified the statutory scheme in the unamended provisions.

9.6.4   The 'ignorance' defence under section 179(7)

This provides that anyone charged under section 179 can raise a defence if:

(a) he has not been served with a copy of the enforcement notice;

(b) the notice is not kept on the register maintained under section 188; and

(c) he shows that he was not aware of the existence of the notice.

All three elements must be proved: the LPA can ensure that this defence is not raised by maintaining the register of enforcement, breach of condition and stop notices.

9.6.5   'Causes or permits'

The information prepared by the LPA must be carefully drafted. Where 'cause or permit' is the phraseology used in the relevant provision (as is the case with the TCPA 1990, section 179(4)) the LPA must take care and be certain as to which is appropriate. Both terms are widely used in the environmental law sphere and so case law from both the planning and non-planning fields needs to be kept under review. Thus the term 'cause' has been the subject of an Attorney-General's reference where that term is used in provisions relating to the pollution of controlled waters[1]. The case law discussed there examines some of the recent decisions involving such language. The court identified five principles that emerged from the case law: one was that the word 'causes' should be given its plain commonsense meaning and was not to be refined by introducing concepts such as proximate or principal cause, effective cause, *novus actus* etc. Another principle was that it required some active participation in the operation or chain of operations resulting in the pollution. This opinion and the decisions cited in it will therefore have a bearing on non-compliance cases where the non-owner is under examination as regards the section 179(4) offence. As regards 'permits' there are two elements to such an offence:

(a) the person liable must have it in his power to forbid the activity in question; and

(b) he must have failed to take reasonable steps to prevent the activity.

The magistrates' court will decide on the 'reasonableness' issue after looking at all the circumstances of the case[2].

1 *A-G's Reference (No 1 of 1994)* [1995] 1 WLR 599, CA.
2 *Ragsdale v Creswick* [1984] JPL 883.

9.6.6 Offences by corporations

It should always be remembered that companies will not necessarily provide a shield against the prosecution of directors etc. Where any offence under the TCPA 1990 is committed by a body corporate and this is proved to have been committed 'with the consent or connivance of, or to be attributable to any neglect on the part of . . . a director, manager, secretary or other similar officer of the body corporate, or . . . any person who was purporting to act in any such capacity' then such person as well as the body corporate 'shall be guilty of that offence'[1]. The prosecuting authority should generally focus on the 'attributable to any neglect' version of the offence since that will be the easiest to prove. The other elements may be suitable bases for a prosecution if evidence is available – they should also give rise to higher fines.

1 TCPA 1990, s 331(1).

9.6.6.1 *Corporate liability and listed buildings etc*

In respect of offences under the P(LB&CA)A 1990 the provisions of section 331 are generally applied by P(LB&CA)A 1990, section 89(1). The one exception to this is the 'intentional damage' offence under section 59 relating to listed buildings. This offence does not, therefore, extend to company directors etc, on the basis of the TCPA 1990, section 331.

9.6.7 Adjournments

One practical problem facing the LPA is the argument from the accused that he is appealing the planning permission etc to the Secretary of State and that therefore the magistrates should adjourn until the administrative process under the TCPA 1990 is completed. This argument had failed in one case and the Court of Appeal held that the magistrates were wrong in not granting an adjournment as the outcome of the appeal was directly relevant to the penalty to be imposed[1]. However, the normal rule is that magistrates should proceed to hear and determine the guilt or innocence of the defendant notwithstanding that a planning application has recently been made[2]. In this case however (where the age, means, state of health of the defendants and substantial delay by the LPA in taking action were such as to make the case exceptional) the magistrates had been justified in departing from the normal procedures because of such wholly exceptional circumstances.

1 *R v Newland* (1987) 54 P & CR 222.
2 *R v Beaconsfield Magistrates, ex p South Buckinghamshire District Council* [1993] COD 357.

9.6.8 The notice – principles of construction

The criminal courts apply a stringent rule of construction. Thus in the case of *Ivory v Secretary of State for the Environment*[1] the contravener appealed to the High Court against the dismissal of his enforcement notice appeal. The Divisional Court (Kennedy J) said this about the construction of terms used in an enforcement notice:

> '... words should not be construed like a statute, but as with byelaws should be benevolently interpreted, at least until they had to be construed within the context of a criminal prosecution[2].'

In 'civil' proceedings – on appeal to the Secretary of State for example – a 'benevolent' interpretation applies. This would also, apparently, be the way of interpreting a notice (if the point arose) in an action for recovery of expenses incurred by exercising the works in default power. When it comes to using the injunctive power to enforce planning control the more stringent rules of interpretation might apply. Thus if the court (when considering contempt proceedings) is asked to find that the contravener was in contempt of court then this would directly affect 'the liberty of the subject' – hence a criminal law standard of interpretation (see also para 9.7 et seq on the injunctive remedy). With criminal law sanctions then the court will be under a duty not 'to make any construction on a benevolent or other basis which favour[s] the prosecution at the expense of the defence[3].' There are therefore two modes of construing a notice that is ambiguous. In a non-criminal law forum the court should be 'benevolent': in a criminal law forum the court has to protect the accused and thus not help the prosecution by interpreting an ambiguous notice in a manner which favours the prosecution. In chapter six (the discussion of deficiencies in form and substance) I suggest that it might be appropriate to describe a notice which cannot support a prosecution because of its failings when subjected to the scrutiny and interpretation of the criminal courts as 'nugatory': it might be intelligible to the Secretary of State and comply with both DOE and LPA policy; it may also be valid to support the works in default power; yet as regards a prosecution it might not be clear enough to pass the stringent interpretation applied by the criminal courts.

1 [1985] JPL 796.
2 Ibid at 798.
3 *Warrington Borough Council v David Garvey* [1988] JPL 752 at 761. This case is a useful overview of the issues of interpretation when the enforcement notice is being scrutinised at a criminal law forum.

9.6.8.1 *Vires arguments*

The defendant contravener may try to assert that the notice is a nullity even when, on its face, there is no obvious flaw. Such latent defects (errors of procedure may be alleged) cannot be asserted by the defendant contravener: the Court of Appeal has indicated that the statutory scheme and case law points towards the administrative appeal process as being the proper place for such challenges[1]. The LPA should not therefore be required to prove regularity in procedure: errors on the face of the notice however will need to be addressed as these are relevant to the approach taken by the criminal courts by virtue of the stricter rules of interpretation that apply.

1 *R v Wicks* (1995) Times, 19 April, CA (see also para 6.7.2.4).

9.6.9 The presentation of cases

The prosecution of offences under the planning regime raises problems of 'familiarity' for lay magistrates in particular. Two problems frequently arise. First prosecuting authorities invariably complain that the penalties imposed by the courts are inadequate. The basis of the problem may well be the failure of prosecutors to set out fully enough the background of the offence (and the rationale for criminal liability). This prompted the editor[1] of *The Magistrate* to write an article (originally appearing in the *Law Society's Gazette* and then reprinted in *The Magistrate*[2]) in which the following comment appeared:

> 'If the case is inadequately presented, it is almost inevitable that the court will err on the side more favourable to the defendant . . . I would invite readers who practise in magistrates' courts to reflect that there are scores of offences which will come before a lay magistrate only once or twice during his magisterial service. Many magistrates may never be called upon to deal with what may be called "rare offences". It is, therefore, all the more necessary that cases which are outside the run-of-the mill category (viz crime and motoring offences) should be presented with great care and particularity.'

The editor of *The Magistrate* then noted eight specific matters which needed to be addressed by the prosecuting authority. These may be listed as:

(a) explain the reason why Parliament made such offences criminal offences;

(b) outline the 'prevalence' of such offences;

(c) outline the steps taken by the LPA to obtain compliance (visits, warnings etc);

(d) identify the level of 'guilt' of the accused – whether the offence was committed on purpose, negligently etc;

(e) assess the gravity of the offence so that the harm to the 'victim' can be gauged by the magistrates – reference to 'illegal' profit will be appropriate here in the case of planning contraventions as this is specifically covered by the statutory provisions regarding penalties;

(f) point out the maximum penalties prescribed by law for the offence and the other sanctions available (eg works in default power);

(g) set out the prosecution's costs.

The second problem is the readiness of some courts to allow proceedings to be adjourned merely because the defendant indicates that he has 'put in another planning application'. On this issue the advice from the editorial pages of *The Magistrate*[3] states:

'Courts that adjourn or otherwise defer a prosecution for this reason alone frustrate effective planning control and fail to have regard to the provisions of section [180(3)] of the Act which specifies that the grant of a subsequent planning permission for the unlawful development alleged does not remove the liability to comply with an enforcement notice until the relevant provision of that notice ceases to have effect.'

As regards inadequate penalties a letter from J A Swanwick MBE, JP (a former Chairman of the Planning Committee of the Association of District Councils) noted some of the problems that commonly arise[4]. The letter finished:

'My purpose in drawing attention to these issues is not to criticise some of my colleagues on the Bench, nor to make or invite invidious comparisons with other offences which regularly come before us. It is to say that planning control deserves to be taken seriously as a means of helping our fellow citizens who are suffering from unlawful, and sometimes intolerable, activities; and it is our job, in my view, to see that those who defy the law in this way are made to pay heavily for it.'

A more recent discussion of the problems raised by planning and environmental law offences (when it comes to the presentation of a case) is to be found in article published in *Justice of the Peace & Local Government Law*, 26 November, 1994[5]. This stresses, inter alia, the importance of supplying the magistrates with the appropriate information that allows them to assess the harm done to the 'victim' and so enables them to come to an informed view on the right 'tariff' for the offence. Such tactics are necessary given the approach to sentencing taken by the Bench. Thus the Magistrates' Association's own 'Sentencing Guidelines' (September 1993) set down the principles by which consistency in sentencing is to be achieved. The two key factors are the assessment of the seriousness of the case and then the determination of a commensurate penalty. This underlines the need to show how a contravention is detrimental to the interests of other owners/occupiers and the community at large in order to lay the basis for an appropriate penalty. Unfortunately the categories of offences noted in this document do not include those relating to planning control. The prosecutor is therefore set the task of educating the Bench and making it aware of the importance of planning control.

1 I would like to thank E Ronald Horsman OBE and his staff at *The Magistrate* for tracking down and supplying these items.
2 *The Magistrate*, March 1983, p 36.
3 *The Magistrate*, August 1983, p 122.
4 Ibid p 130.
5 R Jackson, *Planning and Environmental Law Offences*, vol 158, p 784.

9.6.10   Aiders and abetters etc

This guide is not the place to address in detail principles of criminal law. However, it should be remembered that the statutory criteria regarding liability under the planning legislation need to be seen in the light of general criminal law principles regarding aiders, abetters etc. So although planning law does not itself appear to cast a wide net covering such miscreants the general rules regarding aiders, abetters etc will apply. So anyone who aids, abets, counsels or procures the commission by another person of an offence has the same criminal liability as that person: this applies to both summary offences as well as those triable either way[1]. The elements involved in proving such liability, general issues regarding evidence etc should naturally be well-understood by the prosecutor whose task it is to ensure that the criminal sanction does give effective support to the enforcement of planning control.

1 Magistrates' Courts Act 1980, s 44.

9.6.11   The standard scale of fines

The standard scale of fines currently in force is set out below. This is set out in section 37 of the Criminal Justice Act 1982 (as amended by section 17(1) of the Criminal Justice Act 1991). The Criminal Justice Act 1991, section 17(2)(c) also amends the Magistrates' Courts Act 1980, section 32(9) so that the maximum fine on summary conviction of an offence triable either way is now £5,000.

Level on the scale	Amount of fine
1	£ 100
2	£ 200
3	£ 1,000
4	£ 2,000
5	£ 5,000

9.6.12 Enforcement pressure and the 'repentant' contravener

The concluding section for this discussion of the criminal sanction is an appropriate place to remind the reader of one of the themes of this book. Throughout this discussion of the effective enforcement of planning controls I have stressed the need to consider employing all available sanctions in an efficient manner against the contravener. Such 'enforcement pressure' in conjunction with a persistent presence by the enforcement team (be it by personal visit or letter etc) helps to give the appearance of an efficient enforcing authority. An enforcement strategy that is also highly visible will be its own reward in many cases. As an enforcement episode continues the relentless pressure from the enforcement team will gradually make more and more contraveners comply. Where a breach is profitable and the contravener well-advised this may not come until quite near the end of formal action – perhaps at the door of the magistrates' court. So even at this late stage the LPA should be awake to the possibility of a negotiated compliance and a resolution of the breach by way of an enforcement agreement. It should be clear by now that the LPA should not merely withdraw the prosecution and wait for the contravener to fulfil his promises. The LPA must keep up the enforcement pressure by continuing the prosecution until the contravener has indicated (perhaps by signing an enforcement agreement) that he is sincere about his offers of compromise. This principle carries through to the hearing itself. The contravener may seek to 'plea bargain' with the enforcing authority. Naturally, the handling of such negotiations will depend upon the particular circumstances of the case. However, the LPA must ensure that its hard work leading up to the prosecution should not be wasted by agreeing to drop the prosecution (or offer no evidence) without adequate safeguards.

Sometimes the option may arise of testing the sincerity of the contravener's protestations by the court's deferring sentence. The LPA may therefore show itself to be reasonable by 'suggesting' that the sentence not be determined immediately. If, say, six months is then allowed for the contravener to demonstrate his sincerity by remedying the breach then the punishment prescribed by the court at a later date would reflect the contravener's good behaviour. Such an option ensures that the enforcement pressure continues to be applied to the contravener without the LPA being subject to criticism of being harsh. The strategy of applying persistent and proportionate enforcement pressure against contraveners is one which the LPA should seriously consider. It is under such pressure that compromises can be reached[1]. However, officers should resist the temptation of releasing such pressure as a result of vague promises by the contravener which may well let him off the hook and seriously hamper the taking of effective enforcement against the breach.

1   Similar observations are made in the Carnwath Report.

9.7   INJUNCTIONS

The planning regime provides for administrative remedies where breaches of control have occurred. These naturally allow for appeals etc in order to protect the legitimate interests of owners, occupiers etc. However, such procedures can take time and there may be occasions where such mechanisms (enforcement and stop notices) and sanctions (a fine in the magistrates' court) are too dilatory or of little impact on the recalcitrant contravener that more immediate and forceful action is warranted. In the context of mainstream enforcement the LPA now has the option of seeking the help of the civil courts by way of a planning injunction under the TCPA 1990, section 187B.

9.7.1   Planning injunctions – general

The LPA may apply to either the High Court or the county court for an injunction to restrain:

(a) an actual breach of planning control; or
(b) an apprehended breach of planning control[1].

An injunction may be sought whether or not the LPA has exercised or intends to exercise any other enforcement powers[2]. The power envisages the High Court or county court granting both mandatory as well as prohibitory injunctions and since 'apprehended' breaches of control can be tackled by such action the LPA may also seek the equivalent of a *quia timet* injunction. The case law relating to the power under the Local Government Act 1972, section 222 is not fully relevant to injunctions under section 187B. The specific statutory basis for the new planning injunctions clearly means that the discretion of the courts is now to be considered within the specific statutory framework of this power. This is evident from Court of Appeal decisions: see the next paragraph on the issue of the court's discretion. In terms of the basic ambit of the planning injunction the term 'restrain' should not be construed restrictively: in *Gladden* the Court of Appeal rejected the argument that the statutory reference to 'restraining' breaches of control indicated that mandatory injunctions were not encompassed by the provision[3]. The court's grant of an interlocutory mandatory injunction to remove a replica Spitfire from the roof of G's house is a broad indication of the scope of the new planning injunction.

Injunctions under this provision can only be sought in cases involving a 'breach of planning control': this term is defined in section 171A(1) and means the carrying out of unauthorised development or failing to comply with any condition or limitation subject to which planning permission has been granted. Such injunctions thus relate to breaches of mainstream planning control: contraventions of the subsidiary regimes will, depending on the specific provisions, also be subject to injunctive action. Reference should be made to the appropriate paragraphs in this text in order to address the availability of injunctive relief under the planning acts in respect of such subsidiary regimes. (In some cases, it should be noted, the LPA will still have to rely on the general purpose power under the Local Government Act 1972, section 222 where a special planning act injunction is not available. A discussion of the different case law rules on section 222 is to be found below. Case law addressing the factors relevant to the discretion of the court in considering mandatory injunctions or *quia timet* injunctions may still be of relevance (though the LPA should note the discussion below of the Court of Appeal's approach in interpreting section 187B and its comments on the applicability of section 222 case law) since such factors may still have some relevance even though the planning injunction under section 187B has a specific statutory basis. This is another reason why the discussion of section 222 case law is still relevant to an understanding of the likely legal principles affecting the injunction as an element in effective enforcement.)

1   TCPA 1990, s 187B(1).
2   Ibid.
3   *Croydon London Borough Council v Gladden* [1994] 1 PLR 30.

9.7.2   The court's discretion

The court is given discretion to grant such an injunction as it 'thinks appropriate for the purpose of restraining the breach' – section 187B(2). In exercising this discretion however it is now clear (from Court of Appeal decisions) that the courts will treat the new provisions as more supportive of LPA action against contraveners. In *Runnymede Borough Council v Harwood* and *Croydon London Borough Council v Gladden* the Court of Appeal emphasised that the reforms to the injunctive power have made substantive changes to the legal rules governing this particular weapon in the enforcement armoury[1]. The introduction of a statutory planning injunction is therefore not merely a procedural change that leaves the substantive case law concepts relating to section 222 injunctions unaffected. The Court of Appeal has made it clear that injunctive action under the TCPA 1990 section 187B (and, by implication, the other specialised injunctive provisions relating to hazardous substances, listed buildings etc) is not automatically subject to the more limiting rules developed by the courts in terms of the section 222 power. The rules applicable to section 222 injunctions (eg those taken from *American Cyanamid*) do not therefore apply where interlocutory proceedings in connection with a section 187B injunction are at issue[2]. The Court of Appeal thus stated that Parliament cannot have intended to preserve the status quo of an infringement by refusing interlocutory relief to the LPA when framing section 187B. The court referred to a case where it was accepted that withholding such relief would have the same effect as granting planning permission for the contravening use[3]. This still leaves unanswered the arguments over the mandatory form of planning injunction which requires more than just removal of contravening 'operational development'. A mandatory injunction requiring reinstatement of a structure that was demolished in contravention of control might be more difficult to obtain. As noted below in discussing the section 222 form of injunction it is clear that the case law is more demanding of the applicant in justifying injunctive relief.

1   [1994] 1 PLR 22 and [1994] 1 PLR 30 respectively.
2   *American Cyanamid Co v Ethicon Ltd* [1975] AC 396.
3   *Mole Valley District Council v Smith* [1992] 3 PLR 22, at 33.

9.7.3   Apprehended breaches

The *quia timet* type of injunction is envisaged by section 187B in the use of the 'apprehended breach' terminology. It would seem that there will be two main types of situations where an apprehended breach can reasonably be the basis for an application to the court. A pattern of breaches of control may be established by past action either:

   (a) on a site which is prone to illegal development by a variety of occupiers; or
   (b) by a particular person whose past record indicates a propensity to ignore planning control.

Often these two issues are linked – sensitive sites often attract a particular type of miscreant: endless changes in company names may be a feature of breaches by one person or small groups of people. The illegal mini-cab office which moves around the town centre as enforcement action is taken over the years would be a good example: the green belt site on the edge of urban development is an example of the site-dependent apprehended breach where the landlord would be the target for action. Such are the types of grounds most likely to convince a court to exercise its discretion and grant relief. However, the general principles regarding *quia timet* injunctions (discussed below in relation to section 222 injunctions) are still likely to figure in the court's exercise of its discretion. Such factors also, therefore, need to be taken into account.

9.7.4   Undertakings in damages

Although the court has an inherent discretion to require undertakings in damages even from the LPA it is clear from the House of Lords' decision in the *Kirklees* case that the court will, in its discretion, be unlikely to require such undertakings at the interlocutory stage[1]. The LPA is thus in a position equivalent to that of the Crown in enforcing the law.

1 *Kirklees Metropolitan Borough Council v Wickes Building Supplies Ltd* [1992] 3 All ER 717.

9.7.5 Injunctions against persons of unknown identity

LPAs can often encounter situations where the contravener hides behind a changing shield of intermediaries. If the identity of those intermediaries varies day to day then injunctive action against those directly involved in the contravention may still be possible by way of court rules made under the TCPA 1990, section 187B(3). RSC Order 110 sets out such rules whereby the High Court may grant an injunction against a person whose identity is unknown to the applicant[1]. The applicant LPA must, in its originating summons, describe the defendant by reference to:

   (a) a photograph,
   (b) a thing belonging to or in the possession of the defendant, or
   (c) any other evidence,

with sufficient particularity to enable service to be effected[2]. The applicant LPA must file in support of the originating summons evidence by affidavit:

   (a) verifying that they were unable to ascertain, within the time reasonably available to them, the defendant's identity;
   (b) setting out the action taken to ascertain the defendant's identity, and
   (c) verifying the means by which the defendant has been described in the originating summons and that the description is the best that the applicant LPA is able to provide[3].

It should be noted that the order explicitly notes that these provisions are without prejudice to the power of the court to make an order for substituted service or to dispense with service. These avenues should also be explored when faced with problems of service. Similar rules apply to the county court[4].

1 Inserted by RSC (Amendment) 1991, SI 1992/638.
2 Ord 110, r 2.
3 Ibid r 3.
4 County Court Rules 1981, Ord 49, r 6 (substituted by SI 1992/793).

9.7.6 Injunctions and enforcement policy

The discretionary power given to the court when considering an application for an injunction is a feature of the remedy which can be to the advantage of the LPA. A very wide range of issues will be relevant when the court examines the arguments for and against an injunction. Since we are concerned with an injunction given statutory recognition in the planning legislation then clearly that statutory context and planning arguments in favour of a grant will be of considerable importance. This suggests that the emphasis on the development plan in guiding planning decisions is an important factor from the statutory context which is relevant to the court's exercise of its discretion. This is where the planning trinity perspective again comes into play: the LPA is in a stronger position to persuade the court to exercise its discretion in favour of the LPA if it can rely on enforcement policies whose 'target' is clearly defined. By 'target' I mean those breaches which have a particularly damaging impact on the proper planning of the area: breaches affecting listed buildings, conservation areas, trees etc are examples of such targets which will be relevant for all LPAs. The LPA can then use the statutory context (section 54A) as a further argument in its favour. LPAs should thus bear in mind this factor when considering enforcement policies for their development plans.

9.7.7 Injunctions – wording

The wording of the injunction sought should be given very close attention. The LPA must be awake to the possibility of non-compliance and the options then open to it. Since most LPAs will deal with non-compliance by instituting contempt proceedings the nature of such proceedings must be taken into account. In such proceedings the standard of proof is the criminal standard and so if the LPA is to point to breaches of the injunction it will have to have cast-iron proof of contempt: in providing such proof the LPA will necessarily be restricted by the terms of the injunction – so this means that the injunction must itself be enforceable and precise. If the LPA allows the injunction to be worded in a complex manner with many provisos to protect the contravener then this may mean that enforcement is made very difficult: in a sense this takes the discussion back to the issue of practicality and the court should be made aware of the limitations placed on effective action under section 187B if the injunction is not worded in a relatively clear and enforceable manner.

The terms of an injunction will also have to deal with the ingenuity of the contravener to get around its terms. One way of avoiding injunctions is for the named individual to gain the benefit of the land by selling it to others (not specifically covered by the terms of the injunction). This problem cropped up in the *Ball* case[1]: according to the judgment in *Waverley Borough Council v Hilden*[2] the site in question was still being used in contravention of planning control despite the order made by the Court of Appeal on 17 July 1985. Thus the judge in the *Waverley* case made it clear that the order he contemplated would restrain each defendant from allowing others to station caravans on his or her pitch. Thus a sale of a pitch to another person to be used for the stationing of caravans would represent a breach of the order and place both vendor and purchaser in contempt of court. The various ways of evading the terms of an injunction should therefore be very carefully assessed when an applicant applies for an injunction – the appropriate (watertight) drafting of the injunction should therefore be a key element in the application and not a mere afterthought. In the *Waverley* case the judge was of the opinion that the terms of the injunction should not include an order that the defendants should be required in the injunction to undertake certain works (removal of close board fence, hardcore, huts etc) – that could be done by the authority using its works in default power. In contrast however it should be noted that in contempt proceedings for breach of an injunction relating to a listed building the High Court did secure undertakings from the contravener to pay for restorative and remedial works connected with the breach of the injunction – see para 10.18.1.

1 *Runnymede Borough Council v Ball* [1986] 1 All ER 629.
2 [1988] JPL 175 at 184.

9.7.8 Contempt proceedings

Case law under the section 222 provision (relating to contempt proceedings) will still be relevant to contempt proceedings stemming from a planning injunction. One point to note at the beginning however is that the contemnor's disobedience need not amount to 'stubborn opposition' or 'obstinacy', nor need it be 'rebellious'. All that is necessary is that it was intentional or reckless. Such is the law as stated by the Court of Appeal and the House of Lords in *Heatons Transport Ltd v TGWU*[1]. An example of contempt proceedings relating to a tipping breach is noted in *Planning Magazine*[2] – the injunction was directed at the storing, sorting or spreading of waste and the creation of hardstanding on a site in the green belt and an area of natural beauty. Twenty-nine breaches of the injunction were alleged – the defendant disputed ten of these saying that drivers in his employ had breached the injunction but without his knowledge or consent. Naturally, the deputy judge found this assertion 'incredible'. A four-month jail sentence (suspended for nine months) was imposed. It is also relevant to note that if the injunction is made against an individual or a corporation and a servant or agent fails to comply with the injunction then the individual or corporation may be in contempt. Thus the ordinary test of vicarious liability applies also to the servant or agent acting on behalf of the employer or principal.

The court may commit for contempt those who are not included in the injunction but who help a defendant to commit a breach of that injunction knowing of its existence. The litigation over the *Spycatcher* book provides an example of a situation where parties not named in the injunction could still find themselves in contempt of court for undertaking action which the injunction prohibited[3]. A director of a company the subject of an injunction will be in contempt if he fails to take reasonable steps to ensure that the terms of an injunction are obeyed. If the director could reasonably believe that another officer was taking such steps then he will not have 'wilfully' breached the injunction[4].

1 [1973] AC 15, [1972] 3 All ER 101.
2 15 June 1990, p 7.
3 *A-G v Newspaper Publishing plc* [1988] Ch 333, CA.
4 *A-G for Tuvala v Philatelic Distribution Corpn Ltd* [1990] 2 All ER 216.

9.7.9 Direct action as an alternative to committal proceedings

LPAs should be aware that committal action is not the only option. The court (under RSC Ord 45, r 8) may direct that the *mandatory* elements of an injunction be carried out by the plaintiff or some other person appointed by the court at the defendant's expense. This would be enforced by the court: this may therefore offer the LPA a means of ensuring that a mandatory injunction is obeyed – though gaining a mandatory injunction in the first place is usually more difficult (see the discussion of mandatory injunctions below).

9.7.10 Sequestration

Under RSC Ord 45, r 5 the court may also use sequestration as a sanction against an individual or body corporate for non-compliance with an injunction.

9.7.11 When section 222 rules apply

It should be remembered however that some breaches of control will still only be amenable by action under the more restrictive power – section 222. Section 187B action is only permissible where there is (or is threatened) a breach of planning control. This is defined in section 171A as covering unauthorised development or failing to comply with any planning condition. Breach of a planning obligation (for example) will therefore not be a trigger for a section 187B injunction – the LPA will still be subject to the rules applicable to the section 222 type of injunction. Breaches of advertisement control will also not (unless they also involve breaches of planning control – which can be often the case) be amenable to action under section 187B.

9.7.11.1 *Local Government Act 1972, section 222*

The starting point is section 222 of the Local Government Act 1972. This states:

> 'Where a local authority considers it expedient for the promotion or protection of the interests of the inhabitants of their area

(a) they may prosecute or defend or appear in any legal proceedings, and in the case of civil proceedings, may institute them in their own name . . .'.

Applications to the High Court for an injunction will be by writ or by originating summons[1].

1 Rules of the Supreme Court Ord 5 r 4.

9.7.11.2 *Section 222 principles*

There are two principal cases, one relating to planning control[1] and one relating to construction site noise[2], which set the basis for the principles guiding the court's discretion within the context of section 222. The latter case produced a comprehensive set of 'guiding principles' which should be of general applicability in the field of public law (including planning). First the jurisdiction was to be invoked and exercised exceptionally and with great caution[3]. Second, a mere infringement of the criminal law was not enough for the court to entertain an application[4]. Third the basis for the grant of an injunction was *not* that there was a 'deliberate and flagrant breach' of the law[5], but the inference that the unlawful activity would continue unless and until restrained by the law – and that an injunction was the only effective way of guaranteeing that[6]. In this last case the court focussed on the 'clear evidence of persistent and serious conduct'. It is relevant that the court in the *Bovis* case (O'Connor LJ) said that if the work 'contravened the terms of the notice that was a deliberate contravention, and the judge had been correct to hold that it was proper to grant injunctive relief'. Thus it was not necessary to wait for a prosecution. In contrast, the *Smith* case[7] suggested that if the breach did not involve 'irreparable damage' to the land then a first prosecution would have to be followed by the initiation of a second prosecution before the court would be likely to grant an injunction. Such a position seems to be less tenable now given the more recent cases; the discussion of *quia timet* injunctions would also suggest that the 'irreparable damage' criterion is now inappropriate.

1 *Runnymede Borough Council v Ball* [1986] 1 All ER 629, [1986] JPL 288 and *Runnymede Borough Council v Smith* [1986] JPL 592.
2 *City of London Corpn v Bovis Construction Ltd* (1988) 86 LGR 660.

3 *Gouriet v Union of Post Office Workers* [1978] AC 435, [1977] 3 All
   ER 70.
4 *Stoke-on-Trent Borough Council v B&Q (Retail) Ltd* [1984] AC 754
   at 767 and 776.
5 This was the test that had sometimes appeared in recent decisions
   but was not an accurate summary of the criteria set out in the *B&Q
   Retail* case.
6 *Wychavon District Council v Midland Enterprises (Special Events)
   Ltd* (1987) 86 LGR 83 at 89.
7 See note 1, above.

9.7.11.3 *Quia timet injunctions*

In most cases the type of injunction being sought will be the
prohibitory injunction – one which prevents (for example)
'damage' to important planning interests. However, a reference
in the 'Current Topics' section of the *Journal of Planning Law*[1]
suggests that the High Court will also entertain applications for
injunctions in respect of an imminent breach. The discussion in
the JPL thus noted an unreported case[2] which involved premises
originally used by members of one family as two flats. The
council found that the property was in the process of conversion
for occupation as nine bedsit flats. The LPA got in touch with the
owner and told him that planning application was required but
that it would be unlikely to be granted. He was thus informed
also that enforcement action was being considered. It seems
that the premises were gradually being occupied as bedsits but
the true legal position as to whether enforcement and stop
notices could be used was in doubt. Warnings to the owners were
ignored. The High Court however granted an injunction on the
following bases:

  (i)   that it was expedient for the promotion of the interests of
        the inhabitants of the council's area;
  (ii) that the council was reasonable in considering it expedient
        to seek an injunction;
  (iii) that an injunction was appropriate in the case;
  (iv) that the breach was deliberate and flagrant in that there
        had been a clear breach and that the owner had ignored
        the council's warnings and a breach would occur if not
        restrained by injunction.

Such a remedy has some of the hallmarks of a *quia timet*
injunction (though the report is not clear) and represents an

important development in this particular field. The apparent focus of the court on the 'promotion' limb of the section 222 wording is also highly relevant as LPAs who can call in aid the development plan policy when seeking relief under section 222 can emphasise the importance of 'promoting' the planning interests of their area.

The LPA that can demonstrate that it has good grounds for fearing (thus the link with *quia timet* injunctive relief) that the contravener will merely play the system unless restrained by an injunction may thus be able to get a district-wide prohibition imposed on the contravener. The authority which comes across such a 'roving' breach problem may therefore, on the basis of the *Morris* case referenced in that discussion, have good grounds for seeking an injunction to prevent future breaches of control of a specified kind within the boundaries of the district. *Quia timet* injunctions are only granted where the applicant meets criteria that are stricter than those normally applied: such criteria are the same as those applicable to mandatory injunctions – the next topic for discussion.

1 [1989] JPL 645.
2 *London Borough of Southwark v M L Frow* [1989] JPL 645n.

9.7.11.4 *Mandatory injunctions*

If the LPA is seeking a mandatory injunction based on section 222 (eg to require action under a planning obligation) then, as was noted above in the discussion of *quia timet* injunctions, the courts will apply quite strict standards. In the case of *Redland Bricks Ltd v Morris*[1] Lord Upjohn set out four general principles to be taken into account when a mandatory or *quia timet* injunction is sought. These principles are:

'(1) A mandatory injunction can only be granted where the plaintiff shows a very strong probability upon the facts that grave damage will accrue to him in the future.
(2) The plaintiff must also show that damages will not be a sufficient or adequate remedy if such damage does happen.
(3) Unlike the case where a negative injunction is granted to prevent the continuance or recurrence of a wrongful act the question of the cost to the defendant to do works to prevent or lessen the likelihood of a future apprehended wrong must be an element to be taken into account.

(4) If in the exercise of its discretion the court decides that it
is a proper case to grant a mandatory injunction, then the
court must be careful to see that the defendant knows
exactly what he has to do, and this means not as a matter
of law but as a matter of fact.'

Such principles need necessarily to be construed by reference to
the particular public law context of an application by the LPA
under the Local Government Act 1972, section 222. The LPA's
case will be strengthened by being able to rely upon well
phrased enforcement policies in the local plan which include the
'promote and protect' language of that section – see above.

1 [1970] AC 652 at 665G–666G.

9.7.12 Judicial review

In the *B&Q Retail* case Lord Templeman noted that the exercise
of the power under section 222 would be subject to judicial review.
This would also apply to the LPA's use of section 187B powers. The
standards of decision-making required by administrative law
principles must apply. The well-advised contravener faced with an
application for an injunction may closely examine the decision-
making procedure employed by the LPA for any errors. Such errors
could be the basis of an attack by an application for judicial review.
In order to protect itself against such actions the LPA will need to
ensure that its decision to seek injunctive relief has been taken
after consideration of all relevant options. Thus in seeking relief
under section 187B (or related planning provisions dealing with
specialised regimes) or section 222 the LPA should (if only briefly
in a report to committee) address the other normal enforcement
options such as the use of the works in default powers. The LPA
would also be wise to consider, at least on paper, the severity of the
non-compliance and the inappropriateness of underenforcing by
way of the various powers to withdraw, waive or relax the
requirements of a notice that has taken effect[1]. These and other
powers are all relevant in considering the 'public interest' issues
and the LPA might court legal challenge by way of judicial review
if it was seen to ignore all other courses of action open to it.

1 TCPA 1990, s 173A(1)(a) deals with the withdrawal of an
enforcement notice: exercise of this withdrawal power does not
affect the power to issue a further notice – section 173A(4). TCPA

1990, s 173A(1)(b) allows the LPA to 'waive or relax any requirement ... and, in particular, [they] may extend any period' set down in the notice as the compliance period. These powers may also, of course, be exercised before the notice takes effect: see the TCPA 1990, s 173A(2). When exercising the powers under section 173A(1) the LPA must immediately given notice of such exercise to every person who has been served with a copy of the original enforcement notice - section 173A(3).

10 Listed buildings – enforcement issues

10.1 INTRODUCTION

The listed building regime is probably the most prolific source of enforcement cases after mainstream enforcement. The potential number of breaches is not only high because of the large number of buildings that are listed but also because the regime's enforcement provisions are more 'invasive' and bring into play the option of the criminal sanction right at the beginning. However, despite the extra enforcement teeth that seem to be available the reality is often that enforcing listed building controls is just as difficult as enforcing normal mainstream controls. In some ways it might be said to be more difficult since the objective of the enforcement regime (ensuring that the architectural or historic features of such a building are not harmed) may often come up against breaches of control that involve economic arguments and/or elements of some substance.

10.1.1 English Heritage and enforcement

English Heritage (in respect of contraventions within Greater London) can take enforcement action under the P(LB&CA)A 1990, section 38 and use the works in default powers in section 42[1]. It can also make use of the statutory injunction provisions in the P(LB&CA)A 1990, section 44A in respect of any LPA area[2]. In addition it can institute, in its own name, proceedings to restrain the contravention of any provision of the P(LB&CA)A 1990[3]. English Heritage invariably liaises with the relevant LPA (helping it with technical advice and assistance) rather than using such enforcement powers alone.

1 By virtue of the P(LB&CA)A 1990, s 45.
2 P(LB&CA)A 1990, s 44A(4) extends the definition of 'local planning authority' found in subsection (1) to English Heritage.
3 National Heritage Act 1983, s 33(2A).

10.2 THE WIDER SCOPE OF CONTROL

It should always be remembered that the scope of listed building control is broader than that of mainstream planning control. There are two main reasons for this extended control:

(a) the range of activities that fall within the ambit of listed building control is defined by reference to those 'works' which would affect the features of the building that are important to its 'listed' status. This means that internal works (exempted from planning control by the GPDO) to a listed building can be controlled;

(b) the extended definition given to the term 'listed building' means that objects which might not normally fall within the term 'building' are in fact covered by the listed building regime.

The second point produces some problems for enforcing authorities. The legislation thus treats as 'part of the building':

'(a) any object or structure fixed to the building;
 (b) any object or structure within the curtilage of the building which, although not fixed to the building, forms part of the land and has done so since before 1st July 1948[1].'

A large tapestry fixed to the wall of a listed building is thus 'part of' the listed building. An urn that is secured to the ground would thus be covered by this extended definition. A complication arises where a structure falling within the second category also has 'parts' which are not fixed in a permanent way to the structure itself: the problem then arises whether removal of such a part (eg a statuette merely resting by its own weight on a 'folly' but constituting an integral element of that folly) would be an alteration of that part (the folly) of the listed building. A good case can be made for saying that such a removal is an 'alteration' since, in common sense terms, the removal of such an integral feature does 'alter' that part of the listed building. A problem might arise however, with the term 'works'. Does this term require a scale or type of activity of a certain description? It might be relevant here to look at a detailed analysis of 'operational' development which may well rely on similar fundamental concepts. It is relevant to note that painting a building can constitute 'works for [its] alteration' – *Windsor and Maidenhead Royal Borough Council v Secretary of State for the Environment*[2].

1 P(LB&CA)A 1990, s 1(5).
2 [1988] JPL 410.

10.3 CRIMINAL AND ADMINISTRATIVE SANCTIONS

A preliminary point worth stressing is that in addition to action under the powers to issue a listed building enforcement notice the LPA may find that the following criminal sanctions (under the P(LB&CA)A 1990) can be applied:

(a) prosecution under the P(LB&CA)A 1990, section 9 (available in those circumstances when a listed building enforcement notice can be issued);

(b) prosecution under section 59 (the 'intentional damage' offence).

The 'intentional damage' offence is often overlooked by authorities. This is a serious error as it can cover problems not falling within the scope of an enforcement notice. The sanctions available to the LPA thus may comprise:

(a) listed building enforcement notice;

(b) prosecution ('unauthorised works' and 'intentional damage' offences);

(c) statutory injunction.

A very important aspect of control under this regime is the concept of 'authorised works'. The legislation employs this idea for many purposes: a distinction is made between authorised works for the alteration or extension of a building and authorised demolition works.

10.4 AUTHORISED ALTERATIONS AND EXTENSIONS

Works 'for the alteration or extension' of a listed building are 'authorised' when:

(a) they are carried out in compliance with a listed building consent; and

(b) any conditions attached to a consent are obeyed[1].

Where works for the alteration or extension of a listed building are not so authorised then the LPA is able to employ the various enforcement sanctions. A small point that might be relevant here is the use of the 'for' (rather than 'of') when describing the works which are subject to control. As is suggested later (see para 10.8.2.1) the choice of 'for' in preference to 'of' may be significant.

1   P(LB&CA)A 1990, s 8(1).

10.5   AUTHORISED DEMOLITION

As regards works for the demolition of a listed building there is an extra requirement. Such works must be preceded by the giving of notice[1] of the proposals to the Royal Commission on Historical Monuments for England – in Wales the appropriate body is the Royal Commission on Ancient and Historical Monuments (Wales). The developer must then either:

(a) for at least one month after the grant of listed building consent and before the works are started afford reasonable access to the Commission for the purpose of recording the building; or

(b) have received a statement in writing from the Commission that they have completed their recording of the building or that they do not wish to record it[2].

Where works of demolition have taken place or are about to take place then the LPA may (if the listed building consent requirements have been met) wish to contact the appropriate Commission to check on compliance with the notice requirements. Since the notice provisions cover both partial as well as total demolition the scope of 'control' arising from this requirement is quite wide. LPAs may therefore consider reviewing their system of 'monitoring' this type of control by systematic liaison with the two Commissions whenever 'demolition' of a listed building is involved.

1   P(LB&CA)A 1990, s 8(2)(b).
2   Ibid ss (2)(c).

10.6   ALTERATION/PARTIAL DEMOLITION

There is some dispute as to the difference between works for the alteration of a building and works for its demolition. Since the definition of 'building' includes part of the building then 'partial demolition' is 'demolition' for the purposes of the legislative scheme. However, how does 'partial demolition' differ from 'alteration or extension'. The case law points to some difficulty with divining the legislative intent in construing the relevant provisions and providing a clear answer to this question. A suggestion from an earlier case that the answer depends on whether the application was 'predominantly' concerned with demolition or alteration was seen, by the Court of Appeal, as being 'unworkable at best and meaningless at worst'[1]. The Court of Appeal (by a majority verdict) thus overturned a view of the legislation adopted by the Lands Tribunal which seemed to offer one way out of the legislative muddle. So although many 'refurbishment' schemes (to use a neutral term) might involve demolition of part of a building as an element in a scheme of works that alters the building the Court of Appeal has indicated that the 'demolition' element is not subsumed within the larger scheme. Demolition and alteration on this basis are mutually exclusive categories: the Lands Tribunal approach took the opposite line by suggesting that demolition might only be subsidiary to alteration. (This case was concerned, at base, with compensation liability which is now an historical footnote yet the distinction can still be relevant to the basic operation of listed building control and, consequently, enforcement.) The Court of Appeal's attempt to address this problem is unlikely to be the last word (the case is to be appealed).

1 [1981] JPL 752 at 753.
2 Comments made by Millett LJ (in the majority Court of Appeal judgment in the case of *Shimizu UK Ltd v Westminster City Council* [1995] 23 EG 118) on the approach taken by the High Court in *R v North Hertfordshire District Council, ex p Sullivan* [1981] JPL 752.

10.7 CONTRAVENTIONS

Any contravention of section 9(1) or 9(2) gives the LPA jurisdiction to consider the expediency of issuing an enforcement notice[1]. Such unauthorised works, whether their unauthorised nature arises from the lack of listed building consent or from a failure to comply with a condition also give rise to immediate criminal liability. The LPA should also investigate whether the other ground of criminal liability (causing damage to a listed building

– P(LB&CA)A 1990, section 59) is relevant. In terms of using enforcement powers effectively this dual liability (triple if the 'intentional damage' offence is involved) should be exploited by the authority and all possible enforcement action be taken whenever possible.

1 P(LB&CA)A 1990, s 38(1).

10.7.1 Entry and requisition powers

The P(LB&CA)A 1990, sections 88, 88A and 88B confer powers of entry on any person duly authorised by the LPA, Secretary of State or English Heritage (as regards Greater London) similar in scope to those given under the TCPA 1990, sections 196A, 196B and 196C. Officers investigating contraventions of listed building control should therefore ensure that their written authorisation and the LPA's standing orders etc reflect the different statutory authority. By virtue of the P(LB&CA)A 1990, section 89(1) the powers granted by the TCPA 1990, section 330 to require information as to interests in land are also applied for the purposes of the P(LB&CA)A 1990. The discussion of the TCPA 1990 provisions in chapter two is therefore relevant. The implications of PACE in the investigation of potential breaches of listed building control will need to be taken into account: comments regarding such matters are made in para 9.3.1.

10.7.2 Listed building enforcement notice

The LPA may exercise its discretion to issue a listed building enforcement when the following 'preconditions' are met:

(a) it appears to the LPA that,
(b) any works have been or are being executed,
(c) to a listed building in their area,
(d) and such works involve a contravention of section 9(1) or (2).

These preconditions function in a way similar to the preconditions that govern the exercise of the discretion to take enforcement action in mainstream enforcement. It should be remembered that although action can be taken against works being carried out *in flagrante delicto* there are no special listed building stop notices which can 'bite' before the listed building enforcement notice takes effect. If the breach also involves a breach of mainstream planning control then a stop notice could be issued.

10.7.3 The substantive discretion

Once the preconditions governing the discretion are met the LPA:

(a) may issue a listed building enforcement notice if they consider it expedient to do so,
(b) having regard to the effect of the works on,
(c) the character of the listed building[1].

These issues will be examined below. However, it is pertinent to remember the following point: since many listed buildings are within conservation areas the LPA should also be aware of the impact of the conservation area test in section 72 – see para 10.7.3.4 and chapter eleven.

1 P(LB&CA)A 1990, s 38(1).

10.7.3.1 *May issue etc*

The permissive 'may' clearly underlines (especially when combined with the term 'expedient') that the discretion is widely drawn. In fact the discussion of the discretionary power to take mainstream enforcement action (see para 5.3) is relevant here but must be tempered by the different structure of that power. Those differences relate to the 'relevant considerations' that must be taken into account when assessing 'expediency'. These issues are discussed next.

10.7.3.2 *Having regard to etc*

Again the phraseology stresses that authorities should not automatically take enforcement action if the listed building is harmed. However, this needs to be read in the light of the phraseology in section 1(1) of the P(LB&CA)A 1990 which states:

'For the purposes of this Act and with a view to the guidance of local planning authorities in the performance of their functions under this Act and the principal Act in relation to buildings of special architectural or historic interest, the Secretary of State shall compile lists of such buildings . . .'.

Thus the LPA should be 'guided' by the fact that the building is listed (and given a grading on the list) when exercising its enforcement (and other) powers under the P(LB&CA)A 1990.

10.7.3.3 *The character of the listed building*

Purists might object to the paraphrase here – the legislation does not use the phrase 'listed building': instead the term is 'building . . . of special architectural or historic interest'. This means the same but might usefully be highlighted since the basis of the building's listing might be either 'historical' or 'architectural'. The listing is not a definitive version of the important features of a building. The listing description may not cover important features. Indeed some buildings are listed which, on closer inspection, turn out to be much older (Tudor as opposed to Georgian, for example) than is stated to be the case in the listing. The 'unauthorised works' may well have helped to reveal the true 'character' of the building! It is also important to bear these terms ('special architectural or historic interest') in mind since they provide a good link to the other criteria which may be relevant to this discretion: this is the impact of the conservation area test.

10.7.3.4 *The conservation area test*

A listed building may be within a conservation area. In such a case any exercise of powers under the planning legislation involving enforcement action in respect of the listed building problem will also trigger the application of the conservation area test in the P(LB&CA)A 1990, section 72(1). (See the discussion in chapter 11 of this test and its relevance to the enforcement discretion and the inspector's consideration of the issues on appeal.)

10.8   CONTENTS OF NOTICE

Statute requires that a listed building enforcement notice specify four items:

(a) the alleged contravention;
(b) the steps required;
(c) the period(s) for compliance; and
(d) the date of effectiveness (the 'specified date')[1].

The failure to include any of the above and to specify them with sufficient clarity could mean that the document may be quashed by the Secretary of State on appeal. The comments made in chapter six as respects deficiencies in form and substance of and in chapter seven as regards the powers on appeal to correct errors etc are thus relevant here. Most authorities will set out listed building enforcement notices in a way parallel to the style used for normal enforcement notices – a map and statement of reasons will therefore be included.

1   P(LB&CA)A 1990, s 38(2) and (3).

10.8.1   The alleged contravention

There need only be an 'apparent' contravention. The discussion of this feature of the enforcement power in mainstream enforcement is thus relevant here. There is no 'four-year rule' with these notices. Section 38(1), however, does not apply to any works executed or caused to be executed before 1 January 1969. Works carried out before then cannot be in contravention of section 38(1). This statutory rule depends on a provision in Schedule 24 of the TCPA 1971 which still continues to have effect by virtue of the Planning (Consequential Provisions) Act 1990, Schedule 3, paragraph 3. Thus by virtue of the TCPA 1971, Schedule 24, Part V, paragraph 23 any works carried out before 1 January 1969 cannot be in contravention of section 38(1) of the P(LB&CA)A 1990. In theory, a contravention that occurred after 1 January 1969 could still be the subject of a listed building enforcement notice – problems of proof and 'reasonableness' (before the inspector) might make such action difficult.

One limitation on the enforcement power concerns damage caused to a listed building by a third party. Damage from the impact of a vehicle seems to be a common example. The DOE's view is that such damage by a third party does not fall within the terms of section 7 as 'works for' the demolition, alteration or extension of a listed building[1]. This seems correct in that the owner/occupier can hardly have 'caused' the works if they arise from the impact of someone else's car. Any subsequent works carried out to deal with the damage would then seem likely to fall within the 'defence' that the subsequent works were 'urgently necessary' for safety, health etc[2]. It would seem unlikely that the person actually causing the damage could be prosecuted for the 'intentional damage' offence in section 59 since there is a proviso that only a person 'otherwise entitled' to carry out such works can be found liable – see para 10.17.3. The ordinary offence of 'criminal damage' would be available though.

1 Ministerial decision reported in [1981] JPL 443.
2 P(LB&CA)A 1990, s 9(3).

10.8.2 The steps required

The LPA may requires steps for:

  (a) restoring the building to its former state;
  (b) executing such further (specified) works as it considers necessary to alleviate the effect of the works carried out without listed building consent (where the authority considers such restoration would be undesirable or not reasonably practicable);
  (c) bringing the building to the state in which it would have been if the terms and conditions of any listed building consent granted for the works had been complied with[1].

As regards the first type of 'step' it seems that even though a building is no longer in existence on the original site it can still be 'restored'. The saga of Stagbatch Farm near Leominster in Herefordshire provides two cases which illustrate both this point and the use of injunctions[2]. A timber barn was dismantled and removed from a site (leaving only foundations and footings). An injunction prevented its export from the UK. An enforcement notice was upheld requiring its replacement on the site. Thus even though the barn was just a mass of timbers in shipping crates it was still a 'building' for the purposes of the listed building provisions.

Another point to bear in mind is that any step for a building's 'restoration' cannot validly require action which would be an 'improvement' on its 'former' state. In a case[3] that arose from enforcement action in Bath a listed building had a roof which was made up of Welsh slates and asbestos cement tiles. The owners decided to re-cover the whole roof with asbestos tiles. The council issued a listed building enforcement notice which required all asbestos slates to be replaced with Welsh slates – thus affecting also those asbestos tiles in position before the owner did his retiling. The court held that this was not 'restoration' of the building to its condition before the unauthorised works were carried out but an improvement. The notice was quashed. This construction may not be as restrictive as might be supposed in all cases. If the asbestos slates had been added to the roof after 1 January 1969 then *that* 'alteration' would be a contravention of section 7. Thus a LPA facing a similar problem should try to investigate the site history and see how much of the building has been subjected to 'unauthorised works' since the beginning of 1969 and try to tackle the situation using that date as a starting point.

1 P(LB&CA)A 1990, s 38(2).
2 *Leominster District Council v British Historic Buildings and SPS Shipping* [1987] JPL 350 and *R v Leominster District Council, ex p Antique Country Buildings Ltd* [1988] JPL 554.
3 *Bath City Council v Secretary of State for the Environment* (1983) 47 P & CR 663, [1983] JPL 737.

10.8.2.1 *Alleviating steps – deemed consent*

Where the LPA has required works to alleviate the effect of the breach then section 38(7) grants deemed consent for any 'works of demolition, alteration, or extension of the building executed as a result of compliance with the notice'. Thus where a contravener is carrying out such works he is not required to obtain express listed building consent. An interesting point of construction arises from the phraseology here. In the provision dealing with the need for express listed building consent the phrase used is 'works for the demolition of a listed building or for its alteration or extension'. Yet instead of the phrase 'works for' we have 'works of' in the deemed grant of consent provision. Whether the different phraseology has significance is uncertain.

One argument might be that the 'for' implies that the works were executed with the 'intention' of alteration etc: the Ministerial decision noted in para 10.8.1 regarding the collision of a car with a listed building would tie in with this interpretation. In contrast 'works of' simply indicates a direct physical nexus – the works constitute the alteration etc and there is no need to demonstrate any 'intention' to alter etc.

10.8.3   The compliance period(s)

These must be reasonable and they run from the time when the notice becomes effective. 'Reasonableness' will depend on the complexity of the works – it might even depend on whether skilled craftsmen are available to do the works at the time required.

10.8.4   The specified date

This is the date on which the notice takes effect. It must not be earlier than 28 days after the last date on which copies of the notice are served[1]. The LPA should generally allow a few extra days after service to allow for any problems.

1   P(LB&CA)A 1990, s 38(4).

10.9   SERVICE

Service of copies must take place no later than 28 days after issue[1]. The term 'issue' (just as with normal enforcement notices) appears to be the official production by the proper officer of the council – usually the Chief Executive/Town Clerk – of the notice with all the necessary dates and items of information on it. The methods of service are detailed in chapter six. Service must be on:

   (a) the owner and occupier of the building, and
   (b) any other person having an interest in that building, being an interest which in the opinion of the authority is materially affected by the notice[2].

Again the terminology is similar to that used in mainstream enforcement – see chapter six for comments.

1   P(LB&CA)A 1990, s 38(4).
2   Ibid.

10.10   POINTS OF DIFFERENCE

Although listed building enforcement notices are similar in many respects to ordinary enforcement notices there are significant differences:

(a) there is no four-year or ten-year rule applied to listed building enforcement notices. In theory, any unauthorised works carried out after listing and after 1 January 1969 could be the subject of a listed building enforcement notice;

(b) listed buildings enforcement notices are only concerned with 'works' – and thus they are similar to 'operational' enforcement notices. Uses cannot be (directly) the subject of a listed building enforcement notice;

(c) the issue of a listed building enforcement notice alone cannot be followed by a stop notice to stop the 'activities' (ie the 'unauthorised works') on the land;

(d) the grounds of appeal, and thus the planning arguments, are necessarily flavoured by the particular features of the listed building regime;

(e) the extended meaning given to 'listed building' enables enforcement to cover a wider range of works.

10.11   THE APPEAL

Comments made in the chapter on appeals in respect of ordinary enforcement notices have general applicability here. Thus clearly it is important to assess the grounds of appeal and the supporting evidence upon which the appellant relies. Not only is such scrutiny necessary as regards the proper examination of substantive issues, it is also relevant to the proper formulation of a costs application and the formulation of a defence to such an application. The appeal also offers the LPA the opportunity (where appropriate) to correct flaws in the notice and even take account of new information as regards the damage caused by the breach. The powers of the Secretary of State or his inspector to correct and vary the notice are therefore important aspects of the appeal and the comments in chapter seven regarding the correction and variation powers should be noted.

10.12 APPEAL GROUNDS

A person having an interest in the building to which a listed building enforcement notice relates or a 'relevant occupier'[1] may appeal to the Secretary of State on grounds specified in the legislation. The grounds are similar to those for mainstream enforcement notices; they are supplemented by grounds by which the contravener can, in effect, ask for the building to be de-listed and a ground which contends that the contravening works were urgently necessary in the interests of safety or health or for the preservation of the building. The prudent LPA will, of course, ensure that enforcement action will not be prejudiced by a weak case on any of the grounds of appeal.

1 This term (P(LB&CA)A 1990, s 39(7)) covers a person who occupies the building on the date on which the notice was issued by virtue of a licence and continues to occupy the building when the appeal is brought.

10.12.1 The inspector's powers

The range of powers available to the inspector on appeal are as broad as those available to him when deciding a normal enforcement appeal. As a matter of law he must consider the issue of whether to use such powers. The powers fall into three categories, ie powers relating to:

  (a) the listed building enforcement notice;
  (b) listed building consent;
  (c) the listed status of the building.

10.12.1.1 *Powers relating to the notice*

The standard powers to quash, correct or vary the notice are made available[1]. The discussion of these powers in terms of mainstream enforcement notices is thus relevant. If the notice has flaws then the authority should argue for its correction – see chapter seven. If the trend visible in mainstream enforcement (towards the greater use of the correction power) becomes firmly established then the LPA should ensure that forceful arguments are made to the inspector persuading him to save a flawed notice. This can be done, it would seem, before the appeal is 'determined'. If the corrections are substantial then extra time may be necessary to allow the appellant to amend his grounds and deal with the corrected notice. Such an adjournment may involve the payment of costs (though if the correction was done at an early stage there would not be any 'costs necessarily and reasonably' incurred). Where mistakes have been made in a listed building enforcement notice the LPA may be able to correct all but the most fundamental by making appropriate submissions to the Secretary of State arguing that the power does enable a correction to be made before the substantive issues relating to the appeal are discussed. The existence of these discretionary powers means that the inspector must do all he can to 'get the enforcement notice in order'[2]. The inspector must:

(a) consider amending the notice, and
(b) if he decides not to amend it he should give clear reasons for not so doing.

1 P(LB&CA)A 1990, s 41(1) and (2).
2 *Bath City Council v Secretary of State for the Environment* (1983) 47 P & CR 663, [1983] JPL 737, quoting *Hammersmith London Borough Council v Secretary of State for the Environment* (1975) 30 P & CR 19 at 21.

10.12.1.2 *Powers relating to listed building consent*

The inspector may grant listed building consent or discharge any conditions imposed on a listed building consent[1]. The latter power also carries with it the power to impose extra conditions – these may be more onerous if the inspector considers it appropriate. The LPA may consider suggesting to the inspector that he 'tighten up' some conditions on a listed building consent if it has good arguments to support this: the inspector will, however, ensure that the contravener is aware of this possibility and so the contravener may in fact withdraw his appeal. If the building is in a conservation area then the increased emphasis on furthering the conservation area's features (the conservation area test) might be one basis for making such representations.

1 P(LB&CA)A 1990, s 41(6)(a) and (b) empower the Secretary of State to do so: such powers are granted to the inspector by Sch 3, para 2(1)(b).

10.12.1.3 *Powers relating to the listing of the building*

The inspector may 'de-list' the building[1]. He may also direct that the 'deemed' listing of a building (by virtue of the P(LB&CA)A 1990, Schedule 1, paragraph 1) that is protected solely by a building preservation order (the pre-1969 regime for protecting buildings of note) be nullified[2].

1 The Secretary of State is given this power to amend on appeal the list of buildings of special architectural or historic interest by the P(LB&CA)A 1990, s 41(6)(c); inspectors are given such power by the P(LB&CA)A 1990, Sch 3, para 2(1)(b).
2 P(LB&CA)A 1990, Sch 1, para 2(1) gives the Secretary of State power to do so 'at any time'. This power can be wielded by an inspector by virtue of Sch 3, para 2(1)(b).

10.13 WITHDRAWAL, RELAXATION OF NOTICE

The LPA may withdraw a listed building enforcement notice at any time[1]. On withdrawing the notice the authority has to give notice of the withdrawal to every person who was served with a copy of the notice[2]: where this happens after an appeal has been lodged the LPA should ensure that a copy of the withdrawal is sent to the DOE officer handling the appeal so that appeal proceedings can be halted. This provision also allows the LPA to waive or relax any requirements in a notice.

1 P(LB&CA)A 1990, s 38(5).
2 P(LB&CA)A 1990, s 38(6).

10.14   THE DECISION

The discussion in chapter seven on the appeal decision is of general relevance here. Where difficult issues of law, policy or fact have arisen during an appeal it is important that the LPA thoroughly scrutinises the appeal decision letter to ensure that the decision contains the necessary reasons to justify the determination.

10.15   NOTICE SUPERSEDED BY GRANT OF LISTED BUILDING CONSENT

Unauthorised works may be given retrospective authorisation[1]. The authorisation dates from the date of grant of the written consent. If such a retrospective listed building consent is granted after the issue of a listed building enforcement notice then the notice will cease to have effect in respect of two categories of 'steps' required under the notice. The first category of steps that ceases to have effect comprises those steps which would involve the works given retrospective authorisation being retained in accordance with the retrospective authorisation[2]. The second category of steps that ceases to have effect comprises those steps which require compliance with a condition of a previous listed building consent and the retrospective authorisation permits the retention of works without complying with such condition[3]. These provisions do not affect criminal liability in respect of a failure to comply with the notice before the relevant steps in the notice ceased to have effect[4]. A prosecution under these circumstances would be unlikely to result in a high penalty as the grant of retrospective consent would be pleaded as a factor in mitigation.

1   P(LB&CA)A 1990, s 8(3).
2   P(LB&CA)A 1990, s 44(1)(a).
3   P(LB&CA)A 1990, s 44(1)(b).
4   P(LB&CA)A 1990, s 44(2).

10.16   NON-COMPLIANCE WITH LISTED BUILDING ENFORCEMENT NOTICE

The usual trinity of sanctions can be used against the non-complying contravener:

(a) prosecution;
(b) the works in default power;
(c) injunction.

10.16.1 Prosecution

There is one offence for failure to comply: the owner will be liable
if any steps required has not been taken[1]. The structure of the
provisions are similar to those defining liability for non-
compliance with a mainstream enforcement notice. In subsection
(4) there is both an 'ignorance' defence and a defence that the
owner did everything that he could be expected to do to secure
compliance. In the latter case the important interests protected
by the listed building regime would probably set a high standard.
A 'financial benefit' provision is also included so that the court's
attention is specifically drawn to the profit that might accrue or
has accrued by reason of the offence[2]. In the magistrates' court
the penalty is a fine not exceeding £20,000: in the Crown Court
the fine is unlimited.

1 P(LB&CA)A 1990, s 43(1) and (2).
2 P(LB&CA)A 1990, s 43(6).

10.16.2 *The works in default power*

The works in default power is similar to that provided for
ordinary enforcement notices[1]. However, as the works required
may call for specialist skills then the authority should have at
hand a list of specialist contractors who can do such work.
English Heritage may also be able to advise on problems.
Amenity groups can be useful in providing local knowledge and
expertise. The works in default power arises after the expiration
of the compliance period or such longer period as the authority
may have agreed in writing with the contravener. The points to
bear in mind here are:

(a) the power covers only those works specified in the notice;
(b) any expenses reasonably incurred by the authority may
    be recovered from the person who is the owner of the listed
    building at the time the power is exercised[2];

   (c) there are powers to sell 'materials' removed in reliance on
       the power;
   (d) the liability of agents and trustees to pay the expenses of
       the LPA is limited.

As regards the first point it is important that the conservation
officer in the LPA does not get carried away. The terms of the
enforcement notice must be strictly followed. Stepping outside
the terms of the notice to any material extent would be ultra
vires and possibly prejudice the whole operation, especially the
recovery of expenses – the second point. Expenses are recoverable
as a simple contract debt. The third point (sale of materials) may
be relevant when the exercise of the default power results in the
removal of building materials – see chapter nine. The limited
liability of those 'owners' who are acting on behalf of the 'real'
owner is also covered in chapter nine. The latter two points arise
from the application to the works in default provisions by
regulations made under the provisions of the P(LB&CA)A 1990,
section 42(3)[3].

1 P(LB&CA)A 1990, s 42.
2 P(LB&CA)A 1990, s 42(1)(b)
3 Planning (Listed Buildings and Conservation Areas) Regulations
   1990, SI 1990/1519, reg 11 applies the Public Health Act 1936, ss
   276, 289 and 294 to listed building enforcement notices.

10.16.2.1 *Enforcement agreement*

The works in default power may be easier to use if the LPA has
a list of approved contractors. Such a list is also useful if the
authority is negotiating with the contravener. If the pressure on
the contravener is mounting he may be agreeable to carrying
out the works (with a slightly expanded timetable) in accordance
with an agreement setting out the appropriate terms of work
etc. A list of approved contractors allows the contravener to
select a contractor whilst ensuring (to some extent) that the
LPA can be confident that the work will be of sufficient quality.
The discussion of enforcement agreements in chapter nine is
thus relevant here.

10.16.2.2 *Power of sale*

The expenses recoverable under the P(LB&CA)A 1990, section

42(1) are, until recovered, a charge binding on successive owners of the land covered by the enforcement notice. This (just as is the case with mainstream enforcement notices and the works in default power in the TCPA 1990) means that where the expenses of the LPA have not been recovered then the LPA has the powers of a mortgagee under the Law of Property Act 1925. The LPA can, for example, arrange for the sale of the property in order to meet the expenses so charged on the land[1].

1 Planning (Listed Buildings and Conservation Areas) Regulations 1990, SI 1990/1519, reg 11(2) makes such expenses a charge binding on successive owners: this provision was inserted by the Town and Country Planning (Enforcement Notices and Appeals) Regulations 1991, SI 1991/2804, reg 10. See the discussion in para 9.5.3.1 of the power of sale etc.

10.16.3 Injunction

Non-compliance with a listed building enforcement notice may need injunctive action if the contravener seems unwilling to obey the terms of the notice on the strength of the normal sanctions of the criminal law. The 'strict liability' character of a contravention (see the following sections) indicates that the special interests protected by the listing are such as to support swift action by the LPA. (Non-compliance is not of itself an activity that triggers the new statutory injunction and so the LPA would have to rely on section 222 of the Local Government Act 1972.) Well-phrased enforcement policies that tie in with section 222 language (see the discussion of injunctions under section 222 in chapter nine) will be valuable aids in a successful application for such a remedy.

10.17 IMMEDIATE CRIMINAL LIABILITY FOR CONTRAVENTIONS

As has already been indicated there are in fact two types of offence that may be relevant. Liability under the first arises in circumstances where an enforcement notice could be issued – this offence is therefore concerned with 'unauthorised works'. The second offence is concerned with 'intentional damage'.

10.17.1 The 'unauthorised works' offence

The offence is one of strict liability[1]. It covers the person who:

(a) executes, or
(b) causes to be executed,
(c) unauthorised works to a listed building.

Strict liability means that liability for this offence cannot be avoided merely because the individual or the company being prosecuted was not aware that the building was listed. Thus as long as the other elements of the crime are present ('executes or causes to be executed' the unauthorised works) then the fact that the offender did not know that the building was listed – or even believed it was not listed – is irrelevant to the issue of guilt. The LPA wishing to prosecute someone who may raise the argument that he 'did not know' will have to consider whether his 'defence' will impress the court. If it does the penalty may be minimal. The liability of companies in this respect is important. The reader should study the discussion of directors' liability in the treatment of mainstream enforcement. By way of illustration a prosecution involving 'corporate' liability was noted in the *Journal of Planning Law*. This was a prosecution under the predecessor of section 9 at the Crown Court. It resulted in a company being fined £1,000 on two counts with £1,000 costs. A director of the company was convicted on the same lines and ordered to pay a fine of £17,000 on each of the two counts (£1,100 costs)[2]. Another director was penalised similarly.

1 *R v Wells Street Metropolitan Stipendiary Magistrate, ex p Westminster City Council* [1986] 3 All ER 4, [1986] 1 WLR 1046.
2 The case of *R v Chambers* 3 October, 1988, Cambridge Crown Court (noted in [1989] JPL 229).

10.17.1.1 *'Executes'*

The person actually carrying out the unauthorised works will be liable under the head of 'executes'.

10.17.1.2 *'Causes to be executed'*

Intermediaries (ie the advisors who are between the person owning the property and the contractors who physically carry

out the work) may also be liable to prosecution under this part
of the provision. Their role in instructing those 'on site' may give
rise to criminal liability. If they are in the chain of causation
then it would seem that they, as well as those above giving them
instructions, are liable for any unauthorised works[1]. There is
some protection available in the word 'cause'. The normal
interpretation of this word requires that the person in authority
gives a direction which is then carried out properly by the agent.
If the chain of causation is not broken by the unauthorised
activity of those receiving orders then it would seem that all
those above the actual contractors would come within the scope
of this second offence. The owner who tells his architect 'to get
on with the job' may thus set in motion a chain of events leading
to unauthorised works. The magistrates' court might not feel
too happy about convicting those further up the chain (especially
when they argue that they did not know the building was listed):
so the LPA should consider the practical difficulties of prosecuting
those who give the commands. Where a case is brought against
not only the contractors (for executing the works) but also the
architect and the owner (for causing the works to be executed)
then the LPA should take care to stress the importance of the
breach and the failure of the architect or owner to take adequate
care over the works.

1 See discussion of 'causes or permits' in chapter nine.

10.17.1.3 *Aiders and abetters*

The generally applicable rules of criminal law regarding aiders
and abetters may also be relevant in prosecuting those who
have been involved in the contravention: see chapter nine's
discussion of this issue. The interaction of aiding and abetting
principles with the statutory terms such as 'cause' may be an
area that will need exploration by the courts.

10.17.1.4 *Unauthorised works*

If the 'works' are works for the alteration or extension of a listed
building and require consent the authority will have to show
that they are works that 'affect its character as a building of
special architectural or historic interest'. This would involve

producing the listing of the building: if the listing did not cover the features affected (eg a fine interior) then expert evidence would need to be produced showing that the quoted proviso was met. With works comprising 'partial' demolition the LPA will probably have to deal with arguments as to whether it is 'demolition' or 'alteration'. This issue has been raised earlier in relation to the discussion on what constitutes authorised works. In the context of criminal law the court may take a narrow construction of the term demolition. The authority thus faces the possibility of having two definitions for the same term: one definition for enforcement notice purposes and one for prosecution purposes. The comments made in *Ivory v Secretary of State for the Environment*[1] by Kennedy J are thus pertinent here – see discussion of this issue in relation to mainstream enforcement.

1 [1985] JPL 796 – see para 9.6.8 and also the notion of the 'nugatory' enforcement notice.

10.17.1.5 *Penalties*

The offence is triable either way[1]. Thus before the magistrates' court the penalties are up to six months' imprisonment, a fine of up to £20,000 or both. If the case goes to the Crown Court the penalties up to 12 months' imprisonment, an unlimited fine or both[2]. In determining the fine imposed 'the court shall in particular have regard to any financial benefit which has accrued or appears likely to accrue' to the offender in consequence of the offence[3]. Prosecuting authorities should thus bring evidence (when going to the Crown Court) showing what 'financial benefit' has accrued or is likely to accrue as a result of the offence. A breach of control affecting a listed building may well have quite dramatic financial benefit for the owner of the building. If the building is so altered that its features giving rise to its listing are no longer apparent then it is likely that the building could be de-listed. This would then make the development of the site much more simple and thus more lucrative. A site that had (presumably) been worth considerably less because of the planning constraints (by reason of the listed building) before a major breach of control would therefore increase in value as the planning constraints disappear. Valuation evidence from the authority would be very relevant then in helping the court to reach a sensible figure for the 'financial benefit' arising from the breach of control.

1 Not merely the local authority but any individual or interest group could bring a prosecution. With the growing interest of amenity groups in planning issues there is the increasing likelihood of such groups bringing prosecutions.
2 P(LB&CA)A 1990, s 9(4).
3 Ibid.

10.17.1.6 *The statutory defence*

Where the accused raises the statutory defence set out in the legislation he will have to establish *all* of the following[1]:

(a) that the works to the building were urgently necessary in the interests of:
   (i)   safety,
   (ii) health, or
   (iii) for the preservation of the building;
(b) that it was not practicable to secure safety, health or the preservation of the building (whichever is the case) by works of repair or works for affording temporary support or shelter;
(c) that the works carried out were limited to the minimum measures immediately necessary;
(d) that notice in writing justifying in detail the carrying out of the works was given to the LPA as soon as reasonably practicable.

The LPA should require the maximum specificity of the accused when he attempts to plead this defence. Thus he should be consistent in his choice of 'justification' – is it safety or health or preservation of the building? Were all the works 'urgently necessary' – *not* 'desirable'? Evidence from structural engineers will thus be useful. The LPA must examine carefully the arguments suggesting that temporary support or shelter were not 'practicable': this term covers the reasonableness of any expenditure. The 'minimum measures' argument would be amenable to expert evidence from structural engineers.

1 P(LB&CA)A 1990, s 9(3).

10.17.2   Breach of condition offence

Failure to comply with a condition imposed on a listed building consent is a criminal offence[1]. Breach of an important condition should therefore merit some attention. The prosecuting authority should prepare its case fully so that magistrates are made well aware of the importance of such a condition. As has already been stressed (chapter nine and elsewhere) the proper handling of a prosecution under the planning legislation is of vital importance if an appropriate penalty is to be imposed.

1   P(LB&CA)A 1990, s 9(2).

10.17.3   Intentional damage to a listed building

The person who has control over the listed building where such control enables him to carry out building works to the building may find himself being prosecuted under section 59. Thus a person who:

(a) does or permits the doing of any act,
(b) other than 'excepted works' which,
(c) causes or is likely to result,
(d) in damage to,
(e) a listed building,
(f) with the intention of causing such damage,

commits an offence where 'but for this section [he] would be entitled to do so'.

This latter proviso limits the range of those who can be prosecuted to owners and occupiers who have rights under private law to carry out such works. Trespassers cannot, therefore, be prosecuted under this provision – though they will be guilty of criminal damage. 'Doing' damage to the building will be the easier offence to prosecute. If the LPA has to go against someone who 'permitted' the doing of damage then it will have to show that the person 'permitting' failed to prevent another carrying out the forbidden acts in circumstances where it could reasonably be said that he should have prevented such action[1].

1   *Ragsdale v Creswick* [1984] JPL 883 – see the discussion in chapter nine.

10.17.3.1 *'Excepted works'*

The term 'excepted works' is used here to cover those works which fall within the P(LB&CA)A 1990, section 59(3). This section covers:

- (a) works authorised by planning permission granted or deemed to be granted in pursuance of an application under the principal Act; or
- (b) works for which listed building consent has been given under the P(LB&CA)A 1990.

An act executed in relation to such 'excepted' works does not fall within the ambit of the intentional damage offence.

10.17.3.2 *Listed buildings*

The listed status of the building will have to be proved. Ecclesiastical buildings being used for such purposes and scheduled monuments are excluded from the protection of section 59 by virtue of section 60(1). A building covered by a building preservation notice does not receive the protection of this section – P(LB&CA)A 1990, section 3(5).

10.17.3.3 *Continuing offence*

Where a person convicted of a first offence under the 'intentional damage' provision then fails to take such reasonable steps as may be necessary to prevent any damage or further damage resulting from the offence he commits a further offence[1]. This is also an offence tried before a magistrates' court and the fine is based on a daily penalty of up to one-tenth of level 3 of the standard scale for each day that the defendant fails to take such reasonable steps (see para 9.6.11 for the standard scale).

1   P(LB&CA)A 1990, s 59(4).

10.17.3.4 *Corporations – exclusion from liability*

The TCPA 1990, section 331 deals with offences by corporations. This provision is applied to offences under the P(LB&CA)A 1990 by section 89(1) of that Act. However, an exception to this is made by section 89(2) of the P(LB&CA)A 1990 in respect of the 'damage' offence under section 59. Thus corporate liability does *not* extend to the 'damage' offence under the P(LB&CA)A 1990, section 59.

10.18 STATUTORY INJUNCTION

A provision corresponding to that found in mainstream enforcement allows the LPA to apply to the court for an injunction to deal with actual or apprehended contraventions of the P(LB&CA)A 1990, section 9(1) and (2)[1]. The listed building regime does not include a direct equivalent of the stop notice so this provides an avenue for taking swift action against such contraventions. The existence of enforcement policies (directed at listed buildings) in the development plan will be very useful in supporting the application to the court. Comments made in relation to the mainstream statutory injunction (chapter nine) should be studied.

1   P(LB&CA)A 1990, s 44A.

10.18.1 Contempt proceedings

An example reported in the *Journal of Planning Law*[1] indicates how severe the penalty may be where a contravener is found to be in contempt of court: this related to an injunction under section 222 but the example is still of use. The director of a property investment company was fined £25,000 for illegally rendering the exterior of a distinguished Georgian house in Newmarket. This was a Grade II listed building which the LPA had sought to protect by means of an injunction. In addition to the fine the defendants were also required to undertake to pay for restorative and remedial works to the brickwork of the listed building. Contempt proceedings are not the only sanction that the court can impose: the other sanctions (sequestration and ordering the works to be carried out by someone else) should not be forgotten and the LPA should consider submissions on such issues where appropriate – see discussion of the injunctive power in chapter nine.

1   [1990] JPL 397.

11 Conservation areas – enforcement issues

11.1 INTRODUCTION

The conservation area regime has three main impacts on the enforcement of planning controls:

  (a) in exercising any power under the planning Acts the decision-maker must comply with the statutory criteria in the P(LB&CA)A 1990, section 72(1) with its special emphasis on conservation area considerations;

  (b) a contravention of conservation area consent requirements gives rise to a power to issue a conservation area enforcement notice (with concomitant subsidiary powers);

  (c) a special statutory injunction is also available to restrain actual or apprehended breaches of the conservation area control regime.

The first impact is of greater importance as the latter two only relate to demolition of unlisted buildings in conservation areas[1]. Although the purpose of controlling such demolition is an important aspect of planning control within conservation areas it has much less effect than the conservation area test. The criteria in section 72(1) apply to all enforcement decisions (and other planning powers and functions) relating to land within a conservation area. The conservation area test thus colours all enforcement action taken against breaches of control in a conservation area. It is this wider impact of the conservation area regime that is of greater strategic relevance for the LPA in enforcing control. However, the discussion first deals with the more obvious aspect of enforcement in conservation areas – the failure to obtain conservation area consent for the demolition of an unlisted building.

---

1 P(LB&CA)A 1990, s 74.

11.1.1 English Heritage and enforcement

The enforcement powers which are granted to English Heritage as respects listed building contraventions are also made available to English Heritage in respect of conservation area contraventions (see para 10.1.1)[1].

---

1   P(LB&CA)A 1990, s 74(3) achieves this. The National Heritage Act provisions regarding injunctive relief (s 33(2A)) extend to the contravention of any provisions of the P(LB&CA)A 1990.

11.2   THE SCOPE OF DEMOLITION CONTROL

Before turning to the mechanisms for dealing with a breach it is important to appreciate the scope of control. Since the definition of 'building' in section 336 of the principal Act includes part of a building then the 'demolition' of a building also includes demolition of part of a building[1]. A demolition of this type might be termed 'partial demolition': buildings that fall within the scope of demolition control will thus fall within the scope of control if they are subject to 'partial demolition'. The ability to exercise control over 'partial demolition' underlines the need for effective development control activity. There are a number of categories of building and types of demolition that are exempted from the scope of demolition control. These are noted below.

---

1   Certain definitions from the principal Act are applied to the P(LB&CA)A 1990 by the P(LB&CA)A 1990, s 91(2). This covers 'building'.

11.2.1 Buildings exempted by statute and direction

The most important exemptions cover:

(a)   listed buildings;
(b)   ecclesiastical buildings which are being used for ecclesiastical purposes and for which the ecclesiastical exemption is retained by the Ecclesiastical Exemption (Listed Buildings and Conservation Areas) Order 1994, SI 1994/1771;

(c) a building included in the schedule of monuments compiled and maintained under section 1 of the Ancient Monuments and Archaeological Areas Act 1979[1].

In addition to these major categories there is a list of other buildings and structures specified in a direction[2]. The direction is contained in circular 8/87 (paragraphs 97(a) to (d)) and covers the following:

(a) any building whose total volume is less than 115 cubic metres, or any part of such a building;
(b) any gate, wall, fence or railing less than 1 metre high fronting a highway or open space or 2 metres high elsewhere;
(c) any agricultural building erected after 1914;
(d) up to 10 per cent (or 500 sq metres if greater) of any industrial building.

The other main category (this time focusing on instances where the 'demolition' has been a factor covered by other forms of control) comprises demolition of specified types.

1 Achieved by the P(LB&CA)A 1990, s 75(1).
2 P(LB&CA)A 1990, s 75(1) and (2) are the relevant provisions in the primary legislation.

11.2.2 Types of demolition exempted by direction

Certain types of demolition are thus not covered by the conservation area consent requirements: these are found in circular 8/87 at paragraphs 97(e) to (k). Thus conservation area consent is not required where the demolition is:

(a) required by a discontinuance order;
(b) required by a section 106 agreement;
(c) required by an enforcement notice or a listed building enforcement notice;
(d) required by a condition attached to a planning permission;
(e) under a demolition order under the Housing Act 1985;
(f) under a compulsory purchase order under the Housing Act 1985;
(g) under a pastoral scheme or a redundancy scheme under the Pastoral Measure 1983 – demolition of a redundant Church of England church.

The first four mechanisms (since they come under the planning legislation) should, by virtue of the conservation area test in the P(LB&CA)A 1990, section 72, have dealt with the issues to which conservation area status gives special emphasis. The last three powers are not covered by the conservation area test. As regards demolition required by an agreement it would seem that the term 'require' means that the demolition is actually specified as an obligatory action in the agreement. It should also be noted that the sub-paragraph is solely directed to section 106 agreements – an agreement made purely under other powers would not benefit from the exemption. However, as standard practice in most authorities would be to cite section 106 as well as the other provisions then it would seem that most agreements will fall within this provision. It should also be noted that where the permission (moving now to sub-paragraph (d) of the direction) is granted by the planning authority for its own works then they must seek conservation area consent from the Secretary of State. Finally, the provision relating to compulsory purchase orders only covers those that have been approved by the Secretary of State.

11.2.2 Entry and requisition powers

The powers available to the LPA as regards listed building contraventions are applied for the purposes of the conservation area regime with the appropriate modifications in language. See para 10.7.1.

11.3 CONSERVATION AREA ENFORCEMENT NOTICE

The power to take enforcement action against a breach of the controls relating to conservation area consent is couched in terms similar to those applying to listed buildings[1]. This is because these provisions have been taken from those applying to listed building enforcement: some modifications have been made to the wording to reflect the differences. These changes are effected by regulations – the Planning (Listed Buildings and Conservation Areas) Regulations 1990, SI 1990/1519, regulation 12, Schedule 3 ('the 1990 Regulations')[2].

1 By virtue of the P(LB&CA)A 1990, s 74(3).
2 The 1990 Regulations are made under the above provision.

11.3.1 The precondition – unauthorised demolition

The discretion arises where 'it appears to the LPA that any works have been or are being executed to' a building in their area and are such as to involve a contravention of conservation area consent controls. The phraseology of the 'apparent breach' is thus the same as that used in the listed building regime and the mainstream enforcement regime – see the appropriate paragraphs for details.

11.3.2 The substantive discretion

The terms of the discretion to take enforcement action are also closely modelled on the listed building regime. However, the focus on the area basis of the conservation area regime means that an amendment has been made to the elements in the substantive discretion. Thus a LPA 'may, if they consider it expedient to do so having regard to the effect of the works on the character or appearance of the conservation area in which the building is situated' issue a conservation area enforcement notice – the P(LB&CA)A 1990, section 38 (as applied by the 1990 Regulations). Here then the relevant considerations are the effect of the unauthorised works on the character and appearance of the surrounding conservation area. Two important points are relevant here. First, the conservation area test (P(LB&CA)A 1990, section 72(1)) applies since the exercise of this power falls within its scope. Hence the LPA must pay 'special attention' to the criteria in that test when exercising their enforcement discretion. One effect of this is that the term 'character' therefore covers not only the *visual* elements of the conservation area but also the *use* elements. Second, the provision talks of the effect of the unauthorised works 'on the character and appearance' of the conservation area (emphasis added). Now, it would seem that normally the conservation area regime is concerned to see that any particular exercise of a power in relation to a conservation area takes into account *either* the 'character' *or* the 'appearance' of the conservation area when exercising that power. The decision-maker thus has to make a choice between these elements – this choice depends on those considerations relevant to the conservation area regime. However, in relation to enforcement action the provision has used the word 'and' (not 'or'); this may well indicate that both elements are relevant when enforcement action is contemplated. Thus it would seem to indicate that the authority will have to gauge the effect of the breach by reference to the visual aspects of the conservation area *and* the use aspects. How this ties in with the different emphasis of the conservation area test is unclear since that seems to require a choice to be made between 'character' and 'appearance' and the elements of the other pair comprising 'preserve or enhance'. (The conservation area test is also examined in para 11.6 below.)

The substantive discretion is therefore a little confusing. It may be that the amended section is, in effect, saying that the LPA must 'have regard' to the effect of the breach on both 'character' and 'appearance' (thus covering both design and use issues). Then, if either (or both) features of the conservation area are affected the LPA should assess such effects against the 'preserve or enhance' criteria – choosing the most appropriate criterion on conservation area grounds. The LPA then should be able to conclude which of the various elements set out in the legislation are most relevant to the case at hand. Development plan policy may well, of course, be very useful in setting the broad parameters for the choice of 'preserve' or 'enhance' standards (as well as 'character' or 'appearance'). The role of plan policy in this respect is demonstrated in case law where the inspector was found, by the court, to be fully justified in applying an 'enhancement' standard because the development plan policy framework indicated that this was more appropriate than mere 'preservation'[1].

1 See *Impey v Secretary of State for the Environment* [1995] JPL B20 for an example of an inspector applying an 'enhancement' standard in a case involving installation of uPVC windows in a building in a conservation area. The development plan policy framework had been an important factor in convincing the inspector of the importance of choosing the 'enhancement' criterion.

11.3.3 Contents of notice

A conservation area consent enforcement notice must specify the following:

(a) the alleged contravention;
(b) the steps required;
(c) the period(s) for compliance with those steps;

(d) the date on which the notice becomes effective ('the specified date').

The discussion of listed building enforcement notices is relevant here. However, in addition to that discussion the following should always be borne in mind. The fact that the conservation area test will always apply means that its particular criteria are relevant to the content of the notice. In practice the LPA may find that the test will justify more stringent 'quality' standards and a more demanding timetable for works. Remember that PPG15 itself discusses the problem of unsightly gaps left in conservation areas: it even suggests that this problem merits a planning agreement at the development control stage. This might be the basis for arguing that 'time is of the essence' in cases where breach of control involves total demolition.

11.3.3.1 *The alleged contravention*

The discussion of listed building enforcement notices is relevant – see para 10.8.1.

11.3.3.2 *The steps required*

There are three types of steps that may be required in a notice. These are steps for:

(a) restoring the building to its former state;
(b) for executing such further works specified in the notice for alleviating the effect of the contravening works (this is where the authority consider that restoration would not be reasonably practicable or would be undesirable);
(c) for bringing the building to the state in which it would have been if the terms and conditions of any conservation area consent which has been granted for the works had been complied with.

The first category (restoration works) would enable the authority (within the limits imposed by problems of proof) to require full restoration. This would involve returning the building to its condition before the unauthorised works were carried out. If, however, this would either be 'not reasonably practicable' or 'undesirable' then works to alleviate the effect of the unauthorised demolition may be required.

11.3.3.3   *The compliance period(s)*

The discussion of listed building enforcement notices is relevant
– see para 10.8.3.

11.3.3.4   *The specified date*

The discussion of listed building enforcement notices is relevant
– see para 10.8.4.

11.3.4   Service of notice

The discussion of listed building enforcement notices is relevant
– see section 10.9.

11.3.5   Withdrawal of notice

The discussion of listed building enforcement notices is relevant
– see section 10.13.

11.3.6   The appeal

The grounds on which an appeal may be made are identical to
those relevant to a listed building enforcement notice except in
two respects. Thus the first ground of appeal against a
conservation area enforcement notice is that:

> 'retention of the building is not necessary in the interests of preserving
> or enhancing the character or appearance of the conservation area
> in which it is situated'.

The other difference is that there is no ground of appeal which
argues that the steps required for restoring the unlisted building
to its former state would not serve the purpose of restoration. All
the arguments made at appeal should be framed with 'special
attention' paid to the terms of the conservation area test: its
criteria apply since the appeal function of the Secretary of State
falls within the ambit of that test. Thus the LPA should ensure
that it makes the best available use of the terms of that section
when putting its case in support of its notice. If the LPA has a
development plan policy supporting enforcement action and

also addressing the appropriate factors (eg 'preserve' rather than 'enhance' and 'character' rather than 'appearance') then such statements will be important in persuading the inspector to follow the line taken by the LPA. The conservation area test may also be important as regards the possible exercise of the powers of correction or variation. 'Special attention' (for example) suggests an even greater emphasis on correction in order to ensure that the 'public interest' is not harmed by the adoption of a dogmatic and absolutist interpretation of the 'nullity' argument. The appellate stage is the next topic.

11.3.6.1 *Inspector's powers on appeal*

The exercise of the powers of the inspector is subject to the requirements of the conservation area test[1] since such powers are given by the P(LB&CA)A 1990. If the appellant argues that the inspector should grant conservation area consent for the demolition then the LPA must forcefully argue that the terms of the conservation area test (and, if applicable, the development plan policy applying those considerations to the site in question) be given due consideration. Similarly, any variation or correction of the notice must take full account of the criteria in the conservation area test which give special emphasis to the interests of the conservation area. The LPA should especially consider the line of argument that the inspector should correct any defects in the notice (where, for example, an uncorrected notice might otherwise have to be quashed) along lines suggested by the LPA and then give the appellant sufficient time to amend his grounds of appeal if necessary. The more traditional reluctance of the inspectorate to correct major defects would seem to be inappropriate in a conservation area if corrections can be made and any injustice to the appellant cured by allowing him time to amend his appeal. The discussion of the correction power in chapter seven should be studied.

1 P(LB&CA)A 1990, s 72.

11.3.7 **Subsequent grant of consent**

If the notice is followed by a grant of consent then the effect is similar to that resulting from subsequent grant of listed building consent on a listed building enforcement notice. The provisions of the P(LB&CA)A 1990, section 41 are applied with the necessary modification in wording.

11.3.8 Non-compliance with notice

If the contravener fails to carry out the steps in a conservation area enforcement notice in the specified time then the LPA may use three sanctions. These are the standard trinity of:

(a) prosecution;
(b) works in default power;
(c) injunction.

The normal principles apply. The LPA should employ all the available sanctions if possible. The prosecution sanction is the most favoured of course. However, this sanction is particularly difficult to apply effectively if the breach is quite minor and the case is not explained sufficiently to the magistrates. For them the demolition of a bit of a building (not listed) hardly seems to be a major breach. Care with presentation is thus essential if the breach is not that major. The discussion of such issues in chapter nine is relevant.

11.3.8.1 *Prosecution*

The elements of the offence and the penalties are the same as those for listed buildings with appropriate modifications in wording[1].

1 P(LB&CA)A 1990, s 43 – as applied and amended by the 1990 Regulations.

11.3.8.2 *Default power*

There is also a default power akin to that of the P(LB&CA)A 1990, section 42 to enter the land and execute the steps required by the notice[1]. The power of sale (arising where the expenses incurred become a charge on the land) is also an important feature to bear in mind.

1 Again the 1990 Regulations make the necessary amendments.

11.3.8.3 *Injunction*

The discussion in para 10.16.3 is relevant. The possibility of mandatory injunctions to achieve restoration is something to consider – see the discussion of mandatory injunctions in chapter nine.

11.4 PROSECUTION

If a person executes or causes to be executed any works for the demolition of a building to which conservation area consent controls apply then an offence is committed if those works are unauthorised[1]. Liability also covers failure to comply with a condition of a conservation area consent[2]. A small but important difference between this regime and that for listed buildings is that there is no equivalent of the notice requirements for demolition. Thus notice of the demolition of an unlisted building does not have to be given to the Royal Commission on Historic Buildings and Ancient Monuments. The other elements in the offence remain the same – including the defences. For details of the criminal offence see the discussion of the offence in relation to listed buildings (para 10.17). The LPA would have to prove the following:

(a) that the building was in a conservation area (this would involve producing the minutes of the appropriate decision to designate, the documents (officer's report and map) referenced in the minutes, the local newspaper notice and notice in the London Gazette regarding the designation and the notification sent to the Secretary of State);

(b) that the building was one in respect of which conservation area consent was required;

(c) that the building had been demolished (here there may be legal arguments as to 'partial' demolition);

(d) that the defendant executed or caused to be executed those works.

1 P(LB&CA)A 1990, s 9(1) as applied by the P(LB&CA)A 1990, s 74(3).
2 P(LB&CA)A 1990, s 9(2).

11.5 INJUNCTION

The third sanction is the statutory injunction under provisions whose terms are the equivalent of those in the P(LB&CA)A 1990, section 44A. The discussion in chapter ten is relevant. The court's discretion is more likely to be exercised in favour of the LPA where the conservation area's special status is clear. This should have been further underlined by effective and justifiable plan policies – both conservation area consent and enforcement.

11.6 THE CONSERVATION AREA TEST

As this statutory provision (the P(LB&CA)A 1990, section 72(1)) can affect a wide range of enforcement decisions by the LPA and the appellate decision-maker an understanding of its implications for decision-making is important. There are around 7,000 designated conservation areas so even a mainstream enforcement decision can trigger the conservation area test if it relates to land in a conservation area. The problem is that even with the courts at higher level giving it some attention in recent years the complexity of the provision is still something of a conundrum. The likelihood of erroneous interpretation of the provision and inappropriate application of it to decisions is therefore significant. In terms of the enforcement function this provision is necessarily central to the LPA's defence of its actions on appeal or before the courts. That is why the LPA should be rigorous in both the use of its designation powers (so ensuring that the reasons for designation are clearly set out) and its development control/enforcement powers: all the LPA's functions should be consistently exercised in the light of the particular features of the area so designated.

11.6.1 Careful and full analysis of criteria

One of the most illuminating ways of examining section 72(1) is to see it as posing a series of questions for the decision-maker. The main questions revolve around two pairs of elements. As the legislation indicates the central focus is on the 'preservation' *or* 'enhancement' of the 'character' *or* 'appearance of the area. The decision-maker's consideration of the factors is not framed in terms of the ordinary 'have regard to': there is the more demanding standard imposed – namely that 'special attention shall be paid to' the conservation area issues. This heightened burden of decision-making further emphasises the need to understand the differences between the two pairs of elements that are central to the conservation area test. 'Appearance' covers the visual elements that describe in a comprehensive manner the built (buildings, street patterns, the architectural styles and features etc) and natural (trees, open spaces etc) environment of the area. The interaction and mix of those visual elements would also be relevant when defining the appearance of the area. The 'character' of an area is not to be confused with 'architectural' character: 'character' in the conservation area test is a combination of its 'appearance' and 'use' elements. Thus character requires an assessment of different types of uses (residential, industrial, office etc), their densities and mixes. PPG15 (paragraph 4.2) with its reference to the 'mix' of uses in a conservation area is more illuminating in its analysis of the regime in this respect than was circular 8/87. So the outward flexibility of the law with its 'preserve or enhance' and 'character or appearance' phraseology in fact should be seen as requiring the LPA to make justifiable choices as to which element in each of those pairs applies to the case at hand. In some cases 'preservation' is more appropriate than 'enhancement'[1]. Unless the LPA is able to back up its choice with sound arguments it can expect to be challenged on appeal.

The LPA should also note that 'enhance' has two different meanings: the first is 'enhance by replication' – in other words any consideration of the deemed application for planning permission would be guided by the aim of replacing the items lost by the contravention. However, if 'enhance by contrast' were to be the appropriate standard the LPA may well consider that the breach in fact produces an appropriate 'counterpoint' which, although not replicating the character or appearance of the area, is still acceptable on the basis of this second version of 'enhancement'. In the absence of a clear direction from the development plan it is clearly possible for the appellant to argue 'enhance by contrast' and for the inspector to accept such arguments. (The interaction of the conservation area test with the section 54A 'presumption' is also another factor. The parallel conflict in terms of the listed building test is evident in case law pointing to an error by the inspector in applying plan policy in a case where the preservationist emphasis of the listed building test was overlooked. See the discussion of the *Heatherington* case in para 5.4.2.)

Additionally it should not be thought that the conservation area test 'requires' preservation or enhancement. (The term 'desirable' can be seen as injecting this element of flexibility: ie in some situations it is not desirable to preserve etc.) If other important planning interests are at stake (arguably those which involve a weighty 'public interest' element) then a conservation area can in fact be validly 'harmed' by a development. An example of this from development control is found in the *Wansdyke* case where the inspector validly gave permission for 'harmful' development in an 'ordinary' conservation area on the basis that this would positively benefit a nearby conservation area of international importance[2]. Therefore although conservation area status will normally help the LPA in its enforcement action it is not a factor that will 'trump' the arguments of the appellant in every case.

1 *South Lakeland District Council v Secretary of State for the Environment* [1992] 1 All ER 573, HL indicates that 'preserve' means 'not harm'. This is not, however, a case that thoroughly explores the meaning of the P(LB&CA)A 1990, s 72(1) as a whole: it only examines the question of what is meant by 'preserve' and so fails to address the more complex issues of how the rather convoluted phraseology should be reflected in practice. It thus fails to address in any coherent way the interaction between the term 'desirable' and the other terms used: it also fails to address fully how decision-making should reflect the disjunctive 'or' found in both of the paired elements that are central to the provision.
2 *Wansdyke Borough Council v Secretary of State for the Environment* [1992] JPL 1168.

11.7 CONCLUSION

Conservation area status thus has important consequences for mainstream enforcement as well as enforcement concerned with the conservation area consent regime. It also emphasises the point that the legal details need to be well-understood by the LPA and that this applies to all aspects of the planning trinity. A coherent development plan policy framework that includes policies addressing conservation area issues is particularly important therefore if the LPA intends to set the agenda for any analysis of the planning arguments on appeal. This also applies to the practice of designation: designation reports should include a clear, comprehensive and justifiable analysis of the rationale for designation – so making clear to all what the LPA is seeking to achieve. 'Preserve' or 'enhance', 'character' or 'appearance' are then criteria whose relevance is not something that is open to question: choices will have been made and the LPA's stance will be much more easily defended when it comes to the appeal and countering the arguments of the appellant.

12 The display of advertisements – enforcement issues

12.1 INTRODUCTION

The advertisement regime can be one of the most troublesome areas of 'environmental control'. This is a term used to point out that the activity involved in erecting and maintaining an outdoor advertisement is something which will often fall under both planning control (as 'development') and advertisement control (by virtue of its 'display'). In most circumstances the complexities that could arise from such 'dual control' are avoided by the planning legislation's use of a special statutory rule. This is found in section 222 of the TCPA 1990. This provision grants planning permission (if a display involves the development of land) where such display is 'in accordance with' the advertisement regulations – currently those made in 1992[1]. When the deemed grant of permission in section 222 does not operate the advertiser has to obtain planning permission for any development involved in the display of an advertisement. If permission is not obtained for such development then a breach of planning control has occurred. This is one important point to bear in mind. The other is the complexity of the statutory provisions which, when combined with lingering doubts as to the proper interpretation of some provisions, produce complications when officers attempt to take enforcement action. These problems of interpretation come to the fore with the definition of 'advertisement' itself and the term 'display' – issues discussed next.

1 Town and Country Planning (Control of Advertisements) Regulations 1992, SI 1992/666 ('the 1992 Regulations').

12.1.1 The definition of 'advertisement'

The definition in the TCPA 1990, section 336(1) is very wide ranging – advertisement:

288

'means any word, letter, model, sign, placard, board, notice, awning, blind, device or representation, whether illuminated or not, in the nature of, and employed wholly or partly for the purposes of, advertisement, announcement or direction, and (without prejudice to the preceding provisions of this definition) includes any hoarding or similar structure used, or designed or adapted for use and anything else principally used, or designed or adapted principally for use, for the display of advertisements, and references to the display of advertisements shall be construed accordingly;'.

This definition means that, for example, 'awnings' and 'blinds' that are only partly used for the purpose of advertising become advertisements and are thus subject to the specialist regime with its deemed consent rules etc. If the awning or blind etc do not have deemed consent and their erection involves development then the whole structure can be subject to mainstream enforcement action as discussed above. The related definition of 'display' is somewhat opaque and the courts have, arguably, erred in its interpretation by treating it as the physical structure rather than the activity of displaying[1]. The term 'device' does not mean 'mechanism' or a similar mechanical 'device'. It means 'heraldic' device – the modern version would be 'logo'[2].

1 See my case note in [1990] Journal of Environmental Law 128 on *Westminster City Council v Secretary of State for the Environment and Bally Group* [1990] 1 PLR 30.
2 *McDonald v Howard Cook Advertising Ltd* [1972] 1 WLR 90.

12.1.2 Entry powers

Except for cases where a breach of mainstream planning control is involved the LPA will have to rely on the general powers to enter land under the TCPA 1990, section 324 (see para 2.5.5). That provision also provides for special powers relating to fly-posting contraventions.

12.2 DISCONTINUANCE NOTICES

By virtue of regulation 8(1) of the 1992 Regulations the LPA is empowered to serve a notice requiring the discontinuance of the display of an advertisement or the use of a site for the display of an advertisement where such display benefits from deemed advertisement consent by virtue of regulation 6 and Part I of Schedule 3. It is important therefore to note the elementary fact that discontinuance action only relates to advertisements which benefit from such deemed consent. An advertisement that does not benefit from such deemed consent has to be attacked by other methods such as prosecution under the advertising regime and/or the use of enforcement powers under the planning regime (if the display involves the development of land for which planning permission was not obtained).

12.2.1 The discretion

A discontinuance notice may be served if the LPA is 'satisfied it is necessary to do so to remedy a substantial injury to the amenity of the locality or a danger to members of the public'[1]. This comprises two elements. In order to succeed on appeal, the LPA must therefore be able to demonstrate a 'substantial injury' to the 'amenity' of the local area or else some 'danger' to members of the public. These two issues of 'amenity' and 'safety' are central to the advertisement regime under the 1992 Regulations. Regulation 4(1) further expands upon the term 'amenity'. It thus states[2] that the authority must take particular account (when examining 'amenity') of the 'general characteristics of the locality, including the presence of any feature of historic, architectural, cultural or similar interest, disregarding, if they think fit, any advertisements being displayed there'.

1   1992 Regulations, reg 8(1)(a).
2   Regulation 4(1)(a).

12.2.1.1 *'Amenity'*

The language used here is similar to that which appears in the discussion of listed buildings and conservation areas. It is therefore a salutary reminder that if the advertisement with deemed consent is being displayed on or near a listed building or within a conservation area, then the concerns of those two regimes may well be relevant. This is particularly the case with the conservation area regime. It is important to note that the conservation area test in the P(LB&CA)A 1990, section 72(1) will be relevant in the exercise of powers relating to discontinuance notices. This is because the service of a notice and the examination of that notice at appeal (if any) will involve the exercise of powers under a provision of the TCPA 1990. The delegated legislation under which such discontinuance powers are exercised derives from the TCPA 1990 and thus the ambit of the conservation area test also covers the exercise of powers by virtue of the 1992 Regulations. This not only covers the powers exercisable by the LPA, but also by the Secretary of State. In assessing the 'substantial injury to the amenity of the locality' it is therefore relevant (when the site concerned is within the conservation area) to take account of the interaction between the conservation area test and the wording in the 1992 Regulations. This is important for the LPA since they may be able to justify discontinuance action more easily by reference to the 'preserve or enhance' criteria in the conservation area test. Again, it is important to ensure that officers are aware of the interaction of the conservation area test and the provisions of the advertisement regime in order to make effective use of this particular 'enforcement' power.

12.2.1.2 *Public safety*

The 'public safety' criterion is further expanded in regulation 4(1)(b) to cover the safety of any person who may use any road, railway, waterway (including coastal waters), docks, harbour or airfield. That provision also requires the authority to take particular account of the risk that the advertisement is likely to obscure or hinder the ready interpretation of any road traffic sign, railway signal or aid to navigation by water or air.

12.2.2 Contents of the discontinuance notice

The discontinuance notice served by the LPA must specify the following:

  (a) the advertisement or the site to which it relates;
  (b) the period within which the display or the use of the site (as the case may be) is to be discontinued;
  (c) a period at the end of which a notice shall take effect[1].

The period after which the notice is to take effect may not be less than eight weeks after the date on which it is served – regulation

8(3). The notice must also contain a full statement of the reasons for taking discontinuance action[2]. The comments above regarding 'amenity' arguments in relation to conservation area are particularly relevant to action taken in respect of such areas. The 'full statement' of reasons should therefore cover the relevant conservation area arguments – this will probably need some justification and closely worded argument from the LPA. The analysis of the interaction of the conservation area test and the provisions of the 1992 Regulations is something which will be carefully scrutinised by the DOE and the appellant.

1 Regulation 8(2).
2 Ibid.

12.2.3 Service of notice

The LPA is required[1] to serve a discontinuance notice on the advertiser and the owner and occupier of the site on which the advertisement is displayed. The term 'advertiser' seems (see regulation 2(3) dealing with the interpretation of the 1992 Regulations) to cover the following categories of person:

(a) the owner and occupier of the land on which the advertisement is displayed;

(b) any person to whose goods, trade, business or other concerns publicity is given by the advertisement; and

(c) the person who undertakes or maintains the display of an advertisement.

The LPA has the option (regulation 8(2)(b)) to serve a notice, if they think fit, on any other person displaying the advertisement.

1 Regulation 8(2)(a).

12.2.4 Withdrawal of notice

By virtue of regulation 8(5) the LPA may withdraw a discontinuance notice at any time before it takes effect by serving a notice on the advertiser. If there is no appeal pending they may also vary the notice by extending the compliance period. When using this variation power (and indeed the withdrawal power noted above), the LPA is required to send a copy of such withdrawal or variation to every other person served with a discontinuance notice when serving the withdrawal or variation on the advertiser[1].

1 Regulation 8(6).

12.2.5 Appeal

The appeal regime for discontinuance notices is modelled on the procedures under the Planning Acts for appeals in respect of planning decisions. Modifications to the regime are made, however, by Schedule 4, Parts IV and V. The notice is of no effect pending the final determination or withdrawal of the appeal – regulation 8(4).

12.2.6 DOE policy

PPG19 sets out DOE policy as regards the advertisement regime. Circular 5/92 addresses the mechanics of control and in paragraphs 17–21 the discontinuance power is discussed. As well as giving an overview of the basic stages in the process, the advice also stresses that the period within which the display must be discontinued must be 'reasonable'. This is especially so when the discontinuance action 'is likely to have serious financial consequences for a particular advertiser'. The advice also suggests that the LPA may consider that a modified display would be acceptable. The Secretary of State suggests that if this is the case, then the LPA should so inform the person displaying the advertisement and that this is best done *before serving the notice*.

12.3 ADVERTISEMENTS DISPLAYED IN CONTRAVENTION OF THE REGULATIONS

In the introduction to this chapter it was noted that the displaying of an advertisement can fall under both the controls imposed by the advertisement regime and the planning regime if there is 'development'. This 'dual control' is particularly relevant when the section 222 deemed grant of planning permission does not operate. This exemption does not operate when the advertisement is not displayed 'in accordance' with the 1992 Regulations. In such a case not only do the special controls of the advertisement regulations come into play but also those of the planning regime if there is 'development'. The LPA should always bear in mind that a display of an advertisement that is not 'in accordance' with 'the regulations' can comprise two forms. First there are 'unauthorised displays': thus the display of an advertisement which does not gain express or deemed advertisement consent will be an 'unauthorised display'. Second, an advertisement display which does gain deemed or express advertisement consent may not be 'in accordance' with the regulations by virtue of non-compliance with a condition imposed on such grant. The parallels between the 'unauthorised development' and 'breach of condition' contraventions under mainstream planning control are clear. The LPA should thus be aware of the possibility that the display of an advertisement may involve a breach of the standard conditions set out in Schedule 1 to the 1992 Regulations or the various conditions and limitations set out in Schedules 2 and 3. The first issue to discuss is the criminal offence committed where an advertisement is displayed in contravention of the 1992 Regulations.

12.3.1 Criminal offence

The most obvious sanction available to the LPA where the display of an advertisement is in breach of control is that provided by section 224(3) of the TCPA 1990. It states that:

> '... if any person displays an advertisement in contravention of the regulations, he shall be guilty of an offence and liable on summary conviction to a fine of such amount as may be prescribed, not exceeding level 3 on the standard scale and, in a case of a continuing offence, one tenth of level 3 on the standard scale for each day during which the offence continues after conviction'[1].

The display of different advertisements on one site will involve multiple offences reflecting the number of different advertisements[2]. Subsection (4) states that a person shall be deemed to display an advertisement if:

(a) he is the owner or occupier of the land on which the advertisement is displayed, or

(b) the advertisement gives publicity to his goods, trade, business or other concerns.

This definition ties in with that of regulation 2(3) except that it does not cover the person who undertakes or maintains the display. Such a person is not therefore liable under section 224 where an illegal advertisement is displayed. His position as an aider or abetter, however, may merit examination: the discussion of such liability in chapter nine is relevant here.

1 See para 9.6.11 for the current scale of fines.
2 *Kingston-upon-Thames London Borough Council v National Solus Sites Ltd* [1994] JPL 251.

12.3.1.1 *Defence*

The legislation provides the following defence where a person is accused of an offence under section 224(3)[1]. Thus a person shall:

'not be guilty of an offence under subsection (3) by reason only:
(a) of his being the owner or occupier of the land on which an advertisement is displayed, or
(b) of his goods, trade, business or other concerns being given publicity by the advertisement
if he proves that it was displayed without his knowledge or consent'.

As always, where the accused is required to prove a defence, it is on the balance of probabilities. In this situation the pro forma warning letter has its role to play in effective enforcement. Where the defendant has been informed of the illegally displayed advertisement then it will be difficult for him to plead this defence if he fails to remove the offending advertisement. This is clear from the case of *Preston v British Union for the Abolition of Vivisection*[2]. The use of the warning letter in respect of illegally displayed advertisements is thus a useful tactic in ensuring that this defence cannot be relied on by the advertiser. However, in *Wycombe District Council v Michael Shanly Group Ltd* the court held that even where the defendant had knowledge he could then seek to prove that he did not consent to the display and if he proves that he had neither expressly nor implicitly agreed to the display he should be acquitted[3]. This conclusion is perhaps strange since clearly public policy arguments would suggest that the provisions should be interpreted so as to require the owner who has knowledge to take such measures as are reasonable to remove the illegal display. In a sense the acquisition of knowledge of the display and the failure to take action to remove it means that the owner is no longer just 'deemed' to display the advertisement – he is now (because of the omission to act effectively) actually displaying the advertisement and so can be prosecuted under the TCPA 1990, section 224(3) without reliance on the 'deemed' display rules.

1   TCPA 1990, s 224(5).
2   (1985) 149 JP 740.
3   [1994] 02 EG 112.

12.3.1.2 *Case law*

When prosecuting for the continuing offence, LPAs should note the case of *Royal Borough of Kensington and Chelsea v Elmton Ltd*[1]. Here the advertiser had been convicted and had then taken down the offending advertisement. At a later date the advertisement was put back in position and the council prosecuted for the continuing offence. However, the Divisional Court held that the display of the advertisement constituted a fresh offence and was not linked to the display which had previously been the subject of the successful prosecution. Therefore the council should have treated the display as a new offence rather than a continuing one. A House of Lords case on a matter of interest to many authorities is the interpretation of the regulations relating to 'For Sale' signs. In the case of *Porter v Honey*[2] an estate agent had displayed (with deemed consent) a 'For Sale' sign outside a house. However, a second advertisement was displayed for the same purpose – and the issue was whether this second display took away the deemed consent which had been granted in respect of the first display. The House of Lords held that the terms of the regulations dealing with the display of 'For Sale' signs had to be interpreted so as to read that the subsequent display of a sign (which would not fall within the deemed consent provisions) could not take away the deemed consent rights enjoyed by a first advertisement displayed in accordance with the regulations. For LPAs the case produces problems of proof – they will have to demonstrate which advertisement was the one to benefit from the deemed consent. One way of circumventing this particular problem is for the LPA to prosecute the person who is selling the house.

Such a person would fall within the ambit of section 224 of the
TCPA 1990 as a person 'deemed to display' the advertisement.

1   (1978) 245 Estates Gazette 1011.
2   [1988] 3 All ER 1045, [1988] 1 WLR 1420.

12.3.2 Mainstream enforcement and contravening advertisements

As noted in the introduction to this chapter planning control
and advertisement control are not 'hermetically sealed' regimes
totally independent of each other. The provisions of the TCPA
1990, section 222 'exemption' can operate when the
advertisement is displayed in accordance with the 1992
Regulations: the person displaying the advertisement does not
therefore need to get planning permission for any 'development'
which the display activity may involve. In such circumstances
there is a clear statutory rule which avoids having to consider
the planning regime's impact. However, where this exemption
does not apply and where the display does involve 'development'
then the mainstream planning regime can be relevant and the
opportunity for taking mainstream enforcement action arises.
Therefore, it is important for authorities to realise that in
achieving the effective enforcement of advertisement control,
there may be occasions where the overlap between planning
control and advertisement control enables the LPA to take
enforcement action under *both* regimes. Section 222 is the main
indication of how this may be the case. So, mainstream planning
control can be an option where the advertisement display
involves development requiring express planning permission:
in such a case there is no section 222 deemed grant of planning
permission.

12.3.3 The advantages of mainstream enforcement action

Problems with delays over prosecution and the problems in
winning cases and getting suitable fines, affect the enforcement
of planning control generally. With advertisement cases, such
concerns are more important as the offence is only summary
and the financial gains from the contravening activity can be

considerable. Therefore, if the advertiser is prosecuted but
merely treats the fine as a minor overhead, the LPA may find
that the prosecution process does not actually produce the
desired result – the removal of the advertising display. More
direct action might be needed. This is what the mainstream
enforcement regime offers: the statutory injunction, stop notices
and the works in default power can all be used as a way of
removing the offending advertisement.

12.3.3.1 *'Development' and the display of an advertisement*

It has already been noted that the TCPA 1990, section 222
specifically recognises that the display of an advertisement may
involve development of land. This is given further support in
section 55(5) which deals with a particular form of development
– namely, 'material change of use'. Thus the use 'for the display
of advertisements of any external part of a building which is not
normally used for that purpose shall be treated for the purposes
of this section as involving a material change in the use of that
part of the building'. The provision clearly recognises then that
a display of an advertisement may involve a material change of
use. An example where such a situation arose on appeal against
an enforcement notice (and a listed building enforcement notice)
is to be found in a decision letter dated 2 November 1989[1]. The
enforcement notice, alleging a material change in the use of the
frontage of some premises, was upheld; the deemed application
for planning permission was refused on the basis that the
'Dutch' blind was detrimental to the listed building and was also
inappropriate in the conservation area. It is also interesting to
note that the National Park Committee had produced an informal
policy dealing with 'Sunblinds in the National Park'. In dealing
with the appeal the Secretary of State thus accepted that the
authority could take enforcement notice action against the
breach of mainstream planning control.

Large displays mounted on substantial structures may well
involve 'operational' development. An example of a breach of
planning control arising from the erection of a 48 sheet poster
display is to be found in an enforcement notice appeal arising
from enforcement action taken by the Portsmouth City Council[2].
The contents of the decision letter indicate that the LPA was
somewhat ambiguous in its description of the planning breach
by referring to the 'addition of a 48 sheet poster display and
advertising panel' on a wall without the necessary grant of

planning permission. During the course of the appeal the inspector ruled that the breach involved 'operational' development and was adequately described by the notice. The LPA faced with an unauthorised development of this sort should note that it is safer to be clear as to the type of breach involved. Indeed, this sort of breach would involve not only operational development but also a change of use development (thus involving two enforcement notices) – the material change of use would arise if the land used for the poster display was not already used for such a purpose. Clearly, the LPA is in a stronger position if it can issue a material change of use enforcement notice since then the option of a stop notice may also arise.

In the Portsmouth case the notice was upheld, the inspector found that the panel was an unsightly and incongruous addition to an otherwise attractive building. The panel projected from the building and this increased the detriment to the building and the immediate area. In a similar appeal dealing with a similar situation (London Borough of Greenwich) the relevance of local plan policies dealing with the display of advertisements was noted[3]. An interesting feature of the enforcement notice in this case was that the requirements of the notice covered not only removal of the hoarding itself but also the supporting equipment and fittings. A second enforcement step required the discontinuance of the illegal advertising use. The works in default power can then be used if there is non-compliance with the notice. The erection and retention of an advertisement display on land (be it on a building or on open land) is thus an activity which can fall within both the advertisement regime and the planning regime. If such activity does not benefit from other statutory provisions granting planning permission, then the activity connected with the display of the advertisement will also require planning permission. Where this is not obtained then clearly a breach of mainstream planning control will have taken place.

1   DOE reference APP/C/88/D2700/0015–16; APP/F/88/D2700/0002. The case involved the installation of a 'Dutch' blind on a listed building within a conservation area and an Area of Special Control in a National Park.
2   Decision letter dated 9 March 1990; DOE reference T/APP/C/89/ K1745/06/P6.
3   Decision letter dated 13 April 1989; DOE reference T/APP/C/88/ E5330/25/P6.

12.3.3.2   *Stop notices*

It is clear from the statutory regime (the TCPA 1990, section 55(5)) that the use of an external part of a building for the display of advertisements may constitute a material change of use. There is also the possibility that the erection of an advertisement on land (eg open land on the urban fringe) may involve a change of use of part of the land. (There need not necessarily be a 'building' involved in order to trigger a change of use.) If no planning permission is obtained for that material change of use then the display of an advertisement on the land will involve a breach of mainstream planning control. The unauthorised change of the use thereby arising from such a display is something which can be tackled by an enforcement notice and, more importantly, a stop notice. The LPA which comes across a display which falls within the ambit of mainstream planning control in this manner should therefore consider the possibility of achieving effective enforcement by using its mainstream powers as well as those found in the advertisement regime. If the situation is amenable to stop notice action against the use then the LPA should consider it: since amenity impacts may justify a notice taking immediate effect the LPA's use of such powers is clearly an important avenue to explore.

12.3.3.3   *Works in default power*

The enforcement notice issued in respect of the material change of use should be so worded as to allow the LPA use its works in default power. Removal of the advertisement (and its support structure if that is also in breach of control) can thus be the target of the works in default power should there be non-compliance with the enforcement notice. The 'materials' used in the construction of the advertisement would seem to fall within the special powers derived from the Public Health Act 1936 which enable the LPA to sell 'materials'. The power of sale (as regards the land used for the display) to recover sums due to the LPA is also an option which should be borne in mind. The discussion in chapter nine of this power is relevant.

12.3.3.4   *Injunctions*

An actual or apprehended breach of planning control can also (as discussed in chapter nine) be the basis for a statutory injunction under the TCPA 1990, section 187B. This obviously applies where the contravening advertisement is also in breach of planning control. Given the attitude of the courts to this new weapon in the enforcement armoury it is clearly a very useful tool for dealing with advertisement displays. A prohibitory injunction against the change of use should thus be sought: this can, of course, be tried before any enforcement notice action is taken. Naturally, the LPA will be more likely to succeed if the factual and policy circumstances support their case. If the person involved has a history of such contraventions or the site in question is prone to such activity then the 'apprehended' breach element of the TCPA 1990, section 187B may be relevant. (The discussion in chapter nine is of course important here.) Development plan policies addressing advertisement breaches will be an important support for any application to the court and factors such as section 54A will further support the case for an injunction. There is no special statutory injunction for dealing with a contravention of advertisement control: the LPA could try using a section 222 injunction (also discussed in chapter nine) for this type of contravention. However, the most favourable and effective response will be to use the statutory injunction provisions relating to mainstream breaches of planning control.

12.3.3.5 *Extra-legal pressure*

One of the techniques of effective enforcement is to employ pressure of an extra-legal source where possible. This is possible with advertising contraventions where the company whose goods are being advertised are sensitive about any 'illegality' that may taint their advertising strategy. The company concerned should thus be contacted and informed of the illegal display and the action that the LPA will be taking against the advertiser if this continues. Some authorities find that this approach is quite successful – especially if backed up by comments regarding 'aiding and abetting' and the direct liability of officers of the company where there is 'neglect' on their part. (See chapter nine on such aspects of legal liability). Informing such officers of the illegality will of course make it difficult for them to argue that there was no neglect. In some authorities an additional strategy is used whereby the offending advertisements are themselves the object of attention with advertising strips being applied by the LPA declaring that 'THIS

ADVERTISEMENT IS ILLEGAL' or 'CANCELLED'. In choosing such extra-legal strategies the LPA should also be aware that the large advertising companies will be very sympathetic to any action against illegal displays since invariably it is the small (cowboy) operators who are contravening the controls. Such operators are a threat to the larger firms and so economic interest will often drive the larger operators to side with the LPA in dealing with problems.

12.4 FLYPOSTING

Flyposting provides particular problems for the LPA. If the extra-legal methods described above do not work then the LPA may have to resort to the statutory powers under the TCPA 1990. Flyposting often occurs when the owner of the affected property is unaware and, in fact, may well object to such an activity taking place. The TCPA 1990, section 225 empowers the LPA to 'remove or obliterate any placard or poster' which is illegally displayed. However, before entering the land and taking such action the authority should check to see if the placard 'identifies the person who displayed it or caused it to be displayed'[1]. If the placard or poster *does* identify such a person then the LPA may not remove or obliterate it unless they have taken the following steps. The LPA must thus serve a notice in writing on the 'advertiser' stating that:

'(a) ... in their opinion it is displayed in contravention of regulations made under section 220; and
(b) they intend to remove or obliterate it on the expiry of a period specified in the notice'[2].

The LPA is excused from giving such notice if the placard or poster does not give the address of the person who displayed the placard or poster and the authority do not know the address and, after reasonable enquiry, they are unable to ascertain it. The period specified in the notice must not be less than two days from the date of service of the notice[3].

1 TCPA 1990, s 225(3).
2 Ibid.
3 TCPA 1990, s 225(5).

12.4.1 Placards and posters

Unfortunately there is a slight ambiguity in the regime as regards definitions. The terms 'placard' and 'poster' are not defined in the TCPA 1990. The term 'poster' would seem to be restricted to advertisements that comprise a paper-backing medium and the advertisement 'message' itself. The term 'placard' does occur in the definition of 'advertisement' in section 336(1) of the TCPA 1990 but only as one of a number of items found in limb one of that definition. Ordinary usage would suggest that a placard is a thin piece of cardboard onto which the advertising 'message' has been applied. Often placards are supported on small pieces of wood which are then either fixed to property (eg to form an estate agent's 'For Sale' board) or held aloft by those involved in demonstrations etc. It seems therefore that the range of advertisements that may be tackled by using the powers in section 225 is rather limited. It would seem to cover rather insubstantial (paper and/or cardboard-based) advertisements which are easily attached to buildings etc by the 'advertiser'. Paragraph 50 of the circular on advertisement control suggests that if a placard or poster is displayed by means of securing it temporarily to an 'A-board' then the power in section 225 applies only to the placard or poster and not to the A-board itself. Some authorities, however, do take a rather robust view of the legislation and have taken action against advertisements which would only fall under an expanded interpretation of the provisions in section 225. Those authorities therefore are less constrained by over-cautious interpretations by their legal department in the exercise of their enforcement powers. Whether other LPAs wish to view matters in this light is a matter for them to consider.

12.4.2 Entry powers

The exercise of the power to 'remove or obliterate' any 'placard or poster' which falls within the provision of section 225 triggers a special entry power. This is found under section 324(3) of the TCPA 1990. This states that any person:

> 'duly authorised in writing by the local planning authority may at any reasonable time enter any land for the purpose of exercising a power conferred on the authority by section 225 if –
> (a) the land is unoccupied; and

(b) it would be impossible to exercise the power without entering the land'.

Where the two provisos are met, therefore, the LPA officer proposing to use this power need only ensure that he is 'duly authorised in writing'. The general-purpose card which the officer should carry for the purposes of section 324 should suffice for this purpose.

12.4.3   Highways Act 1980, section 132

Highway authorities have power under this provision to remove pictures or signs affixed to trees, structures or works on the highway. This power, like that under section 225 of the TCPA 1990 thus allows the authority to use its own resources to clean up environmental problems.

12.4.4   Injunctive relief

The persons who put up the posters may often be employed on a part-time basis by one or two specialised agencies dealing with this sort of work. It may be most appropriate for the LPA to take action (perhaps in conjunction with the police) by seeking injunctive relief against the agencies to prevent such activity. (This would be under the Local Government Act 1972, section 222 as normally there would be breach of mainstream planning control unless the 'change of use' type of development was involved because of large-scale flyposting on a wall etc.) Injunctive action may therefore be a long-term solution to such activity in contrast to the short-term expedient of action under the TCPA 1990, section 225. The manner in which the company and its controlling members etc are to be tackled is something to which considerable thought has to be given. Clearly, the financial benefit accruing to such persons from such activity is a powerful incentive to ignore the minor inconvenience of prosecutions, and thus the injunctive remedy may possibly offer the only effective redress against organised flyposting. The discussion of 'roving' use breaches and injunctive relief in chapters three and nine should also be noted.

12.5 ADVERTISEMENTS AND LISTED BUILDINGS

Breaches of 'environmental control' with an advertising element that affect listed buildings deserve particular mention. The first point to note is that the deemed grant of permission that may operate by virtue of the TCPA 1990, section 222 only covers planning permission – it does not cover listed building consent. Hence, if the act of displaying the advertisement involves unauthorised works to a listed building and those works 'affect' the 'character' of the listed building then a breach of listed building control will have occurred[1]. The LPA may also be able to prosecute on the basis of the 'damage' offence under the P(LB&CA)A 1990, section 59. These issues will be examined in a little more detail below. The more detailed discussion in chapter ten dealing specifically with listed building enforcement issues will also be relevant.

1 P(LB&CA)A 1990, s 7.

12.5.1 Listed building enforcement notices

The most obvious sanction in respect of an advertisement-related breach will be the listed building enforcement notice. As long as the elements of a listed building breach are evident the LPA will be in a position to issue such a notice. The key terms – 'works' and 'character' – will be the focus of attention when the LPA is considering whether a breach arising from an illegally displayed advertisement can be tackled by means of a listed building enforcement notice.

The content of the notice will necessarily reflect the particular type of breach. It would therefore contain something like the following in the schedule dealing with the required steps:

'(1) The removal of the unauthorised works.
 (2) Repair and reinstatement of that part of the listed building affected by the breach of control to its condition before the unauthorised works took place.'

The 'unauthorised works' would have been defined earlier in the notice when setting out the nature of the breach of listed building control. Failure to comply with the requirements of a listed building enforcement would then give rise to another prosecution sanction (P(LB&CA)A 1990, section 43) and also the works in default power (P(LB&CA)A 1990, section 42). The discussion of these sanctions in chapter ten is relevant: for present purposes however a few words regarding the works in default power are in order.

12.5.1.1 *Works in default power*

This power enables the authority to ensure that the advertisement display is physically removed from the building. There is of course the power to take any 'materials' and sell them to meet the cost of the works – if the owner does not claim and collect them within three days of their removal (see chapters ten and nine). So clearly, the use (or probably just 'reminding' the contravener) of such powers will often achieve the desired result – removal of the offending display. The power of sale over the land used for the display which arises where sums due are a charge on the land is something to bear in mind (see chapter ten on this aspect of the works in default power).

12.5.2　Statutory injunction

An injunction under the P(LB&CA)A 1990, section 44A may also be a possibility if the advertisement display involves a breach of listed building control. This will be a relatively speedy and effective sanction and given the importance of protecting listed buildings the court will look sympathetically on any application: comments made elsewhere regarding the value of clear and justifiable development plan policies dealing with enforcement are naturally relevant.

12.5.3　Prosecutions under the P(LB&CA)A 1990, section 9

The fixing of an advertisement to a listed building will often involve 'works'. If those works fall within the ambit of section 7 (that is, they 'affect' the 'character' of the listed building) then the failure to obtain listed building consent for such works will involve a contravention of listed building control. Merely resting an advertising display against the building (or, perhaps hanging it from some existing projection) may not constitute 'works'. The term thus may be interpreted to cover only those activities which involve some physical alteration to the material of the building itself. The practicalities of prosecution will then be important issues to consider. The comments made in para 9.6.9 regarding the need for a full and clear presentation of the relevant issues (bearing in mind that this sort of problem may not be that familiar to lay magistrates) will be essential to effective action.

12.5.4 Prosecutions under the P(LB&CA)A 1990, section 59

The 'damage' offence under section 59 of the P(LB&CA)A 1990 will need to be assessed carefully. Again the display must have some tangible effect on the material of the building: it may be small (eg a nail driven into a wall) but it must be apparent – see the discussion in chapter ten.

12.6 CONCLUSION

The effective enforcement of advertisement control illustrates many of the themes appearing throughout this book. One such theme is to view breaches of control as 'environmental problems' which can be tackled with a variety of sanctions supported by the adroit use of legal and planning knowledge. In particular, the enforcement of advertisement control illustrates the obstacles that sometimes beset the enforcing authority by reason of gaps and inconsistencies in the statutory wording itself. The overlap between the various regimes within the planning fold is another factor that affects enforcement choices. The effective use of the various sanctions (including the full and clear presentation of cases before magistrates) is something which necessarily must be taken on board by the LPA if it wishes to achieve the effective enforcement of planning control. When considering the use of planning powers to deal with such problems we are also reminded that the other two aspects of the 'planning trinity' (forward planning and development control) must be well co-ordinated in order to make the enforcement of control a viable proposition. The injunctive remedy may be a realistic option if the court is given a clear idea of the policy framework adopted by the LPA to deal with the problem at hand. Advertisement control can also be one example where the use of extra-legal strategies can lead to the resolution of a problem. Advertisement control can be a complex and confusing subject for LPA officers, however, the considered use of a number of different strategies and sanctions can achieve effective results if enough thought and pre-planning are devoted to the problem from the start.

13 The protection of trees – enforcement issues

13.1 INTRODUCTION

Trees can form a very important element in the amenity of the rural and urban environment. Indeed, the TCPA 1990 devotes Chapter I of Part VIII to the subject of trees – the constituent provisions of that chapter are the focus of this discussion. The controls can be discussed by reference to three separate categories. These categories comprise:

(a) trees protected by conditions attached to planning permissions;
(b) trees protected by tree preservation orders; and
(c) trees in conservation areas.

However, before addressing these issues it should be borne in mind that there is no authoritative statement by the courts indicating that felling a tree does not of itself constitute development. There may be occasions where the LPA would consider testing this argument by issuing an enforcement notice against such an activity: 'arboricultural operations' involved in felling (followed by the related 'engineering operations' involved in taking away a tree of substantial size) could arguably constitute one of those 'other operations' noted in the TCPA 1990, section 55(1). Further discussion of this is provided in my Lawyer's Aside column in *Planning*, 25 March 1994.

13.1.1 Entry powers

Entry with a view to investigating breaches of planning conditions will be possible under the special enforcement power in the TCPA 1990, sections 196A, 196B and 196B. If the LPA suspects a breach of a tree preservation order or the controls relating to trees in a conservation area then the special entry powers under the TCPA 1990, sections 214A, 214B and 214C apply: these are the equivalent of the specialist entry powers for mainstream enforcement so the discussion of those powers in chapter two provide an indication of their ambit.

13.2 TREES PROTECTED BY CONDITIONAL PLANNING PERMISSION

Enforcement starts with effective development control practice. This is particularly the case with trees as LPAs are required by section 197 to take into account the need for the preservation or planting of trees when granting planning permission. That section also requires the LPA 'to make such orders under section 198 as appear to the authority to be necessary in connection with the grant of such permission, whether for giving effect to such conditions or otherwise'. The LPA should therefore ensure that its development control procedure adequately takes account of such issues and that standard conditions and standard reasons for refusal reflect the importance of this particular amenity issue. In circular 36/78, section X, authorities will find advice as to handling development proposals in the light of the importance of trees. Thus paragraphs 72–77 contain valuable advice on taking into account the use of conditions for preservation and planting of trees. Appendix 4 to that circular includes model planning conditions. Circular 1/85 also deals with the related issue of landscaping – Appendix A, model conditions 20 and 21. Authorities that have taken full account of the problems of adequately protecting trees by means of precisely worded conditions will then find that enforcement of such controls will be made easier.

13.2.1 Breaches of planning conditions relating to trees

Conditions that may be breached are those which deal with the protection of trees during works of development, ensure the planting of trees as agreed with the LPA and the replanting of such trees that become diseased or severely damaged etc. Enforcement difficulties may indicate the need to use planning agreements at the development control stage. Central

Government advice supports such a line – paragraph 75 of circular 36/78 states that the 'retention or planting of trees may be ensured by agreements with developers'. Such considerations are given more emphasis if the development proposals relate to land within a conservation area. Here then the conservation area test (see chapter ten) will apply and give greater scope for the protection and preservation of trees by means of planning agreements. Where such planning agreements are then breached the LPA is in a much stronger position by virtue of its contractual relationship with the developer (or his successor in title) to enforce the provisions of the agreement (see chapter fourteen's discussion of the enforcement of planning agreements). Where planning conditions or agreements have been breached then the LPA should take into account its power to issue enforcement notices and/or seek a remedy in the High Court. Such conditions and agreements may also be in addition to other protective mechanisms such as a tree preservation order or the special controls over trees within a conservation area. If the other mechanisms are relevant then they too should be examined and the authority should consider using such sanctions as are thereby made available.

13.3 TREES PROTECTED BY TREE PRESERVATION ORDER

Any tree which comes under the protection of a TPO receives protection under the TCPA 1990, section 206. Section 206 applies to such a tree if it is removed, uprooted or destroyed in contravention of the order or, secondly, if it is removed, uprooted or destroyed or dies when its cutting down or uprooting is authorised only by virtue of the provisions of section 198(6)(a) of the TCPA 1990. The ambit of section 198(6)(a) is noted in para 13.4.1.1.

13.3.1 Replanting duty

Where the protection of section 206 is triggered then a duty is imposed by that section on the owner of the land to plant another tree of an appropriate size and species at the same place as soon as he can reasonably do so. In *Bush v Secretary of State for the Environment*[1] the court held that the duty to replant at the same 'place' was to be ascertained by referring to the description and plan contained in the relevant tree preservation order. Section 206 does not contain a sanction for non-compliance: the LPA must turn to section 207 at first to enforce this duty. The duty to replace the tree by another appropriate tree falls on that person who is the owner at the time. This means that the LPA can take enforcement action against subsequent purchasers of the land. The enforcement of this duty is the next topic for discussion.

1   [1988] JPL 108.

13.3.2   Replanting notice

The authority may issue such a notice requiring the owner to plant a tree or trees of such size and species as may be specified in the notice. This must be done within four years of the date of the alleged failure to comply with the provisions of section 206. This power also applies to the failure to comply with any *condition* in a consent given under a tree preservation order which required the replacement of trees. It would seem that a mandatory injunction *cannot* be sought by the LPA since the TCPA 1990, section 207(5) states that the tree replacement duty under section 206(1) can only be enforced by section 207 'and not otherwise'.

13.3.2.1   *Contents of notice*

A replanting notice must contain the following:

(a) a period for compliance with the replacement duty[1];
(b) a period at the end of which the notice takes effect (this may not be less than 28 days after the service of the notice)[2];
(c) a specification of the tree or trees, their size and species[3].

1   TCPA 1990, s 207(1).
2   TCPA 1990, s 207(3) and (4).
3   TCPA 1990, s 207(1).

13.3.2.2 *Service*

The person who should be served with the notice is the 'owner of the land' at the date of service. See chapter six on methods of service.

13.3.2.3 *Appeals*

The person who is served with such a notice may appeal to the Secretary of State. One of the grounds for appeal – TCPA 1990, section 208(1)(b) – is that the requirements of the notice are unreasonable in respect of the period, size or species of the trees specified in the notice. This would seem to indicate that the local authority should give a reasonable amount of time in order to allow the owner to locate and plant the required trees. It also seems to indicate that it may sometimes not be reasonable to require the person to plant trees of exactly the same size or species as those that have been uprooted. Another ground of appeal – section 208(1)(c) – is that the planting of a tree or trees in accordance with the notice is not required in the 'interest of amenity' or would be contrary to the practice of good forestry. The authority should thus ensure that they have adequate grounds for demonstrating that amenity interests do require such a notice to be issued and that good forestry practice is not compromised[1]. The final ground of appeal is that the 'place on which tree or trees are required to be planted is unsuitable for that purpose'. In order to counter such an appeal the authority has to ensure that expert evidence is available to rebut this contention. These issues should be covered in the report to the committee (or officer) to whom the power to authorise action is given.

1 The 'amenity' issue may involve the use of the *Helliwell* formula – see para 13.3.4.2.

13.3.2.4 *Suspension of notice*

Where an appeal is made to the Secretary of State the notice is of no effect pending a final determination or withdrawal of the appeal[1]. This provision mirrors that found in the mainstream enforcement regime and so has similar effect.

1 TCPA 1990, s 208(6).

13.3.2.5   *Powers of Secretary of State / inspector*

On determination of an appeal the Secretary of State may either quash the notice or vary its terms[1]. He may also 'on such appeal' correct any informality, defect or error in the notice or give directions varying its terms if he is satisfied that the correction or variation can be made without injustice to the appellant or the LPA[2]. Again, these powers mirror those found in the mainstream enforcement regime and so similar considerations apply here: the issue of nullity should therefore be addressed in the light of the comments made in that discussion.

1   TCPA 1990, s 208(7).
2   TCPA 1990, s 208(8).

13.3.3   Works in default power

Where the owner fails to comply with a replanting notice then the LPA may use a works in default power granted to it by the TCPA 1990, section 209(1). The terms of this power mirror those of the works in default power of mainstream enforcement. The reader should therefore refer to that discussion for details. The LPA may enter the land and plant the trees specified in the notice and recover from the person who is then owner of the land any expenses reasonably incurred in doing so[1].

1   TCPA 1990, s 209(1).

13.3.4 Contravention of a tree preservation order – offence

Contravention of a tree preservation order also gives rise to criminal liability[1]. Any person in contravention of a tree preservation order who 'cuts down, uproots or wilfully destroys a tree or wilfully damages, tops or lops a tree in such a manner as to be likely to destroy it' commits an offence. Another offence under section 210 is committed where any person contravenes a tree preservation order otherwise than in the manner above[2]. In this instance the offence is purely summary – the penalty is a fine not exceeding level 4 on the standard scale (see para 9.6.11 for the current standard scale).

1   TCPA 1990, s 210(1).
2   TCPA 1990, s 210(4).

13.3.4.1   *Wilful destruction*

As can be seen from the above quotation the 'wilful destruction' of a tree or 'wilful damage' in such a manner as to be likely to destroy it are alternative offences. The 'wilfully destroys' type of offence would seem to have been committed where a tree has been rendered useless in the sense of having ceased to have any amenity use or as something worth preserving[1]. The case law also suggests that if a 'competent forester', taking into account the nature of the injury and the situation of the tree (for example its proximity to a highway), is of the opinion that it ought to be felled then the person who inflicted that injury will have 'wilfully destroyed' the tree[2]. In arriving at this assessment as to the meaning of the term 'destroy' the court referred to the dictionary definition of that term – which included the equivalent phrase 'to render useless'. This allowed the court to look at the underlying purpose of the relevant legislation which was to protect trees and woodland for their amenity and thus decide that if a tree ceases to have any amenity use then it is 'destroyed' for the purposes of the statutory regime.

The reference in the *Barnet* case to the relevance of the tree's 'amenity' value may also indicate that the contribution made by the tree to amenity is important in assessing the 'harm' caused to the 'victim' (ie the environment) when determining the appropriate fine to be imposed. Although the statutory scheme makes special reference to the 'financial benefit' to the defendant this does not mean that the 'victim' should be forgotten. Indeed, from the viewpoint of effective prosecution it is a central aspect of the prosecution case that the 'victim' (ie the environment) be a central element in arguments that address the gravity of the offence. The *Helliwell* system (discussed below) is one way of giving monetary values to the harm caused to this particular 'victim'.

1   *Barnet London Borough Council v Eastern Electricity Board* [1973] 2 All ER 319, [1973] 1 WLR 430.
2   Ibid.

13.3.4.2   *Penalties*

The penalty for committing an offence under section 210(1) is, on summary conviction, a fine not exceeding £20,000[1]. If the case goes to the Crown Court then the fine is unlimited[2]. In determining any fine to be imposed 'the court shall in particular have regard to any financial benefit which has accrued or appears likely to accrue' to the convicted person in consequence of the offence[3]. The LPA should therefore bring forcefully to the attention of the court the likely financial benefits or actual financial benefits which will arise or have arisen by virtue of the offence. If the clearance of the site in an urban setting means that the value of the land is dramatically increased then this increased development value should be the basis of the LPA submissions to the court.

A further component however should not be forgotten when dealing with such a prosecution. As noted above the financial component of any penalty reflecting the harm to the 'victim' is also, on general principle, relevant even if not explicitly stated in the planning legislation. This element of the case should be addressed as it provides an opportunity for educating the Bench as to the nature of planning and other related environmental law offences. Although the statutory reference to 'financial benefit' will often result in a monetary figure of some significance the LPA prosecutor should also attempt to quantify the harm caused to the 'victim' – the environment. In seeking to achieve a meaningful assessment of such harm the LPA should perhaps use the *Helliwell* system. This involves assessing seven different issues which have a bearing on the public amenity value on a tree. These include the size of the tree, its useful life expectancy, its form and other special factors. The tree in question is then assessed according to each of the seven categories and points are awarded in each category according to the importance of that tree as regards each specific interest. The points from each category are then multiplied together and the resulting figure is multiplied by a monetary value which is inflation-proofed. The resulting figure produces a monetary value which reflects the public amenity value of the particular tree. A similar exercise is also suggested for woodlands. The LPA should therefore contact the Arboricultural Association at the address below for information on the *Helliwell* system together with examples of how the courts have relied upon this particular method to assess the amenity value of trees. Thus in one case involving the felling of six trees covered by a tree preservation order the *Helliwell* formula produced a value of £3,594. A fine of £5,400 was imposed which was reduced on appeal to £4,000. If the LPA has an arboriculturalist then this method can be employed without the need for expert evidence from a private firm of specialists. The address of the Arboricultural Association is: Ampfield House, Ampfield, Nr Romsey, Hants SO51 9PA.

1 TCPA 1990, s 210(2)(a).
2 TCPA 1990, s 210(2)(b).
3 TCPA 1990, s 210(3).

13.3.4.3 *Strict liability*

If the accused has cut down etc a tree but does not know that it is subject to a tree preservation order then he will still be liable. The offence is one of strict liability – *Maidstone Borough Council v Mortimer*[1]. However, if the LPA has failed to put a copy of the tree preservation order on deposit for inspection (as required by the regulations) then it is unlikely that a prosecution would stand. Such a situation was considered in the case of *Vale of Glamorgan Borough Council v Palmer*[2]. LPAs must be aware of the limitations of the strict liability doctrine. If the owner of the land employs an independent contractor to carry out works and expressly tells that independent contractor not to interfere with the tree then the owner is not liable if the independent contractor does in fact contravene the tree preservation order: he would also fall outside the scope of liability relating to aiding and abetting etc. The case that illustrates this is *Groveside Homes Ltd v Elmbridge Borough Council*[3]. The independent contractor will of course be liable since he falls within the scope of section 210(1); the owner, however, cannot be prosecuted. LPAs in such a situation should therefore attempt to prosecute the contractor rather than the owner. (The possibility of using the principles regarding aiding and abetting should not be overlooked.)

1 [1980] 3 All ER 552. See also the Court of Appeal (Criminal Division) in *R v Alath Construction Ltd* [1991] 1 PLR 25.
2 (1982) 81 LGR 678, [1984] JPL 334.
3 [1988] JPL 395.

13.3.4.4 *Injunction*

The TCPA 1990, section 214A provides a special statutory injunction whose terms are similar (though there is one major difference) to those of the TCPA 1990, section 187B injunction relating to mainstream control. The TCPA 1990, section 214A applies to any 'actual or apprehended offence under section 210 or 211'. The injunction is therefore only available where the contravention of control would itself constitute a criminal offence under those provisions. It does not apply to breaches of conditions relating to trees (these can be handled via the TCPA 1990, section 187B). Non-compliance with the duty to plant a replacement tree (TCPA 1990, section 213) is not directly amenable to injunctive action at all (see the discussion of the replanting duty).

13.4 TREES WITHIN A CONSERVATION AREA

The designation of a conservation area gives rise to a special form of protection for trees that are not otherwise protected by a tree preservation order. The carrying out of certain activities without having given prior notice is a criminal offence. The activities which are caught by this particular offence are the cutting down, topping, lopping, uprooting, wilful damage, or wilful destruction of trees. The basis of control in this particular part of the TCPA is slightly unusual in that the prohibited activity is very widely drawn but then a defence[1] is provided. This defence constitutes, primarily, a prior notice procedure; the accused must also show that the activity in question was then done with the consent of the LPA or after the expiry of six weeks from the date of notice but before the expiry of two years from such date[2]. The penalties for contravening the control imposed by section 211 are those that arise on a section 210 offence. Thus the TCPA 1990, section 211(4) applies the provisions of section 210 to an offence under section 211 in the same manner as such provisions apply to the contravention of a tree preservation order.

1 TCPA 1990, s 211(3).
2 TCPA 1990, s 211(3)(b).

13.4.1 Exempted activities

The scope of this provision has been limited by regulation – the empowering provision for which is the TCPA 1990, section 212[1]. Therefore the prohibition does not apply where the person under investigation has done an act which comprises:

'(i) the cutting down, uprooting, topping or lopping of a tree in the circumstances mentioned in subsection (6) of s [198];

(ii) the cutting down of a tree in the circumstances mentioned in para (1) or (2), or the cutting down, uprooting or lopping of a tree in the circumstances mentioned in para (3) of the Second Schedule to the Form of Tree Preservation Order contained in the Schedule to the Town and Country Planning (Tree Preservation Order) Regulations 1969 (as amended by these regulations);

(iii) the cutting down of a tree in accordance with a felling licence granted by the Forestry Commissioners;

(iv) the cutting down, uprooting, topping or lopping of a tree on land in the occupation of a LPA and the act is done by or with the consent of that authority; or

(v) the cutting down, uprooting, topping or lopping of a tree having a diameter not exceeding 75 millimetres, or the cutting down or uprooting of a tree having a diameter not exceeding 100 millimetres where the act is carried out to improve the growth of other trees, the reference to 'diameter' herein being construed as a reference to diameter, measured over the bark, at a point 1.5 metres above the ground level.'

1 Town and Country Planning (Tree Preservation Order)(Amendment) and (Trees in Conservation Areas)(Exempted Cases) Regulations 1975, SI 1975/148, reg 3.

13.4.1.1 *Dead, dying or dangerous trees*

Certain activities relating to trees are given exemption from the special controls (both trees subject to tree preservation orders and trees in conservation areas) under Chapter I of Part VIII. Thus in the TCPA 1990, section 198(6) it is stated that:

'Without prejudice to any other exemptions for which provision may be made by a tree preservation order, no such order shall apply –

(a) to the cutting down, uprooting, topping or lopping of trees which are dying or dead or have become dangerous, or

(b)   to the cutting down, uprooting, topping or lopping of any trees
in compliance with any obligations imposed by or under an Act
of Parliament or so far as may be necessary for the prevention
or abatement of a nuisance.'

The extent of the 'have become dangerous' exemption has been
examined in the case of *Smith v Oliver*[1]. That case seems to
indicate that the term 'dangerous' should be construed not only
by reference to persons but also property. This is clear from the
judgment of Tudor Price J at 4. The leading judgment by
Farquharson J is important as it examines the manner in which
the magistrates' court should approach the situation to see if the
accused can validly claim that the trees he has cut down or
lopped 'have become dangerous'. He said:

'The approach which they should make is the everyday sensible
approach of a prudent citizen looking at the trees in question and
deciding in his own mind whether he can properly say those trees
are dangerous. The existence of the danger must be a present
danger. He must be able to say that the existing condition is one of
danger in relation to the tree or trees which he is examining. Of
course that does not mean that the danger which has been threatened
has actually occurred. It is not necessary to show that the tree has
fallen or that its roots have disturbed the foundation of the house,
fence or the pavement nearby. The justices must be in a position to
say to themselves that "having regard to the state of the tree, its
size, its position and such effects as any of those factors have so far
had, we can properly come to the conclusion that the tree has now
become dangerous". It may be that the condition of the tree itself is
perfectly healthy, but because of those other factors the magistrates
may be able none the less to say that the tree is in the condition
described by the subsection, that is to say it has become dangerous.
    In deciding that question, the magistrates are entitled to look at
what is likely to happen. If the tree has already shown signs of
disturbing a fence or a pavement or indeed the house itself, it does
not need the justices or indeed anyone concerned with the treatment
of the tree to wait for those events actually to occur, namely for the
fence to fall down on some passing pedestrian or the condition of the
pavement to be such that somebody falls and is injured or that the
house begins to subside. The present danger is one that is constituted
by the conditions at the time the tree is being examined, and the fact
that these other matters may shortly arise is something that can
properly be taken into account when the justices come to their
decision.'

The burden of establishing either of the section 198(6) exemptions
lies on the defendant[2]. Only where a provision creates a negative

ingredient of an offence does the burden of proof rest upon the prosecution.

1   [1989] 2 PLR 1.
2   *R v Brightman* [1990] 1 WLR 1255, CA.

13.4.2   Replanting duty

Where a tree in a conservation area is removed, uprooted, or destroyed in contravention of section 211 or is removed, uprooted, or destroyed or dies at a time when its cutting down or uprooting is authorised only by virtue of certain regulations then a duty is placed on the owner of the land to plant another tree of appropriate size and species at the same place as soon as he reasonably can[1]. Again, this replacement duty may be waived by the LPA upon application of the owner. This duty may be enforced against the current owner of the land in the manner provided for by section 207 – see para 13.3.2. The section 213(1) duty can only be enforced by tree replacement notices and the works in default power 'and not otherwise'[2].

1   TCPA 1990, s 213(1).
2   TCPA 1990, s 213(3).

13.4.3   Planning conditions/agreements

If any act is also in breach of a condition and/or an agreement relating to the development of land then the LPA may use its powers to deal with contravention of these controls.

13.4.4   Conservation area test

Since by definition we are concerned with trees in conservation areas then:

(a) the issue of an enforcement notice under section 172 of the TPCA 1990, and
(b) the issue of a tree replacement notice,

will both trigger the conservation area test. Thus the impact of the prohibited act on the conservation area's 'appearance' and 'character' will be relevant. The interests of the conservation area are important – as indicated by the wording of the conservation area test (see chapter eleven).

13.4.5 Compliance checks – entry powers

The rights of entry (discussed above) in sections 214B, 214C and 214D also apply to contraventions of the duties arising under section 211[1]. Please refer to the above discussion of those sections.

1   TCPA 1990, s 214B(1)(b).

13.5 INJUNCTIONS

As noted earlier section 214A makes provision for a special statutory injunction for restraining offences under both section 210 and 211. Since the provisions of this section are very similar to those in section 187B the discussion of the statutory injunction provisions relating to mainstream enforcement is relevant. However, the possibility of using a mandatory injunction is limited by section 207(5). This provides that the duty under section 206(1) may only be enforced by the replanting notice procedure. The statutory injunction procedure cannot therefore be used directly to address:

   (a) breach of a tree preservation order; or
   (b) a consent given under a tree preservation order requiring the replacement of trees.

The LPA must first issue a replanting notice. However, if that remedy is unsuccessful the LPA would appear to have the option of then seeking a statutory injunction to secure compliance with that notice – as well as taking proceedings in the criminal courts. Injunctive relief has been a quite common feature of enforcement of controls relating to trees[1].

1 *Kent County Council v Batchelor* [1978] 3 All ER 980 is a well-known example of injunctive action against a particularly infamous contravener.

14 Miscellaneous enforcement issues

14.1 WASTELAND NOTICES

14.1.1 Introduction

A wide-ranging 'enforcement' power is found in the TCPA 1990, section 215. This is the wasteland notice. The term 'wasteland' is used here although the 1990 legislation does not employ that term: the original (much amended) provisions did use the term and so it retains currency among planning officers and planning lawyers. In time, of course, usage may change but the advantages of using this label are considerable – even if puzzling to someone coming anew to the provision in its current form. This power is at the periphery of the planning system, however, some LPAs have begun to use it as a means of dealing with an environmental problem arising from dereliction or accidents such as a fire destroying a building and leaving a site in an unacceptable state. It can thus operate to impose a positive duty on a landowner to ensure the 'proper maintenance of land' – as the sidenote to section 215 puts it.

14.1.2 Entry powers

As noted in para 2.5.4 the LPA officer wishing to enter the site in question will have to rely on the powers in the TCPA 1990, section 324 since section 196A etc does not extend to this particular type of problem.

14.1.3 The power to serve

Under section 215 the LPA may serve a 'wasteland' notice on the owner or occupier of land if 'it appears to the local planning authority that the amenity of a part of their area, or of an adjoining area, is adversely affected by the condition of land in their area'. Such a notice may deal with 'buildings' as well as unbuilt land since the definition section of the TCPA 1990 defines 'land' in broad terms. The breadth of the term 'amenity' and the need for only an 'apparent' adverse effect on such amenity underline the wide degree of discretion given to the LPA by this power. As noted below there is an appeal provision allowing the recipient to challenge the notice in the magistrates' court. The risk of such an appeal should be taken into account by the LPA in drafting such a notice: however, a robust enforcement approach is often taken by LPAs using this power and if an appeal is not made then a notice which might have been challenged successfully (in whole or in part) on appeal can often achieve the aims of the LPA.

14.1.3.1 *Contents of the notice*

The notice must contain the following:

  (a) the steps for remedying the condition of the land[1];
  (b) the period within which such steps should be taken[2]; and
  (c) the period at the end of which the notice shall take effect[3].

The period after which the notice takes effect cannot be less than 28 days after the service of the notice[4]. The LPA should be careful with the 'steps' required by the notice. As will be discussed later the appeal (to the magistrates' court) can be made on a number of grounds: one of these deals with the 'reasonableness' of those steps. This would probably involve a mixture of the 'public interest' importance of the problem and the resources etc of the recipient of the notice.

1 TCPA 1990, s 215(2).
2 Ibid.
3 TCPA 1990, s 215(3).
4 TCPA 1990, s 215(4).

14.1.3.2 *Service*

The notice must be served on the owner and occupier of the land[1]. Service details are similar to those for mainstream enforcement notices – the 28-day minimum period allowed from service to date of effectiveness is thus the same. The LPA should therefore allow a few extra days to take account of problems in late service that might otherwise prejudice effective service. There are no appeal forms to send out with the notice.

1 The term 'owner' is analysed in the discussion of service requirements in chapter six.

14.1.4 Appeal

An appeal against such a notice may be made to the relevant magistrates' court before the notice takes effect. Those entitled to appeal are:

(a) those served with the notice, and
(b) any other person having an interest in the land to which the notice relates[1].

Once an appeal is lodged the notice's effect is suspended pending 'the final determination or withdrawal of the appeal'[2]. There is also provision for a further appeal to the Crown Court – available to both parties[3].

1 TCPA 1990, s 217(1).
2 TCPA 1990, s 217(3). The equivalent phraseology in respect of enforcement notice appeals suggests that such notices may similarly be 'suspended' by appeals to higher levels.
3 TCPA 1990, s 218.

14.1.4.1 *Grounds of appeal – amenity*

The first ground refutes the assertion that there is an adverse effect on the amenity of the area[1]. Here the LPA will have to contend with a mixture of planning and common sense arguments which the appellant will deploy. It will be necessary therefore to have clear evidence of the adverse effect (eg neighbour complaints etc) on the local amenity: professional assessments from planning staff will help but these should not be overly technical – the unfamiliarity of the Bench with such appeals means that clear and understandable evidence should be given.

1 TCPA 1990, s 217(1)(a).

14.1.4.2 *Grounds of appeal – 'ordinary condition'*

The second ground asserts that the condition of the land is such as arises from the ordinary use of the land – a use which is not in contravention of Part III of the TCPA 1990[1]. The key elements to cover here are:

(a) identifying the range of uses of the land which can be carried out without contravening Part III of the 1990 Act;

(b) examining the impact 'in the ordinary course of events' of such uses on the land.

One approach by the appellant is to give as full a definition as possible of those uses which would not require planning permission and then show how the condition of the land is not unusual in the light of what it could be used for. His definition of what impacts such uses would have 'in the ordinary course of events' is thus something which the LPA will have to analyse carefully. This aspect of this ground is much more a common-sense issue. The LPA should therefore be able to give 'homely' examples to the magistrates of 'ordinary' impacts arising from the non-contravening uses of the land – stressing what might reasonably be expected of the landowner in keeping a site tidy etc. Evidence of breaches arising in other environmental regimes (noise/pollution) might be useful in helping the authority demonstrate that the impacts are not 'normal'.

1 TCPA 1990, s 217(1)(b).

14.1.4.3 *Grounds of appeal – requirements exceed the necessary*

The third ground would need expert evidence as to what is 'necessary' to deal with the 'adverse effect' on the land[1]. It might be relevant to note that there is no qualifying adjective (such as 'reasonably') before the word 'necessary'. The LPA which have to be clear about the 'necessity' of the action required in order to rebut this ground.

1 TCPA 1990, s 217(1)(c).

14.1.4.4 *Grounds of appeal – unreasonable compliance period*

The appellant arguing this ground will often bring into play
issues of 'hardship' etc. The expense (in time and money) of
complying with the notice will thus be issues which the LPA will
have to answer. The other side of the coin is, of course, the
'environmental' damage arising from the 'condition' of the land.
The 'public interest' versus the 'private interest' equation is
thus the focus here. Neighbour complaints are useful to have as
evidence on the harm to the 'victim'. Comments in chapter nine
regarding the need for special care with planning law offences
when dealing with the magistrates are relevant here: they will
be swayed by their normal case load of criminal law infractions
where harm to the 'victim' and the 'guilt' of the defendant can be
assessed relatively easily. In addressing the magistrates
therefore in the context of an appeal the LPA will have to take
account of the problems caused by the perceptions of the Bench
towards such 'victimless crimes'. Personal appearances by such
neighbours will thus be very useful in substantiating the case
of the LPA. As regards the authority's other environmental
powers it may be relevant to employ environmental health
arguments as ancillary evidence on this and the preceding
issues.

14.1.4.5 *Magistrates' powers on appeal*

The magistrates' court may:

  (a) correct the notice[1];
  (b) quash the notice[2];
  (c) vary the terms of the notice[3].

The magistrates may correct 'any informality, defect or error in
the notice if satisfied that the informality, defect or error is not
material'[4]. This wording is very similar to that used in the
correction power relating to enforcement notices *before* the
current 'without injustice' standard was introduced. On a literal
interpretation the correction power implies that a material
error – an error which is central or fundamental to the notice –
would cause the notice to fail. A notice that is vitiated in this way
would seem to be a nullity and of no effect. However, it might be
important to note that Lord Denning was of the opinion[5] that
the 'material' error standard should be interpreted to cover

situations where a correction could be made without causing injustice to the appellant. In discussing the correction power granted to the minister in relation to enforcement notices it was said that if the error[6]:

'. . . does not go to the substance of the matter and can be amended without injustice, it should be amended rather than that the notice should be quashed or declared a nullity. In this way the legislature has disposed of the proposition that there must be "a strict and rigid adherence to formalities"'.

Thus it may be possible to argue that a flaw can be corrected under section 217(4) if the correction would not cause injustice (in all the circumstances) to the appellant. The discussion of the correction power granted to inspectors in relation to mainstream enforcement notices may also be of relevance in arguing for the more liberal interpretation of this power – so enabling the magistrates to cure a wider range of defects than might be thought possible.

The power to quash arises on 'the determination of'[7] an appeal under section 217. The magistrates would use this power when the appeal has succeeded on the amenity ground or the 'ordinary condition' ground. The variation power (again exercisable on 'the determination of' an appeal) seems to be appropriate where the magistrates wish to deal with arguments that the notice contains an unreasonable compliance period or requirements that exceed the necessary. Thus the magistrates may agree with the need to remedy a situation by means of a wasteland notice but consider that the particular form of notice before them is not appropriate. The variation power thus enables the magistrates to make suitable changes to a notice which will then become operative. The variation power, it should be noted, may only be exercised where this will be 'in favour of the appellant'[8].

1 TCPA 1990, s 217(4).
2 TCPA 1990, s 217(5)
3 Ibid.
4 TCPA 1990, s 217(4).
5 *Miller-Mead v Minister of Housing and Local Government* [1963] 2 QB 196, [1963] 1 All ER 459. See also the discussion in chapter six of this case and other relevant case law.
6 Ibid at 467.
7 TCPA 1990, s 217(5).
8 TCPA 1990, s 217(5).

14.1.5 Non-compliance with notice

The TCPA 1990, section 324(1) remains the relevant provision granting entry powers to monitor compliance: see paragraph (c). If there is non-compliance with an effective notice then three sanctions become available. These are:

(a) criminal prosecution;
(b) the exercise of the default power;
(c) injunction.

14.1.5.1 *Criminal sanction*

Where the recipient (owner or occupier) of a notice fails to comply with it a criminal offence (summary only) is committed[1]. If there is continuing non-compliance after a first offence then a cumulative fine may be imposed which will be based on a maximum daily penalty of one-tenth of level 3 on the standard scale[2]. Where the LPA has taken proceedings against someone who was not the owner or occupier of the land at the time of service of the notice then they may find the 'new' owner/occupier employing a special 'substitution' procedure in order to have the original miscreant brought before the court[3]. If failure to comply is through no fault of the defendant then the person who is responsible may be convicted instead.

1   TCPA 1990, s 216(2). The fine is set at level 3 on the standard scale – see para 9.6.11 for the current scale.
2   TCPA 1990, s 216(6). See note 1 above for the current scale.
3   TCPA 1990, s 216(3) (original owner) and (4) (original occupier).

14.1.5.2 *Default power*

By virtue of the TCPA 1990, section 219 a default power to carry out 'any steps required by the notice' is given to the LPA. This is very similar to that given in respect of enforcement notices – thus the LPA may recover from the person who is then the owner of the land any expenses reasonably incurred by them in doing so[1]. This would seem to allow some dispute as to the expenses 'reasonably incurred'. Perhaps putting out the job to tender would help with this problem – though ensuring that the contract did cover precisely what the notice required. Establishment charges and provisions enabling 'materials' to be sold are also included via delegated legislation triggering provisions in the TCPA 1990, section 219(3)[2]. These same regulations (which provide that expenses relating to enforcement notice direct action are a charge on the land) do not extend such a charging provision to expenses relating to wasteland notices.

1   TCPA 1990, s 219(1).
2   TCPA 1990, s 219(3) is the empowering section and relates to provisions in the Public Health Act 1936. Consequential amendments are made to the wording of the provisions via the Town and Country Planning General Regulations 1992, SI 1992/1492, reg 14.

14.1.5.3   *Injunction – section 222 power*

The third of the familiar trinity of sanctions may have to be used to deal with obstinate contraveners. The LPA will have to rely on section 222 of the Local Government Act 1972 as the special planning injunction under section 187B does not cover 'proper maintenance' problems: see discussion of the injunctive powers in chapter nine for a discussion of the section 222 power in the light of the case law principles. A mandatory injunction to force action by the contravener would be necessary in order to ensure his compliance with those steps in the notice that require positive action: where the steps require the cessation of activity then a prohibitory injunction would be appropriate.

14.1.6   Enforcement against subsequent owner

The LPA should ensure that a wasteland notice is registered as a local land charge[1]. This will help to put pressure on a 'contravener' who is attempting to sell the land – solicitors acting for potential purchasers should react cautiously to such a charge and this would make the land less marketable. If the land is sold then action can be taken against subsequent owners – however, as suggested earlier, this may be more troublesome (given the substitution procedure etc) and give rise to delay.

1   Local Land Charge Rules 1977, r 2(2).

14.1.7 Central government advice

The applicable advice is found in circular 19/86, Annex, paragraph 3. This suggests that LPAs should use these powers 'with discretion, as a means of dealing with relatively isolated, severe cases of neglected or unsightly land'. It should be noted that the normal 'enforcement' mechanism for advice in a circular (an appeal to the DOE at which the government policy/advice will be applied) is absent as the appeal is to the magistrates' court – not to the Secretary of State. As long as the LPA considers the elements of the relevant discretion in the proper manner their decision will not be challengeable even though it has involved them in giving only minimal weighting to DOE advice.

14.1.8 Judicial review etc

There is a statutory rule in the TCPA 1990, section 285(3) which restricts the basis on which a wasteland notice may be challenged in 'any proceedings whatsoever'. This provision states that the validity of such a notice which has been served under section 215 on the owner and occupier of the land shall not except by way of appeal to the magistrates' court 'be questioned in any proceedings whatsoever on either of the grounds specified in section 217(1)(a) or (b)'. These two grounds are the 'amenity' and 'ordinary condition' grounds discussed earlier. However, this bar does not operate where a person is prosecuted for non-compliance with a wasteland notice[1] and that person was not served with the notice but has held an interest in the land since before the date when the notice was served on the owner and occupier of the land and where he did not appeal against the wasteland notice in section 217. The general bar in section 285(3) does not operate to prevent challenges on the grounds of ultra vires action. Indeed the LPA may face arguments as to ultra vires action both before the magistrates' (or Crown) court and by way of judicial review proceedings under RSC Order 53. In the case of *R v Oxford Crown Court, ex p Smith*[2] a wasteland notice was issued requiring the clearance of part of a scrap metal site. There was an appeal to the magistrates and a further appeal to the Crown Court. Issues as to vires were raised in the Crown Court but the court declined to hear such arguments. This decision was challenged in the Divisional Court where it was held that an allegation of ultra vires action could be made both when appealing to the magistrates and the Crown Court and by way of judicial review.

1   Under TCPA 1990, s 216.
2   (1989) 154 LGR 458.

14.2 PLANNING OBLIGATIONS AND AGREEMENTS

14.2.1 Introduction

The enforcement of obligations under section 106 (or its predecessors) should be a more straightforward matter than using the administrative sanctions of enforcement notices etc. There will be the practical legal issues such as getting the case to court and being able to rely on clear terms in an agreement. However, despite the greater legal input required the enforcement of obligations arising under such agreements is generally an easier task than the enforcement of planning control by the normal method of enforcement notices etc. Indeed, central government advice at various stages (eg in relation to developments affecting the historic environment) acknowledges the value (from the point of view of enforcement) of using a planning agreement to supplement the normal development control power.

14.2.2 Clarity and precision of terms

The authority has to ensure that the drafting of planning agreements (especially if they are complex and novel) is undertaken by experienced legal staff. One problem which may occur is the careless use of planning terminology in legal agreements. A phrase may seem to be crystal clear to a planning officer but when viewed critically by a lawyer it might be found to admit several interpretations. Legal advisers in LPAs should therefore be aware of this problem: their close involvement with planning officers may actually increase the risk that they adopt uncritically the phraseology used in daily practice by the planning fraternity.

14.2.3 Monitoring provisions

Agreements that are solely concerned with 'one-off' obligations (such as the transfer of land or money) may possibly be handled so that the planning permission is granted only when that one-off obligation has been met. Continuing obligations (eg the upkeep and maintenance of soft landscaping) can present a more difficult problem since here the question is one of the LPA's knowing whether that obligation is being met. Continuing obligations may therefore need to be accompanied by provisions in the planning agreement that (inter alia) set up a 'monitoring' system. The authority, taking the example of the landscaping agreement, might be able to get the developer to agree that the initial landscaping works and their maintenance are kept under review (perhaps at periods specified in the agreement) by a reputable landscape architect. Such a monitoring provision in an agreement would therefore mean that the planning authority would receive reliable and regular information as to compliance with the terms of the agreement. Of course, the nature of such monitoring provisions is a matter for negotiation between the parties and the authority will need to pay some attention to the content of such provisions if they want to ensure that they will achieve the purpose for which they are designed. In some cases long-term obligations may pose almost insurmountable problems of monitoring for the LPA as controls over (for example) occupation may require regular checking and this can of course be difficult with limited resources. Innovative monitoring provisions may therefore be needed in certain cases where long-term obligations are contemplated. Liaison with other agencies, reliance on information from other forms of control may therefore be required where other regimes provide regular information which can be used by the LPA to assess compliance with a planning obligation.

14.2.4 Breach of an agreement

When an authority is made aware that an agreement is being breached its approach will vary according to the nature of the breach and the enforcement options open to it. Where the contravener has to dispose of property which is encumbered by a breach of a planning agreement then the 'legal' nature of that obligation can work to the advantage of the LPA. The authority can rely on the fact that the agreement will be registered as a local land charge. This should mean that when the developer tries to sell the property the intending purchaser's solicitor should notice the existence of a planning agreement and then make inquiries as to whether its terms have been fulfilled. The prudent solicitor who has not been given a satisfactory answer would then advise his client not to complete the purchase. This means that normally the developer will find that the sale of the property on to a final purchaser is made much more difficult because of the failure to meet the obligations imposed by the planning agreement. Where there is no subsequent transfer of the land then normal principles of contract law apply and the authority can take action against the other party for breach of contract.

14.2.4.1 *Successors in title*

If subsequent purchasers of the land subject to a planning agreement take up the burden of compliance with the planning agreement then the local authority must use the special provisions under which the agreement was expressed to be made in order to enforce the agreement against subsequent purchasers. Here the distinction between negative obligations and positive obligations is important. Although the term 'section 52 agreement' is commonly used (even after the 1990 consolidation) to describe most forms of planning agreement this does in fact confuse the issue. Agreements that are solely made under section 106 before 25 October 1991 may only be enforced against subsequent purchasers to the extent that the obligation being enforced deals with 'restricting or regulating' the development or use of land. (Naturally, if positive obligations are enforceable by virtue of the Local Government (Miscellaneous Provisions) Act 1982, section 33 or other powers having been used then those other provisions will be relevant to the enforcement of such provisions.) Similar considerations apply to agreements made under the TCPA 1971, section 52.

14.2.4.2 *Injunction*

Unless the contravention of the obligations constitutes of itself a breach of mainstream planning control the LPA cannot use the statutory injunction under the TCPA 1990, section 187B. Injunctive relief will therefore normally be subject to the section 222 principles which are discussed in chapter nine. It is not necessary to deal with the breach by way of the normal enforcement procedures of the planning regime[1]. This case also indicates that in normal circumstances the remedy would be an injunction rather than damages.

1　*Avon County Council v Millard* (1985) 83 LGR 597, [1986] JPL 211, CA.

14.2.4.3　*Works in default provisions*

In addition to the enforcement of positive obligations (both under the section 33 power and the amended section 106 power) by action in the courts there is also available (by virtue of the LG(MP)A 1982, section 33(3) and the TCPA 1990, section 106(6) respectively) to the LPA a statutory 'works in default' power. The precise terms of the section 33 power must be well understood since these affect the enforcement of agreements expressed to be made under the section. Thus where there is a non-compliance with the covenant to carry out works or 'to do any other thing on or in relation to' land then the 'principal council' must first give 21 days' notice of their intention to enter their land to any person:

(a)　who has for the time being an interest in the land on or in relation to which the works are to be carried out or other things are to be done; and

(b)　against whom the covenant is enforceable whether by virtue of section 33(2) or otherwise.

After giving such notices the principal council may then carry out the works or do anything which the covenant requires or remedy anything which has been done and which the covenant requires to be done. The council may then recover from any persons against whom a covenant is enforceable any expenses incurred by the council in the exercise of their powers under section 33(3). Provisions of the Public Health Act are applied to the exercise of powers under section 33 by virtue of section 33(6). These provisions include the power to charge expenses on the land and power to order payment by instalments. These provisions will rarely be relevant to planning agreements/

obligations entered into after 25 October 1991 since section 33 cannot now be used as an empowering provision in agreements where the development of land is involved[1]. (The prohibition probably extends to agreements which address enforcement problems.) Since that date the provisions of the amended section 106 include enforcement of positive obligations found in instruments made thereafter.

1 Planning and Compensation Act 1991, Sch 7, para 6.

14.2.4.3 *Local act powers*

Authorities should also examine any local act powers which may bestow upon them contractual powers enabling them to control development (either positively or negatively). A good example of this is found in the Greater London Council (General Powers) Act 1974, section 16. This power covers both unilateral undertakings and bilateral agreements. Any undertaking given by an owner of land or an agreement between such an owner and a London borough which are given or made under seal in connection with the land and are expressed to be given or made in pursuance of the section are thus enforceable not only against the owner but also against any successor in title and any person claiming through or under such a person. Again, the borough must be certain that the technical requirements are met. If the person offering the undertaking or agreeing to the agreement is not the owner of a legal estate in land then it will be necessary to conclude a preliminary agreement requiring that (on his obtaining a legal interest in the land) he will give the undertaking or make an agreement under seal in the appropriate manner.

14.2.4.4 *Undertakings*

The use of planning obligations in the context of both resolving enforcement problems and (via the planning contravention notice) encouraging the contravener to back up his promises by legally enforceable means has already been noted. In the context of planning appeals it is also relevant to note that offers from the appellant (often through his advocate) 'undertaking' to do or desist from carrying out some activity should be formalised by way of a section 106 obligation. In this way an undertaking that may impress the inspector can be turned into a concrete obligation: the LPA should insist on this or else require a condition achieving the same.

14.2.4.5 *Modification and discharge of planning agreements*

The options available to the LPA as regards enforcement must take account of the opportunities given to the owner to modify or discharge any obligation arising under a planning agreement/ obligation. With those obligations arising under agreements entered into before 25 October 1991 there is the Lands Tribunal route under the Law of Property Act 1925, section 84 (as amended by the Law of Property Act 1969, section 28). This power only applies to *restrictions* imposed by a planning agreement. Action in the courts to enforce such a restriction may thus be countered by the owner seeking a stay pending a determination by the Lands Tribunal. In *Re Martin's Application*[1] the discrete nature of the two regimes was emphasised. Thus the issues which the Secretary of State deals with on appeal will not necessarily be those which will concern the Tribunal. Thus the Tribunal had held that the detriment to visual amenity which will arise from the erection of a house in contravention of the restriction would cause 'an injury to the council in its capacity as custodian of the public interest'. In *Re Kentwood Property Ltd's Application*[2] the Tribunal noted that in its discretion it will not make an order in favour of the applicant where he had been guilty of a flagrant, cynical and continuing breach of covenant. In *London Borough of Tower Hamlets v Stanton Rubber and Plastics Ltd*[3] it was stated that if a restriction in an agreement was also mirrored by a similar restriction in a planning permission then any reference to the Lands Tribunal to discharge and modify the restriction was premature until a planning appeal against the counterpart condition had been decided.

With planning obligations entered into after 25 October 1991 there is the statutory procedure (akin to that allowing an applicant to seek modification or discharge of a planning condition) contained in the TCPA 1990, section 106A and B. This supplements the mutually agreed variation of planning obligations under the TCPA 1990, section 106A(1)(a). The elements of the statutory procedure are naturally relevant where a planning obligation has been contravened near the five-year limit set by section 106A(4) beginning with the date on which the obligation is entered into. Again the civil courts would be swayed by the argument that the statutory procedure (in progress or imminent) should perhaps be allowed to take its course. A contrary argument may be that delaying a decision would be tantamount to a finding that the planning arguments favoured the contravener: such a finding would implicitly involve the court making judgements about planning merits when this is clearly a matter for the Secretary of State or inspector. The five-year hiatus (preventing early application for discharge/modification) is clearly of relevance to the LPA's use of section 106. One-off obligations should be worded such that they are timetabled for implementation well before the five-year period ends. Maintenance and other long-term obligations will have to be 'appeal-proof' and capable of being sustained on their planning merits. One option which may be open to the LPA is to argue for a series of back-to-back planning obligations each of which has, say, a four-year life. In this way a long-term obligation is in fact composed of linked multiple planning obligations – each of which 'renews' the relevant obligation before the five-year period can bite. Naturally, most owners would try to resist this if the obligation in question was onerous.

1   [1988] 3 PLR 45.
2   [1987] JPL 137.
3   [1990] JPL 512, CA.

14.2.4.6   *Secretary of State modification / discharge / recision*

Planning agreements made under the TCPA 1932 have different rules regarding modification etc. Where the LPA is seeking to enforce the provisions of an agreement made under the TCPA 1932, section 34, then it is important to note that any restrictions in such agreement may, on application to the Secretary of State, be modified or discharged. Such an agreement may also be rescinded or modified by means of an arbitration procedure. The provisions relating to these particular procedures are found in paragraph 88(3) and (4) of Schedule 24 to the TCPA 1971. The 1990 consolidation has not totally repealed the provisions of Schedule 24: thus the Planning (Consequential Provisions) Act 1990, Schedule 3, paragraph 3 states that the provisions of Schedule 24 continue to have effect. The LPA should therefore take care with old agreements since the owner of land against whom they are considering enforcement action by way of a civil remedy may well apply for a stay of proceedings in order to invoke the procedures under paragraph 88 of Schedule 24.

14.2.4.7 *Ultra vires obligations*

One difficult issue that necessarily is of relevance when construing a planning agreement and assessing whether any of its terms are ultra vires is the multiple use of empowering provisions by the LPA. In one sense the LPA is wise to ensure that an agreement is 'watertight' as regards the need to cite the appropriate empowering provisions. However, in analysing a situation in respect of different types of obligation it is relevant to note that where the enforcement of such obligations against successors in title depends upon non-Planning Act provisions then the use of non-Planning Act powers might involve a different analysis of the exercise of that contractual power. The position would be clearer if an agreement were made solely under (for example) the LG(MP)A 1982. Also, if the LPA merely quoted section 111 of the Local Government Act 1972 (and relied purely on the contractual nexus between it and the original contracting party) then such agreements might have a wider scope than would an agreement made solely under section 106. However, many agreements cover obligations which (as regards their later enforcement against successors in title to the original contracting parties) rely upon the 1990 Act, in respect of restriction, and the 1982 Act in respect of positive obligations. The picture becomes even more confused when private Acts (for example the powers under section 16 of the Greater London Council (General Powers) Act 1974) are utilised.

An assertion therefore that a planning agreement or a term within a planning agreement is ultra vires the planning authority cannot be meaningfully assessed in abstract. The authority will, where seeking to enforce an obligation, come up against the vires argument in the form of a defence; the contravener will thus be seeking to raise vires as a shield against the remedy sought by the authority. Complications have arisen in the past with the courts failing to separate policy in circulars (eg circular 16/91) from the legal parameters of the powers in section 106 and section 70. More recent judgments have started to approach the problems in a more coherent way thus finding that planning obligations containing elements in conflict with the policy advice are not thereby ultra vires the LPA[1]. A proper analysis of the situation at hand may well depend upon many factors including the following:

(a) the identity of the party alleging ultra vires (original contracting party or successor in title);
(b) the existence of valuable consideration or some other factor giving rise to questions of 'equity';
(c) the degree to which the party can be said to have assumed the obligation which is under consideration with full knowledge as to the implications of that obligation;
(d) the impact upon the 'public interest' or 'good administration' of finding that the permission or the agreement is tainted – this relates to the above issue as regards the tie-up between the agreement and a planning permission;
(e) whether the related permission has been implemented;
(f) the possibility of severing ultra vires provisions.

These and other issues will all raise points that will be relevant in any particular case. There will of course be occasions where an agreement is clearly ultra vires. An obligation which has no clear link to a local government function (let alone the planning function) would not be well-received by the courts. On the other hand development plan policies that establish a nexus between the planning permission, development and the contents of the planning obligation can perhaps establish a link which would otherwise fail the case law test that the obligation 'fairly and reasonably relate' to the permission. (This test is not necessarily one which is proof against criticism.) In this vein it is relevant naturally to keep up to date with the latest case law. For critiques of the House of Lords' decision in *Tesco* see my Lawyer's Aside column in *Planning*, 26 May 1995 and an article in *Local Government Chronicle*, 9 June 1995. The courts appear to be taking a less interventionist approach when approaching the narrow question of what can lawfully be included in a planning obligation. As long as the obligation is not *Wednesbury* unreasonable, relates to planning and falls within section 106(1) the courts will not strike down the obligation: this is clear from *Tesco*. As yet the courts have not fully and convincingly explored the more difficult question of how they will police the necessary interaction between the LPA's determination of the related planning permission (which is subject to the rules regarding what is a 'material consideration') and the terms of the planning obligation. Terms in the planning obligation that are legally valid for the purposes of section 106(1), etc may not be 'material considerations' for the purposes of the section 70 determination. What role can development plan policy play in making a planning obligation 'material' to a grant of permission when otherwise it would be irrelevant? Will the courts simply accept the LPA's word that such factors were ignored by the planning committee? (Lord Hoffman appears to think that the UK courts should not delve too far into the negotiations etc: he prefers to leave such matters to the political mechanisms (call-in, appeals and elections presumably) found in the planning system.)

1   *Tesco v Secretary of State for the Environment* [1995] 2 All ER 636, HL. The case of *R v South Northamptonshire District Council, ex p Crest Homes plc* [1995] JPL 200 stresses that the criteria employed for computing appropriate financial payments need not ensure exact proportionality between the size of the contribution and the purpose for which that contribution is sought.

14.2.4.8   *Conditional planning obligations*

The TCPA 1990, section 106(1) defines the legal parameters of planning obligations. The TCPA 1990, section (2)(a) then allows such obligations to be 'subject to conditions'. A problem may be encountered where this provision is, in effect, used to override the statutory limitations imposed by section 106(1). The most common way of doing this (eg to use a planning obligation as a vehicle for making payments to a third party – section 106(1)(d) only allows planning obligations to require sums to be paid to the LPA) is to introduce a *Grampian*-style condition into the obligation. The owner is thus prevented, for example, from using or occupying the land until the payment is made to the third party. Although widely used this particular strategy would seem to be in direct conflict with the statutory scheme and so susceptible to legal challenge by an amenity group (for example) who objected to the whole arrangement. The courts could well be persuaded to stamp down on this long-established practice (clearly in conflict with the statutory intent) where surrounding circumstances indicate a clear possibility of abuse. LPAs entering into negotiations that involve payments to third parties (or other obligations justifiable on planning grounds but falling outside the ambit of section 106(1)) should perhaps consider the risks that this rather transparent device may create.

14.3 COMPLETION NOTICES

14.3.1 Introduction

Since the grant of planning permission is 'permissive' the LPA may find that either the permission is not acted upon or, in some cases is only implemented 'gradually'. This is particularly likely in recession where funds for different phases can only be raised on the sale of earlier ones. The long, drawn-out development of land in this way can be damaging to amenity. Yet it is very unlikely that the relevant permission will have a condition requiring completion of the development within a stated time. Thus the only real option to 'enforce' planning control in this situation may be to invoke the completion notice procedures under the TCPA. (Of course, where financial difficulties have led to a development being half completed it may even be the case that the completion notice procedure will be unlikely to have much effect.) DOE advice (circular 1/85, paragraph 50) discusses problems relating to conditions requiring that the whole of the development be completed. That paragraph usefully summarises some of the issues that relate to this sort of problem:

> 'A condition requiring that the whole of the development permitted be completed is likely to be difficult to enforce. If a development forming a single indivisible whole, such as a single dwellinghouse, is left half-finished it may be possible to secure completion by a completion notice under section [94] of the Act. If, however, the reason for failure to complete is financial difficulties experienced by the developer, neither a completion notice nor enforcement of conditions would be likely to bear much fruit; in such circumstances the only practical step open to the local planning authority, if they wish to secure the completion of the development, may be the acquisition of the land. If a large development such as an estate of houses is left half-complete, this may well be because of market changes (for example, a shift of demand from four-bedroom to two-bedroom houses), and it would clearly not be desirable to compel the erection of houses of a type for which there was no demand or need. Conditions requiring the completion of the whole of a development should therefore not normally be imposed'.

With the development of 'deregulated' planning regimes – simplified planning zones and enterprise zones – the completion notice system has also been extended to cover developments begun in accordance with planning permissions under those particular regimes but have then 'stalled'. The completion notice system thus now covers not only developments that have not been completed within the normal 'expiry'[1] period but also the 'expiry' periods relating to simplified planning zone schemes and enterprise zone schemes.

The LPA may therefore issue a 'completion notice' if it is 'of the opinion that the development will not be completed within a reasonable period'[2]. This notice must state that the planning permission will cease to have effect at the expiration of a further period specified in the notice. This period cannot be less than 12 months after the notice takes effect[3].

1 This would normally be the five-year period set out in section 91 of the TCPA 1990 and automatically imposed on grants of full planning permission by that section.
2 TCPA 1990, s 94(2).
3 Ibid.

14.3.2 Service of completion notice

The notice must be served on the owner and occupier of the land and on any other person 'who in the opinion of the LPA will be affected by the notice'[1]. This notice takes effect only when it is confirmed by the Secretary of State[2].

1 TCPA 1990, s 94(4).
2 TCPA 1990, s 95(1).

14.3.3 Contents of notice

The notice must specify a period (being not less than 28 days from the service of that notice) within which any person on whom it is served may require the Secretary of State (before confirming the notice) to hold a hearing. The notice must refer to the planning permission to which it relates[1]. It is advisable for authorities to set out the permission in the notice so as to avoid any confusion.

1 TCPA 1990, s 94(2) implies that reference is made to 'the permission' in the notice.

14.3.4 Appeal

Both the LPA and any person on whom a completion notice is served may request a public inquiry to be held before the Secretary of State confirms the notice[1]. The Secretary of State (if he decides to confirm the notice) may substitute a longer period for that specified notice after which the planning permission lapses[2].

1 TCPA 1990, s 95(3).
2 TCPA 1990, s 95(2).

14.3.5 Effective completion notice

When a completion notice takes effect (and this can only be when and if the Secretary of State confirms it) then the planning permission which is the basis of the notice becomes invalid except as far as it authorises any development carried out in compliance with the notice up to the end of the expiration period stated in the completion notice[1]. Therefore development carried out after the permission becomes invalid is subject to enforcement action. The DOE has accepted that a partially built structure (the planning permission for which has expired by virtue of an effective completion notice) can be subject to an enforcement notice requiring removal of the *whole* of the structure[2]. Thus in one enforcement notice appeal the LPA alleged that there was a breach of planning control in that the partially built structure did not accord with the plans which showed a completed dwelling. The inspector accepted this and upheld the notice which required demolition of the building and removal of all materials. Authorities that wish to rely on this interpretation should, however, be prepared for litigation as it is somewhat surprising!

1 TCPA 1990, s 95(5).
2 DOE reference – APP/5083/C/83/86 (*sic*), [1985] JPL 496.

14.3.6 Withdrawal

The LPA may withdraw a completion notice at any time before the expiration of the period specified in the notice after which the planning permission becomes invalid. The authority is required to give notice of the withdrawal 'immediately' to every person who was served with the completion notice[1].

1 TCPA 1990, s 94(5).

14.3.7 Enforcement of completion notices

A completion notice operates so as to encourage the developer to finish the development for which he has permission within a stated time. If this is not done then the authority may take enforcement action against works carried out in breach of planning control. Since the DOE has accepted (see above) that enforcement action may actually require removal of the entire structure as not being in compliance with the plans accompanying a planning permission, then the 'enforcement' of a completion notice can have quite an impact.

14.4 DISCONTINUANCE ORDERS

14.4.1 Introduction

The discontinuance order enables an authority to deal with a planning problem which is prejudicial to the 'proper planning' of the area: LPAs may, in the era of sustainable development, even consider using such powers to address sites whose current activity is 'unsustainable'. Such an order effectively writes the final page in the current 'chapter in the planning history' of a site. However, the compensation provisions that are triggered on the exercise of this particular power may well deter most authorities from ever using a discontinuance order. This may explain why LPAs are empowered also to grant permission for development of the land subject to such an order: such permission in effect allows a new chapter in the planning history of that site to start.

14.4.2 The discretion

A LPA may issue a discontinuance order requiring:

(a) the discontinuance of a use;
(b) that conditions should be imposed on the continuance of a use; or
(c) the alteration or removal of buildings or works.

By virtue of section 102(1) of the TCPA 1990 they may do so if it appears 'expedient in the interests of the proper planning of the area (including the interests of amenity)'. Regard must be had to the development plan and to other material considerations: this indicates that section 54A applies to the LPA's exercise of this discretion. A broad reading of the term 'use' was given by the Court of Appeal in *Parkes v Secretary of State for the Environment*[1]. Thus the sorting and storing of scrap was held to be a 'use' which could then be subject to a discontinuance order. As regards the term 'amenity' it was held in *Re Lamplugh*[2] that the LPA could take into account the possible future detriment to amenity.

1 [1979] 1 JPL 33.
2 (1967) 19 P & CR 125.

14.4.3 **Minerals**

The power to require the discontinuance of mineral workings is covered by Schedule 9 to the TCPA 1990. A mineral planning authority may issue such a discontinuance order dealing with a use of land for development consisting in the winning and working of minerals. The details of the special procedures relating to discontinuance orders affecting mineral workings is outside the scope of this work, however, it should be noted that Schedule 9 also deals with suspension and supplementary suspension orders which are of particular importance to the minerals regime.

14.4.4 **Confirmation**

The Secretary of State must confirm a discontinuance order if it is to take effect. The Secretary of State's confirmation may be without modification to the order or may include such modifications 'as he considers expedient'[1]. The modifications that the Secretary of State may make include modifications as to any provision of the order granting permission[2]. Any modification may also operate so as to include in the order any grant of planning permission which might have been included in the order as submitted to the Secretary of State[3]. When the LPA submits an order to the Secretary of State for his confirmation it must serve a notice on the owner and occupier of the land affected by the order and on any other person who in its opinion will also be affected. Such notice must contain a period (not less than 28 days from the service of the notice) within which any person on whom the notice is served may require the Secretary of State to hold an inquiry[4]. If the Secretary of State confirms the discontinuance order then the LPA is required to serve a copy of the order on the owner and occupier of the land to which the order relates[5]. A discontinuance order is registrable as a planning charge (Part 3 of the Register) under the Local Land Charges Rules 1977, SI 1977/985, r 2(2).

1 TCPA 1990, s 103(1).
2 TCPA 1990, s 103(2).
3 Ibid.
4 TCPA 1990, s 103(4) and (5).
5 TCPA 1990, s 103(7).

14.4.5 Residential premises

Where a discontinuance order affects residential premises then the LPA is placed under a special duty. The existence of this duty (discussed below) may therefore colour the consideration of the power when the problem is carefully analysed. Thus if an order involves the 'displacement of persons residing in any premises' then the authority is obliged to secure the provision or accommodation in advance of the displacement[1]. This duty arises to the extent that there is no other residential accommodation available on reasonable terms suitable to the 'reasonable requirements' of the persons so displaced. The extent of this particular duty was analysed in *R v East Hertfordshire District Council, ex p Smith*[2] where the authority had secured temporary bed and breakfast accommodation for the persons displaced by the discontinuance order. The court held that such accommodation was 'suitable' – the local authority was also discussing with the residents longer-term arrangements for rehousing.

1 TCPA 1990, s 102(6).
2 (1990) 22 HLR 176.

14.4.6 Grant of planning permission

Compensation liability will be decreased if the order grants planning permission – as it may under the legislation[1]. The order may specify conditions[2]. The conditions may be for the retention of buildings or works constructed or carried out before the date on which the order was submitted to the Secretary of State[3]. The planning permission may also be for the continuance of a use of land instituted before the date on which the order was submitted to the Secretary of State[4]. (The LPA may be able to bargain with the owner and use a planning obligation to achieve a use-swap which deals with the problem caused by the undesirable use by relocating it to another site. By giving permission on another site and enforcing the move by way of a planning obligation the LPA can more flexibly achieve an appropriate result with minimal cost in terms of compensation.)

1 TCPA 1990, s 102(2).
2 Ibid.
3 TCPA 1990, s 102(4)(a).
4 TCPA 1990, s 102(4)(b).

14.4.7 Contraventions of discontinuance order

Where a discontinuance order under section 102 (and also the various orders made in respect of mineral workings under Schedule 9) are contravened then a criminal offence is committed. The convoluted terms of that offence are set out in section 189(1) and (2) of the TCPA 1990. The foundation of criminal liability is the use of land or causing or permitting its use in contravention of such orders without planning permission. There is a defence available in section 189(4) and so the prosecuting authority will naturally wish to ensure that the accused will not be able to rely on such a defence in court.

14.4.8 Defence

A person charged with an offence under section 189 may use the statutory defence that he took 'all reasonable measures and exercised all due diligence to avoid the commission of the offence by himself or by any person under his control'[1]. If that defence is relied on and this involves an allegation that the commission of the offence was due to the act or default of another person or due to reliance on information supplied by another person then the defendant (unless leave of the court is given) shall not be entitled to rely on the defence unless he has served (within a period ending seven clear days before the hearing) on the prosecutor a notice in writing giving such information identifying or assisting in the identification of the other person[2].

1 TCPA 1990, s 189(4).
2 Ibid ss (5).

14.4.9 Penalties

Any person guilty of an offence under section 189 is liable on summary conviction to a fine not exceeding the statutory maximum[1] and on conviction on indictment to an unlimited fine[2].

1 This is £5,000.
2 TCPA 1990, s 189(3).

14.4.10 Works in default power

A second option open to the LPA is to use the works in default power in relation to certain types of 'steps' which have not been taken within the period specified in the order. The LPA is given powers to enter the land and take such steps which should have been carried out as required by an order under section 102 or paragraph 1 of Schedule 9 of the TCPA 1990. More specifically, this covers:

(a) any step to be taken for the alteration or removal of any buildings or works or any plant or machinery;
(b) any steps required in an order under paragraph 3 of schedule 9 of the TCPA 1990 required to be taken,
  (i) for the alteration or removal of any buildings or works or any plant or machinery, or
  (ii) for the removal or alleviation of any injury to amenity;
(c) any step for the protection of the environment required to be taken by a suspension order or a supplementary suspension order[1].

The provisions of section 276 of the Public Health Act 1936 apply[2] – thus allowing the authority to sell 'materials' if not claimed and removed by the owner within three days. The discussion of the use of the default power in the enforcement of mainstream planning control in chapter nine deals in more detail with the works in default power.

1　TCPA 1990, s 190(1).
2　TCPA 1990, s 190(5).

14.4.11　Injunctive relief

The LPA could seek an injunction under section 222 of the Local Government Act 1972 (not the TCPA 1990, section 187B) in cases where, for example, a use had not been discontinued despite prosecution of the guilty party. The discussion in chapter nine of injunctive relief is relevant.

14.4.12　Compensation

The exercise of this power gives rise to compensation liability and this may explain why the power is rarely used by LPAs. Compensation is less of a problem however where a notice is used to deal with a breach of planning control. Compensation liability is less in respect of uses that are in breach of control by virtue of the wording of the Land Compensation Act 1961[1]. This states that if a use is 'contrary to law' then any increase in value of the land attributable to that use should not be taken into account when assessing compensation. However, case law indicates that a use which is an established use or which can benefit from a certificate of lawful use is not 'contrary to law' and so that use's value must be reflected in any computation of the compensation payable.

1　Land Compensation Act 1961, s 5(4).
2　*Hughes v Doncaster Metropolitan Borough Council* [1991] 1 AC 382.

14.5　ENFORCEMENT AND CROWN LAND

14.5.1　Introduction

'Crown land' has a special status in the planning system. Planning officers may already be familiar with the special procedures that apply to development proposals affecting Crown land so it will not come as a shock to learn that such special status also affects the enforcement function. The term 'Crown land' it must be noted has a specific meaning. Such land is land in which there is a Crown interest or a Duchy interest[1]. Crown interest means an interest belonging to Her Majesty, or belonging to a government department or held in trust for Her Majesty for the purposes of a government department. Duchy interest means an interest belonging to Her Majesty in right of the Duchy of Lancaster or belonging to the Duchy of Cornwall[2]. Where a breach of planning control affects Crown land there are special rules. These are discussed below. Annex 6 of circular 16/91 discusses enforcement affecting Crown land and also includes a model enforcement notice.

1 TCPA 1990, s 293(1).
2 Ibid.

14.5.2 Development by Crown interests

There is an exemption given to development carried out by or on behalf of the Crown on land which was Crown land at the time the development was carried out. Such development, although it may appear to be in breach of planning control, cannot be attacked by an enforcement notice[1]. However, the enforcement provisions of the planning Acts do apply to Crown land 'to the extent of any interest in it for the time being held otherwise than by or on behalf of the Crown'[2]. This means that although a superior interest (usually the freehold) is held by the Crown an inferior non-Crown interest will be subject to control. Thus leaseholders (for example) will still be subject to enforcement action even though they are on Crown land.

1 TCPA 1990, s 294(1).
2 TCPA 1990, s 296(1)(c).

14.5.3 Contraventions on Crown land (non-Crown interests)

Enforcement can be taken against contraventions of planning control for which non-Crown interests are responsible. The 'Crown land' label is thus not determinative of the position – the more important aspect of a situation is the nature of the interest in the land – is it a Crown interest or not? But even where a non-

Crown interest is responsible for the breach the LPA still has to obtain the 'consent' of the 'appropriate authority' before it can issue an enforcement notice[1]. The term 'appropriate authority' covers the body that will be in day-to-day control of the land and administer it for the Crown[2]. Normally this will be a government department. So the LPA will have to approach the proper body and formally request its permission. Naturally, the body concerned may try to sort out the breach of control by means of private law mechanisms – relying on the landlord/tenant relationship normally. The LPA may therefore face a little delay. Indeed, it may often be necessary to indicate some sort of deadline for a response from the 'appropriate authority'; otherwise, the LPA may find that no decision is forthcoming. The authority is thus in a position similar to that of a developer waiting for a development control decision but with no 'deemed refusal' rule.

1   TCPA 1990, s 296(2)(a).
2   TCPA 1990, s 293(2) sets out in more detail the definition.

14.5.3.1 *Trespassers and squatters*

As the 'consent' of the appropriate authority is required for ordinary enforcement action under the TCPA 1990 in respect of non-Crown 'interests' in land the ambit of the term 'interests' is important. It thus covers instances where the person in breach occupies the land by virtue of a licence in writing[1]. It is clear however, that trespassers and squatters do not have an 'interest' as that term is used in the above provisions. Breaches of control that arise from the activities of such people may trigger the 'special enforcement notice' procedures. These provisions dealing with 'squatters' will thus be relevant where a breach affects motorways and trunk roads. The 'mobile cafe' problem (discussed in chapter three) thus will involve Crown Land issues and the use of a special enforcement notice.

1   TCPA 1990, s 293(3).

14.5.3.2 *Special enforcement notices*

Legislation in 1984[1] was enacted to deal with situations where there was no 'interest' held by the person causing the breach of control and no person was entitled to occupy the land by virtue of a private interest. The authority may serve a 'special enforcement notice"[2] to deal with the breach. Again the consent of the 'appropriate authority' is necessary[3]. The detailed procedures for such notices are set out in delegated legislation[4]. Although the procedures are modelled on mainstream enforcement procedures there are differences – for example, there is no 'works in default power' available. It should be noted that the terms of section 294(2) restrict the use of such notices to those situations where the only interest in the land is a Crown interest. If a squatter/trespasser commits a breach of control when a private interest allows a person to occupy the land then ordinary enforcement notices should be used: naturally the consent of the 'appropriate authority' is still required.

1 Town and Country Planning Act 1984, s 3, now the TCPA 1990, s 294(2) et seq.
2 Ibid subsection (3).
3 Ibid subsection (4).
4 Town and Country Planning (Special Enforcement Notices) Regulations 1992, SI 1992/1562.

14.5.3.3 *Contents and service*

A special enforcement notice must specify the following matters:

- (a) the matters alleged to constitute development;
- (b) the steps required to be taken for,
    - (i) restoring the land to its condition before the development took place, or
    - (ii) discontinuing any use of the land which has been instituted by the development;
- (c) the date on which the notice is to take effect ('the specified date'); and
- (d) the period(s) for compliance with the notice[1].

There are no standard appeal forms to be sent out with copies of the notice. There are some 'notes for appellants' (cf listed building enforcement notice procedures) which should accompany copies. Those to be served are:

- (a) the person who carried out the development alleged in the notice;
- (b) any person who is occupying the land when the notice is issued; and
- (c) the appropriate authority[2].

Where the LPA are unable to identify or trace the person who carried out the development alleged in the notice after 'reasonable inquiry' then they need not serve a copy of the notice on him[3].

1 TCPA 1990, s 294(5) and (6).
2 TCPA 1990, s 295(1).
3 TCPA 1990, s 295(2).

14.5.3.4 *Appeal against special enforcement notice*

The contravening 'squatter' may appeal against a notice – if he is occupying the land on the date on which the notice is issued; the person who carried out the development alleged in the notice may also appeal[1]. The appellant need not have been served with a copy of the notice in order to appeal[2]. There is no 'deemed application for permission' when an appeal is made against a special enforcement notice. The grounds of appeal are that the matters alleged in the notice:

  (a) have not taken place; or
  (b) do not constitute development.

1 TCPA 1990, s 295(3).
2 TCPA 1990, s 295(4).

14.5.4 Stop notice

Where the breach involves an activity which is undesirable the LPA may serve a stop notice. The stop notice power exercisable in respect of special enforcement notices is based on the standard stop notice of mainstream enforcement. Some of the minor differences will be outlined here. A stop notice may be issued against any 'activity which is, or is included in, a matter alleged by the notice to constitute development'[1]. The stop notice may be served on any person who appears to the authority to be occupying the land or to be engaged in any activity prohibited by the stop notice[2]. The stop notice is not invalidated by a failure to serve a copy of it as required by the 1990 Act if the LPA demonstrates that it took all such steps as were reasonably practicable to effect proper service[3]. There is no requirement on the LPA to obtain the consent of the appropriate authority before issuing a stop notice.

1 TCPA 1990, s 183(1)(b), as modified by the Schedule to the Town and Country Planning (Special Enforcement Notices) Regulations 1992, SI 1992/1562.
2 TCPA 1990, s 183(6), as modified by the Schedule to the Town and Country Planning (Special Enforcement Notices) Regulations 1992, SI 1992/1562.
3 TCPA 1990, s 184(8), as modified by the Schedule to the Town and Country Planning (Special Enforcement Notices) Regulations 1992, SI 1992/1562.

14.5.4.1 *Compensation*

The provisions dealing with compensation in respect of 'ordinary' stop notices are applied with minor modification. The modification affects the circumstances when compensation may be claimed. The provisions of the TCPA 1990, section 186(1)(a)–(d) are amended so a person may claim compensation where any of the following apply:

    (a) the special enforcement notice is quashed;
    (b) the special enforcement notice is varied, so that matters alleged to constitute development cease to include one or more of the activities prohibited by the stop notice;
    (c) the special enforcement notice is withdrawn by the LPA;
    (d) the stop notice is withdrawn.

14.6 MONUMENTS

14.6.1 Introduction

Where the LPA is concerned with a problem affecting a monument it will firstly have to deal with the problems of definition. The first point to note is that the term 'monument' includes not only buildings or ruins but also earthworks, burial mounds, crosses, fortifications etc. The term also covers the remains of such items and the sites comprising the remains of any 'vehicle, vessel or aircraft or other movable structure'[1]. The definition of 'monument' is expanded by the legislation (the extended definition given to the term 'listed building' is another example of where the legislation introduces definitions which give broad protection to a particular planning interest); thus references in the AMAAA 1979 to a monument include references to the site of the monument and to a group of monuments or any part of a monument or group of monuments[2]. By virtue of section 61(9) the site of a monument includes not only the land in or on which it is situated but also any land comprising or adjoining it which appears to the local authority (or the Secretary of State or English Heritage) to be essential for the monument's support and preservation. This extended definition given to the term 'monument' is something which the authority should therefore note when exercising any enforcement powers in relation to contraventions of the legislation. In addition to the wide range of physical objects which fall within the term 'monument' it is also important to note that there are three specific categories of monument. These comprise:

(a)　ancient monuments;
(b)　scheduled monuments;
(c)　protected monuments.

In terms of the enforcement function the key definitions are 'scheduled monument' and 'protected monument'. The latter term is relevant since it occurs in the provisions dealing with the special 'criminal damage' offence under section 28(1) of the AMAAA 1979 – see para 14.6.5. The term 'scheduled monument' is defined as any monument which is for the time being included in the schedule of monuments compiled and maintained for the purposes of the AMAAA 1979 by the Secretary of State.

1　AMAAA 1979, s 61(7).
2　AMAAA 1979, s 61(10).

14.6.2　Scheduled monuments

A 'scheduled monument' is protected by the provisions of section 2. Thus any person who 'executes or causes or permits to be executed any works' that fall within the terms of that section will commit an offence. Only where such works are authorised under the AMAAA 1979 will that person escape liability. Such authorised works primarily comprise those carried out in compliance with a scheduled monument consent or in reliance upon a consent granted by delegated legislation[1]. The offences under section 2 fall under two headings. Thus there is the 'unauthorised works' type of offence and the 'breach of condition' type of offence.

1 Ancient Monuments (Class Consents) Order 1994, SI 1994/1381.

14.6.2.1 *Unauthorised works*

Criminal liability attaches to the following types of works:

(a) any works resulting in the demolition or destruction of or any damage to a scheduled monument;
(b) any works for the purpose of removing or repairing a scheduled monument or any part of it or of making any alterations or additions thereto; and
(c) any flooding or tipping operations on land in, on or under which there is a scheduled monument'[1].

In respect of the carrying out of works falling within (a) above the legislation provides two defences. Thus it shall be a defence for the accused to prove that he took all reasonable precautions and exercised all due diligence to avoid or prevent damage to the monument. A second defence available in relation to this particular charge is that the defendant did not know and had no reason to believe that the monument was a scheduled monument. In any proceedings for an offence under section 2 it shall be a defence to prove that the works were urgently necessary in the interests of safety or health and that notice in writing of the need for the works was given to the Secretary of State as soon as reasonably practicable. A prosecution may, however, be difficult if the documentation used to prove the fact of scheduling does not clearly indicate the precise delineation of the scheduled monument. In many cases the scale of the plan and the thickness of lines meant to show the boundary of the site so scheduled will make the task of precisely delineating the margin between scheduled and non-scheduled land very difficult. When this has a bearing on criminal liability then the exacting standards imposed by the criminal courts will make the task of the prosecutor in such a case almost impossible. (It may be useful to talk of the scheduling, in such a case, as being 'nugatory' in the sense I use that term in para 9.6.8). Problems with interpreting the schedule were thus at the heart of the case in

R v Jackson where the Court of Appeal (Criminal Division) was critical of the clarity of the documentation in question[2]. The conviction was quashed in that case because the scheduling documentation did not meet the standard of clarity demanded by the criminal law process and so could not substantiate the charge of demolishing (part of) the scheduled monument.

1 AMAAA 1979, s 2(2).
2 (1994) Independent, 23 May.

14.6.2.2 *Breach of condition offence*

By virtue of section 2(6) of the AMAAA 1979 if any person executes or causes or permits to be executed any works to which a scheduled monument consent relates and fails to comply with any condition attached thereto then an offence will be committed. The subsection also sets out the defence that the defendant 'took all reasonable precautions and exercised all due diligence to avoid contravening the condition'.

14.6.2.3 *Penalties*

A person guilty of an offence under section 2 of the AMAAA 1979 shall be liable:

  (a) on summary conviction to a fine not exceeding the statutory maximum; or
  (b) on conviction on indictment to a fine.

14.6.3 **Liaison with English Heritage**

It is important that LPAs recognise the role that can be played in prosecutions by English Heritage. It will be prudent in any event to obtain the necessary proof as to the 'scheduling' of a monument when presenting a case before the magistrates. A guidance note 'Damage to Ancient Monuments: Guidance to Prosecution' was prepared by English Heritage and endorsed and issued by the Association of County Councils on 22 June 1988. English Heritage is also empowered to prosecute any

offence under Part I (the ancient monuments provisions) of the
AMAAA 1979[1].

1 National Heritage Act 1983, s 33(2A).

14.6.4 Metal detectors

The abuse of metal detectors is a problem that can affect
monuments. The site of a scheduled monument or any other
monument under the ownership or guardianship of the Secretary
of State, English Heritage or a local authority is a 'protected
place' for the purposes of offences under the AMAAA 1979,
section 42 involving metal detectors[1]. Thus if any person without
written consent removes any object of archaeological or historical
interest which is discovered by the use of a metal detector in
such a place then an offence will be committed. The offence is
triable either way. Before the magistrates' court the fine is up
to the statutory maximum and if the case goes to the Crown
Court the fine is unlimited[2]. The mere use of a metal detector in
'a protected place' without the written consent of English
Heritage gives rise to a summary offence punishable by a fine
of up to £200[3]. Written consents under section 42 may be
granted subject to conditions. Consequently the failure to comply
with a condition can give rise to liability on the basis of a simple
'use' offence or a 'removal' offence. Thus non-compliance with a
condition on written consent in the use of a metal detector
attracts a penalty identical to that of unauthorised use under
section 42(1). Non-compliance with the condition in connection
with the 'removing or otherwise dealing with any object' which
has been discovered by the use of a metal detector in a 'protected
place' gives rise to a liability identical to that found in section 42(3).

1 AMAAA 1979, s 42(2)(a).
2 AMAAA 1979, s 42(3). See para 9.6.11 for the standard scale of fines.
3 AMAAA 1979, s 42(1).

14.6.4.1 *Defences*

By virtue of section 42(6) where the accused is prosecuted under
section 42(1) (the 'use' offence) and he proves that he used the

metal detector 'for a purpose other than detecting or locating objects of archaeological or historical interest' then he will be acquitted. If the accused is prosecuted under section 42(1) or section 42(3) then he can raise the defence that he had taken 'all reasonable precautions to find out whether the place where he used the metal detector was a protected place and did not believe that it was'[1].

1 AMAAA 1979, s 42(7).

14.6.5 Damaging a 'protected monument'

Anyone who destroys or damages a protected monument is guilty of an offence if that person:

(a) knows that it is a protected monument and either intends to destroy or damage the monument, or
(b) is reckless as to whether it would be destroyed or damaged[1].

The term 'protected monument' covers any scheduled monument and any monument under the ownership or guardianship of Secretary of State, English Heritage or the local authority. The fine before the magistrates' court can be up to the statutory maximum (ie £5,000), a prison sentence of up to six months, or both: before the Crown Court the fine is unlimited, the prison term may be up to two years, or both.

1 AMAAA 1979, s 28(1).

14.6.6 Compensation orders, community service orders

The criminal courts are given powers to make compensation orders against a person convicted of an offence for any 'loss or damage' resulting from the commission of such an offence[1]. The convicted person may thus be ordered to pay compensation to, usually, the owner of property damaged by the defendant. Where the LPA is 'guardian' of a monument in respect of which an offence falling under the compensation order powers has been committed, then a compensation order can be made in favour of the LPA as 'guardian'[2]. Although the court may make such order on its own motion it would be better for the LPA to make an express application. A more creative form of sentencing is available in the form of community service orders: the Powers of the Criminal Courts Act 1978, section 14 could therefore be used where 'rehabilitation' (rather than 'punishment' or 'retribution') is to be the main aim. In such cases the offender's attitude to the historic environment could perhaps be changed by an appropriate programme of community service involving restoration etc of the historic environment.

1 Powers of Criminal Courts Act 1973, s 35.
2 AMAAA 1979, s 29.

14.7 HAZARDOUS SUBSTANCES CONTROL

This regime is a recent addition to the planning stable. I will not discuss the details of the system of control as circular 11/92 provides a useful overview of the system and the links with the controls exercised by the Health and Safety Executive (HSE) under separate regimes (Annex B particularly). Annex A to the circular sets out the detail and enforcement personnel should study it for the basic structure while referring to the following for a discussion of those factors of particular importance to the enforcement regime.

14.7.1 Contraventions and the HSE – general issues

Contraventions of control under this regime can arise in two situations – situations which follow a pattern familiar to those experienced in handling contraventions of planning control. First a contravention can arise where there is or has been an 'unauthorised presence' of a hazardous substance on land[1]. This can arise when there is no hazardous substances consent for the presence of the substance or if the quantity of the substance in question present exceeds the maximum permitted by such a consent[2]. This naturally involves the hazardous substances authority (HSA) being able to apply the rules regarding the amounts, locations and substances etc that can be stored under any relevant consent or without the need for express consent. The second type of contravention is failure to comply with a condition imposed on a hazardous substances consent – a 'breach of condition' contravention[3]. There may, of course, be parallel forms of control (eg a planning obligation entered into with the LPA[4]) which may be relevant so the HSA may have to consider how action under other forms of control should be taken. This also involves consideration of the parallel regime for controlling hazardous substances which is exercised by the HSE. As in other special cases therefore (eg noise problems, waste tipping and environmental-health contraventions) the authority will have to consider the options for enforcement made available by other environmental law regimes. Liaison with different agencies may therefore be an issue to address in terms of the basic organisational response at the early stages of investigation etc. The enforcement manual dealing with hazardous substances contravention should perhaps address this is issue head on: working arrangements with the HSE should be established so that the parameters and responsibilities of the two agencies are established and clearly set down. (The HSE has to be consulted on every application for hazardous substances consent so the HSA will necessarily have to establish some relationship with the HSE[5].) Circular 11/92 (which addresses the new system) also makes specific reference to the importance of liaison with the HSE over enforcement issues: see paragraph A-86.

1 HSA 1990, s 23(2)(a). The basis of the regime (control over the 'presence' of a hazardous substance) appears to be fundamentally different from all other planning regimes. Normally the legislation controls the 'minded' activity of the owner etc who is 'carrying out development' or 'demolishing an unlisted building in a conservation area' etc. In other words the focus is on someone who is intentionally engaged in some activity. In the hazardous substance regime however the legislation (instead of using a concept such as 'storing' or 'keeping' which directly involves the minded activity of the owner etc) uses the impersonal term 'presence'. This may suggest that the regime is fundamentally different and is not concerned at a basic level with whether the person in control of the land or activities on it intentionally caused such a 'presence'. Though (because of the various defences involving 'intention' to criminal liability) this rather unusual conceptual basis to the regime is not followed through in terms of the criminal law provisions it may still have some relevance to the way in which the civil and criminal courts approach this regime. See further on this point my Lawyer's Aside column in *Planning*, 7 August 1992.

2 HSA 1990, s 23(2)(a)(i) and (ii) respectively.
3 HSA 1990, s 23(2)(b).
4 The HSA as such has no power to enter into a planning obligation as that is a power contained in the TCPA 1990 – not the HSA 1990: there is no special 'hazardous substances obligation' provision equivalent to that found in TCPA 1990, s 106. The HSA could probably enter into simple contracts with operators under the Local Government Act 1972, s 111 but these would not of themselves run with the land. If the authority (as LPA) was also considering a planning application at the same time then the authority (as LPA) could negotiate a section 106 obligation addressing the planning issues raised by the parallel application.
5 Planning (Hazardous Substances) Regulations 1992, SI 1992/656 ('the 1992 Regulations'), reg 10(1)(a).

14.7.2 HSE and conditions

The special role of the HSE in terms of decision-making under the legislation is symbolised by provisions which set out specific conditions which may be imposed on a grant of consent. The conditions may deal with:

(a) how and where any hazardous substance is to be kept or used;
(b) the times between which any substance may be present;
(c) the permanent removal of any substance –
    (i) by a date specified in the consent,
    (ii) before the end of a period set out in the consent, and commencing on the date of the grant of consent;
(d) state that the consent is conditional on the commencement or implementation (in whole or in part) of a planning permission specified in the condition[1].

The legislation limits the HSA's ability to control the keeping and use of hazardous substances by condition to situations where the HSE has advised that such a condition be imposed[2]. The HSA is required also to 'have regard' to the advice of the HSE in determining applications[3].

1 HSA 1990, s 10(1).
2 HSA 1990, s 10(2).
3 HSA 1990, s 9(2)(e).

14.7.3   Entry powers and investigation

Rights of entry similar to those granted for mainstream enforcement are provided by HSA 1990, sections 36, 36A and 36B. There is no equivalent of PCNs provided though the HSA does have power to require information as to interests in land in the manner of a section 330 notice under the TCPA 1990: this provision is applied to the HSA 1990 by section 37(1). Service of such notices and contravention notices is possible also under TCPA 1990, section 329 as applied to this regime by section 37(1). Since immediate criminal liability arises when a contravention occurs the HSA investigator will need to be aware of the PACE code regarding interviews: see chapter nine.

14.7.4   The sanctions

This form of planning control has fundamental similarities to the specialist regimes such as listed building control since the issues addressed can be particularly important to the community. There is therefore a three-fold option for the HSA when faced with a contravention (additionally, of course, the HSA should explore, as suggested above, action by the HSE):

(a) prosecution;
(b) hazardous substances contraventions notice; and
(c) statutory injunction.

14.7.5   Criminal offence

The person liable is termed the 'appropriate person'[1]. This covers:

(a) the person in control of the land;
(b) any person knowingly causing the substance to be present;
(c) any person allowing it to be so present.

Since such substances may be delivered to the site by other companies the HSA may find that both the company in control of the site and a second (supplier) company will be covered by this definition and possibly the transport company involved in the actual transportation of the substance. Therefore when the fine is being assessed by reference in particular to the 'financial benefit' standard the HSA will need to provide evidence about the 'profit' element accruing to a range of different corporate entities[2]. The maximum fine on summary conviction is £20,000 and on indictment it is unlimited.

1 HSA 1990, s 23(3).
2 HSA 1990, 23(4A) requires that, as with many other enforcement offences under the planning legislation, the 'financial benefit' factor be particularly addressed by the court. Naturally, the prosecutor will need to ensure that the gravity of the offence is made clear to the court and so the discussion in chapter nine of the presentation of cases will be relevant.

14.7.5.1 *Defence*

The defences available depend, largely, on the specific form of the offence. However, there is a general defence available. So if the accused proves, in relation to any of the offences under the section, that:

(a) he took all reasonable precautions and exercised all due diligence to avoid commission of the offence, or

(b) that commission of the offence could be avoided only by the taking of action amounting to a breach of a statutory duty

then he will be acquitted[1]. More specific defences are given. So if the offence charged is one of 'unauthorised presence' by virtue of no consent having been granted then the accused can avail himself of the following defence. He must prove that at the time of the alleged commission of the offence he did not know, and no reason to believe, that the substance was present or that it was present in a quantity equal to or exceeding the controlled quantity[2]. If the 'unauthorised presence' offence is based on there being an excessive quantity of a hazardous substance then the accused must prove that at the time of the alleged commission of the offence he did not know, and had no reason to believe, that the substance was present in a quantity exceeding the maximum permitted[3]. As regards the second category of contravention ('breach of condition') then if the accused proves that he did not know, and had no reason to believe, that there was a failure to comply with the condition then he will be acquitted[4].

1   HSA 1990, s 23(5).
2   HSA 1990, s 23(6)(a).
3   HSA 1990, s 23(6)(b).
4   HSA 1990, s 23(7).

14.7.5.2 *Corporate liability – extended to subsidiaries etc*

The familiar provision from the TCPA 1990, section 331 which deals with the liability of directors etc of companies found liable under that act are applied to this regime by virtue of HSA 1990, section 37(1). Further refinements are however introduced by HSA 1990, section 39(3): thus bodies corporate which are interconnected for the purposes of the Fair Trading Act 1973 are to be treated as being one 'person' for purposes of sections 4 to 21 and 23 to 26. As the latter series of provisions deal with contraventions this means that where a company is a subsidiary of another or both are subsidiaries of a third then both subsidiary and holding companies qualify as a 'person' for the purposes of this regime[1]. The use of the Fair Trading and Company Law legislation broadens the impact of the regime considerably: the 'interconnected company' test thus cuts through the corporate 'veil' between companies that are intimately linked together. The HSA should thus note the interaction between this provision and that of TCPA 1990, section 331 as applied to this regime. This liability, when combined with the 'inter-connected company' provisions from the Fair Trading legislation means that criminal proceedings may be taken against directors etc of related companies.

1   The term 'subsidiary' is defined in the Fair Trading Act by reference to the Companies Act 1985, s 736.

14.7.6   Contravention notice

The second sanction is the contravention notice – modelled on the enforcement notice of the mainstream planning regime[1]. (Circular 11/92 provides a useful discussion of the system so this discussion will not repeat the points made there.) However, there are some important differences between mainstream enforcement and hazardous substances enforcement that should be borne in mind. First, there is a special limitation on the power to take action: the HSA 'shall not issue a hazardous substances contravention notice where it appears to them that a contravention of hazardous substances control can be avoided only by the taking of action amounting to a breach of a statutory duty'. (This special limitation also appears as an alternative defence to the 'due diligence' defence in HSA 1990, section 23(5) – see above.) This is potentially a very wide-ranging limitation and experience will tell as to whether the limitation is too widely drawn. Second, the HSA cannot issue a contravention notice if there is a temporary exemption direction issued by the Secretary of State using his powers under HSA 1990, section 27. Third, there is no explicit reference in the power to the development plan (even though this is mentioned as a relevant factor in making hazardous substance consent decisions)[2]. Fourth, 'nothing in any hazardous substances contravention notice ... shall require or allow anything to be done in contravention of any ... prohibition notice or improvement notice served' under the health and safety legislation[3]. The contravention notice procedure is otherwise very similar to that for mainstream enforcement. There is even an 'under-enforcement' element since section 24(1)(b) indicates that the HSA may require such steps to be taken 'to remedy wholly or partly the contravention'.

The removal of the substance from the land may be required[4]. In addition to section 24 the 1992 Regulations also prescribe some matters and apply the supplementary provisions relating to appeal etc from the TCPA 1990. The 1992 Regulations require that the notice must identify the land to which the notice relates; it must also be accompanied by a statement of, first, the HSA's reasons for issuing the notice and, second, the right of appeal to the Secretary of State[5]. As well as service on the owner and those who appear to be 'materially interested' there must also be service on 'any person other than the owner who appear to the hazardous substances authority to be in control of the land'. Regulations 18 to 22 apply the various provisions of the TCPA 1990 to the hazardous substances code and so appeals, criminal liability for non-compliance, subsequent grants of consent etc are dealt with by way of the 1992 Regulations. Enforcement personnel will find Schedule 5 of the 1992 Regulations particularly useful as it contains the provisions from the TCPA 1990 as modified, namely, sections 174 – 179, 181, 188, 285 and 289.

1   HSA 1990, s 24.
2   HSA 1990, s 9(2)(d).
3   HSA 1990, s 29(1). Subsection (2) provides that the notice shall be void to the extent that it contravenes this principle.
4   HSA 1990, s 24(6).
5   Planning (Hazardous Substances) Regulations 1992, reg 17(1) and (3) respectively.

14.7.6.1 *Non-compliance with notice*

The prosecution option is available: the penalties and provisions are directly applied from the TCPA 1990. In addition there is a works in default option: however, it would not seem that the HSA has the power to sell the land concerned as is the case with mainstream enforcement since no regulations have been made which make the expenses recoverable a charge on the land. See chapter nine on the mainstream works in default power.

14.7.7   Statutory injunction

The HSA 1990, section 26AA provides, in terms similar to those of other planning injunctions, for a statutory injunction for actual or apprehended contraventions of hazardous substances control. The discussion of the mainstream planning injunction in chapter nine is relevant.

Appendix 1
PACE Code C

CODE OF PRACTICE FOR THE DETENTION, TREATMENT AND QUESTIONING OF PERSONS BY POLICE OFFICERS

1 General
[Omitted]

2 Custody records
[Omitted]

3 Initial action

(a) Detained persons: normal procedure

[Omitted]

(b) Detained persons: special groups

[Omitted]

(c) Persons attending a police station voluntarily

3.15 Any person attending a police station voluntarily for the purpose of assisting with an investigation may leave at will unless placed under arrest. If it is decided that he should not be allowed to do so then he must be informed at once that he is under arrest and brought before the custody officer, who is responsible for ensuring that he is notified of his rights in the same way as other detained persons. If he is not placed under arrest but is cautioned in accordance with section 10 below, the officer who gives the caution must at the same time inform him that he is not under arrest, that he is not obliged to remain at the police station but that if he remains at the police station he may obtain free and independent legal advice if he wishes. The officer shall point out that the right to legal advice includes the right to speak with a solicitor on the telephone and ask him if he wishes to do so.

3.16   If a person who is attending the police station voluntarily (in accordance with paragraph 3.15) asks about his entitlement to legal advice, he should be given a copy of the notice explaining the arrangements for obtaining legal advice. [See paragraph 3.2]

(d) Documentation

3.17   The grounds for a person's detention shall be recorded, in his presence if practicable.

3.18   Action taken under paragraphs 3.6 to 3.14 shall be recorded.

4 Detained persons' property
[Omitted]

5 Right not to be held incommunicado
[Omitted]

6 Right to legal advice
[Omitted]

7 Citizens of Independent Commonwealth countries or foreign nationals
[Omitted]

8 Conditions of Detention
[Omitted]

9 Treatment of detained persons
[Omitted]

10 Cautions

(a) When a caution must be given

10.1   A person whom there are grounds to suspect of an offence must be cautioned before any questions about it (or further questions if it is his answers to previous questions which provide the grounds for suspicion) are put to him regarding his involvement or suspected involvement in that offence if his answers or his silence (ie failure or refusal to answer a question or to answer satisfactorily) may be given in evidence to a court in a prosecution. He therefore need not be cautioned if questions are put for other purposes, for example, solely to establish his identity or his ownership of any vehicle or to obtain information in accordance with any relevant statutory requirement (see paragraph 10.5C) or in furtherance of the proper and effective conduct of a search, (for example to determine the need to search in the exercise of powers of stop and search or to seek cooperation while carrying out a search) or to seek verification of a written record in accordance with paragraph 11.13.

10.2 Whenever a person who is not under arrest is initially cautioned or is reminded that he is under caution (see paragraph 10.5) he must at the same time be told that he is not under arrest and is not obliged to remain with the officer (see paragraph 3.15).

10.3 A person must be cautioned upon arrest for an offence unless:

(a) it is impracticable to do so by reason of his condition or behaviour at the time; or

(b) he has already been cautioned immediately prior to arrest in accordance with paragraph 10.1 above.

(b) Action: general

10.4 The caution shall be in the following terms:

'You do not have to say anything. But it may harm your defence if you do not mention when questioned something which you later rely on in court. Anything you do say may be given in evidence.'

Minor deviations do not constitute a breach of this requirement provided that the sense of the caution is preserved. [See *Note 10C*]

10.5 When there is a break in questioning under caution the interviewing officer must ensure that the person being questioned is aware that he remains under caution. If there is any doubt the caution should be given again in full when the interview resumes. [See *Note 10A*]

Special warnings under sections 36 and 37 of the Criminal Justice and Public Order Act 1994

10.5A When a suspect who is interviewed after arrest fails or refuses to answer certain questions, or to answer them satisfactorily, after due warning, a court or jury may draw such inferences as appear proper under sections 36 and 37 of the Criminal Justice and Public Order Act 1994. This applies when:

    (*a*) a suspect is arrested by a constable and there is found on his person, or in or on his clothing or footwear, or otherwise in his possession, or in the place where he was arrested, any objects, marks or substances, or marks on such objects, and the person fails or refuses to account for the objects, marks or substances found; or

    (*b*) an arrested person was found by a constable at a place at or about the time the offence for which he was arrested, is alleged to have been committed, and the person fails or refuses to account for his presence at that place.

10.5B   For an inference to be drawn from a suspect's failure or refusal to answer a question about one of these matters or to answer it satisfactorily, the interviewing officer must first tell him in ordinary language:

    (*a*) what offence he is investigating;
    (*b*) what fact he is asking the suspect to account for;
    (*c*) that he believes this fact may be due to the suspect's taking part in the commission of the offence in question;
    (*d*) that a court may draw a proper inference if he fails or refuses to account for the fact about which he is being questioned;
    (*e*) that a record is being made of the interview and that it may be given in evidence if he is brought to trial.

10.5C   Where, despite the fact that a person has been cautioned, failure to cooperate may have an effect on his immediate treatment, he should be informed of any relevant consequences and that they are not affected by the caution. Examples are when his refusal to provide his name and address when charged may render him liable to detention, or when his refusal to provide particulars and information in accordance with a statutory requirement, for example, under the Road Traffic Act 1988, may amount to an offence or may make him liable to arrest.

(c) Juveniles, the mentally disordered and the mentally handicapped

10.6   If a juvenile or a person who is mentally disordered or mentally handicapped is cautioned in the absence of the appropriate adult, the caution must be repeated in the adult's presence.

(d) Documentation

10.7 A record shall be made when a caution is given under this section, either in the officer's pocket book or in the interview record as appropriate.

Notes for Guidance

10A In considering whether or not to caution again after a break, the officer should bear in mind that he may have to satisfy a court that the person understood that he was still under caution when the interview resumed.
10B [Not Used]
10C If it appears that a person does not understand what the caution means, the officer who has given it should go on to explain it in his own words.
10D [Not Used]

11 Interviews: general

(a) Action

11.A An interview is the questioning of a person regarding his involvement or suspected involvement in a criminal offence or offences which, by virtue of paragraph 10.1 of Code C, is required to be carried out under caution. Procedures undertaken under section 7 of the Road Traffic Act 1988 do not constitute interviewing for the purpose of this code.

11.1 Following a decision to arrest a suspect he must not be interviewed about the relevant offence except at a police station (or other authorised place of detention) unless the consequent delay would be likely:

  (a) to lead to interference with or harm to evidence connected with an offence or interference with or physical harm to other persons; or
  (b) to lead to the alerting of other persons suspected of having committed an offence but not yet arrested for it; or
  (c) to hinder the recovery of property obtained in consequence of the commission of an offence.

Interviewing in any of these circumstances shall cease once the relevant risk has been averted or the necessary questions have been put in order to attempt to avert that risk.

11.2 Immediately prior to the commencement or re-commencement of any interview at a police station or other authorised place of detention, the interviewing officer shall remind the suspect of his entitlement to free legal advice and that the interview can be delayed for him to obtain legal advice (unless the exceptions in paragraph 6.6 or Annex C apply). It is the responsibility of the interviewing officer to ensure that all such reminders are noted in the record of interview.

11.2A   At the beginning of an interview carried out in a police station, the interviewing officer, after cautioning the suspect, shall put to him any significant statement or silence which occurred before his arrival at the police station, and shall ask him whether he confirms or denies that earlier statement or silence and whether he wishes to add anything. A 'significant' statement or silence is one which appears capable of being used in evidence against the suspect, in particular a direct admission of guilt, or failure or refusal to answer a question or to answer it satisfactorily, which might give rise to an inference under Part III of the Criminal Justice and Public Order Act 1994.

11.3   No police officer may try to obtain answers to questions or to elicit a statement by the use of oppression. Except as provided for in paragraph 10.5C, no police officer shall indicate, except in answer to a direct question, what action will be taken on the part of the police if the person being interviewed answers questions, makes a statement or refuses to do either. If the person asks the officer directly what action will be taken in the event of his answering questions, making a statement or refusing to do either, then the officer may inform the person what action the police propose to take in that event provided that that action is itself proper and warranted.

11.4   As soon as a police officer who is making enquiries of any person about an offence believes that a prosecution should be brought against him and that there is sufficient evidence for it to succeed, he shall ask the person if he has anything further to say. If the person indicates that he has nothing more to say the officer shall without delay cease to question him about that offence. This should not, however, be taken to prevent officers in revenue cases or acting under the confiscation provisions of the Criminal Justice Act 1988 or the Drug Trafficking Offences Act 1986 from inviting suspects to complete a formal question and answer record after the interview is concluded.

(b) Interview records

11.5

    (*a*) An accurate record must be made of each interview with a person suspected of an offence, whether or not the interview takes place at a police station.

    (*b*) The record must state the place of the interview, the time it begins and ends, the time the record is made (if different), any breaks in the interview and the names of all those present; and must be made on the forms provided for this purpose or in the officer's pocket-book or in accordance with the code of practice for the tape-recording of police interviews with suspects (Code E).

    (*c*) The record must be made during the course of the interview, unless in the investigating officer's view this would not be practicable or would interfere with the conduct of the interview, and must constitute either a verbatim record of what has been said or, failing this, an account of the interview which adequately and accurately summarises it.

11.6 The requirement to record the names of all those present at any interview does not apply to police officers interviewing people detained under the Prevention of Terrorism (Temporary Provisions) Act 1989. Instead the record shall state the warrant or other identification number and duty station of such officers.

11.7 If an interview record is not made during the course of the interview it must be made as soon as practicable after its completion.

11.8 Written interview records must be timed and signed by the maker.

11.9 If an interview record is not completed in the course of the interview the reason must be recorded in the officer's pocket book.

11.10 Unless it is impracticable the person interviewed shall be given the opportunity to read the interview record and to sign it as correct or to indicate the respects in which he considers it inaccurate. If the interview is tape-recorded the arrangements set out in Code E apply. If the person concerned cannot read or refuses to read the record or to sign it, the senior police officer present shall read it over to him and ask him whether he would like to sign it as correct (or make his mark) or to indicate the respects in which he considers it inaccurate. The police officer shall then certify on the interview record itself what has occurred. [See *Note 11D*]

11.11   If the appropriate adult or the person's solicitor is present during the interview, he shall also be given an opportunity to read and sign the interview record (or any written statement taken down by a police officer).

11.12   Any refusal by a person to sign an interview record when asked to do so in accordance with the provisions of the code must itself be recorded.

11.13   A written record shall also be made of any comments made by a suspected person, including unsolicited comments, which are outside the context of an interview but which might be relevant to the offence. Any such record must be timed and signed by the maker. Where practicable the person shall be given the opportunity to read that record and to sign it as correct or to indicate the respects in which he considers it inaccurate. Any refusal to sign should be recorded. [See *Note 11D*]

(c)   Juveniles, mentally disordered people and mentally handicapped people

11.14   A juvenile or a person who is mentally disordered or mentally handicapped, whether suspected or not, must not be interviewed or asked to provide or sign a written statement in the absence of the appropriate adult unless paragraph 11.1 or Annex C applies.

11.15   Juveniles may only be interviewed at their places of education in exceptional circumstances and then only where the principal or his nominee agrees. Every effort should be made to notify both the parent(s) or other person responsible for the juvenile's welfare and the appropriate adult (if this is a different person) that the police want to interview the juvenile and reasonable time should be allowed to enable the appropriate adult to be present at the interview. Where awaiting the appropriate adult would cause unreasonable delay and unless the interviewee is suspected of an offence against the educational establishment, the principal or his nominee can act as the appropriate adult for the purposes of the interview.

11.16   Where the appropriate adult is present at an interview, he should be informed that he is not expected to act simply as an observer; and also that the purposes of his presence are, first, to advise the person being questioned and to observe whether or not the interview is being conducted properly and fairly, and secondly, to facilitate communication with the person being interviewed.

Notes for Guidance

11A [Not Used]

11B It is important to bear in mind that, although juveniles or people who are mentally disordered or mentally handicapped are often capable of providing reliable evidence, they may, without knowing or wishing to do so, be particularly prone in certain circumstances to provide information which is unreliable, misleading or self-incriminating. Special care should therefore always be exercised in questioning such a person, and the appropriate adult should be involved, if there is any doubt about a person's age, mental state or capacity. Because of the risk of unreliable evidence it is also important to obtain corroboration of any facts admitted whenever possible.

11C It is preferable that a juvenile is not arrested at his place of education unless this is unavoidable. Where a juvenile is arrested at his place of education, the principal or his nominee must be informed.

11D When a suspect agrees to read records of interviews and of other comments and to sign them as correct, he should be asked to endorse the record with words such as 'I agree that this is a record of what was said' and add his signature. Where the suspect does not agree with the record, the officer should record the details of any disagreement and then ask the suspect to read these details and then sign them to the effect that they accurately reflect his disagreement. Any refusal to sign when asked to do so shall be recorded.

12 Interviews in police stations
[Omitted]

13 Interpreters

(a) General

13.1 Information on obtaining the services of a suitably qualified interpreter for the deaf or for persons who do not understand English is given in *Note for Guidance 3D*.

(b) Foreign languages

13.2 Except in accordance with paragraph 11.1 or unless Annex C applies, a person must not be interviewed in the absence of a person capable of acting as interpreter if:

  (*a*) he has difficulty in understanding English;

(b)   the interviewing officer cannot himself speak the person's own language; and

(c)   the person wishes an interpreter to be present.

13.3   The interviewing officer shall ensure that the interpreter makes a note of the interview at the time in the language of the person being interviewed for use in the event of his being called to give evidence, and certifies its accuracy. He shall allow sufficient time for the interpreter to make a note of each question and answer after each has been put or given and interpreted. The person shall be given an opportunity to read it or have it read to him and sign it as correct or to indicate the respects in which he considers it inaccurate. If the interview is tape-recorded the arrangements set out in Code E apply.

13.4   In the case of a person making a statement in a language other than English:

(a)   the interpreter shall take down the statement in the language in which it is made;

(b)   the person making the statement shall be invited to sign it; and

(c)   an official English translation shall be made in due course.

(c)   Deaf people and people with a speech handicap

13.5   If a person appears to be deaf or there is doubt about his hearing or speaking ability, he must not be interviewed in the absence of an interpreter unless he agrees in writing to be interviewed without one or paragraph 11.1 or Annex C applies.

13.6   An interpreter should also be called if a juvenile is interviewed and the parent or guardian present as the appropriate adult appears to be deaf or there is doubt about his hearing or speaking ability, unless he agrees in writing that the interview should proceed without one or paragraph 11.1 or Annex C applies.

13.7   The interviewing officer shall ensure that the interpreter is given an opportunity to read the record of the interview and to certify its accuracy in the event of his being called to give evidence.

(d)   Additional rules for detained persons

13.8   All reasonable attempts should be made to make clear to the detained person that interpreters will be provided at public expense.

13.9   Where paragraph 6.1 applies and the person concerned cannot communicate with the solicitor, whether because of language hearing or speech difficulties, an interpreter must be called. The interpreter may not be a police officer when interpretation is needed for the purposes of obtaining legal advice. In all other cases a police officer may only interpret if he first obtains the detained person's (or the appropriate adult's) agreement in writing or if the interview is tape-recorded in accordance with Code E.

13.10   When a person is charged with an offence who appears to be deaf or there is doubt about his hearing or speaking ability or ability to understand English, and the custody officer cannot establish effective communication, arrangements must be made for an interpreter to explain as soon as practicable the offence concerned and any other information given by the custody officer.

(e) Documentation

13.11   Action taken to call an interpreter under this section and any agreement to be interviewed in the absence of an interpreter must be recorded.

Note for Guidance

13A   If the interpreter is needed as a prosecution witness at the person's trial, a second interpreter must act as the court interpreter.

14   Questioning: special restrictions
[Omitted]

15   Reviews and extensions of detention
[Omitted]

16   Charging of detained persons
[Omitted]

ANNEX A: INTIMATE AND STRIP SEARCHES (See paragraph 4.1)

[Omitted]

ANNEX B: DELAY IN NOTIFYING ARREST OR ALLOWING ACCESS TO LEGAL ADVICE

[Omitted]

ANNEX C: VULNERABLE SUSPECTS: URGENT INTERVIEWS AT POLICE STATIONS

[Omitted]

ANNEX D: WRITTEN STATEMENTS UNDER CAUTION (See paragraph 12.13)

(a) Written by a person under caution

1.   A person shall always be invited to write down himself what he wants to say.

2.   Where the person wishes to write it himself, he shall be asked to write out and sign, before writing what he wants to say, the following:

> 'I make this statement of my own free will. I understand that I do not have to say anything but that it may harm my defence if I do not mention when questioned something which I later rely on in court. This statement may be given in evidence.'

3.   Any person writing his own statement shall be allowed to do so without any prompting except that a police officer may indicate to him which matters are material or question any ambiguity in the statement.

(b) Written by a police officer

4.   If a person says that he would like someone to write it for him, a police officer shall write the statement, but, before starting, he must ask him to sign, or make his mark, to the following:

> ' I, ..., wish to make a statement. I want someone to write down what I say. I understand that I do not have to say anything but that it may harm my defence if I do not mention when questioned something which I later rely on in court. This statement may be given in evidence.'

5.   Where a police officer writes the statement, he must take down the exact words spoken by the person making it and he must not edit or paraphrase it. Any questions that are necessary (eg to make it more intelligible) and the answers given must be recorded contemporaneously on the statement form.

6. When the writing of a statement by a police officer is finished the person making it shall be asked to read it and to make any corrections, alterations or additions he wishes. When he has finished reading it he shall be asked to write and sign or make his mark on the following certificate at the end of the statement:

> 'I have read the above statement, and I have been able to correct, alter or add anything I wish. This statement is true. I have made it of my own free will.'

7. If the person making the statement cannot read, or refuses to read it, or to write the above mentioned certificate at the end of it or to sign it, the senior police officer present shall read it to him and ask him whether he would like to correct, alter or add anything and to put his signature or make his mark at the end. The police officer shall then certify on the statement itself what has occurred.

ANNEX E: SUMMARY OF PROVISIONS RELATING TO MENTALLY DISORDERED AND MENTALLY HANDICAPPED PERSONS

[Omitted]

ANNEX F
COUNTRIES WITH WHICH BILATERAL CONSULAR CONVENTIONS OR AGREEMENTS REQUIRING NOTIFICATION OF THE ARREST AND DETENTION OF THEIR NATIONALS ARE IN FORCE AS AT 1 JANUARY 1995

[Omitted]

Appendix 2
Effective enforcement: the ten commandments

Effective enforcement requires a new way of thinking and working. Although the legal regime may now, in general, be reasonably effective at preventing most contravenors from 'playing the system' this does not mean that enforcement activity is a piece of cake. (The determined contravenor, as with any other professional criminal, cannot be caught on every occasion he commits a crime. Effective enforcement must accept the potential for failure when faced with this sort of problem.) Effective enforcement still requires the organisation, resources, staff and attitudes which can make the system provided by the planning legislation work effectively. A summary of many of the issues that need to be addressed can be expressed in the form of the ten commandments for effective enforcement.

The ten commandments and a 'translation' for these biblical pronouncements are set out on the following pages. The commandments can be photocopied (with enlargement) onto an A4 page as a way of reminding enforcement personnel of some of the main themes of effective enforcement.

Effective Enforcement

The Ten Commandments

1. Thou shalt spurn Tumult and Confusion.

2. Thou shalt cooperate with thy Brethren.

3. Thou shalt hark unto the Complainant.

4. Thou shalt commune with Chief Officers.

5. Thou shalt tarry not.

6. Thou shalt heed the Word of the Law.

7. Thou shalt converse with the Magistrate.

8. Thou shalt consult the Timetable.

9. Thou shalt enforce the Obligations.

10. Thou shalt covet the Manual.

1 Organise for enforcement and ensure that administrative systems are up to the mark. Computerisation and routinisation of the different stages and processes are key issues to consider.

2 Working with colleagues in the Planning Department (forward planning and development control) will produce benefits for enforcement and these other two aspects of the planning trinity. Similar liaison with other parts of the Council and even other agencies (Customs & Excise) will need to be addressed.

3 Keeping the complainant informed of progress is important: engaging the complainant in enforcement activity can help substantiate a case before the inspector or the criminal courts.

4 Obtaining support for organisational reform, resources etc will need the help of senior levels of management within the authority. This will require a planned strategy aimed at Chief Officers, elected members and others in positions of influence.

5 Each enforcement case should progress smoothly – lose momentum and you lose the battle.

6 The legal limitations need to be understood: however, the law can also provide innovative solutions if the opportunities to use the law creatively are grasped.

7 When a prosecution is at stake the Magistrate will invariably have to be 'educated' about planning control and enforcement. Only then can the court appreciate the importance of planning, the impacts of the contravention on the 'victim' (the environment, the complainant etc) and so assess the 'guilt' of the contravenor in terms that will then be reflected in an appropriate sanction.

8 When action is required action should be taken: the Enforcement Manual and its timetable should be reflected in action on the ground.

9 Planning obligations (and some important planning conditions) may need to be monitored: if they are 'self-monitoring' (a job for development control) then enforcement will be much easier.

10 The Enforcement Manual should be comprehensive, updated and effective in giving not only a clear structure for dealing with cases but also offering advice on the different options that are available at various stages.

Index